DOING PRAGMATICS

THIRD EDITION

DOING PRAGMATICS

PETER GRUNDY

LONDON AND NEW YORK

First edition published in Great Britain in 1995
Second edition published in 2000
This third edition published in 2008
By Hodder Education

Published 2013 by Routledge
2 Park Square, Milton Park, Abingdon, Oxon OX14 4RN
711 Third Avenue, New York, NY, 10017, USA

Routledge is an imprint of the Taylor & Francis Group, an informa business

British Library Cataloguing in Publication Data
A catalogue record for this title is available from the British Library

Library of Congress Cataloging-in-Publication Data
A catalog record for this book is available from the Library of Congress

ISBN 13: 978-0-340-97160-4 (pbk)

Typeset in 8.5pt Stone Serif by Servis Filmsetting Ltd, Stockport, Cheshire
Printed and bound by CPI Group (U) Ltd, Croydon, CR0 4YY

Contents

Preface (and how to get the best out of this book)

Some students find that learning pragmatics and learning syntax are mirror images of one another. Because pragmatic data consist of everyday utterances, the first impression of pragmatics tends to be that it's really quite easy: the examples and the ways they are described seem to accord closely with our intuitions about everyday talk. In contrast, when we study syntax for the first time, the formal representation of the examples often seems very challenging. But as time goes on, we realize that the underlying ideas in pragmatics are really very difficult indeed, whereas the underlying ideas in syntax have a simplicity and elegance that make syntax seem less difficult the more we study it. My main motive in writing this book has been to try and extend the sense felt in the early stages of pragmatics, that it's really a very accessible area of linguistics, to the second stage when we have to grapple with the more challenging underlying ideas.

There are now several very good pragmatics textbooks available: for this reason I've recommended chapters from several of them in the suggestions for further reading which appear at the end of each chapter. If this book is different, I hope it's because you'll feel that it's a genuine entry-level book with a wide coverage and with a suitable degree of challenge too. I also hope it justifies its title, *Doing Pragmatics*, which is meant to reflect its strong pedagogic orientation. Wherever possible, I've tried to use real examples of talk that I've collected over the years rather than rely on invented examples. A book about the use of language ought to work with 'live' examples.

The materials in this book have been extensively trialled over several generations of students. I've been fortunate to have had the opportunity to teach pragmatics at undergraduate and postgraduate levels for many years and to have benefited from large and extremely lively lecture and seminar groups where I've frequently been caught out and corrected by clever students. And I have to admit that reading pragmatics essays and projects is often a learning experience too – students frequently have insights and react to data in ways that I've found enlightening and shaming.

As well as all the faults that are owed to me, in this book you'll also find many insights that are owed to generations of students. In particular, I've acknowledged some by name in the text of the book: Laurence Brushi, Andrew Caink, Roger Maylor, Csilla Szabo, and especially Kelly Glover, who contributed ideas to and read and commented insightfully on parts of the manuscript of the first edition all those years ago, thereby saving me from a number of mistakes. I also owe a considerable debt to Joanne Burdon, Charlotte Harper, Zhang Lin and Susan Millington, who've generously allowed me to use data which they collected and analysed in particularly insightful ways. Several of my former colleagues in Hong Kong have also helped, both practically with data collection as well as with their insights, especially Annie Au, Phil Benson, Philip Bolt, Winnie Cheng, Hiroko Itakura, Yan Jiang and Martin Warren. But because this is pragmatics, I'm sure that as you read this book you'll see things that I've missed and even got wrong – please write and let me know when this happens.

In fact, one of the real pleasures I've enjoyed since the first edition came out in 1995 has been receiving so many thought-provoking comments from readers and users. I've tried to act on all the helpful suggestions I've received for this edition and gratefully acknowledge them here.

I also owe a great deal to the readers who commented anonymously on the proposals for this and previous editions. I appreciate the real trouble they took. The further refinements and new materials in this edition owe much to their helpful and generous work.

Although I never had a colleague at Durham who was first and foremost a pragmaticist, I was fortunate enough to work alongside stimulating colleagues in a department that took its linguistics seriously and in which all our different interests and approaches were understood to be independent and yet to have the same ultimate goal. As with deixis, the point of origin has been important to this book. All the more pity that in a moment of utter foolishness the powers-that-were decided to close the once outstanding Linguistics Department at Durham, a decision which so many linguists around the world have deplored.

I also owe a debt to my editors at Hodder Education, Lesley Riddle, who threw caution to the winds in allowing me to write this book in the first place, and Naomi Meredith, who bore with me when the first edition took longer than it should have done. Naomi also suggested the title, which is much better than those I'd toyed with and which has often been praised by other pragmaticists. Christina Wipf-Perry, the second edition editor, shamed me into trying to match her constant efficiency and at the same time gave me real confidence. For the third edition I've been fortunate to have Tamsin Smith and Bianca Knights to guide me and tidy up ever so many loose ends. Their kindness and attention to detail have been inspirational. I've also been very fortunate in having had Susan Dunsmore as copy editor for both the second edition and for this edition. No one could have made a better job of turning a less than tidy manuscript into the beautiful book you hold in your hand.

How to get the best out of this book

As you work your way through *Doing Pragmatics*, you'll notice that there's a movement from the study of short utterances in the early chapters to the study of more extended conversations in the later chapters. It's not only the data type that change, but the approach to pragmatics too. In the early chapters, you'll learn about the central areas of linguistic pragmatics. You can then use this knowledge in the later chapters as you develop the ability to handle larger pieces of data in a more 'empirical' way. Towards the end of the book, you'll find yourself progressively invited to take a stance in the various debates about approaches to pragmatics. You'll also notice that examples which we work with in the earlier chapters sometimes turn up again in the later chapters. This gives you a sense of familiarity as you meet old friends again, but also shows that more than one way of accounting for a single example is often appropriate. As you'll see, things aren't always as simple as they appear at first sight.

Most of the chapters have a common structure, beginning with a simple example which is repeated in each chapter and evaluated from a chapter-specific perspective. This is then followed by a description of the essential principles of the area under consideration, which sets the scene for an examination of real-world uses. I hope this structure will soon become familiar and help you to navigate your way successfully not only through the book but also through each of the areas of pragmatics.

Another motive in writing this book has been the hope that it may help you to do your own pragmatics. There are four ways in which this book overtly addresses this motive:

As you read this book, you'll encounter *Checking Understanding* exercises at regular intervals. It's important that you attempt these exercises. Not only will they help you to confirm your understanding of what you're reading, but the Key containing suggested answers often includes ideas which supplement those in the main text of the book.

Second, at the end of every chapter there are a number of *Raising Pragmatic Awareness* activities which you can try for yourself, or with friends, or in a tutorial group. These are sensitizing activities which involve you in tasks like eavesdropping on conversations and reporting your findings to your colleagues or writing entries for a dictionary of pragmatics. Each of these activities is meant to be do-able either as a task set by your lecturer or on a self-study basis.

Third, as well as *Raising Pragmatic Awareness*, at the end of each chapter you'll also find several topics which can be used to stimulate tutorial discussion (or, if you must, essays).

Finally, Chapter 12 contains several suggestions for possible types of *Project Work*, and in particular gives advice on data collection and transcription techniques. It also contains a case-study which shows how conversational data can be collected and analysed in the light of pragmatic theory. I hope this chapter will help you in planning and carrying out your own project work.

I've tried to make this book a good read – so sit back and enjoy yourself.

Peter Grundy
March 2008

1 Using and understanding language

We all know what light is; but it is not easy to tell what it is.
(Sam Johnson, in James Boswell's Life of Johnson, *11 April 1776)*

Keywords:

accommodation, appropriateness, context, deixis, implicature, indeterminacy, indirect meaning, inference, reflexivity, relevance, speech act

1.1 Introduction

In this first chapter, I'm going to write about some of the aspects of language use that are of particular interest to pragmaticists like you and me. At several points in the chapter, I'll make suggestions about the essential concerns of pragmaticists which will help you to define pragmatics.

Let's begin with a scenario. Walking at a brisk pace along the footpath, I pass a mother with a small boy in a pushchair and a small girl trotting along beside them. As I pass, this exchange occurs:

(1) SMALL BOY: Man
ME: Is that your brother
SMALL GIRL: Yes
ME: It takes all sorts
MOTHER: It certainly does

Unexceptional, you might think, but from a pragmaticist's point of view, this exchange, like any other, is far from uninteresting. Let's look at it utterance by utterance.

SMALL BOY: Man
Although this utterance consists only of a single noun, the speaker uses it for a purpose – to demonstrate to himself or to his mother or to his sister or perhaps to all three of them his ability to recognize objects. Perhaps even to show off this ability. As pragmaticists, we see that the form of his utterance (its grammar) and its literal semantic meaning fail to determine its pragmatic function, which we have to work out for ourselves.

ME: Is that your brother
Although I'm not addressed by the small boy and have never met him before, it feels inappropriate to continue walking past without a response, and I find myself opting for a relatively neutral question to his sister. I suppose my use of 'that' rather than 'he' might encode my wish to get my own back on the small boy who's drawn attention to me and caused us all just a little embarrassment. And because I choose the formula 'your brother', rather than, say, 'her brother', I select the small girl as the person who must respond.

SMALL GIRL: Yes
The small girl's minimal answer perhaps suggests that she doesn't think the mild criticism implicit in 'that' is appropriate. Or perhaps that she thinks it's unfair that I've picked her out to respond in a slightly awkward situation.

ME: It takes all sorts
Although I don't identify the person referred to, my idiomatic suggestion that we've a character in our midst is readily taken to refer to the small boy. The utterance also functions as a kind of compliment because it implies that a small infant whose contribution to the exchange has been only a single word has a distinct character and that his small sister is clever enough to understand this pragmatic meaning.

MOTHER: It certainly does
Like 'it takes all sorts', the children's mother's utterance is also indirect, that's to say, she confirms that her small son is a character although she doesn't say this explicitly. Although her comment might in theory be taken to refer to me, in which case it would certainly be an insult, it never occurs to us to take it this way. Thus an exchange that had begun badly for all of us with a small boy making an audible comment about a total stranger ends with everyone feeling good.

Here's another scenario which also had an awkward element to it, but which ended happily. I'm standing at the bar of our local pub having a quiet drink. Two large men have just come in and are standing next to me. The barman is serving them when the barmaid appears and says

(2) BARMAID: Are you two both together – well you know what I mean
ME: I was wondering too
ONE OF THE MEN: That's how rumours get started

Again, if we look at this exchange utterance by utterance, we see that our ability as pragmatically skilled conversationalists to recognize meanings that are implicit rather than explicit is crucial to our understanding.

BARMAID: Are you two both together – well you know what I mean
It's clear from the barmaid's 'you know what I mean' that the optimal meaning of 'are you two both together' is not the meaning she intends. Those familiar with the British pub context know that *Are you together* functions as an offer to serve a person standing beside someone who is already being served. On this occasion, the barmaid fails to produce this optimal form, so her untypical utterance prompts us to search for another possible meaning. Perhaps it's a combination of the slightly dismissive 'you two' and the redundant 'both' which causes the barmaid to realize that she might be thought to be asking the men if they are a gay couple. Her use of 'well' is also crucial – imagine the quite different force the utterance would be likely to have without it. It seems that 'well' mitigates the force of 'you know what I mean' and goes some way to apologizing for the speaker's unfortunate choice of words.

ME: I was wondering too
Although what's just happened has nothing to do with me, I can hardly pretend I haven't heard what was said. Even keeping quiet might be taken to imply that I'm at least considering whether the men standing next to me could be a couple, so it seems safer to speak. Fortunately, my utterance is regarded as a joke rather than as

an assertion of the couple theory. Perhaps the use of 'too' aligns me with the barmaid and her mistake – somehow her pragmatically inappropriate choice of words seems less problematic when someone else states, but does not mean, that they could have made the same mistake.

ONE OF THE MEN: That's how rumours get started
Just as the barmaid commented on the unintended pragmatic meaning of her own utterance, so the customer also refers to her utterance, from which he distances himself with the use of 'that'. And in his use of 'rumours', he implies that he isn't gay. It's also noticeable that it's important to clear up the possible misunderstanding before attending to the matter of whether or not the two men are together and whether one of them may or may not need serving.

Such simple observations about some of the pragmatic properties of these brief, trivial exchanges show how subtle even the most apparently straightforward uses of language are. Pragmatics is about explaining how we produce and understand such everyday but apparently rather peculiar uses of language.

Checking understanding (1.1)

Before we move on, perhaps you would like to try your hand at coming to some conclusions about what is going on in two simple conversations of the kind we have just examined together. The first exchange occurred when I asked for a particular brand of cold capsule at the chemist:

(3) PHARMACIST: Do you usually have this sort
PETER: Yeh I think so
PHARMACIST: They make you drowsy mind
PETER: Oh are there others that don't

The second exchange occurred when I was buying fruit in the market from a female stallholder:

(4) STALLHOLDER: Do you want two boxes of grapes for 80p
PETER: No I don't think so. There aren't any black ones at the moment, are there
STALLHOLDER: No they're just green ones
PETER: No my wife's very saucy
STALLHOLDER: <laughs>
PETER: No I didn't mean that – you know what I mean
STALLHOLDER: It's just the way you said it

If you want to check your ideas against my suggestions, look at the answer section at the back of this book.

The more you work on conversations like (1)–(4), the more you come to see that it is not so much what the sentences literally mean that matters when we talk as how they reveal the intentions and strategies of the speakers themselves. This point is very well made by Atkinson, Kilby and Roca, who define pragmatics as being to do with "The distinction between what a speaker's words (literally) mean and what the speaker might mean by his words" (1988: 217).

1.2 Properties of everyday language

In the rest of this chapter I am going to discuss some of the features of everyday language use which are important in pragmatics. When we get to the end of the chapter I shall be more systematic and make a number of observations about utterances with the aim of signposting our way through the first few chapters of this book. Meanwhile, the first feature I want to discuss is appropriateness.

1.2.1 Appropriateness

Not very long ago I was standing by the photocopier talking to a female colleague when a female stranger approached us and asked my colleague

(5) Where's the ladies' room

I suppose the speaker judged 'the ladies' room' the most appropriate formula for the **context** and that it would have been inappropriate to explain the reason for her wanting this information. She also clearly thought it appropriate to address her request to my female colleague rather than to me. On the other hand, directing her request at just one rather than both of us seems to encode an awareness of gender. This raises the question of whether encoding or constructing gender is appropriate on university premises, although on balance, I guess the stranger did find the most appropriate formula for the context.

Similar examples of **appropriateness**-driven utterances are easy to find. On another occasion at work I was standing by the porter's office dressed in similar navy blue trousers and pullover to the porter's uniform, when a female student walked up to me and said:

(6) You're not the porter are you

Obviously, there are few contexts in which it's appropriate for a student to say this to a lecturer. But on this occasion, the speaker could hardly stand around waiting for the porter when, judging by the way I was dressed, I might just be the person she was looking for. But as I probably didn't look organized enough to be the porter, and not wanting to make a mistake by asking the wrong person for help, she chose a pessimistic formula as the most appropriate way to frame her inquiry.

At one stage in my career I had a senior colleague who had the bad habit of saying

(7) Are we all here

at exactly the moment a meeting was due to start and only if he could see that we were not all there. His utterance was perfectly attuned to the situation and always had the same effect, that of causing a younger member of our department to get up and go on a missing colleague hunt. On another occasion when we were waiting for a colleague without whom a meeting couldn't start, another colleague said to the person sitting next to her

(8) Shall we go and get Mike

whereupon the person addressed dutifully got up and went to look for him.

Or when I begin a lecture I often call for attention by uttering loudly

(9) Right, shall we begin

which I take to be the most appropriate utterance in the context. When I am feeling mischievous I sometimes begin a first-year pragmatics lecture by saying

(10) May I speak English

This always causes a moment of consternation when the students think their lecturer might have lost the plot. But this beginning enables me to make the neat point that 'May I speak English' is not the appropriate way to begin a pragmatics lecture in Britain. And to make the still neater point that when I say 'May I speak English' in a shop in Italy, the commonest response (I know, I have done the research) is 'A little'. This response indicates that the addressee, struggling with limited English, takes me to be saying the more appropriate or expectable 'Do you speak English?'

And then there used to be a service manager at the garage where I take my car for servicing, who could never remember my name and knew he should, so he signalled it every time I went with

(11) What's your name again

Now that everything is stored on computer, they ask your car number first and the screen obligingly tells them who you are. But the new service manager is much more efficient than his predecessor and has begun to say

(12) What's the number again

as though he knows that he should be able to remember it.

And when I stayed for two nights in a bed-and-breakfast and had the same waitress each morning, she used two different ways of asking me whether I'd like tea or coffee. You can surely guess which of the following utterances she used on the first morning and which she took to be more appropriate on the second:

(13) Is it tea or coffee
(14) Would you like tea or coffee

The law in Britain requires anyone selling alcohol to make sure that they sell it only to an adult, which they usually check with the formula

(15) Are you over twenty-one

Technically, an adult in Britain is anyone over eighteen, but the less confrontational formula 'Are you over twenty-one' is felt more appropriate because it allows answers like *No, but I am over eighteen* or *I'm nineteen actually* and not just the bald yes or no required by 'Are you over eighteen'. Sometimes, they put the 'over 21' question to people who are manifestly adults, perhaps as a kind of joke or, to people my age, even a kind of compliment. The first time this happened to me, I was rather taken aback, as the following exchange indicates:

(16) CHECKOUT LADY: Are you over twenty-one – for your alcohol
PETER: It's for my Dad
CHECKOUT LADY: That's what they all say

Seeing me look puzzled by her question, the checkout lady added an explanatory 'for your alcohol'. Having been a bit slow in the uptake, it seemed important to find an appropriate way of responding. My response then enabled the checkout lady to show solidarity with me by 'othering' under-eighteen would-be purchasers of alcohol with the use of 'they'. I'm now wise to the question and have tried to find a formula which maintains the joke but, unlike my response in (16), puts me on the right side of the law and thus removes the checkout lady's need to find an appropriate response to my response. So usually the conversation goes like this:

(16′) CHECKOUT LADY: Are you over twenty-one
PETER: Last week

This response also has the advantage of implying that I take the question to be an appropriate way of asking if I'm over eighteen.

I cite these few examples because they are immediately recognizable as appropriate ways of using language to get business done. One of the features of language use that is of interest to pragmaticists is its appropriateness in relation to those who use it and those they address.

1.2.2 Non-literal or indirect meaning

As well as being appropriate to the contexts in which they occurred, many of the utterances in the last section were also **indirect** in the sense that their literal meanings were not all the speakers intended them to convey. So

(7) Are we all here

and

(9) Right, shall we begin

both purport to be questions in terms of the forms in which they are expressed, yet both are clearly intended to have other functions. Indeed, I would be rather cross if someone took 'Shall we begin?' as a real question and replied with a negative rejoinder.

Sometimes the literal meaning is very far removed from the indirect meaning. Thus you would have to have seen the classic television comedy *Fawlty Towers* to know that

(17) He's from Barcelona

is a way of saying that someone is stupid and undeserving of sympathy. But usually the indirectness is much more subtle than this, so that it takes a bit of working out to realize that

(18) Radion removes dirt AND odours

is an indirect way of saying that other washing powders are good at getting the dirt out but leave your clothes smelling bad. And when the BBC referred to

(19) The campaign group called the Freedom Association

listeners had to do quite a lot of work to come to the conclusion that the BBC was indicating indirectly that it did not necessarily share the philosophy of the Freedom Association and that the name 'Freedom Association' might give a false impression.

Often indirectness is motivated by a wish to allow the person we address a way of appearing to take what we say directly while responding to its indirect meaning. There was a block of flats up the road from where I lived in Hong Kong with a sign on the gate which read

(20) This building has a no visitors car park

Similarly, the in-flight announcement

(21) May I draw your attention to the fact that smoking is not allowed in this aircraft by law

is presumably not taken only at face value by smokers.

We are remarkably clever at interpreting indirectness. I once had a Head of Department who showed me the draft of a letter which he had written to the Dean. The draft contained the sentence

(22) Meanwhile, Peter Grundy has just told me of his long conversation with you earlier today

I asked for 'long' to be removed from the sentence because 'long conversation' is a marked, or unexpected, description and might seem to the Dean to be an indirect way of referring to what had in fact been a disagreement between us.

So we see that indirectness too is typical of real-world language use, and that literal or stated meaning is only one aspect of the meaning conveyed in an utterance – and not always the most important one.

1.2.3 Inference

One question worth asking is how we get from a string of words that appears to have a literal meaning (for example, 'long conversation') to an understanding of its indirect meaning (disagreement). We obviously have to draw **inferences** or come to conclusions as to what the speaker is intending to convey. So although we are not told that other washing powders leave our clothes smelling bad, we can work out that this is a conclusion we are meant to draw from the stress on 'AND' in

(18) Radion removes dirt AND odours

In a similar way, 'called' in

(19) The campaign group called the Freedom Association

triggers an inference. Why, we ask ourselves, did the BBC not say 'The campaign group, the Freedom Association', or, more simply still 'The Freedom Association'? 'Called', we decide, must be telling us something about the title 'the Freedom Association', and so we infer that it may be slightly suspect.

This suggests that communication is not merely a matter of a speaker encoding a thought in language and sending it as spoken or signed message through space, or as a written message on paper, to a receiver who decodes it. This is clearly insufficient – the receiver must not only decode what is received but also draw an inference as to what is conveyed beyond what is stated.

Sometimes this inference is quite dramatic and much more interesting than the literal meaning itself, as when one of my colleagues said

(23) I'm a man

Nothing remarkable in that, one might think at first sight, except that the speaker was a woman. Here the meaning she intended to convey was much more important than the literal meaning of her utterance, which in any case was patently false. In fact, when you think about it, if someone says something that's obviously true (for example, a man says 'I'm a man') or obviously false (for example, a woman says 'I'm a man'), they must intend us to infer a hidden meaning.

Sometimes the inference just repairs or explicates a message that is in some way unclear. This is often the case with advertisements, which draw our attention with apparently exotic uses of language which we repair with inferences. Our local department store window is a ready source of such language:

(24) Spring into Summer

and the sign displayed next to smartly dressed male mannequins

(25) We have designs on your man

shout the need to draw inferences to work out the intended meaning, as does the comment of the BBC theatre critic talking about the opening night of a new musical

(26) I looked at my watch after two hours and realized that only twenty minutes had passed

It's also interesting to notice how some speakers feel that when they are speaking metaphorically, they sometimes need to use the term 'literally'. It's as though language really were a matter of literal meanings that could be encoded and despatched by the speaker and received and decoded by the addressee without any inference being required. I heard a nice example of this on the *Today* programme on BBC Radio 4 when a reporter said

(27) The Conference trade has literally helped turn Brighton around

In fact, every utterance seems to invite an inference, so that the addressee has to determine whether an utterance such as

(28) I was wondering too

is sincere or ironical.

1.2.4 Indeterminacy

Regarding some meanings as matters of inference has one important consequence. It implies that the utterances we hear are in some ways unclear, or, as linguists sometimes say, under-determined. By this we mean that an utterance might typically have one of several different possible meanings and that the inferences we draw determine which of these possible meanings is the one the addressee thinks the speaker is intending. An example of an under-determined utterance in the previous section is

(23) I'm a man

We clearly need to draw an inference in order to determine which of several different possible understandings is the right one.

In her book *Understanding Utterances*, Diane Blakemore (1992: 83) draws our attention to how under-determined the possessive is in English and gives a long list of examples which, although they share the same grammatical form, are all determined quite differently. Her list includes

(29) I have borrowed *Jane's car*
I would hate to have *Simon's job*
Yesterday's events really shocked *the country's president*
Jane's father has bought her a car

There are many other structures besides possessives that are typically under-determined. I remember that my daughter was very upset when she first noticed the sign *Pet mince* outside our local butcher's shop. Indeed butcher's signs are a rich source of such indeterminacy: how fortunate it is that a *Family Butcher* does not do to families what a *Pork Butcher* does to pigs!

When the sculpture *The Angel of the North* was first erected on a hilltop near Gateshead, a road-sign appeared beside the road which runs past it. The message on the road sign was *Angel parking*. Were passing motorists being advised that there was an angel parking? Or that there was a parking place for angels? Or that they could park their angel? Or that there was a place where motorists could park to view the sculpture of an angel?

Sometimes the problem is to do with determining which word in a two-word phrase is the head word, so that although *a child actor* is a child who acts, the meaning of *a child psychiatrist* cannot be determined by analogy. Similarly, in *additive free*, the headword is 'free', whereas in *50% extra free*, '50% extra' is head.

In my capacity as an external examiner, I once found myself writing an examiner's letter which, on re-reading, I saw contained one particularly pompous sentence that might be understood in either of two quite different ways. The sentence was

(30) There must therefore be a very good case for not allowing anyone to proceed to Year 3

The word that gave the trouble was clearly 'anyone' – it was meant to mean *a particular person* rather than *every person*. A similar problem occurs with 'the team that won in mid-week at Everton' in the following sentence which I heard on BBC Radio 4's *Today* programme

(31) Wimbledon are playing the team that won in mid-week at Everton

Were Wimbledon to play against the team that won at Everton? Or are Wimbledon the team that won at Everton and intending to field the same players against their new opponents? Similarly, the newspaper headline

(32) Bergkamp wants to end his career at Arsenal

might mean that Bergkamp wants to move to another club or that he wants to stay at Arsenal for ever. Whether we process 'paid for' as active or passive in the *Sunday Times* headline

(33) Bin Laden paid for Bali bombing

helps us to determine a pragmatic meaning that neither the superficial syntax nor the semantics alone determine adequately.

I once had an interesting intercultural experience of this sort. It was at the time when I first went to live in Germany and was a couple of lessons into my German course. Arming myself with a phrasebook and a good deal of misplaced confidence, I took myself off to a bar for a drink. Although I seemed to order my first beer with some success, I was less successful with the second one, which involved consulting my phrasebook for the German word for *another*. In English, *another* is indeterminate between *another of the same type* and *another of a different type*, but in German these two notions are represented by different formulas. This explains why when I thought I was ordering 'another beer', the barman gave me a hard look and a beer that was distinctly different from the previous one.

And I cannot resist telling you about a party where someone was telling a story about her holiday. The story contained the sentence

(34) We were woken up at three o'clock in the morning by a drip in our bedroom

Of course, she meant that water was dripping into her room. But if you know that *drip* is a British English slang expression for someone without much personality, then you'll appreciate why we found the indeterminacy entertaining.

Typically the context helps us to determine the meaning. When most people say

(35) I've just finished a book

we take them to mean that they have just finished reading a book. But when a university lecturer says 'I've just finished a book', they usually mean that they have just finished writing one. So knowing who the speaker is will help us to determine what is meant. A colleague of mine once made what we thought was a good joke when someone at lunch said that a particular member of his department had just finished a book, and my colleague asked, 'Reading one or writing one?' This would only be a joke in a context where the determination of *has just finished a book* could be problematical. And in fact, another of Diane Blakemore's examples is

(36) Should I read *your book*

where 'your book' is clearly ambiguous between the book you own and the book of which you are the author.

Although we may often think that what we say has one clear, determinate meaning, the examples above show us just how indeterminate our utterances actually are. Pragmatics is partly about trying to account in systematic ways for our ability to determine what speakers intend even when their utterances are so dramatically under-determined.

1.2.5 Context

In the paragraph before last we discussed how context can help in determining the meaning of an utterance. Another way to think through this issue is to think of all the contexts in which you might utter the same words. Take the case of the utterance

(37) I'm tired

If I say it late at night, it may count as a way of excusing myself and getting off to bed before my wife. Or she may perhaps take it as a hint that I want her to come to bed too. Either way it means that I want to go to bed. But if I say *I'm tired* when the alarm clock goes off at ten-to-seven the next morning, it probably means that I do not want to get out of bed and will hopefully be interpreted by my wife as a hint that she should get out of bed and make the coffee. In fact, we could think of as many meanings for *I'm tired* as we could think of contexts in which it might be uttered; or put another way, as many contexts for it as meanings that it might have. The same point could be made about

(38) I've got a flat tyre

In a garage, this might be taken to mean that I need help; or if addressed to a friend with a car, that I need a lift; or as a response to a request for a lift from a friend without a car, that I can't give them a lift; or indeed a wide range of other things in all the other contexts in which you might imagine it being uttered.
Similarly

(39) Can you open the door

is usually taken as a polite, conventionally indirect way of requesting someone to open a door for us. But imagine a non-typical context: you and I are robbing a bank and you are struggling with an oxy-acetylene cutter while I am keeping an anxious look-out. If I were to say *Can you open the door* in such a context, it would probably be a genuine question rather than an indirect request.

Even the physical context in which a written message occurs can play an important part in helping to determine its meaning. Just to the left of the entrance to the Department of Politics at Newcastle University, there's a sign that reads 'WELCOME TO POLITICS'. On the door itself, there's a second sign 'Staff and students please use swipecards. Visitors please use intercom.'

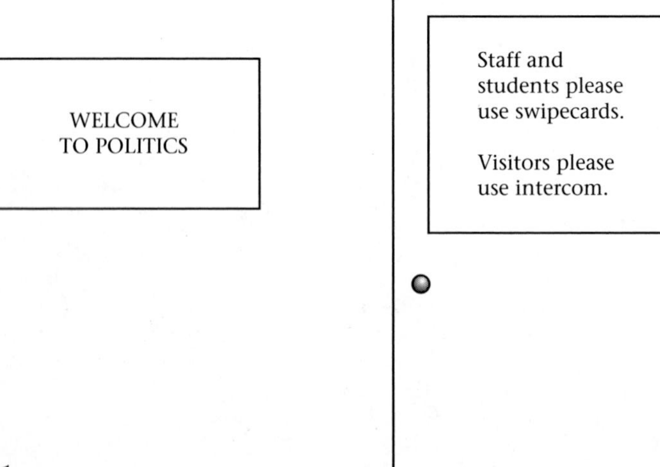

Figure 1.1

Because of their relative placing, we read 'WELCOME TO POLITICS' first. But imagine that 'WELCOME TO POLITICS' was to the right of 'Staff and students . . .'

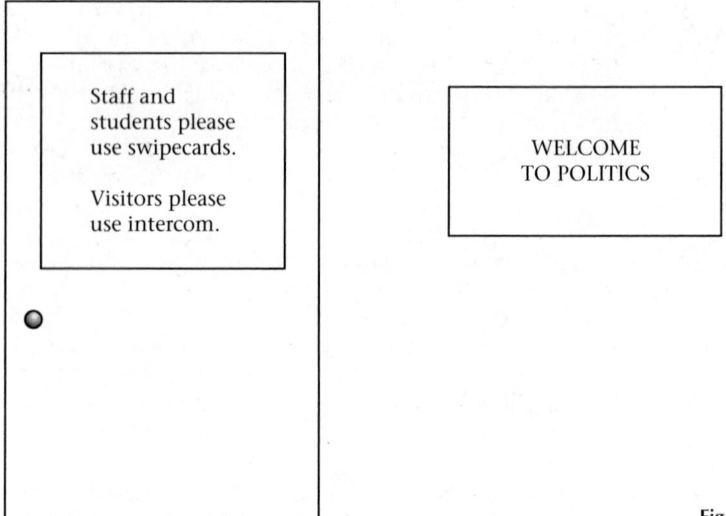

Figure 1.2

Arranged like this, the meanings of both 'welcome to' and 'politics' would be determined quite differently.

I found myself thinking very hard about the context when I had to give a lecture in a university in China on 4th June, the anniversary of the Tiananmen massacre. The title of my talk, which was about second language learning, was 'Listening to Learners'. I began with this sentence

(40) I suppose today it's especially important to be thinking carefully about what our students say to us

There was a perceptible tension as the audience struggled for a moment to determine whether 'today' was a reference to 4th June specifically or to the more general contemporary language teaching methodology scene. I let them consider which of the two contexts was most appropriate for a fraction of a second before going on to explain why listening to our learners is important in language teaching. Had I referred to the Tiananmen context? For some people, perhaps yes; for others, perhaps no.

Sometimes it's interesting to try and guess the context of an utterance. Someone once said to me

(41) Have you got a plastic bag?

Can you guess the context? The same utterance may well have been addressed to you on some occasion in the past. I was once foolish enough to ask a lecture theatre full of students to try and supply the context in which this utterance occurred. Someone shouted out 'You'd just had a colostomy?'

In fact, the real context was much more interesting. It was seven o'clock one Saturday night in Warsaw at the time of military rule in the 1980s. I was with a Polish colleague who was looking after me and we were on our way to a party. I suggested that we should buy a bottle of wine to take with us, which caused her to say rather pityingly, 'You must be joking!' She explained that General Jaruszelski, the then President, did not approve of drinking and so had decreed that no alcohol was to be sold after 5 pm on Saturday afternoons, not even in the hotels where at every other time of the week hard currency would buy you alcohol. So we hit on the idea of playing the stupid foreigner. Entering the restaurant across the road, I asked whether they spoke English (no) or German (nein). So I explained that I would speak English and that my friend would translate: 'Translate please, Maria,' I said, which she duly did. I then explained that I had had a meal in the restaurant two days before and had enjoyed a bottle of most excellent wine. Again Maria translated. As we were going to the birthday party of a very special friend, I was wondering whether it would be possible to have another bottle of their excellent wine to take as a present. Maria translated again, and this time the lady behind the bar obligingly replied 'Have you got a plastic bag?' Luckily I had, and passed it across the bar. Her reply is especially interesting because in the context in which it occurred it counted as an agreement to break the law, and could in theory have landed her (and perhaps us) in quite serious trouble.

My daughter provided another nice example of how context helps us to determine what an utterance means. When she began to be too big for her first pony, I suggested that she should sell the pony and get a bigger one. She replied

(42) I'll never sell her

It took me several months of persuasion, but in the end she agreed that the time had come and we put an advertisement in the paper. After two or three time-wasters had been to see the pony, my daughter said once again 'I'll never sell her', but of course she meant something entirely different this time.

The postmaster in our local post office is an endless source of pragmatically interesting utterances. One morning I overheard a customer complaining that the money he had been given was dirty. The postmaster leaned forward and said

(43) Be careful you don't trip over the step on your way out

What's really interesting about this utterance is that there isn't a step on the way out of our post office. Once you have this little bit of contextual information, you can begin to think about what the postmaster meant by what he said.

Another way in which we try to make the way we say things reflect context is in our use of politeness strategies. We know that

(44) Could you let me have a bit of paper by any chance

is a way of lessening our request and much more likely to be acceded to than

(45) Give me a sheet of paper

Not all contexts are real world. Often, as in the case of 'WELCOME TO POLITICS', it's co-text which constitutes the context for our interpretation. I once read a newspaper report which included the sentence

(46) People living nearby said Mr Neale would go away on 'lengthy business trips'

I expect your interpretation of this sentence is quite different when you know its linguistic context. The previous sentence was 'Neither would the police comment on whether Mr Neale had recently served time in prison'. It's also worth noting that the use of upper case in 'WELCOME TO POLITICS' and scare quotes in 'lengthy business trips' alert us to the kinds of determination that are more likely to be relevant.

As we review the examples in this section, we might ask ourselves whether the taken-for-granted view that the context we find ourselves in determines the language we choose is in fact right. Could it be the other way round, with the language we use creating context? Do I say 'I'm tired' because I want my wife to get out of bed in the morning and make coffee (i.e. the context determines what I say), or does my saying 'I'm tired' construct a context in which a kind wife would get out of bed and make coffee for a still-tired husband?

As these examples show, the relationship between context and language is central in pragmatics. One of the things you'll have to make up your mind about as you study pragmatics is whether the context determines the way we use language or whether the way we use language determines the context. Let me give you another example to help you think this through. My daughter used to take a teenage magazine for girls called *19*. One morning at breakfast she asked me if I wanted to hear my horoscope, and taking silence to mean yes, read out

(47) You are obsessing about a lad but you don't know how to show him how you feel

I said that it wasn't a very appropriate horoscope but she defended it on the grounds that I might be 'going gay'. For me, the context was given – *19* was a teenage magazine for girls and I didn't want to hear the horoscope because I knew it wouldn't be appropriate to a teenage girl's father. But Eleanor, on the other hand, tried to find a context which would make sense of what was written.

Because pragmaticists are interested in the meanings of utterances, they are also interested in the contexts in which utterances occur, since, as we have seen, these contexts help us to determine the meaning of what is said to us.

1.2.6 Relevance

In the previous section we showed how understanding

(40) I suppose today it's especially important to be thinking carefully about what our students say to us

depended on choosing the most relevant of two possible meanings. Deciding on the most appropriate reference for *today* is really a matter of deciding whether a reference to 4th June as the anniversary of the Tiananmen massacre or a reference to present times in general is more relevant. Usually it's a fairly simple matter to decide on the most relevant way to take an utterance, so that in the case of 'I'm tired', we can readily discount all but two or three of the possible pragmatic meanings, on the grounds that none of others could be relevant to the situation obtaining at the time of the utterance. And usually it's relatively easy to tell which of these two or three possible meanings is the most relevant.

We know that relevance is important to understanding because there are mechanisms that enable us to check that we have achieved the most relevant understanding. For example, shortly after half-term in my son's first term at secondary school, he said one day

(48) I'm enjoying school much more now

I was unclear about the reference of 'now'. Did he mean that he was enjoying the second half of his first term at secondary school more than the first half, or did he mean that he preferred secondary school to primary school? Because I could see no way of determining which was the more relevant understanding, I had to ask him to clarify.

Relevance has been seen by Sperber and Wilson (1986, 1995) as the most important principle in accounting for the way we understand language. Since we take every utterance as relevant, we understand utterances in whatever way will make them as relevant as possible. Thus for weeks there was a broken chair in our corridor at work with a notice pinned to it which said

(49) Sit down with care
Legs can come off

It was obviously more relevant to assume the legs belonged to the chair than to the person sitting down.

Sometimes we change our minds about how to take an utterance. A nice example occurred when I worked in Hong Kong. One of the Hong Kong radio stations invented a little jingle

(50) Hong Kong's original channel, 567, Hong Kong's Radio 3 – is there anything else

Whoever thought it up obviously intended 'is there anything else' to be most relevantly understood as an assertion that there couldn't be anything else as good to listen to. But as the weeks went by people began to make jokes about it and roll their eyes heavenwards while saying 'is there anything else'. Their despairing tone indicated that 'anything else' would be better than Radio 3. Not long after, the jingle ceased to be broadcast.

1.2.7 Accommodation

As we try to determine what people mean by what they say, we usually need to accept, or accommodate, a good deal of information which we feel is known to both the speaker and ourselves. This background knowledge or **accommodation** is essential to making sense of exchanges like this one that occurred when the public address system burst into life while I was waiting in the queue at the builders merchant

(51) PUBLIC ADDRESS: Will Bobby Thompson please report to reception
PETER: A bit late
MAN IN FRONT OF PETER IN QUEUE: Perhaps they need cheering up in reception

As you read this, you are probably finding it very hard to understand either me or the man in front of me. This is because we have a vital piece of background knowledge – Bobby Thompson is also the name of a well-known local stand-up comic who died several years earlier. Without this knowledge, you won't be able to make sense of our remarks. Nor would you fully understand the comment

(52) I didn't hear that

made by Evander Holyfield, the World Heavyweight Boxing Champion, on being told that a renewal of Mike Tyson's boxing licence was under consideration unless you could accommodate the crucial piece of background information that Tyson had lost his boxing licence for biting off a piece of Holyfield's ear. Like our comments at the builders merchant, Holyfield's comment is relevant in a special way because his audience can accommodate a vital piece of background information.

I once received an email from a colleague at another university, which contained the sentence

(53) There are rumours that Will's looking for a chair at Cambridge [I've substituted Will for the actual name used]

Given the academic context, it was natural for me to equate 'chair' with professorship, an accommodation which enabled me to reply sarcastically 'If this is true, then I think his best chance is to go to IKEA'. Similarly, there wouldn't be much point in the advertisement board on our local station which read

(54) Back a winner by train: at Beverley, Doncaster, Hexham, Newcastle, Redcar, Thirsk and York

unless those who read it knew that there were racecourses and railway stations at the places listed. And unless readers also knew that trains in Britain had a deplorable punctuality record, still less point in the graffiti added by some wit

(55) Get there in time to see the last race

Such cultural knowledge makes it difficult for us to understand pragmatic meanings when we find ourselves in new cultures or among groups with whom we don't share a great deal of common knowledge. You'd need to know quite a lot about football correctly to determine the meaning of 'all systems go' as *previous plans/systems abandoned* rather than as the more usual, idiomatic *everything is ready and working*, to understand the newspaper headline that accompanied England's problematic preparations for the 2006 World Cup

(56) All systems go as Eriksson enters unknown territory

And you'd need to know quite a lot about manager Eriksson's personal life to enjoy the newspaper headline above a story speculating on the future of Beckham, the then captain

(57) No one is safe from Sven's chopper

I hope you agree that there's a subtle difference between accommodating a background belief and identifying a relevant context. What makes saying 'a bit late' appropriate following the public address announcement asking for Bobby Thompson to report to reception is the shared knowledge that the famous Bobby Thompson is dead. In just the same way, what makes saying 'I'm tired' appropriate when the alarm goes off is the belief my wife and I accommodate that someone has to make the coffee. Identifying the context in which my wife is that person is what makes my utterance relevant.

1.2.8 Reflexivity

Frequently one part of what we say provides some sort of comment on how our utterance fits into the discourse as a whole or on how the speaker wants to be understood. For example, 'therefore' in

(30) There must therefore be a very good case for not allowing anyone to proceed to Year 3

tells the reader how this sentence relates to the one(s) before. Or 'I suppose' in

(40) I suppose today it's especially important to be thinking carefully about what our students say to us

advises the audience that the speaker isn't absolutely certain that what he says is right.

At the beginning of one academic year, I saw two first-year students in conversation in the corridor. One was listing the courses she was taking. She mentioned courses with conventional titles like *Introduction to Logic*, and then said

(58) and er is it Knowledge and Reality

Her 'er is it' conveys to the hearer that she isn't at all sure that she's got the title right.

The then American President, Bill Clinton's statement of 18 August 1998 contained the following sentence:

(59) Indeed, I did have a relationship with Ms Lewinsky that was not appropriate. In fact, it was wrong.

Notice how 'Indeed' and 'In fact' tell you of Clinton's commitment to the truth of what he is saying, as does the emphatic use of 'did'. And notice how 'it was wrong' glosses 'that was not appropriate' and how both comment on the 'relationship'. Clinton simultaneously tells us something (that he had a relationship), comments on what he tells us (that it was wrong) and assures us of his veracity (the function of 'in fact').

When speakers advise us of how they want us to take what they say, they make the task of understanding easier. This is why **reflexive** uses of language are so common.

1.2.9 Misfires

There was the wonderful Admiral Stainforth who nominated the independent candidate Ross Perot for the American Presidency in 1992. He began his nominating speech with the weedy shriek

(60) Who am I? Why am I here?

and must have been astonished at the howls of laughter that greeted what seemed to his audience to be all too real questions. He had made a calculation that this ringing start to his oration would have a particular pragmatic effect, which unfortunately for him it did not have. It was a kind of pragmatic 'misfire'. Pragmatic misfires are important because they tell us that there are expected norms for talk by showing us the effect of not achieving the norm. If you think back over the last few hours, you will probably be aware that several of your utterances did not have quite the effects you would have wished, or at least so it seems when you judge from the reactions of those you were addressing.

In the days before the building I worked in became a no-smoking zone, one of the secretaries put a notice on her office door which read

(61) Thank you for not smoking

This was taken rather amiss by one or two people who should have known better but who clearly did not like being ordered about by the secretary.

This reaction suggests that misfires are a kind of pragmatic failure which results from language being used in a way that is not felt to be appropriate to the context. Thus the last sentence of the letter from the optician reminding me that I was due for an eye-test would have been perfectly appropriate from anyone else:

(62) We look forward to seeing you soon

Or the handbill I picked up at the IBIS hotel which was intended to convey indirectly that the hotel food was of excellent quality prompted quite an opposite understanding

(63) Once you've experienced a meal at IBIS, you'll never want to eat anywhere else

In a similar vein, every time the *Moonlight Exquisite Tandoori Restaurant* puts its leaflet through our letter-box I'm tempted to determine 'want to repeat' in a way unintended by the author

(64) Come and sample the delights of Moonlight. You won't be disappointed and we can guarantee it'll be an experience you'll want to repeat

No doubt the propagandizing former Minister of Education wished her statement on the BBC *Today* programme had been less pragmatically ambiguous

(65) Reading and writing have improved immeasurably

Similarly ill-conceived was the CNN plug for an upcoming programme which promised

(66) a concrete plan to revive the world's dwindling coral reefs

And the student branch of the NatWest bank I visited might perhaps have considered more carefully the possible determination of their leaflet entitled

(67) Feel the need for speed?

As well as helping us to identify pragmatic norms, these misfires also remind us of the role of the addressee, who sets out to recover an optimal meaning for utterances, and remind us of the care speakers need to exercise so as to convey successfully the meanings they intend.

Finally, it should be added that misfires are rare. In fact, speakers are able to convey and addressees to recover meanings other than those explicitly stated with remarkable consistency as a matter of course.

Summary

What have we said so far? We have listed a number of features of talk which are at the heart of pragmatics. They include the notions of appropriateness and relevance, on the one hand, and our liking for non-literal and indirect meaning, on the other. We have seen that there is a crucial relationship between what we say and the context in which it is relevant, including the background beliefs that addressees are expected to accommodate. All this is made possible by the indeterminacy of language and the role of inference in language understanding. And frequently, speakers use language reflexively to indicate how they want what they say to be understood.

Although for convenience I have treated each of these features as distinct, it is already apparent that they are really a bundle which typically appear together. Take the barmaid's botched offer to serve that we considered earlier

(2) BARMAID: Are you two both together – well you know what I mean

In our earlier discussion we commented on the different effects of the *appropriate* 'Are you together' as an *indirect* way of offering to serve someone standing at a bar when the person standing next to them is being served. And we noted the contextually *inappropriate* use of 'Are you two both together'. As a form of words, 'Are you together' is *indeterminate* and in a different *context* would be expected to have a different meaning. The most *relevant* way to take the contextually inappropriate 'Are you two both together' is that the two men are being asked if they are a couple, an *inference* which depends on our ability to *accommodate* the possibility that two men standing together at a bar may be in a relationship. The second part of the barmaid's utterance, 'Well you know what I mean', acts *reflexively* by referring to what has just been said and the possibility that an unintended meaning may have been conveyed, or, in other words, that a pragmatic *misfire* has occurred.

Checking understanding (1.2)

Consider how each of the following utterances relates to the notions of appropriateness, indirectness, inference, indeterminacy, context, relevance, accommodation and reflexivity discussed in this chapter:

(68) Even Presidents have private lives (Bill Clinton, 18 August 1998)
(69) I don't know how you say this in English but for me it was ooh-la-la-la (The French jockey, Olivier Peslier, on the first occasion when he rode the winning horse in the *Prix de l'Arc de Triomphe*)

And for those who understand cricket

(70) Shane Warne can't bowl from both ends (Radio commentator at an England vs Australia Test Match)

1.3 Deixis, speech acts, implicature

I'm now going to try and round this chapter off in the more systematic way promised at the beginning of the previous section by looking at the pragmatic properties of a single utterance and a two-turn exchange. As we'll see, it's one thing to describe the pragmatic properties of utterances as we have been trying to do in this chapter, but quite another to explain how we understand under-determined utterances more or less in the way the speaker intends. We can all recognize the degree to which an utterance is appropriate just as we don't need to be academics to know what light is, but, to echo Sam Johnson's comment with which this chapter began, explaining phenomena like light or appropriateness is far from simple.

The utterance

(71) I'm here now

which Kaplan (1978) discusses in his long and difficult paper on demonstratives, looks straightforward. But for a pragmaticist it has three very problematical properties:

1 *Deixis*
The first of these is to do with an indeterminacy that can only be resolved when we look at the context, and particularly at three aspects of that context, **who** the speaker is and **where** and **when** the sentence is uttered. This indeterminacy stems from the speaker's use of the words 'I', 'here' and 'now'. Although the meaning of the word *I* is perfectly clear and not at all problematical, the reference that is effected each time it is uttered clearly depends on who utters it. In this respect *I* is a quite different kind of description from *Agatha Christie*, which always refers to the same person. Just the same point could be made about *here*. Its meaning is clear enough but its reference depends on the location of the speaker when the sentence is uttered, so that *here* might refer to *Durham* or *Durban* or *Marks and Spencer* or the speaker's kitchen. Similarly the reference of *now* is determined by the time at which the sentence is spoken. This property of a small set of words like *I*, *here* and *now* to pick out an aspect of the context in which they are uttered is called **deixis**, the topic area we will study in the next chapter.

2 *Utterances as speech acts*
The second problematical property of 'I'm here now' stems not only from the natural indeterminacy of the utterance and from the context, but also from considerations of what it most appropriately counts as doing. So if I had heard that a relative had been injured and taken to hospital, I might race there as quickly as possible and say on arrival 'I'm here now', which would count perhaps as a comforting reassurance. On the other hand, if I get home from work and see my children larking about instead of getting on with their homework and say 'I'm here now', it counts as a stern warning. Or if I were to arrive late for a meeting and knew that I had kept my colleagues waiting, uttering 'I'm here now' might count as an apology or as a signal to start the meeting. Utterances like *I'm here now* not only describe situations, they also count as **doing** something, be it reassuring, warning, apologizing or whatever. This is why we call them **speech acts**. After all, there isn't much point on saying *I'm here now*, which must be readily apparent to all and sundry anyway, unless you intend to do something by saying it.

3 *Implicature*
The third problematical property of 'I'm here now' stems not only from the natural indeterminacy of the utterance but also from the context and from considering what inference ought to be drawn to make the utterance maximally relevant. Imagine the utterance being used by two different students talking to themselves on the day they arrive in Newcastle to begin their Linguistics degree course. The first student comes from Southampton and uses 'here' to refer to Newcastle; the second student comes from China and had been looking forward to studying overseas for several years – for this student 'here' refers to Britain. The point is that both references for 'here' are equally consistent with any correspondence the sentence might be thought to have with states of affairs in the world. But knowing which is the right one is a matter of working out which understanding is the most relevant and might be thought to be the one being implied by the speaker. A similar point could be made about 'now', which for one speaker might refer to a particular date and for another might mean something more like *at last*.

But this isn't all: sometimes 'I'm here now' conveys something like *There's no need to worry any more* (the hospital context), sometimes something like *Stop messing about and get on with your homework* (the kids larking about context) and sometimes something like *I'm sorry I've held you up* (the meeting context). And of course these three meanings are only a tiny subset of the possible meanings that a speaker saying 'I'm here now' might be intending to convey. Thus one of the properties of language is that in addition to expressing an invariant meaning, propositions also frequently convey an implied meaning which the addressee must infer. This kind of meaning is called an **implicature**.

Now for a two-turn exchange from a real conversation. For the moment, I won't reveal the context:

(72) A: Are you working this afternoon
B: I'm going back to the office

Deixis: unless you know the speakers involved in the exchange, you don't know who 'you' and 'I' refer to. Unless you know whether the exchange takes place in the morning or once the afternoon has already commenced, you don't know whether 'this afternoon' picks out the whole of the afternoon or the remaining part of it. And unless you know on which date the exchange takes place, you don't know which afternoon is referred to.

Speech acts: If A and B are a couple, A might be requesting B to do some shopping; or if A is B's boss, A may be hinting that it's time B went back to work; or if A knows that B has two workplaces, the question may count as a request to be told where B is working; or if B has a car and A works near B's office, A might be asking for a lift. In other words, there are as many potential speech acts as there are contexts.

Implicatures: In fact, I was A and B was someone I'd never met before who I got talking to at a publisher's lunch. Other important elements of the context are that we had been given several glasses of wine to drink and it was a Friday. The lunch was in London and B knew I lived in Newcastle and therefore wouldn't be working in the afternoon. My question was intended to imply that I would feel sorry for him if he had to go back to work. I took his reply to mean that he didn't expect to be doing any work in any case.

To sum up, pragmaticists study the way in which language is appropriate to the contexts in which it is used. Fortunately, language is under-determined enough to allow us to infer the way in which an utterance is to be understood in the context in which it occurs. Often speakers comment reflexively on what they say (as I did with 'fortunately' in the previous sentence) so as to assist hearers in determining how to take utterances. In the rest of this book, we will investigate the crucial relationship of language use and context, which is the essential subject area of pragmatics.

Raising pragmatic awareness

1 This exercise works well if you do Step 1 individually and Steps 2 and 3 in your tutorial or with a group of friends.

(1) Write a very short dialogue between two imaginary characters.
(2) Dictate each utterance to your colleagues. As you dictate, they write down, not what you say but the contexts in which they imagine each utterance being spoken.
(3) Ask each person to read out what they have written down and discuss the pragmatics of the utterances in relation to the contexts which have been imagined for them.

Raising pragmatic awareness *cont.*

2 This exercise works best in a tutorial or with a group of friends. Choose an item from the following list and brainstorm all the contexts in which you could utter it: *I'm tired, I'm sorry, Is it me, I thought so, Don't.* Why do you think a single proposition can function as so many different speech acts?

3 Get together with a few friends. Each person should recall something surprising which someone once said to them. The other members of the group try to guess the context by asking Yes/No questions.

4 This exercise works best in pairs. You and your partner each find three or four sentences from different newspaper stories or captions for newspaper photographs which invite the reader to draw an inference. (For example, 'The husband of the doctor who disappeared last week refused to comment. Meanwhile, the police continued digging in their garden.') When you have each found your sentences or captions, see whether your partner draws the same inferences as you and try to work out what triggers them. (Acknowledgement: this is Andrew Caink's idea.)

5 This exercise works well in a tutorial group. Before the tutorial, cut out three or four magazine pictures and pin instructions to them which test pragmatic skills. For example, if you cut out a picture of a romantic couple looking out over the sea at night, your instruction might be 'Ask these two for a cigarette / if they've lost a pen you've just found / where they get their hair done'; or if you cut out a picture of someone with a gun, the instruction might be 'Ask her/him for the gun'; or a picture of a toddler, 'Get this person to admire your shoes / to call you Mummy'. Take the pictures and instructions to your tutorial and ask the other members of your group how they would carry out the instructions.

Discussions and essays

Based on what you already know about pragmatics, discuss the relative merits of each of the following views:

- While semanticists study the basic meanings of words, pragmaticists study what speakers mean on the particular occasions when they use words.
- Pragmatic uses of language require addressees to take context into account in order to understand what speakers mean.
- All non-literal meanings are by definition pragmatic.
- We tend to be much better at describing literal meaning than pragmatic meaning because, unlike literal meaning, pragmatic meaning does not depend on form and is therefore largely invisible.

Further reading

Blakemore, 1992:3–23; Cutting, 2007: 1–8; Levinson, 1983: 1–5; Mey, 2001: 12–18; Thomas, 1995: 1–23; Yule, 1996: 2–3.

2 Deixis – the relation of reference to the point of origin of the utterance

SPEAKER A: Here today, gone tomorrow
SPEAKER B: You said that last time
(Two cynics discussing the possible future of a new manager at Newcastle United Football Club)

Keywords:

anaphora, antecedent, common ground, context, deictic centre, deictic change, deixis, demonstrative, discourse deixis, embodiment, gesture, honorific, index, indexicality, membership, person deixis, place deixis, point of origin, reference, social deixis, time deixis

2.1 Introduction

Pragmatic meanings are determined by context; in the case of deictic reference, the critical contextual element is the point of origin of the utterance. In an exchange like

(1) A: When will you be back
B: I should be back by eight but you know what trains are like

you, the reader, don't know who A's use of 'you' and B's use of 'I' refers to. Nor do you know the location referred to by A's use of 'back'. Nor, until B speaks, do you have any idea of the possible time-frame that might be referred to by 'will'; and even when B answers, although you know the time of day ('around eight'), you still don't know on which day or date B 'should by back'. These uses of language pick out a person, a place and a time which can only be determined by someone either present when the exchange occurred or informed of the context in which it took place. Since you were not present when the exchange occurred, you can only determine the referents of 'you/I', 'back' and 'will' if I tell you that A is my wife and B is me, and that the conversation takes place at our home in Newcastle just after breakfast on Saturday 19 May. By providing the original context of the exchange, I have remedied the semantic deficiency of 'you', 'I', 'back' and 'will' as you would have done for yourself, had you been present.

Because expressions such as *you* and *I* constitute a particularly obvious way in which **context** determines interpretation, they seem to be an obvious place to begin our serious study of pragmatics.

The chapter you are about to read contains three further sections, each of which includes several sub-sections:

- *Deictic reference,* which discusses the properties of deictics and the way we understand deictic reference.
- *Deixis in the real world,* which describes a number of actual uses including several typical of Hong Kong contexts.

- *Indexicality, grammar and meaning*, which discusses issues raised by the study of indexicals.

2.2 Deictic reference

2.2.1 Indexical signs

Two scenarios: In the first, you ring my doorbell, and I open the door and say

(2) Do come in

In the second, we approach my house together. I take out my key, open the door and, standing aside, say to you

(3) Do go in

In both cases you are going to go from the same point A to the same point B. But my instruction differs in each case because the relationship between where I stand and where you are to go differs. In other words, there is a common element of meaning which *come* and *go* share, but they differ in the way in which they encode the context – although you are to move to the same place, in the case of (2) you are to move towards me and in the case of (3) you are to move away from me.

In this chapter we will be exploring the way in which a small number of words, such as *come* and *go*, and *I* and *here* and *now*, require an addressee to be able to pick out a person, place or time so as to determine how the word refers. Because *I*, *here* and *now* enable us to identify referents particular to the context, we call these words **indexical** and this function of language **deictic**, a word of Greek origin meaning *pointing to* or *picking out*. Thus the property of language we are studying is called **indexicality**, and the lexical items which encode context in this way are called **deictics**.

A third scenario: Imagine you finally get through the front door and into my house. As you stand in the hall, this is what you see:

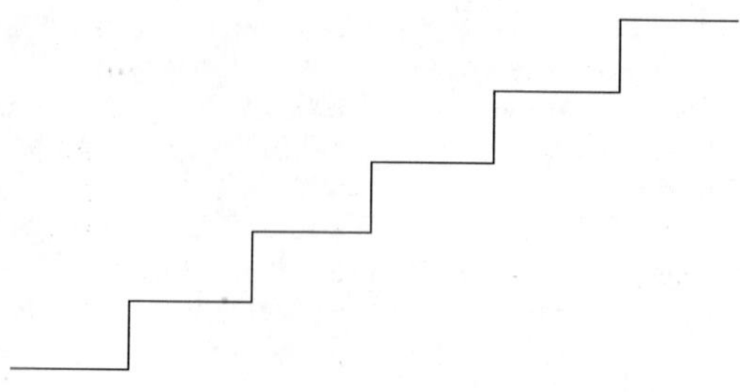

Figure 2.1

leading to the floors above. Unlike the case of *come* and *go*, the word you might use to describe what you see, 'stairs', does not depend on where we are each standing. And it doesn't matter whether you use the word 'stairs' or draw the diagram above, in each case I will know what is referred to. The philosopher Peirce drew a distinction between signs like the one you see in the diagram above, which he called icons, and signs in the form of words, which he called symbols. As well as icon and symbol, Peirce also identified a third sign-type which he called **index**. An index is a pointing device – hence 'index finger', the finger we use for pointing; hence the long list of words and phrases at the end of this book which point to or 'index' different places in the text. In just the same way, the word *I* is an index which points to a person, *here* an index which points to a place and *now* an index which points to a time. Because of their pointing function, we call such words **demonstratives.**

Imagine we are now in the hall of my house and you have come to stay with me. I might say to you

(4) Let's go up and I'll show you your room

The word 'up' is also an index because unless you happen to be in a particular place, such as my house, you cannot know which location it points to. If we were standing at the bottom of a ladder propped against the outside wall of my house and I said

(5) I'll go up if you hold the ladder

the indexical sign 'up' would not pick out the same location as in (4). Similarly, the people referred to when I say '<let>'s' and 'I' and 'you' are all contextually determined, as is the room indicated by 'your room', a description which a colleague might well have used earlier in the day to refer to the office in which you work.

2.2.2 Indexicals: the role of context in helping to determine reference

Consider the following:

(6) I know you'll enjoy reading the chapter
(7) When I say you have to read the chapter, I mean YOU have to read it and YOU have to read it and YOU have to read it
(8) With a book like this, you never know whether to read every chapter or skip one or two

In (6) 'you' picks out a particular but different person on each separate occasion when the sentence is read. On this occasion it is, yes, you, my friend, who is picked out as the referent. And if by any chance there are two of you out there working together as a team reading the book aloud and saying things about me the author, then on this particular occasion 'you' picks out both of you.

Similarly, if in a lecture I were to deliver (7), the three stressed 'YOU's in the second part of the utterance would be accompanied by gestures (nodding, pointing, eye-contact, etc.). Each use would pick out a different referent whose identity would be known only by those present at the time of my utterance.

But in

(8) With a book like this, you never know whether to read every chapter or skip one or two

'you' has a much more general reference. In fact, being present when the sentence was uttered wouldn't help you to identify a referent. This generalized use of 'you' is therefore non-deictic.

Of course 'YOU' isn't the only pronoun in (7). The three uses of 'it' also refer, but to an **antecedent**, 'the chapter', within the utterance. Once again, this use is non-deictic – we don't need to be present at the time of the utterance to identify the referent.

These uses can be represented diagrammatically:

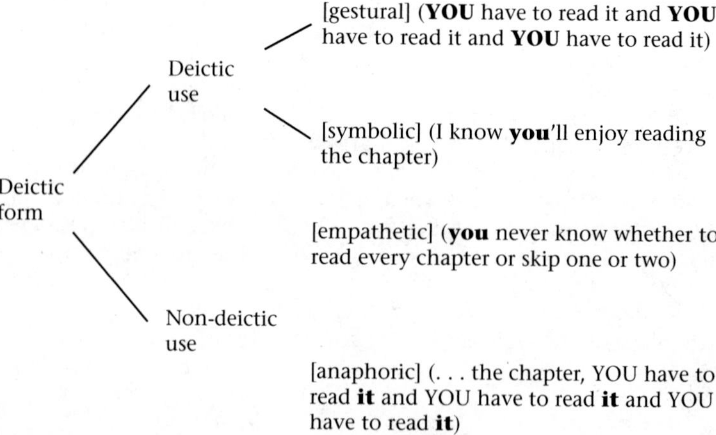
Deictic form
Deictic use
Non-deictic use
[gestural] (**YOU** have to read it and **YOU** have to read it and **YOU** have to read it)
[symbolic] (I know **you**'ll enjoy reading the chapter)
[empathetic] (**you** never know whether to read every chapter or skip one or two)
[anaphoric] (. . . the chapter, YOU have to read **it** and YOU have to read **it** and YOU have to read **it**)

Figure 2.2

Precisely because deictics are semantically deficient, gestures often help us to identify the referents. We use the term 'symbolic' for indexical uses which point to a referent without an accompanying gesture. Although there are cases where gestures seem obligatory and others where they would be very unlikely, the boundary between gestural and symbolic uses of some deictics appears to vary from speaker to speaker and from one social context to another. You can probably imagine saying 'Speaking for myself' with a physical gesture, with an intonational gesture, with both, and with no gesture at all, depending on the context. One kind of gesture we often use to help to determine a precise reference is contrastive intonation, as in

(6′) I know YOU'll enjoy reading the chapter

where I set out to delimit the reference of *you* and imply that others wouldn't enjoy the chapter.

Just as the boundary between gestural and symbolic use is sometimes difficult to determine, it can also be difficult to distinguish symbolic and non-deictic use: although the term 'empathetic' is intended to reflect our ability to see the world from our addressee's perspective, can you always be sure whether the use of 'you' is deictic or non-deictic when people say things like

(9) You're not supposed to say that

When (9) is used as a response to a previous utterance, does 'that' refer deictically or anaphorically? Perhaps deictically when the reference is to an idea and anaphorically when the reference is to the exact words used? Or perhaps it refers both anaphorically and deictically?

One more important distinction. If I ask

(10) How long ago did the last bus leave

'the last bus' is clearly a deictic used to index whichever bus had left most recently before the time of speaking, so that the expression could in principle be used to refer to every bus throughout the day. This use contrasts with the intrinsic use in

(11) The last bus leaves at 23.30

Here 'The last bus' always refers to the same timetable slot in a non-demonstrative way so that identifying the referent does not depend on knowing the time of the utterance.

Finally, deictics are a closed class, i.e. there is a limited set of such words to which we cannot (readily) add. As with other closed class categories, deictics are semantically deficient. This makes them especially useful as a limited set of indeterminate lexical items (such as *you*) whose references are determined in the context of face-to-face interaction and which act as a shorthand for a potentially infinite number of referents (such as every possible grouping of all the people anyone would ever address). However, there is a trade-off: the economy of *you* as a means of referring comes at the price of being able to access a context that enables its reference to be determined. In the next three sections, we'll follow the usual practice of categorizing deictics according to the three fundamental semantic criteria that are a necessary part of every context we experience: *person, place* and *time.*

Checking understanding (2.1)

1 Try to think of utterances in which the words *this, now* and *behind* might be used (a) gesturally and deictically; (b) symbolically and deictically; and (c) non-deictically.

2 Write five or six sentences containing either the word *that* or the word *then* which you could place on a cline from very obviously deictic to non-deictic.

3 If a friend handed you a copy of *Doing Pragmatics* open at Chapter 2 and said 'You just have to read this chapter', how would you categorize his/her use of 'you' and 'this'?

4 Imagine you are out walking with a friend. Can you think of any circumstances in which you can use the phrase *the last mile* intrinsically?

2.2.3 Person deixis

The phenomena: First and second person pronouns and noun phrases determined by first and second person possessives are typically indexical, as in

(12) I don't think your sister likes me

Although third person pronouns may be used indexically, as in

(13) Look at her

they are typically used anaphorically to index a referent in the earlier discourse, as in

(14) Just look at Mary. Where's she been?

The use: We've already seen how *you* can be used both deictically and non-deictically. In English, *you* is used in a much wider range of social contexts than would be represented by a single second person reference term in most other languages. For example, most languages have at least two second person forms, an informal or familiar one for use when talking to friends and a more formal one used for showing respect to the person addressed, typically because they are older or more important than the speaker. In many languages the second person plural form (e.g., *vous* in French) or the third person plural form (e.g., *Sie* in German) has this honorific function, so that in German

(15) Ich danke Ihnen
I thank them (dative)
'Thank you'

is a formal way of thanking and at the same time showing respect to the person one is speaking to. In discussing this **honorific** use of language, following Comrie (1976), Levinson (1983: 90), points out that deictics like *vous* and *Sie* are oriented to a referent (person being referred to) rather than to an addressee (person being addressed). This explains why it makes sense to describe the person we are talking to as 'you' (pl.) or 'they' without appearing contradictory: we address our equals and refer to our superiors. To a native speaker of English this may seem exotic at first; but of course there are similar strategies in English, such as saying 'Shall we do *x*' or 'We could do *y*' when steering someone more important than oneself towards some course of action. Here the interrogative form and the use of the modal auxiliaries 'shall' and 'could' also convey respect to the addressee. In Polish, it would be usual for a ticket collector to show respect to a passenger in the humiliating position of being ticketless on a train by including him/herself in the reference as a sign of respect:

(16) Nie mamy biletu
not have (1st pl) ticket
'You haven't got a ticket?'

In English this inclusion of self in a reference in such a situation is usually sarcastic rather than respectful:

(16′) We haven't got a ticket (then)

Although English appears to have only one deictic address word, *you*, the use of *you two* commented on in the previous chapter and *you-all* (for example, by teachers when talking to groups of students) suggests that speakers do indeed want to encode distinctions that are impossible when there is only a single form available.

Notice that if you and your friend are lost and you say

(17) I'm going to ask someone to help us

your use of 'us' includes your friend as addressee in the reference. But when you approach a stranger and say

(18) Excuse me, can you help us

your use of 'us' does not include the addressee. Many languages grammaticalize exactly this distinction between addressee-inclusive and addressee-exclusive uses of *we*.

First and second person pronouns refer exophorically, i.e. to persons outside the discourse. Third person pronouns typically refer endophorically, either to antecedents, persons/objects already mentioned in the discourse in the case of anaphoric reference, or occasionally to persons/objects about to be mentioned (cataphoric reference). As semantically deficient items, all pronouns index either a *demonstratum*, something that can be pointed to or picked out in the context, or an antecedent in the co-text.

Checking understanding (2.2)

1 Spend a few minutes trying to decide whether *we* and *our* can be used non-deictically.

2 When the Iranian *fatwa* was pronounced on the author Salman Rushdie following the publication of his novel *The Satanic Verses*, he made a written statement apologizing for the distress his book had caused. Consider the following sentence taken from this apology:

(19) Living as we do in a world of so many faiths, this experience has served to remind us that we must all be conscious of the sensibilities of others.

Try to decide whether you think he meant to use 'we' and 'us' inclusively or exclusively, or even non-deictically.

2.2.4 Place deixis

The phenomena include demonstrative noun phrases (*this way, those people*, etc.), demonstrative adverbial expressions (*here, there, where, up, down, behind, ahead, on your left*, etc.) indicating location whose reference can only be determined in relation to the location of the utterance in which they occur, and certain verbs which encode an aspect of location or directionality such as *come, go, bring, take*. For most but not all speakers of English, there is a proximal demonstrative (*this/these*), and a distal demonstrative (*that/those*). Each may be used either as a pronoun or in combination with a noun. The archaic indexicals *hither, hence, thither, thence, whither, whence, yonder* suggest that the number of single-word deictics is reducing. Although demonstratives encoding two degrees of proximity to the speaker, such as *this* and *that* in English, is the commonest pattern across languages (Diessel, 1999), three degrees of proximity is by no means uncommon, with some languages distinguishing proximity to the speaker and to the addressee.

The use: As already noted, *come* usually encodes movement towards and *go* movement away from the speaker. However, if I was speaking on the telephone to my London-based son from my home in Newcastle, I'd be much more likely to say

(20) I'm coming to London on Friday

than

(20′) I'm going to London on Friday

because I'm seeing my movement from his perspective. Notice that I can't do this the other way round: if I'm in Newcastle, I can only say

(21) Are you coming to Newcastle at the weekend

not

(21′) Are you going to Newcastle at the weekend

And the expressions *up north* and *down south* commonly used in Britain can only be used by speakers about their own travel plans when they are not themselves in the locations indexed.

Like *go*, for most speakers, *take* encodes movement away and *bring* movement towards a given location. So a teacher reminds us to *bring* our homework to school and our parents remind us to *take* it there.

In countries like Britain where people drive on the left, the *nearside* of the car is on the driver's left and vehicles travelling in the opposite direction approach on the driver's right. In countries where people drive on the right, the *nearside* is also on the right. Since what's on my *left* is on the *right* of people facing me, we sometimes need an intrinsic way of distinguishing, as in the theatre where *stage-left* and *stage-right* always describe stage locations seen from the actor's point of view, or in a car where *left-hand-drive* means that the steering wheel is on the left from the perspective of people sitting in the car, and in medicine where doctors are careful to talk about *the patient's left/right* hand, kidney, etc. Similarly, the expression *local time* in reports of news stories originating overseas is intended to clarify the time at which the events actually occurred. So *at midnight* is usually assumed to be at midnight in relation to the time in the country where the news is being broadcast, and *at midnight local time* refers to midnight in the country in which the news story originates.

The extent to which context is involved in determining the reference of these items is well illustrated by what used to happen in a building I once worked in. Students looking for the Literature Department office would often climb the stairs to our floor only to find the Linguistics Department office at the top of the stairs directly facing them. When they asked our secretary where the Literature office was, she would sometimes reply

(22) Just along the corridor on your left

and sometimes

(22′) Just along the corridor on your right

This wasn't because she wanted to be difficult – quite the contrary in fact, but because she thought 'Just along the corridor on your left' more helpful for students standing in the doorway facing her directly with the Literature office to their left

Figure 2.3

and 'Just along the corridor on your right' more helpful for students looking through her door over their right shoulders with the Literature secretary's office further along on the right-hand side of the corridor down which they were already facing.

Figure 2.4

Checking understanding (2.3)

1 Under what circumstances would it be appropriate to say

(23) I'm going to John's party
(23′) I'm coming to John's party

2 This exchange took place when I attempted to cross the square in front of the Baltic Art Gallery in Gateshead one afternoon when to all intents and purposes things were just as they always are:

(24) SECURITY GUARD: Can you go round that way sir – a tent's going up and this area's classed as a building site now
PETER: I just want to go across there (indicating the far side of the square)

Draw a map marking the speakers and the two routes. Share it with your neighbour and justify your decisions.

3 You are looking at a school photograph with Mark in the middle:

Figure 2.5

Checking understanding (2.3) *cont.*

If I described one of the other people as being

(25) to the left of Mark
(26) on the left of Mark
(27) on Mark's left

which uses would be deictic and why?

4 What do you think are the unmarked locations of speaker, addressee and, where relevant, third party for each of the following utterances?

(28) If I come back to Durham
(28′) If I return to Durham
(29) If you come back to Durham
(29′) If you return to Durham
(30) If she comes back to Durham
(30′) If she returns to Durham

2.2.5 Time deixis

The phenomena include demonstrative adverbial expressions (*now, then, ago, later, soon, before, this Monday, last week, next year, at the weekend, today, tomorrow, yesterday*, etc.) and tense markers indicating points of time whose reference can only be determined in relation to the time of the utterance in which the tense markers occur.

The use: Although making a list of time deictics is relatively simple, the use of time deictics is not always so straightforward. For example, if a student says in September

(31) I hope this year's going to be good

'this year' probably refers to the academic year. If she says the same thing on 1st January, it refers to the calendrical year. And if she says it on her birthday, it refers to the twelve months until her next birthday. A related phenomenon occurs in the case of utterances including the deictic item *today*. If I say

(32) Today's always a bad day

as I get out of bed on a Monday morning, 'today' refers to Monday. But if I say

(33) I'll see to it today

or

(34) I filled up with petrol today

'today' refers to some unspecified moment in that portion of the day that remains unexpired (33) or has already passed (34). The use of *yesterday, today* and *tomorrow* is also privileged over the use of the name term for the days, so that we cannot say

(35) I'm going to finish this book on Thursday

if either today or tomorrow is Thursday. English has only a three-member set of single-word, pre-emptive terms of this sort, although we also use the phrases *the day before yesterday* and *the day after tomorrow*. There are languages that have five, seven and even a few languages with many more such terms.

In languages like English that encode tense, almost every sentence makes reference to an event time by means of tense and, sometimes, aspect markers. This event time can then only be determined in relation to the time of the utterance of the sentence. Thus when Alf Ramsay, the former manager of the England football team, said repeatedly in 1965 and the spring of 1966

(36) England will win the World Cup

he was referring to an event which he thought would be accomplished in 1966. Now it only makes sense to refer to that event with a past form such as

(37) England won the World Cup

or to make the utterance non-deictic by saying

(37′) England won the World Cup in 1966

Checking understanding (2.4)

1 In the last paragraph, you read a sentence beginning with the words 'Now it only makes sense . . .', repeating the formula used in the first edition of *Doing Pragmatics*. In the second edition, this sentence began with 'Half-a-lifetime later, it only makes sense . . .' Why do you think I made these changes?

2 Some weeks after his first wife died, Thomas Hardy wrote the poem *After a Journey*. It included the line apparently addressed to his deceased wife

(38) What have you found to say of our past

Or to be accurate, it included this line and the word 'now' – but for the moment I'm not telling you where he placed 'now'. How many grammatical positions can you find for *now* in the line? Consider each position and decide whether *now* is used deictically or non-deictically, and if deictically whether it is used gesturally. Can you draw any conclusions about the relationship between where *now* is placed in the line and deictic use in general?

2.2.6 Meaning and deictic reference

It's important to distinguish the invariant meaning of a deictic like *here* or *now* from its variable reference. Thus, Hanks suggests 'the region immediate to you' as one of the principal meanings of *here* and 'the time immediate to this utterance' as one of the principal meanings of *now* (1992: 52). It isn't these propositional meanings that change when a deictic occurs, but the place or time picked out or referred to which shifts as the context changes – hence the name 'shifter', which is sometimes applied to deictics. So when we look at the sign in the Mazda showroom

(39) The car you saw today and intend to buy tomorrow, somebody saw yesterday and intends to buy today

we realize that the 'somebody' who saw the car yesterday and intends to buy it today referred to what is now today as 'tomorrow' when they made the decision to buy the car. Thus knowing which day is picked out or referred to by deictics such as *yesterday, today* and *tomorrow* depends upon knowing the time of utterance – and gives rise to the adage 'Tomorrow never comes'.

You may have noticed that I have been using slightly opaque descriptions, such as 'picked out or referred to', when discussing the function of deictics. In fact, we need to distinguish the demonstrative act of indicating from actually referring. An index such as *this* is really an instruction to identify a referent to which the index is merely a pointer. At one time it was thought that uttering a deictic effected a reference directly, so that to say *this chapter* was to refer directly to the chapter indicated. More recently, however, Nunberg has rejected the index-referent identity hypothesis that "the referents of indexicals are the very things picked out by their linguistic meanings, or by their meanings taken together with the demonstrations that accompany their use" (1993: 6). Instead he proposed a theory of deferred reference which distinguishes between the index (e.g., *this chapter*, which acts as an instruction to identify the relevant chapter) and the interpretation (the chapter actually referred to). Imagine that after you have made yourself comfortable in the spare bedroom in my house, you come downstairs and join me for a glass of wine. In the course of our conversation I point to the wine bottle and say

(40) These are on special offer in the supermarket at the moment

I point to a single bottle and yet I use the plural form 'these' so I'm clearly not referring to just the single bottle you see. The index, *these*, and my gesture direct your attention to the single bottle in front of us, the *demonstratum*. The referent/s, the *demonstrandum/a*, is/are many in number and to be found elsewhere. The indexical expression 'these' thus instructs you to instantiate a set of objects similar to the one I point to. One interesting question is whether you construct a mental image of the bottle I point to or of the bottles I refer to – but we'll leave that problematic issue for another day!

2.2.7 The deictic centre

When we hear a deictic, we typically make a number of assumptions about the context. So if you say

(41) She lives across the road

the addressee will need to determine the location indexed by 'across the road'. If you are talking about where you live, your addressee will assume you are talking about someone who lives 'across the road' from you, but if you are talking about the new house your addressee has just moved to, they will assume that you are talking about someone who lives 'across the road' from them.

The default deictic centre is the speaker's location at the time of utterance, as in

(2) Do come in

But as we saw in

(22) Just along the corridor on your left

and

(22′) Just along the corridor on your right

the deictic centre has shifted. How does this happen?

The use of 'on your left' and 'on your right' is deictic since the same location is being indicated by two different descriptions and can only be determined by knowing the context, in this case, the direction in which the addressee is facing. The co-text associated with 'left' and 'right', the lexical item 'your', advises the addressee that the spatial deictic centre has shifted from the unmarked norm (the location of the speaker) to a marked alternative (the location of the addressee). Sometimes a shift is accomplished without co-text, the context itself being sufficient to prompt the addressee to draw the inference that their location rather than the speaker's is the deictic centre, as in

(20) I'm coming to London on Friday

If I am the hider in a game of hide-and-seek, for example, I might decide to give the seeker a clue by calling out

(42) Behind the tree

It's to be hoped that the seeker would draw the inference that I was behind the tree in relation to themselves rather than in relation to myself!

It's also common for a speaker to update the deictic centre in more extended discourse. So if I am giving you directions, I may punctuate them with expressions like 'after the traffic lights' or 'when you get to the post office'. These are signals to you to update the deictic centre and to interpret succeeding directions in relation to this new centre. We do the same with time when we say things like 'and then' and 'after that', which provide a new temporal deictic centre in relation to which subsequent utterances are to be understood.

As we saw, when a student says

(31) I hope this year's going to be good

knowing which of the three possible referents is intended, school year, calendrical year, year from birthday to birthday, is determined by knowing which of the three possible points of origin of the utterance obtains. So that when an addressee knows the point of origin of an utterance, they will be able to infer the temporal reference intended by the speaker. This is why we get annoyed when someone leaves a back-in-ten-minutes note on their door. Our annoyance stems from not being able to calculate precisely when the writer will return because we don't know the temporal deictic centre. Similarly, we find a there-are-empty-seats-at-the-far-end-of-coach-C public address message frustrating as we get on a crowded train because we don't know the spatial deictic centre. I was listening to the radio on one occasion when the announcer said of a humorous panel game that was about to be broadcast

(43) This edition was recorded last summer

As that day's date was 7th September, I assumed 'last summer' referred to the previous year. But I also wondered whether the announcer might be preparing us for the upcoming panel game by making a joke about British weather and suggesting that the current summer was already over.

2.2.8 Deictic change

As you probably know, English once had a *tu/vous* honorific system. Modern English uses the once formal *you* and no longer has the once familiar second person pronouns and possessives *thou, thee, thine, thy*. The social relation encoded in French *tu* or *vous* raises a question about the extent to which language use in general encodes a social relation and whether utterances and items within utterances index social status. When a speaker chooses a particular way of conveying a proposition, might their decision be motivated by social context? Think for a moment about your reaction to one of the earlier examples in this chapter:

(6) I know you'll enjoy reading the chapter

Try to recall how you felt about the relationship that was assumed between yourself as reader and me as writer when you read it. Perhaps you felt that I was constructing a relationship between us with myself as a slightly patronizing senior partner. I don't suppose I would have conveyed the proposition in the same way if the addressee had been a member of the British Royal Family – or even a member of my own family, come to that. This suggests that utterances themselves have indexical properties in that they encode a social relation between speaker and addressee. The term **social deixis** is sometimes used to describe the way speakers index the social status of their addressees relative to the place in a social structure where they locate themselves.

Location denoting forms like *hither, thither* and *yonder* are also largely archaic. Some place deictics which are no longer used in face-to-face interaction have, however, found a place in the 'new' context of written communicative discourse. *Hence* and *thence* and the compounds *hitherto* and *henceforth*, like *now, then, earlier, later, in an earlier chapter, above, in the paragraph above, already, next, in the next section*, are frequently used to index points in a text determinable only in relation to a discourse deictic centre. The term **discourse deixis** is sometimes used to describe the way a writer indexes places in a discourse relative to the point of writing.

Two problems posed by discourse deixis are knowing (a) whether the deictic centre of any particular written (or even recorded) discourse is writer-oriented or follows the reader-oriented default suggested earlier, and (b) whether expressions that would be indexical in spoken use are necessarily indexical in written form. As my clever student, Julie Plumb, pointed out, the out-of-office recorded message

(44) I'm not here now

is possible precisely because 'now' (but not 'I' or 'here') indexes a temporal referent determined relative to the reader's rather than the writer's deictic centre. With this in mind, consider the out-of-office message that a colleague's computer sent me recently

(45) Sorry! I am currently out of the office for a couple of days

Although the deictic centre is clearly author-oriented, as evidenced by 'I', the author was presumably was not 'currently out of the office' at the time she composed the message, so that the temporal deictic centre appears to be reader-oriented. And although 'for a couple of days' has back-in-ten-minutes properties, because my colleague's computer sent it to me each time I sent her a message and each time tagged with a different 'sent at' time, I began to think of it in the same way as I think of *here today gone tomorrow*, as a non-deictic formula no longer connected to a deictic centre. (And I begin to wonder whether I should make my millions by suggesting to Microsoft that all out-of-office messages should be tagged with time of composition so that their deictic centres are unambiguously established and the exchange of useful information facilitated.)

2.3 Deixis in the real world

Because we use deictics to encode a relationship between persons, times, places and ourselves as speakers, we expect individual uses to vary. For example, if you are a student, you may sometimes use 'we' to refer to the university community of which you are a member. What you are doing when you use *we* in this way is encoding **membership** or affiliation. Similarly, when you say 'this is a problem', you almost certainly mean that it appears to you to be more of a problem than when you say 'that's a problem'. Glover (2000) reports a planning negotiation in which two different suggested routes into a proposed housing development are both referred to as 'this way' rather than as 'this way' and 'that way'. Glover argues that 'this way' indicates the problematic status of both routes from the speaker's point of view:

(46) I mean if you come this way you're into there's a road here and there's a circulating ring road and if you come this way there's a very tight corner here

If individual uses vary, we should also expect cross-cultural variation in the way that speakers encode the relationships of themselves to the world around them. In this section, I'm going to share a number of uses of deictics which I encountered in English utterances in Hong Kong and which surprised me, I think because I was an outsider and these uses encoded relations between speakers and context that were different from those I was accustomed to, and which therefore seemed exotic to me.

2.3.1 The dining room example

(47) Please do not enter the dining room unless you are going to eat there

Nothing surprising about this, you might think – just the kind of notice you might expect to find in the lobby of a hotel. But I saw it on the dining room door in the United Services Club in Hong Kong when I was taken there once by a member. What I found odd was this: if the notice had been displayed in the lobby, I'd have taken 'there' as anaphoric and 'the dining room' as its antecedent. But standing right in front of the dining room, I found myself thinking that the proximal *here* would have been more appropriate. In other words, because the notice was on the door of the room referred to, I was trying to take 'there' deictically, and the use seemed exotic. So here's my hypothesis: members of the club had decided that the dining room should only be used for those wanting to eat, and a member of staff had been given the delicate task of enforcing this rule. The situation may have been complicated by the members being mostly influential expatriates and the staff being mostly local. Perhaps (47) had been tried on the notice-board, yet still non-eating members persisted in using the dining room, so that a sign on the door became necessary. In choosing (47) rather than

(47′) Please do not enter the dining room unless you are going to eat here

the staff member had tried to state a general rule rather than a particular prohibition. I suppose I had stumbled on a cultural practice which reflected a local social context with which I was unfamiliar and which encoded indirectly the differing statuses of the local staff and the expatriate club members.

2.3.2 The railway announcement example

I encountered one particular deictic use on my very first day in Hong Kong which kept me thinking for months. I was travelling south on the overground commuter train, the KCR, on my way into work and heard the following announcement:

(48) The next station is Kowloon Tong. Passengers may change there for MTR trains

All I noticed the first time I heard it was that the use of 'there' was unlike what was at that time the default announcement in Britain:

(49) The next station is Newcastle. Passengers for Sunderland, Middlesbrough, Carlisle and the Newcastle Metro should change here

Some days later, I noticed that the announcement occurred at the beginning of the two-and-a-half-minute journey from Tai Wai, the station before Kowloon Tong, just before the train entered the tunnel that takes it under the Lion Rock. So perhaps 'there' was appropriate because the announcement was made a long way away so as to avoid it being drowned out by the noise of the train in the tunnel. And perhaps the announcement reflected the notion that the next station was the other side of a mountain.

And then one day as I was travelling home, i.e. approaching Kowloon Tong from the opposite direction, I realized that although I had heard the announcement many times before, I hadn't registered that it was the same when travelling north, although there was no tunnel and no mountain. So bang went my hypothesis.

Figure 2.6

And when I asked my Chinese colleagues, I discovered that the Cantonese announcements also used *there* rather than *here*.

And then another idea occurred to me: the KCR is the overground train linking China with Hong Kong. It brings people from the country areas in the north into Kowloon. At Kowloon Tong there is an interchange with the underground (MTR) which serves Hong Kong Island, the rich international business area to the south.

Figure 2.7

So another way of looking at the two systems is to see the KCR as the country boys' line and the MTR as the line travelled by city slickers. This made me wonder whether the KCR announcement might be encoding psychological rather than physical distance. So what announcement would I hear on the MTR if I took a train to Kowloon Tong? Try to imagine my excitement as the MTR got closer and closer to Kowloon Tong: I was about to test my hypothesis as I strained to hear the announcement over the babble of passenger talk. And this is what I heard:

(50) The next station is Kowloon Tong. Passengers should change here for KCR trains

So it seems that approaching Kowloon Tong is a different experience for the passengers on the two railway networks, and my second hypothesis, that it's scarier for country boys to approach the interchange with the MTR than for city slickers to approach the interchange with the KCR, may hold.

Checking understanding (2.5)

1 Compare the three versions of the announcement – KCR, default British and MTR. What conclusions do you draw? Do you think there's a possibility that 'there' in (48) and 'here' in (49) and (50) are anaphoric rather than deictic?

2 In 2006, the KCR announcement I had first heard twelve years earlier was replaced with

(51) The next station is Kowloon Tong. Passengers please change to MTR trains at Kowloon Tong

Do you think this change reflects a change in the way the relationship of the KCR and MTR routes is conceptualized?

2.3.3 The newspaper headline example

Another example of a deictic use that surprised me as I crossed cultures (and which I must admit that I didn't notice until one of my colleagues drew it to my attention) concerns the use of *local*. Nunberg calls *local* a 'contextual' (1993: 36) because sometimes it requires knowledge of context to be interpreted (i.e. it's used indexically) and sometimes it doesn't (i.e. it's used intrinsically). Imagine a crime story appearing in a newspaper under the headline

(52) New York murder – local man arrested

Would you expect the man arrested to be from New York (the intrinsic use) or from whichever town the newspaper was printed in (the indexical use)? I suppose the answer partly depends on the newspaper, so that in a strictly local newspaper you would perhaps expect the deictic interpretation and in a national newspaper you might expect the intrinsic interpretation. So if I was reading the London *Times*, I'd expect the man arrested to be American rather than British. But in Hong Kong, *local* in this sort of headline is almost always deictic. Does this mean that Hong Kong newspapers are local rather than national? Or does the compactness of Hong Kong favour a reading consistent with the strong sense of community that the deictic reading implies? Or is there such a strong sense of Chinese ethnicity that whenever possible events are interpreted as involving compatriots? Who knows the answers to these questions, but once again I was surprised by a deictic use that from my cultural perspective seemed unexpected and which tells you something about the culture in which it occurs.

2.3.4 The bare past example

One Sunday afternoon I was at a country bus terminal in Hong Kong and saw this sign displayed on a sandwich board:

(53) Last bus had departed

It struck me as strange that the past perfect rather than the present perfect had been used. At the time I put it down to the ideolect of the writer and thought no more about it. But then I began to notice other written public address messages where the past was used rather than what to me was the more expected present. Here are two more examples, the first a sign displayed at a KCR station and the second a sign displayed beside some road works:

(54) This section of the platform had been cordoned off. Sorry for any inconvenience caused.
Vivien Lok
Station Manager

(55) This lane was closed temporarily

As I thought more about these uses, it occurred to me that the more expectable present implies that whoever wrote the sign has some responsibility for the message it conveys – perhaps they have put the sign up because they have closed the platform or started to mend the road. But the Hong Kong cases seem to imply that the event reported has occurred before the notice is displayed, thus disassociating the writer of the notice from responsibility for causing an inconvenience. If this analysis is right, we might want to draw conclusions about the attitude to accepting individual responsibility in different cultures. Once again, we see how a deictic use, here tense, indicates cultural membership. (For a more detailed discussion of this use, see Grundy and Jiang, 2001a.)

2.3.5 The radio interview example

The last real-world example discussed in this section is taken from a radio interview recorded and transcribed in Hong Kong for the *International Corpus of English*. In the broadcast, a Chinese interviewee, Annie Wong, is asked to describe how to make the special kind of dumpling eaten during the Dragon Boat festival. Here's a typical example of the way she talks about making the dumplings:

(56) you wash and you soak it for about two hours and apart from that one other thing that we like especially the Chinese kong shin chong [leaf-wrapped steamed dumplings] is that we we like to have the shelled green beans right and you take about uh half . . .

What's noticeable about the way Annie talks is that she constantly switches from non-deictic 'you' to exclusive deictic 'we', using 'we' to refer to the Chinese community of which she is a member and to exclude the expatriate community who are her overhearing audience. It seems that non-deictic 'you' is favoured for general instructions and exclusive 'we' for the particular practices of the expert dumpling makers. Notice also how the first switch from general instruction to particular practice is signalled by 'apart from that one other thing' and the switch back to a general instruction is signalled by 'right'. What Annie does is to show two kinds of affiliation: with her use of non-deictic 'you' she affiliates to her overhearing audience and with her use of deictic 'we' she shows her affiliation to the Chinese community.

Checking understanding (2.6)

Here are five more real-world uses of demonstratives. What do you make of them?

(57) No cars beyond this point (on one side of a sandwich-board displayed at Newcastle station at the point where the car park and the platform meet. Sometimes the sandwich-board is placed so that it faces the car park and sometimes so that it faces the platform.)

(58) If the applicant's native tongue is not English, would you please comment on the applicant's standard of proficiency in that language (Instruction to referees issued by University of Cambridge Board of Graduate Studies)

(59) FRENCH BUILDER: Jeudi ou Vendredi
'Thursday or Friday'
ENGLISH SUB-TITLE: Just a few days (when asked on a Friday on a British television programme how long he would take to finish a building job)

(60) We are stopping at Airport Terminal 2 (LED display in the carriage when the train from Tokyo to Narita Airport had arrived at Terminal 2)

(61) The world's local bank (HSBC advertisement)

2.4 Indexicality, grammar and meaning

The previous sections of this chapter have been about the deictic properties and some of the real-world uses of a closed class of demonstratives that include personal pronouns and possessives, determiners like *this* and *that*, and some time and place adverbials. In this final section, we consider how grammaticalization and conceptualization interface with indexicality.

2.4.1 Common ground and indexicality

In this chapter we've been exploring the way in which the use of a particular set of linguistic forms enables an addressee to determine a referent in a shared context or **common ground** typically anchored to the speaker's location at the time of utterance. This property of linking a referent to a context is what causes us to categorize these indexical uses as pragmatic: indexicality provides clear evidence that language is not just an autonomous or self-contained phenomenon but that aspects of context are organized as grammatical systems.

What then is the nature of this common ground in relation to which a referent is identified? One very important point is that there are far fewer options for elaborating the common ground than for elaborating the index. This is to be expected when we recall that the common ground is a speaker/hearer shared phenomenon and that referents are variable figures. Consider the first half of one the sentences you read earlier in the chapter

(62) And if by any chance there are two of you out there working together as a team reading the book aloud and saying things about me the author . . .

It's readily apparent that the indexical expression 'out there' can be elaborated much more easily than the common ground description. Thus I might have written 'out there in the real world' or 'out there at your desks' or 'out there in a library'. I would have been much less likely to have written ?'out there miles away from me' or ?'out there in relation to me'.

The fixedness of the common ground is indicated in situations where we use different indexical expressions to refer to the same referent from different common ground perspectives. Thus if the 'two of you out there' were to decide to write me about some point, you might begin the letter

(63) There are two of us here who . . .

My 'two of you out there' and your 'two of us here' index an identical referent. The different lexical items we each choose indicate the different points of origin of our two descriptions. When two people say to each other

(64) A: I love you
B: I love you

each uses 'I' to pick out the referent that the other picks out with 'you'. The referents are identical in each case, but the deictic centres are different. And when I move to the left to kiss you on your cheek, you think I move to the right.

The fixedness of the deictic centre poses a particular problem when we want to quote what others have said to us. Imagine your friend William says to you

(65) Why don't you want to come to the cinema with me

When you report his utterance to me, you have a choice of several ways of representing its deictic properties. You might say any of the following:

(66) Will said, 'Why don't you want to come to the cinema with me?'
(67) Will asked why I didn't want to come to the cinema with him
(68) Will complained that I didn't want to go to the cinema with him

In (67) the deictic centre is partly projected from Will's original perspective to yours – you encode this projection in your use of 'I' and 'didn't' and 'him' while your use of 'come' remains faithful to the deictic centre of Will's utterance. Reported speech, and especially fully projected examples of reported speech like (68), are important evidence of the existence of an unmarked deictic centre, which, as (65) and (68) show, is that of the speaker's perspective even when in the case of (68) the speaker is representing the speech of another person.

Our identification of this fixed deictic centre reveals an important pragmatic principle – that we are able both to assume shared knowledge of the background deictic centre and to foreground what is new in each particular utterance, so that what is new appears as a kind of figure in relation to the ground.

Because of the role of assumed knowledge in determining reference, indexicals are typically denotations with limited descriptive power. Thus the pronouns *you* and *me* and *us* are semantically deficient tokens in the sense that they lack the descriptive power that the names of the people they refer to have. In English, only third person singular pronouns are marked for gender and, significantly, usually stand in anaphoric rather than deictic relation to an antecedent. Notice too that many place and time deictic adverbials are reductions of preposition phrases. Sometimes these reduced preposition phrases are deictic while the non-reduced originals are both descriptions with more semantic content and, frequently, non-deictic:

deictic	non-deictic
up	up the hill (note *up the street*, which may be either deictic or non-deictic)
down	down the pipe, down a rabbit hole
above	above John, above the water-line
below	below the window
in front	in front of Mary, in front of the children
behind	behind my house (but not *behind Rover, behind the tree*, which are deictic)

It's also significant that these are all noun-reduced preposition phrases (i.e. their nouns are gapped) and therefore more semantically reduced than preposition-reduced phrases such as *right* (itself reduced from *to the right [side]*). Nor is the deictic status of preposition reduced adverbials altered by reconstituting them as whole phrases (e.g., *to the right*). Notice that the collapsed preposition phrases *today, upstairs*, etc. which function adverbially are also deictic.

2.4.2 Grammaticalization and deixis

Leading on from the discussion of grammatical phenomena at the end of the previous section, in this section we illustrate Hanks's view that deictics "constitute key points of juncture between grammar and context" (1992: 47).

Consider examples (36) and (37) again:

(36) England will win the World Cup
(37) England won the World Cup

Each of these statements encodes two moments in time, the time of the utterance and the time of the event. The first, the time of the utterance, is the deictic centre. This is the present, as we would expect. The second is the time of the event referred to – in the case of (36) some time in the future and in the case of (37) some time in the past. The following sentence is slightly more complicated:

(69) Because England had won the World Cup in 1966, they were granted an automatic place in the 1970 finals

In this sentence, we can distinguish three overt points in time, the time of utterance (present), the time of the first event referred to (longer ago in the past than the time of the second event – in fact, 1966), and the time of the second event referred to (a past time intermediate between the time of utterance and the time of the earlier event referred to – in fact, 1970). In this way the highly grammaticalized system of tense and aspect auxiliaries in English enables the speaker to refer from a present deictic centre to events at two points of distance in time.

Of particular interest in (69) is the time of the second event, expressed by the use of the past tense. This is also the time of the other events which the speaker will refer to in a continuing discourse:

(70) . . . they were granted an automatic place in the 1970 finals, but were knocked out by Germany who came from behind to win

Examples (69) and (70) show that 1970 is the time the speaker refers to with the past tense and that this point of time, the time of the continuing discourse, is the deictic origo for 1966, the time referred to by the past perfect. This suggests that even in a sentence like

(71) I'm reading

which describes a present event, there are in fact three different time types encoded, even though in this utterance they are all present time: the time of the utterance, the time of the event referred to and the time the speaker refers to in the discourse as a whole. In case discourse time is an unclear idea, imagine adding *now* to (71) to give

(71′) I'm reading now

This use of 'now' clearly indicates that the speaker is referring to the present. This is even clearer when we consider the function of the present perfect. In

(72) I've read most of the chapter now

we can distinguish the utterance time (present), the event time (past, indicated by 'read'/rɛd) and the discourse time that the speaker refers to (present, indicated by 'now').

2.4.3 The semantics of space and time: embodiment

We've seen how deictics index a referent established in relation to a point of origin which is usually taken to be the location of the speaker at the time of utterance. So when we are standing outside my front door and I say

(3) Do go in

'go' indexes a direction of movement determined by considering things from my perspective. I might equally have said

(3′) Shall I go in front

or

(3″) Do go ahead

indexing by means of the deictic 'in front' or 'ahead' my perception of the desired relative positions of you and myself as we enter the house. Each of these two-part indexicals is made up of a preposition and a body-part term, 'in' + 'front' (the archaic word for *face* or *forehead*) and Old English 'a' + 'head'. It's as though I conceptualize the space around me as an extension of my body, using body-part terms likes *behind, back, left-hand side*, etc. Most (perhaps all?) languages designate some proximal locations as though they were extensions of our bodies. Nor is this limited to deictic reference – non-demonstrative expressions may also involve body-parts, as in *afoot, eye up, cheek by jowl, yardarm, brow of a hill, toe the line*, etc. This suggests that our bodily experience influences the way we conceptualize phenomena like location. It also accounts for the use of spatial deictics to index temporal phenomena. Because we experience space as a physical reality, we extend this way of perceiving to the non-physical temporal domain, asking questions like 'how long will it take' and thinking of the future as *ahead, to come, from now onwards*, and of the past as *behind, up to now, over*. Several of the deictics listed in our discussion of time deixis in Section 2.2.5 appear to have a spatial origin: *ago, before, this <Monday>, next <year>, at <the weekend>, tomorrow.*

2.4.4 Index, context and text: determining referents

Perhaps at the beginning of things all deictic use required gesture. Now, as noted earlier, gestures sometimes help us to index referents but just as often linguistic signs alone are sufficient. For obvious reasons, gestures are very rarely used to index time reference, and in the case of discourse deixis, physical gestures are obviously impossible. Continuing to speculate on the evolution of deictics, we might suppose that person indexicals came first and then place indexicals, with non-gestural time deixis and finally discourse deixis coming later. We might also suppose that deixis precedes anaphora in the evolution of language: first, we learn to point in the physical world with gesture and accompanying linguistic sign, and then we learn to use indexical signs as pointers to discourse antecedents. Because third person pronouns such as *he* and *she* refer heterogeneously to persons not involved in the interaction and therefore not present in the physical context, it's natural to treat them as instructions to look for discourse antecedents. This raises the interesting question of the cognitive process that occurs when we hear an item like *he* or *she* that typically indexes a referent not present in the physical context. Presumably we are carrying a discourse context with us and so we understand a third person pronoun as an index of/pointer to a previously mentioned semantically replete token with matching gender and number features. But what happens when we encounter a description such as *there*, which may refer deictically or anaphorically. This is precisely the issue explored in our discussion of

(48) The next station is Kowloon Tong. Passengers may change there for MTR trains

What kind of cognitive structure might be hypothesized that allows an addressee to search both extra-linguistic context and co-text for the item indexed by the use of 'there'? Does the addressee search first for a referent in the extra-linguistic context or first in the co-text? Does saying that the reference is both deictic and anaphoric, a possibility raised at one point earlier in the chapter, reflect a credible psychological reality? (For a more detailed discussion of these fascinating questions, see Grundy and Jiang, 2001b.)

Summary

In this chapter we have seen how single lexical items such as *I*, *here* and *now* are part of a highly grammaticalized system and assume addressee knowledge of the identity, the spatial location and the temporal location of the speaker, which are used to identify referents indexed in relation to this point of origin. Crucially, the references effected can only be understood by an addressee who is able to reconstruct the speaker's viewpoint. The study of pragmatics is precisely about accounting for the ability of speakers and addressees to invoke a common context in relation to which a very wide range of language uses can be interpreted. This kind of interpretation is necessary because basic, literal meanings are radically under-determined and, in the case of deictics in particular, semantically deficient.

Well, you've just about made it to the end of the chapter. I hope my initial assertion that you'd enjoy reading was an accurate prediction. As the visit's over, let me show you to the door of my house. To get to the bus stop, you need to turn left, and then right at the T-junction. But if I lived in Beijing, I'd be telling you to go south and then west. In Britain, for the most part, we use deictics such as *left* and *right* when we give directions, although some people still talk about *going up to London* from whichever direction they approach it, as though it were a central hub. But in some cultures, absolute terms such as points of the compass rather than deictic terms are used to give directions. Whichever system you are familiar with, the other takes as bit of getting used to.

Raising pragmatic awareness

1 Form a small group which includes at least one person with a good knowledge of a language other than English. Ask this person to translate utterances containing a range of deictic phenomena into their other language and explain any problems or differences to you.

2 This exercise works well in tutorial groups. Ask each member of the group to come with two consecutive sentences chosen from this book or some other whose indexical properties they are prepared to discuss.

3 This makes a good vacation task. If you get the opportunity to travel, watch out for uses of deictics that surprise you, as I did in Hong Kong. If you aren't able to travel, try to mix with unfamiliar groups and see how they use *we* to show membership, or listen out for uses of *this* and *that* to encode psychological distance. Try to note down exactly what you heard or read and then report it to your tutorial group at the first meeting of the new term.

4 Identify an occasion when you might expect to hear a variety of deictic ways of communicating what appears to be the same message. In Britain, announcements on trains are particularly interesting as each railway company, and even each individual announcer, tries to encode their own notion of the common ground you and they share. Note down what you hear and present an analysis to your tutorial group.

5 Which of the features of talk identified as typically pragmatic in Chapter 1 play an important part in indexicality: accommodation, appropriateness, context, indeterminacy, indirect meaning, inference, reflexivity, relevance?

Discussions and essays

Based on what you know about deixis, discuss the relative merits of each of the following views:

- The assertion that 'Agatha Christie wrote books' will always be true, and the assertion that 'Agatha Christie wrote books about pragmatics' will always be false. This is a matter of semantics, or the relation of statements to states of affairs in the world. However, if someone says 'I wrote books' or 'I wrote books about pragmatics', they will sometimes be making a true statement and sometimes a false one depending on who they are. This is pragmatics.
- Deictics are "expressions whose meaning can best be viewed as a function from context to individual by assigning values to variables for speaker, hearer, time and place of utterance" (Horn, 1988: 116).

Discussions and essays *cont.*

- The indexical element of language exploits the knowledge speakers and hearers share of their location/s in space and time at the moment of utterance.
- Deictics enable the same utterance to convey different propositions in the mouths of different speakers.
- "The referents of deictic expressions are constantly shifting as the relationship between utterance and context changes" (Duranti and Goodwin, 1992: 43).
- Indexicals are semantically deficient referring expressions which function as instructions to identify features of context or co-text needed to complete their semantic determination.
- Deictic reference inevitably tells you something about the membership status of the speaker, and the degree of their affiliation to the culture as a whole and to sub-groups within it.

Further reading

Textbooks

Levinson, 1983: 54–96; Yule, 1996: 9–16.

Advanced reading

Levinson in Horn and Ward, 2004: 97–121.

More challenging – research-based reading

Hanks in Duranti and Goodwin, 1992: 43–76; Levinson in Bloom *et al.*, 1996: 109–69.

3 Presupposition – accommodating background knowledge

He that hath knowledge spareth his words.
(Proverbs 17.27)

Keywords:
accommodation, background assumption, defeasibility, entailment, factivity, metalinguistic negation, pragmatic presupposition, presupposition trigger, projection problem, semantic presupposition

3.1 Introduction

This chapter is about information that is accommodated by the addressee as part of the non-controversial **background** necessary for utterance to be a sensible or an appropriate thing to say. Sometimes these accommodations seem to be triggered by a particular grammatical structure or lexical item, sometimes their recovery appears to be required for pragmatic reasons. Traditionally, the accommodated beliefs necessary for an utterance to make sense are known as **semantic presuppositions** and the accommodations needed for an utterance to be appropriate are known as **pragmatic presuppositions.**

Take the Saturday morning exchange between me and my wife:

(1) BRANKA: When will you be back
PETER: I should be back by eight but you know what trains are like

When Branka says 'When will you be back?', she doesn't regard my coming back as controversial. We both take this for granted. What she wants to know is when this presupposed event will occur. When I say 'you know what trains are like', I expect her to accommodate a non-controversial view of trains which I know she already holds and don't therefore need to spell out. In addition, there's clearly something in the *wh*-structure '*what* trains are like' that triggers the presupposition that <trains are like something>, the belief which I want my wife to accommodate. Notice this is not what I assert, it's what I presuppose – I assert that she 'knows' what trains are like. Indeed, I could have said

(2) You don't know what trains are like

In this case, I'd be asserting that the addressee doesn't know what trains are like. But with respect to the presupposition, nothing changes. Both 'you know . . .' and 'you don't know what trains are like' are only sensible things to say if the addressee is willing to accept as non-controversial the background belief apparently triggered by 'what trains are like' that <trains are like something>.

The chapter you are about to read contains three further sections:

- *Presuppositions as shared assumptions*, which discusses some of the properties of semantic and pragmatic presupposition as well as several presupposition triggering phenomena.

- *Presupposition in the real world,* which describes a number of situations in which presuppositions have significant effects.
- *Presuppositions as pragmatically conditioned assumptions,* which discusses issues raised by the study of presupposition and its problematic halfway house status as both a linguistic and a non-linguistic phenomenon.

3.2 Presuppositions as shared assumptions

A presupposition is a meaning one accommodates alongside an utterance. This accommodated meaning may be triggered by a linguistic form (e.g., a definite description such as 'my dentist' presupposes the existence of such a person) or because the linguistic form would be inappropriate otherwise (e.g., 'my dentist said he needed to take an X-ray' is only appropriate if my dentist is male). We call the first kind of accommodation semantic and the second pragmatic, although as we shall see as the chapter progresses, this distinction may be problematic.

3.2.1 Accommodated knowledge

The following exchange occurred on a train from Exeter to London after I'd given the ticket inspector my seat reservation ticket rather than my regular ticket:

(3) TICKET INSPECTOR: Have you got your other ticket
PETER (searching for ticket): I don't know why National Express give you three tickets. GNER used to give you one
TICKET INSPECTOR: This isn't National Express, this is First Great Western. National Express is a bus company

The ticket inspector wants to see my other ticket, whose existence she presupposes. I wonder about the reason for a situation that's already happened, the issuing of three tickets. The ticket inspector's definite description 'your other ticket' and my embedded *wh*-question 'why National Express give you three tickets' trigger the acceptance of what's denoted by these two formulas as presupposed. And like the presuppositions triggered by the Saturday morning exchange, the presuppositions in this exchange aren't affected by the positive or negative status of the containing sentences:

(4) Have you got/not got your other ticket

both presuppose the existence of my other ticket, and

(5) I know/don't know why National Express give you three tickets

both presuppose that National Express give you three tickets.

The usual expectation is that a speaker responds to the 'new' or asserted part of the other speaker's utterance rather than to any presupposition it triggers. So the ticket collector might expect me to say something like 'It must be in my other pocket' or 'Let me have a look for it' as I address her question 'Have you got your other ticket'. And I might expect her to say something like 'It's their policy' or 'I haven't a clue' as she addresses my comment 'I don't know why National Express . . .'. However, this isn't how things work out. The ticket inspector's response seems to presuppose that (a) I think I'm travelling with National Express and (b) I think that National Express is a train company. Unless she held such beliefs, she'd be very unlikely to say (a) 'This isn't National Express, this is First Great Western' and (b) 'National Express is a bus company'. Presuppositions of this sort are said to be pragmatic because unless they are accommodated, our utterances don't make proper sense, appearing inconsistent with the context, not fully relevant and, therefore, inappropriate.

If an addressee doesn't accommodate the necessary presuppositions, then a misunderstanding is likely. My utterance

(6) I don't know why National Express give you three tickets. GNER used to give you one

assumes the accommodation of several background beliefs

- National Express is a train company.
- National Express has very recently taken over a railway franchise from GNER.
- Some passengers will be unfamiliar with the new systems, including ticketing policy.
- Passengers who buy their tickets on the internet may buy them from one company but travel for some or all of their journey on the trains of another.

None of these beliefs is triggered by what is said – they are simply things I assumed the person I was talking to would know. And since I was talking partly to myself, it's perhaps not surprising that I hadn't fully taken into account the extent to which these presuppositions would be accommodated by the ticket inspector.

Presupposition affords us economy. It's very convenient that we can rely on addressees to accommodate beliefs that would otherwise have to be elaborated. Imagine an exchange like

(3′) TICKET INSPECTOR: You have another ticket. Have you got this other ticket
PETER: National Express is a train company. GNER is a train company. National Express has very recently taken over a railway franchise from GNER . . .
TICKET INSPECTOR: You believe you are travelling on National Express. This isn't National Express, this is First Great Western. You believe National Express is a train company. National Express is a bus company

Another way in which presupposition assists understanding results from the way in which it enables different pieces of information to be perceived as having different levels of salience. Talmy (1978) suggests that main sentence assertions and embedded temporal sentence presuppositions are a linguistic realization of the figure/ground *gestalt* mentioned in the previous chapter. Thus in an example like

(7) Since you started this book, you must have paused several times for thought

I take it for granted that you started this book and against this background I make an assertion. If you respond to my claim, it'll be the figure or more salient piece of information ('you must have paused for thought') that I expect you to comment on, not the background ('since you started this book'). Similarly, if you say

(8) When I started this book, I thought I'd never finish it

you'd take a reply such as 'I knew you would' to relate to the more salient figure ('I thought I'd never finish it') and not to the ground ('when I started this book'). Of course, there are times when for various reasons speakers focus on the background assumption rather than the figure, as in the conversation between the ticket inspector and myself. But this is relatively rare and, as in the ticket exchange, often results in dysfunctional talk.

We should notice that it's not only pragmatic presuppositions whose accommodation may be problematic. Quite often we're unsure about whether a particular linguistic form or structure does trigger a presupposition. This problem is well illustrated by a letter in *The Times*:

(9) Sir, My local paper reports that in cases of canine hepatitis "in most dogs the first sign of this illness is unfortunately death". What (one wonders) is the second sign?

The writer seems to take the view that 'first' triggers the presupposition of at least a second item. Do you agree? Or can one say things like

(10) I'll just have a first course

and

(11) The match was abandoned after the first goal

Utterances like these seem to problematize the distinction between a linguistically triggered semantic presupposition which can't be detached from a form or structure and the extent to which our knowledge of the world is taken into account is deciding whether a structure does in fact trigger a presupposition. Is it a property of language or is it something we know about driving tests that causes us to read 'first' as presupposing at least one more attempt in (12) but not in (12′)?

(12) She failed first time
(12′) She passed first time

This is an issue to which we'll return in the final section of the chapter.

3.2.2 Shared assumptions and linguistic form

So far we've seen that semantic presuppositions are triggered by various forms and structures including

- *wh*-questions: 'When will you be back'
- embedded *wh*-constructions: 'You know what trains are like'
- definite descriptions: 'Have you got your other ticket'
- and perhaps the lexical item *first*.

Checking understanding (3.1)

Can you identify what is presupposed in the following utterances and the linguistic structures that trigger these presuppositions?

(13) Where's the ladies' room
(14) That's what they all say
(15) May I draw your attention to the fact that smoking is not allowed in this aircraft by law
(16) You are obsessing about a lad but you don't know how to show him how you feel

Other structures that give rise to presuppositions include

- iteratives:

  (17) *another* piece of bad news for the Government

  which presupposes that there had been at least one previous piece of bad news for the Government.

- temporal clauses:

  (18) I thought I was a lucky man *before/after/until/when* I got married

  which presuppose that the speaker got married.

- change of state verbs:

  (19) I *began/took up* jogging last summer

  which presuppose that the speaker didn't jog before, and

  (20) I *continued/stopped/gave up* smoking after the doctor warned me of the consequences

  which presuppose that the speaker smoked before being warned of the consequences.

- clefts, where the embedded sentences are presupposed:

  (21) It was the Scots who invented whisky

  presupposes that someone invented whisky.

- pseudo-clefts, which give rise to an existential presupposition:

  (22) What's important is that we all understand

  presupposes that something is important.

- counterfactual conditionals, which presuppose that affirmative propositions contained in the *if*-clause did not occur and negative propositions contained in the *if*-clause did occur:

  (23) If I had won the lottery on Saturday, I wouldn't be here now

  presupposes that I didn't win the lottery on Saturday, and

  (23′) If I hadn't won the lottery on Saturday, I would be here now

  presupposes that I did win the lottery on Saturday.

- stress:

  (24) Radion removes dirt AND odours

  presupposes that other washing powders don't remove odours, and

(25) IF music be the food of love, play on

This original interpretation of the first line of *Twelfth Night* in a production I once saw had the effect of turning the real conditional into a counterfactual, with the resulting presupposition that music, or at least the tuneless rendering being played at the time, was not the food of love.

- implicative verbs such as *remember, forget, manage and happen*:

(26) Reading and writing have improved immeasurably

which presupposes a low base, and

(27) I forgot/didn't remember to send my mother a card

which presupposes that the speaker should have sent his/her mother a card, and the headline in *The Times*

(28) Mr Cool manages to avoid doing a Henman

which presupposes that it wasn't easy for Mr Cool to avoid doing a Henman and asserts that he succeeded in avoiding doing it. (In case this headline is obscure, the story below was about one of those rare occasions when the erratic British tennis player Tim Henman managed to keep a cool head, hence the label 'Mr Cool'.)

- focus and presupposition:
We've already seen that *wh*-questions and embedded *wh*-constructions give rise to presuppositions. So

(29) How many tickets do National Express give you

presupposes that National Express give you tickets. Unlike *wh*-questions, *yes/no* questions like

(30) Do National Express provide tickets

do not trigger presuppositions (except, in this case, the existential presupposition associated with the definite description 'National Express' that arises independently of the question). However, answers like

(31) No, they provide vouchers

(31′) They collect fares once you're on the train

and

(31″) Everything is electronic

treat different parts of the question as presupposed. Table 3.1 shows how different proportions of these answers are divided between presupposition (to the left) and focused, or 'new', information (to the right):

Presupposition	Focus
They provide	vouchers
They	collect fares once you're on the train
	Everything is electronic

Table 3.1 Presupposition and focused information

Checking understanding (3.2)

1 Can you identify what is presupposed in the following utterances and the linguistic structures that trigger these presuppositions?

(32) You said that last time
(33) What's your name again
(34) If you return to Durham
(35) . . . you wash and you soak it for about two hours and apart from that one other thing that we like

2 Identify the semantic presuppositions in the following first lines of Shakespeare plays:

(36) In delivering my son from me, I bury a second husband (*All's Well That Ends Well*)
(37) Come here my varlet, I'll unarm again (*Troilus and Cressida*)
(38) When shall we three meet again, in thunder, lightning, or in rain? (*Macbeth*)
(39) Who keeps the gate here? ho! (*Henry IV, Part II*)
(40) Who's there? (*Hamlet*)
(41) I wonder how the king escaped our hands (*Henry VI, Part III*)

3 What is presupposed and what focused in the following answers to the question 'Do you have any dogs going cheap' asked by a customer in a pet shop?

(42a) No, they're all expensive
(42b) We only have cats
(42c) They all go bow-wow
(42d) Our birds go cheep

4 How many presuppositions can you identify in the following letter published in *The Times* following a demonstration in Gothenburg during a visit by President Bush?

(43) I wager the young lady who bared her shapely backside for President Bush would not have been so daring had Mr Clinton still been President

Another spectacular example of presupposition was described by Kiparsky and Kiparsky (1971), who detailed the properties of what they termed **'factive' predicates**. Kiparsky and Kiparsky show that a fact-S, like *the fact that Shakespeare spelt his name in several ways*, will be presupposed in the highly restricted set of structures in which they may appear either as the subject or the complement of a factive predicate. Thus all the following examples contain a factive predicate (italicized) and a presupposition (indicated by angled brackets):

(44) <The fact that Shakespeare spelt his name in several ways> *is trivial*
<The fact of Shakespeare's spelling erratically> *is surprising*
<That Shakespeare couldn't spell consistently> *is depressing*
<Shakespeare's spelling/having spelt erratically> *matters* to pedants
It*'s tragic* <that Shakespeare couldn't spell his own name>
His admirers *regret* <the fact that Shakespeare was an erratic speller>
Only scholars *are aware of* <Shakespeare's erratic spelling>

Thus *is trivial, is surprising, is depressing, matters, is tragic, regret* and *are aware* are members of a much larger set of factive predicates. Apart from the extraposed structure *It's x that y*, none of these structures is possible with non-factive predicates like *seem, believe* and *turn out*, whose subjects or complements are not presupposed. (You can demonstrate this for yourself by trying *seem, believe* and *turn out* in place of the factive predicates in the examples above.) On the other hand, these non-factive predicates have their own set of structures which are ungrammatical for factives.

3.2.3 Shared assumptions and negation

As we've already seen, presuppositions 'survive' **negation**. You can easily confirm this for yourself by negating (43)

(43′) I don't wager the young lady . . .

As you'll see, all the presuppositions you identified earlier remain unaffected by the negation. Since presuppositions are background assumptions that the addressee accommodates as non-controversial, this is as we would expect. Indeed, the standard definition of semantic presupposition is often considered to be its ability to survive negation, so that a presupposition is a proposition that is true if the sentence in which it occurs is true and is also true if the sentence in which it occurs is false. So if his admirers say either that it's a matter of regret or that it is not a matter of regret that Shakespeare was an erratic speller, and whether in either case they actually regret or do not regret this, that Shakespeare was an erratic speller is always presupposed:

(44′) His admirers regret/do not regret that Shakespeare was an erratic speller

Treating the proposition *<His admirers regret x>* as A and the proposition *<Shakespeare was an erratic speller>* as B, this may be schematized in the following way:

A is true A is not true not-A is true not-A is not true	B is true

Pragmaticists use the term **defeasible** to mean that a proposition can be cancelled or denied.

(45) Manchester United won

is a defeasible proposition that I deny by saying

(45′) Manchester United didn't win

If presuppositions are conventional semantic meanings that are detached from contexts, we wouldn't expect them to be defeasible, since, by definition, no **entailment**, or meaning that arises in every context, can be denied or cancelled without giving rise to a contradiction. For example, we can't deny the entailment of *win*, which in the context of football is something like <score more goals than the other side>. We can't say

(45″) *Manchester United won and scored fewer goals than their opponents

This is why presuppositions 'survive' negation – they are entailments of the utterances within which they arise.

However, there are occasions when we want to comment metalinguistically on the status of a presupposition. For example, there doesn't seem to be anything wrong with saying

(19′) I took up jogging last summer, although to be strictly accurate I'd jogged a bit before

In this utterance, the presupposition triggered by 'took up', <the speaker hadn't jogged before last summer>, appears to be negated. But notice that this is a metalinguistic correction, as indicated by 'to be strictly accurate', rather than a logical negation. We can also comment on the extent to which the presupposition should be accommodated, as in

(28′) Mr Cool manages to avoid doing a Henman, not that it was that difficult given the opposition

Or we can go a step further and suspend the presupposition, as in

(21′) It was the Scots who invented whisky – in as far as anyone can be said to have 'invented' whisky

where the scare quotes in (21′) clearly draw attention to the inappropriateness of 'invented'. Burton-Roberts (1989: 235–8) argues that metalinguistic negation operates on the mention of a proposition rather than truth-functionally on the proposition itself. Thus the speaker of (21′) is objecting to the term 'invented' rather than denying the truth of a presupposed proposition. Horn defines metalinguistic negation as "a device for objecting to a previous utterance on any grounds whatsoever, including the conventional or conversational implicata it potentially induces, its morphology, its style or register, or its phonetic realization" (1989: 363).

Distinguishing in this way between objecting to the mention of an item and denying the truth of a presupposed proposition might seem like splitting hairs, but it has the important consequence that it allows a theory of semantic presupposition to be maintained.

3.3 Presupposition in the real world

3.3.1 *Some* and *any*

You may have noticed that small children acquiring English as a first language and some second language learners frequently produce utterances like

(46) I've locked the door so someone doesn't get in

rather than

(47) I've locked the door so no one gets in

Such utterances are entirely logical if you take the view that 'someone' presupposes the existence of a potential intruder while 'no one' (= not anyone) doesn't. Only an idiot (or an adult native speaker of English) would lock a door if there was no presupposition that someone might get in.

Here's an exchange I noted down between an air-hostess and a passenger:

(48) STEWARDESS: Would you like something to drink
PASSENGER: <reading>
STEWARDESS: Madam would you like something to drink
PASSENGER: Sorry
STEWARDESS: Something to drink
PASSENGER: Yes please I'd like coffee

I've a large collection of such exchanges. Although there's a great deal of variety in the precise formula used, 'something' is very strongly favoured over 'anything', which occurs only very infrequently. Why should this be?

Like 'someone' in (46), the use of 'something to drink' in (48) triggers an existential presupposition in a way that 'anything to drink' doesn't. It's therefore more inviting. For this reason, the hospitable host asks whether guests would like 'some more *x*' rather than 'any more *x*'. Notice also the pragmatic presupposition in (48) that most travellers know what drinks are available on which kinds of flight and so it's not necessary for the stewardess to list them. Indeed, the passenger asks for coffee, without coffee being specifically offered. This kind of world knowledge seems to encourage the use of 'something', with specific drink offers made only as a repair strategy, as in

(49) STEWARD: Madam something to drink for you
PASSENGER: <looks confused>
STEWARD: Coffee tea juice

'Anything' is also less inviting for another reason. *Any* is a negative polarity item which can only occur in negative or hypothetical constructions (conditionals, interrogatives, etc.).

Because of the hypothetical context required by negative polarity 'any', following roadworks we expect the road-sign

(50) Sorry for any delay

rather than the anomalous

(50′) Sorry for some delay

And when we haven't been held up, we think how courteous it is of the Ministry of Transport to apologize, especially when an apology is unnecessary. But when we have been held up, we find the road-sign infuriating precisely because it doesn't presuppose that there has been the delay which we have just experienced. Under these circumstances,

(50″) Sorry for the delay

might be more appropriate. But this sign is only very occasionally posted, presumably because it would be inappropriate when no delay had occurred and when no referent for the existential presupposition could be identified.

McCawley observes that "sentences with *any* do not commit the speaker to the proposition that the domain of the quantifier is not empty, whereas sentences with *every* and *all* do" (1981: 112). In saying this, he's claiming that, unlike *every* and *all*, the use of *any* does not presuppose that there are at least some examples of the description quantified by *any*. Thus

(51) All drinks are free

and

(51′) Every drink is free

each semantically presupposes that drinks are free, whereas

(51″) Any drink is free

pragmatically presupposes that drinks are free.

When I worked with American colleagues, I noticed that they would sometimes privilege *some* over *any* in situations where my British preference would be for *any*. On one occasion, my American Head of Department asked for information to take with him to a meeting, adding by way of explanation

(52) in case I have to say something to somebody

I inferred (wrongly as it turned out) that he had someone in mind for a telling off. This made me wonder whether the association of an existential presupposition with the use of a linguistic form such as *some* or with a definite description might depend on the speaker rather than on the form itself.

3.3.2 Presupposition in court

Earlier in this chapter we considered examples such as

(7) Since you started this book, you must have paused several times for thought

I suggested that if you responded to this claim it would be the figure ('you must have paused for thought') that I would expect you to comment on, and not the non-controversial background ('since you started this book'). But imagine a situation in which someone says to you

(53) Were you married to Mr So at the time you appeared in court

and the background assumption that you appeared in court has no basis in fact and is therefore far from non-controversial. How would you respond to the question asked, bearing in mind that whether you answer yes or no, you seem to accommodate the background presupposition that you appeared in court? So before you respond to the question, you need to reject the embedded presupposition that isn't consistent with real word facts.

In this sub-section, we'll look at what happens when a speaker tries to introduce presuppositions that have no basis in fact into a discourse. The discourse in question is a court record collected in Hong Kong as part of the *International Corpus of English*. A defence council, Mrs Panesar, is cross-examining a prosecution witness, Mrs Wong. The data are set out in the left-hand column and my commentary on them is set out in the right-hand column

(54)	PANESAR: Madam Wong, during the plea and mitigation, your lawyer urged that you be given a suspended sentence on humanitarian grounds, and those grounds were that you had been in Hong Kong just 10 days. Is that right?	Mrs Panesar sets out a situation and then by means of the higher level predicate 'is . . . right' asks if it is true.
	WONG: I don't know.	
	PANESAR: Do you remember your lawyer telling the magistrate that you had married a Hong Kong resident in China earlier that year in 1991?	Sometimes *remember* is factive and sometimes non-factive. If taken as factive, the content of the sentence 'your lawyer . . . in 1991' is presupposed.
	WONG: This is not true. My previous marriage, it was a man in China.	Mrs Wong does not answer the question 'Do you remember . . .' but denies the validity of the presupposition that she married a Hong Kong resident.
	COURT: It's not true that you told your lawyer that?	The judge ('Court') intervenes to clarify whether Mrs Wong had ever given her lawyer the information which Mrs Panesar's question presupposes.
	WONG: I did not say that to my lawyer.	
	PANESAR: Was your lawyer making up things?	
	COURT: No, she can't answer that.	
	PANESAR: Were you married to Mr So at the time you appeared in the magistrates court?	The presupposition that Mrs Wong appeared in the magistrate's court goes unchallenged, presumably because it's consistent with what is known in the discourse context.
	WONG: We were then cohabiting.	
	PANESAR: But you weren't married to him. Is that right?	Again Mrs Panesar advances a proposition and then by means of the higher level predicate 'is . . . right' asks if it's true.
	WONG: Not yet – I mean the marriage was not yet registered.	
	PANESAR: And you had only met Mr So here in Hong Kong a few months before?	Mrs Wong doesn't challenge the presupposition that she met Mr So.
	WONG: Yes.	
	PANESAR: Did you tell your lawyer you came here in order to take care of your husband's 92-year-old mother?	Like *remember, tell* is sometimes factive and sometimes non-factive. If taken as factive, the complement sentence 'you came here . . . 92-year-old mother' is presupposed.
	WONG: I did not say that to my lawyer. In fact what I said to him was my present husband was introduced to	Mrs Wong denies the presupposition that she came to Hong Kong to take care of her

me by some friend and I was aware that he had a mother of that age. In fact I did not see my husband before I came to Hong Kong.
COURT: You are talking about Mr So?
WONG: Yes, So.
PANESAR: Did you say to your lawyer you came to Hong Kong to take care of your elderly mother-in-law?
WONG: No, I said nothing of that sort.

husband's mother since she did not know her husband-to-be at the time.

Again, on some readings Mrs Panesar's question might be taken to presuppose (a) that Mrs Wong had a mother-in-law and (b) that she came to Hong Kong to take care of her.

Presuppositions embedded in questions put to witnesses are particularly damaging in courtrooms because the witness is supposed to answer the question asked. In answering the question, the witness necessarily implies that any presupposition it contains is non-controversial. Despite the difficulty of denying presuppositions embedded in questions, notice how skilfully Mrs Wong deals with Mrs Panesar's presuppositions in her answer

(55) I did not say that to my lawyer. In fact what I said to him was my present husband was introduced to me by some friend and I was aware that he had a mother of that age. In fact I did not see my husband before I came to Hong Kong.

'In fact', the presupposition triggering pseudo-cleft 'what I said to him' and the factive predicate 'was aware' are used to indicate just exactly what Mrs Wong can agree to in Mrs Panesar's question. 'In fact' is then used again in a sentence that denies one of Mrs Panesar's presuppositions and acknowledges the presupposition that is uncontested, that Mrs Wong came to Hong Kong.

Checking understanding (3.3)

You might like to work on the use of presupposition in the following extracts from the cross-examination of Mrs Wong. To help you, presuppositional and potentially presuppositional data of particular interest are italicized and, where appropriate, suggestions and comments are made in parentheses.

(56) PANESAR: Is this right, *when you met the defendant on the 24th and 25th*, did you tell him *this flat had been bought for you by Mr So*?
WONG: I did not say that. (Would the answer 'I did not' have been different with respect to the potential presupposition inherent in the question?)
PANESAR: Madam Wong, isn't it right that it was *when you told Mr Lau here, the defendant, Mr So had bought you a flat and the defendant said 'Well, now that you have got a flat, surely you can afford to return my $50,000'*? (Pay special attention to several presuppositions and presupposition triggers: temporal clause introduced by 'when', definite descriptions, complement sentence following 'said', temporal clause introduced by 'now that', the iterative 'return'.)
WONG: No, not true. I did not have a flat for my own and I never borrowed such money from the defendant.

Checking understanding (3.3) *cont.*

PANESAR: What *excuse* did you give the defendant for *leaving* him? (This is a rape case in which Mrs Wong alleges that her former landlord, Mr Lau, raped her after she left her accommodation to move in with Mr So, whom she subsequently married. It's important for Mrs Wong's case that she should not be portrayed as having had a relationship with Mr Lau between first meeting Mr So and marrying him. Notice the implicatives 'excuse' and 'leave'. 'Leave' is also implicative in Cantonese, the language in which Mrs Wong's evidence is given.)
COURT: For leaving him?
(Another notable feature of the use of presuppositions in cross-examinations of this sort is how quickly the judge intervenes to protect the witness.)
PANESAR: For leaving him.
AITKEN: Leaving him when? (Aitken is the prosecution lawyer and Mrs Wong is his principal witness. How does he deal with the implicative nature of 'leave'?)
COURT: Yes, when?
PANESAR: When you *left* the defendant *for* Mr So. (How does 'for' support implicative 'leave'?)
AITKEN: Wait a minute.
COURT: What do you mean by that? She doesn't say, she doesn't admit that she was ever *with* the defendant. (How does 'with' support implicative 'leave'? Notice how 'admit' is a speech act description consistent with the presupposition Mrs Panesar seeks to establish.)
PANESAR: Well, perhaps I can rephrase my question then, my Lord.
PANESAR: What *excuse* did you give the defendant *when you left the rooftop hut to go and live with Mr So at the new address*? (As well as the temporal clause, there are the two implicatives 'excuse' and 'live with'.)
WONG: *At that time when we were having tea together,* I told the defendant *that I had met a man, I wanted to marry that man,* and I *gave him back* the keys to that hut on the roof-top and requested him to write a note to me and I said I would not stay in that hut *anymore.*
PANESAR: Madam Wong, I suggest *what you said to the defendant* prior to your departure on or around 28 October 1991 was that you were *leaving* him to go and reside with *your brother.*
COURT: Leaving him to go and reside . . .
PANESAR: To go and reside with *her brother, Madam Wong's brother.*
WONG: No, I've got no brother.
PANESAR: Well, you may have no brother but did you *give that reason* to the defendant? (Does Mrs Panesar presuppose that Mrs Wong would have needed to give some reason at least?)
WONG: No, not true. On that day I gave him the keys and I told him, I said 'Look, this is my phone number. You may call me in future if there's anything you want to contact me.'

3.3.3 Making sense of existential assertions and presuppositions

How do you feel about the various fire warning notices you see in lifts? Personally, I prefer

(57) If there is a fire, do not use the lift

to

(57′) When there is a fire, do not use the lift

Both assert the existence of fire with the formula 'there is a fire' but only (57′) presupposes that the situation in which a fire exists will occur. And what about

(58) In case of fire

and

(58′) In the event of fire

Do you agree that the preferred reading of (58) is closer to our understanding of (57) and the preferred reading of (58′) closer to our understanding of (57′)? While (57) and (58) describe possible worlds, the default reading of (57′) and the likely reading of (58′) are descriptions of the real world. Notice also that the definite description 'the fire' isn't possible in any of these cases: *If there is the fire . . .; *When there is the fire . . .; *In case of the fire; *In the event of the fire. In (57) and (57′) the definite description is impossible because of the logical incompatibility of *there*, which asserts the existence of its complement, and a complement containing a definite description which triggers an existential presupposition. And in (58) and (58′) only exophoric references are possible (e.g., 'In the event of the fire spreading . . .'). Since there's no existing fire, there cannot be a definite description in the warning notice.

Sometimes what works as an exophoric reference for one person doesn't work for another. In the days when Marxist ideology was in favour in some places, visitors to Britain from Socialist countries often found it hard to accept that when they referred to 'the bourgeois society', their British friends had no idea what they were talking about. Although the existence of a referent is presupposed by the use of the definite description, the referent was unidentifiable to people who had no familiarity with the necessary ideology. Unlike 'Mind the table', where the referent may not be known to the addressee but the utterance is taken as an instruction to locate it (Hawkins, 1978: 113), addressees unfamiliar with the referent of the description 'the bourgeois society' have no ready means of identifying a referent, with obvious consequences for their view of the reliability of the speaker.

The contexts created when speakers exercise choice in the kinds of noun phrase determination they favour often tell us something about them. Why did I say

(1) I should be back by eight but you know what trains are like

rather than

(1′) I should be back by eight but you know what the trains are like

Clearly 'the trains' presupposes the existence of a set of trains known to both of us to which I refer. 'The trains' narrows the context – I have to choose between criticizing trains in general and affiliation to the addressee. I could even have said

(1″) I should be back by eight but you know what these trains are like

Here the empathetic 'these' seems to me to make trains disproportionately important. What do you think?

I might have added to 'you know what trains are like'

(59) Have the children got plans for the evening

In saying 'the children', a speaker presupposes the existence of a set which may include two or three or four or, even, if we're teachers, thirty-four. It obviously wouldn't make sense to talk about or refer to 'the children' unless those involved in the conversation could accommodate the presupposition triggered by the definite description and identify the unique set of children referred to. Saying 'the trains' or 'the children' is like saying 'these trains' or 'these children', except that when we use 'these' indexically (rather than empathetically), some set of actual trains is indexed and must be identified in the physical context. In the case of 'the trains' we're content to take it for granted that the set referred to exists without going to the trouble of actually picking them out.

Summary

The real-world uses of presupposition triggering constructions discussed in this section show that things aren't simple. For some speakers *some* doesn't always trigger existential presuppositions. Mrs Panesar makes use of predicates like *remember* and *tell* which sometimes trigger presuppositions and sometimes don't. While a definite description will match a real-world referent for one person, it may not for another. We may therefore be tempted to argue that the recovery of presuppositions is pragmatically conditioned, a topic we explore in more detail in the final section that follows.

3.4 Presuppositions as pragmatically conditioned assumptions

This chapter has considered three kinds of accommodated meaning:

- semantic presuppositions that appear to be triggered by one of a set of particular linguistic forms and which are held to be non-defeasible

(5) I know/don't know why National Express give you three tickets (presupposing <National Express give you three tickets>)

- pragmatic presuppositions that are directly recoverable from what is said and which, from a common sense perspective, are also non-defeasible

(5′) This isn't National Express, this is First Great Western (presupposing <the addressee thinks he's travelling with National Express>)

- pragmatic presuppositions or background beliefs that are necessary for an utterance to be seen as appropriate

(6) I don't know why National Express give you three tickets. GNER used to give you one (presupposing <some passengers will be unfamiliar with the new systems, including ticketing policy>)

We've spent more time on semantic presupposition which relies on the hypothesis that a particular form may be an autonomous way of conveying a conventional meaning (a presupposition) that cannot be denied and is non-controversial because it reflects what an addressee knows or is willing to accept. But this seems to be a counter-intuitive notion. A speaker can only guess at and can never actually know what is non-controversial for someone else. And of course there's nothing to stop a speaker exploiting an apparently autonomous way of generating a meaning, as Mrs Panesar does, in order to presuppose propositions that are far from non-controversial.

The evidence suggests that Strawson's (1950) classic view of presupposition as an entailment that survives negation doesn't sufficiently reflect real-world uses of language and the non-linguistic background assumptions required to render utterances appropriate. Shared or non-controversial knowledge cannot be a conventional meaning just because of the form in which it's expressed. It isn't enough for there to be a rule of the language that associates a presupposition with a lexical item or grammatical construction for a presupposition to occur. Something more is required, a rule of use if you like. Seuren puts it well when he says

> The defining feature of presuppositions seems to be the fact that a sentence B_A (i.e. B presupposing A) is fit for use only in a discourse that already contains the information carried by A. A discourse or, more properly, a discourse domain is seen as a cognitive 'working space' for the interpretation of new incoming utterances. The information carried by each new utterance is added to the information already stored in the discourse domain. The technical term for this specific form of 'adding' information to a given discourse domain is *incrementation* . . . What counts here is that a sentence B_A is considered unusable in a discourse not allowing for the incrementation of A. (1998: 439–40)

The evidence shows that sentences of the form B_A do sometimes occur in discourse not allowing for the accommodation of A. Their rejection shows that the use of presuppositions is at least subject to pragmatic checking.

In the sub-sections below, we'll consider a number of issues that problematize the autonomous generation of so-called semantic presupposition.

3.4.1 The projection problem and holes that get plugged

The projection problem is the term used for the issue raised by utterances like Mrs Panesar's questions

(60) Do you remember your lawyer telling the magistrate that you had married a Hong Kong resident in China earlier that year in 1991

and

(61) Did you tell your lawyer you came here in order to take care of your husband's 92-year-old mother

It's unclear whether (60) gives rise to the presupposition that Mrs Wong's lawyer told the magistrate that she had married a Hong Kong resident and (61) to the presupposition that Mrs Wong came to Hong Kong to take care of her husband's mother. Thus predicates like *remember* and *tell* sometimes trigger presuppositions and sometimes don't, depending on pragmatic considerations. For this reason, they're known as **filters**. The problem arises because the meaning of *remember* can be determined in more than one way, as either *remember that* or *remember whether*. Exactly the same is true of *tell*, which usually invites a presupposition but is sometimes used as an alternative to *say*. While *remember* and *tell* are filters, constructions that trigger presuppositions are known as **holes** because they allow presuppositions through. Non-factives like *believe* are known as **plugs** because they plug potential holes and prevent presuppositions from arising.

Uses like *first* in

(12′) She passed first time

plug a hole which would in other circumstances allow a presupposition through and are therefore filters. What turns a hole into a filter must though be a pragmatic condition. One frequently cited example is the apparently inconsistent effect when the verb *die* occurs in temporal clauses:

(62) He suffered a series of illnesses before he made a will

presupposes that he made a will. However,

(63) He died before he made a will

does not. Clearly what we know about the world, that when you've died you can no longer make a will, accounts for the absence in (63) of the presupposition in (62). In other words, this suggests that the presupposition of (62) is a meaning we recover as a result of bringing together a linguistic form, a temporal clause, and an understanding of the world, that you can (and perhaps should) make a will after a series of illnesses. The pragmatic nature of this inference is confirmed by the fact that *he died before x* does not necessarily pre-empt a presupposition, as

(64) He died before he reached the hospital

shows. In the case of

(65) She left before she ate her cake

both the she-ate-her-cake and she-did-not-eat-her-cake readings are possible, although the she-did-not-eat-her-cake reading is perhaps favoured. Our interpretation clearly depends on the context we construct, so that the presupposition triggering property of the structure is in fact pragmatically conditioned. The status of the gerund as a vehicle for conveying factivity, as argued by Kiparsky and Kiparsky (1971: 360), also depends on pragmatic conditioning. In fact, the proposition that she ate her cake seems still less favoured in (65′) than in (65):

(65′) She left before eating her cake

In the real world, factive predicates are often not accepted as such in everyday speech. When he was Archbishop of Canterbury, I once heard Robert Runcie say on television

(66) I contest the fact that the church is more divided

Although this may sound contradictory, we all know what he meant, that the fact-S sentence triggered by the factive predicate *contest* isn't presupposed as far as this speaker is concerned. Indeed, semantically *contest* is a 'factive' predicate that casts doubt on whether its complement is a fact at all. Thus, although Kiparsky and Kiparsky suggest two syntactic frames, one for assumed knowledge and one for non-assumable knowledge, we see that pragmatic considerations also need to be taken into account and that the assumed knowledge frame does not autonomously trigger a presupposition.

Change-of-state verbs are not immune from pragmatic conditions either. I once heard someone say

(67) At least we won't have to give up sex

But the speaker wasn't presupposing that he was having sex (and implying that he enjoyed it). The speaker was a Catholic priest who was contemplating unwelcome changes that he foresaw in the future and seeing this one silver lining on the cloud. Our knowledge of the world tells us that the expectable presupposition does not go through in this case – in fact, the humour derives precisely from the fact that the utterance has a different pragmatic effect on this occasion from the one it would usually have.

Checking understanding (3.4)

1 Can you think up your own examples of temporal clauses, factives, definite descriptions and change-of-state verbs which do not give rise to the presuppositions we might typically expect to find associated with them? As you do this, it may help you to remember that

- temporal clauses are introduced by conjunctions such as *after, before, when* and *while;*
- Kiparsky and Kiparsky's list of factive predicates includes *grasp* (in the cognitive sense), *realize, take into account, bear in mind, ignore, make clear, mind, care (about);*
- definite descriptions are determined by the definite article, possessives, the demonstratives *this/these* and *that/those;*
- change-of-state verbs include *carry on, continue, cease, commence, begin, start, stop, leave off, go on.*

2 Do you think that *be concerned about* is a filter or a hole? Is the complement of 'are concerned' presupposed in this sentence from a news report of a case of sexual abuse at a London school:

(68) Two boys are concerned that they might have contracted the HIV virus from Father David Martin

3.4.2 Grammar and presupposition

To what extent is it possible to make generalizations about the relationship between grammatical constructions and presuppositional phenomena? A long time ago now, Kiparsky and Kiparsky (1971) argued that factive and non-factive predicates and their complements were distinct syntactic structures and hypothesized that these distinct structures could be related to wider syntactic paradigms. In arguing the need for pragmatic checking, we aren't necessarily denying a relationship between syntax and presupposition, only arguing against a syntax that determines presupposition autonomously. At a descriptive level, the association of presupposition with embedded sentences is striking – both with subject clauses and object complements of factive predicates and with temporal clauses. Similarly, we can compare the presupposition triggering functions of higher level predicates like 'is true' and higher level open propositions like *wh*-question structures.

Although not embedded, appositional clauses are not fully part of what a speaker sets out to assert either. Different researchers have taken different views with regard to whether such clauses are auxiliary assertions or whether they are the raw material of, or have actually become, presuppositions. So you'll have to decide for yourself whether the non-restrictive relatives 'who were clever' and 'who were cleverer still' in (69) are asserted or presupposed

(69) The Greeks, who were clever, invented geometry; the Arabs, who were cleverer still, invented algebra

Notice that restrictive relatives never give rise to presuppositions, so that in (70) 'who were clever' and 'who were dim' restrict the class of Greek described and contribute to the truth-value of the containing sentence

(70) While the Greeks who were clever were inventing geometry, the Greeks who were dim were visiting the oracle

It's not surprising that information that occurs in an embedded sentence should contain material that is presupposed, with the higher sentence predicate being used to assert deniable propositions. Another interesting and perhaps iconic relationship seems sometimes to exist between syntactic position and the presuppositional status of some adjectives. Many years ago, Bolinger (1967) drew attention to the tendency of *-able/-ible* adjectives and past participles to convey characteristic meaning when used attributively in pre-nominal position and to convey occasion-specific meaning when used predicatively in post-nominal position. Thus *the responsible man* is characteristically responsible and *the man responsible* is the one we hope the police will arrest. I don't know whether you'd agree that the 'open' signs one sometimes sees on shops work in just this way. Thus

(71) Now open

is used when a new shop opens and wants to announce to the world that it's open-for-business. This can be contrasted with

(72) Open now

the usual sign indicating that the current time falls within the shop's opening hours. The use of open-for-business 'now' in (71) comes closer to describing a characteristic property than the use of opening-hours 'now' in (72), which describes a temporary state. Thus the sign 'Now open' often remains in place for weeks or even months, whereas 'Open now' is displayed and removed each day. Notice that these meanings seem to be presuppositions, at least in as far as the two meanings of 'now' appear to be indefeasible. 'Not now open' is expectably odd and, in as far as it's usable, seems to mean that a once open-for-business enterprise is no longer open-for-business. 'Not open now' merely means that the enterprise is closed because the current time falls outside business hours. This kind of example, like 'live with' in the court data discussed earlier, suggests that apparently conventional implicative meanings may be more widespread than one might at first think.

Earlier I called the placement of 'now' iconic. In pre-head position, adjectives like 'responsible' and adverbs like 'now' might be expected to have a *characteristic* meaning, while post-head position is associated with *occasional* meaning. This is iconic because post-head linear word order reflects the extent to which *occasional* meanings are added relatively late in the day. This perhaps suggests that the structures we use are adapted to the purposes for which we wish to use language, so that grammar, rather than being autonomous, is also a matter of use. Like what we say, how we say it also needs to take account of pragmatic conditions.

3.4.3 Being non-controversial

In creating a presupposition, a speaker has to make judgements about which propositions are readily accommodated by the addressee. Clearly the presupposition that might have been invited by the use of 'give up' isn't intended by the priest who says

(67) At least we won't have to give up sex

The way in which pragmatic checking is used to license a potentially accommodatable meaning is illustrated by the use of stress, as in

(24) Radion removes dirt AND odours

(25) IF music be the food of love, play on

Stress in utterances like (24) and (25) is used to invite presuppositions where the structure would not otherwise trigger them. The relationship between contrastive stress and presupposition is discussed by Lakoff (1971: 333), who points out that

(73) John called Mary a Republican, and then SHE insulted HIM

presupposes that calling someone a Republican is an insult. Notice that this presupposition passes the non-defeasibility test

(73′) John called Mary a Republican, but SHE didn't insult HIM

We might argue that this presupposition is easily accommodated, or in fact perhaps even arises, because of the use of 'called'. This is because *call* in the sense of *call someone a name* is an implicative verb whose entailment is <label> and whose presupposed meaning is <label negatively>. However, anything can be an insult if so regarded by an addressee. So provided being offered baked beans is credible as an insult, a speaker will feel justified in using contrastive stress to invite the accommodation of this belief:

(74) John offered Mary baked beans, and then SHE insulted HIM / but SHE didn't insult HIM

Examples like this are important because they show the speaker conveying meaning at the level of phonetic realization, and are truly pragmatic in the sense that the meaning conveyed is independent of the meaning of the lexical items themselves.

Indeed, everyday utterances are full of cases where we say things that invite presuppositions because of the situation we find ourselves in, or which fail to invite presuppositions for pragmatic reasons. For example, when a colleague and I were discussing whether to wait for our train on the platform at Nagoya station on a humid day in September and I said

(75) It's cooler outside

I certainly didn't intend my utterance to presuppose that it was cool inside. Nor does

(76) Can I ask a more serious question

usually presuppose that previous questions were serious, in fact quite the contrary. And the sentence I once read

(77) Hong Kong was a British Colony before 1 July 1997

seemed to me to invite the presupposition <as well as after> because of the use of 'before' rather than 'until'. However, I know enough about recent history not to accommodate such a belief. And a teachers newsletter I receive often prints at the bottom of its pages the legend

(78) Have YOU ever written an article for the Newsletter?

This seems to me to pragmatically presuppose that the reader hasn't written an article for the Newsletter. Does 'YOU' turn it into a semantic presupposition? Or when we hear an attributive description, we decide whether to accommodate an existential presupposition or not. I had no difficulty accommodating such a presupposition when I read a travel review containing the sentence

(79) Whoever said that Kent is the garden of England could easily have been staying at Broome Park

But I know from what my wife tells me that 'the suit that fits me' doesn't exist.

The point that emerges is that a speaker has a good deal of choice in deciding whether and how to invite the addressee to accommodate background meanings. Because such meanings aren't part of what is conveyed at the level of deniable proposition, they need to be non-controversial, which in turn implies that a speaker needs to take into account the perspective of the addressee in calculating how to convey meaning.

Summary

In the first half of this chapter we saw how 'semantic' presuppositions were triggered by morphemes, lexical items or structures and appeared to pass an independent test of their status, their ability to survive negation. We then considered a number of cases where the expected presupposition did not arise because it would be inconsistent with the discourse context or with the addressee's beliefs about the world. Thus the discourse context and the addressee's encyclopedic knowledge determine whether a presupposition triggering structure or lexical item actually triggers a presupposition. This suggests that presuppositions are pragmatically licensed and that pragmatic checking is always required to confirm the intention of a speaker to invite the accommodation of a background belief.

Presupposition can also be compared to and contrasted with deixis. In both cases, the speaker intends to refer or denote. But whereas in the case of deixis it's necessary to identify a *demonstratum* in relation to the indexical ground in order to effect reference, in the case of presupposition the hearer is content to take the existence of a proposition on trust. These background assumptions, or presuppositions, together with the linguistic form of the utterance itself, then enable us to draw further inferences as to what the speaker meant by what they said, whether these are speech acts (the area explored in Chapter 4) or implied meanings (the area explored in Chapters 5 and 6).

Raising pragmatic awareness

1 Working by yourself, collect a few advertising slogans containing presuppositions and bring these to your tutorial group for discussion.

2 Work with a partner. Choose any lyric with a strong story-line – Beatles songs work particularly well – and agree on three or four lines that you and your partner will work with. Then, working separately, each draw the scene depicted in the lyric in such a way as to represent all the presuppositions. Come back together to compare drawings and discuss the way you each represented the presuppositions. (Acknowledgement: this idea was thought up by Csilla Szabo.)

3 This exercise works best in a small group. Each person should think up a sentence containing a presupposition and dictate it to the group. As each sentence is dictated, you each write down a product which it could be used to advertise and the reason why it could be used in this way.

4 Working in a small group, choose a short news story from a newspaper and together rewrite it as a feature article making as much use of presupposition as you can.

5 Which of the features of talk identified as typically pragmatic in Chapter 1 play an important part in presupposition: accommodation, appropriateness, context, indeterminacy, indirect meaning, inference, reflexivity, relevance?

Discussions and essays

Based on what you know about presupposition, discuss the relative merits of each of the following views:

- Presuppositions are invoked by or contained in utterances. They are not interpretations of utterances.
- Presuppositions are speaker-invited, mutual contextual beliefs without which utterances would lack the background against which they need to be understood.
- In some cases presuppositions seem to be tied to particular expressions or constructions. A better way to explain this phenomenon is to recognize that there are constraints on the appropriate use of certain constructions.
- Semantic presuppositions are preconditions on utterances making sense, and pragmatic presuppositions are preconditions on utterances being appropriate.

Further reading

Primary texts

Green, 1996: 72–86; Levinson, 1983: 167–225; Seuren, 1998: 423–41.

Classic text

Strawson, 1950.

4 Speech acts – language as action

Suit the action to the word, the word to the action.
(Hamlet III.ii.20)

Keywords:

activity type, direct speech act, entailment, felicity condition, form and function, idiom theory, illocutionary act, illocutionary force, indirect speech act, intention, literal meaning, locutionary act, (explicit) performative, perlocution, proposition, speech act, speech event, truth-conditional semantics, truth value, usage, use, utterance

4.1 Introduction

Pragmatic meanings are operations on context. **Speech acts**, the topic of this chapter, alter the prevailing context in a way that the succeeding speaker will need to take into account. In an exchange like

(1) BRANKA: When will you be back
PETER: I should be back by eight but you know what trains are like

I cannot ignore the new context that Branka's question creates. Is it what on the surface it appears to be, an inquiry as to the time of my return? Or is it more than this? Is it an offer to have a meal on the table when I get back? Is it a complaint about my being away from home on a Saturday? Is she checking to see when she has to return to wife mode?

Nor I hope will Branka ignore the new context that I intend my answer to create. I'm accepting her offer to have a meal on the table when I get back (and excusing myself from having to help with the cooking). I'm slagging off trains. And given that it's a Saturday and the draw for the National Lottery takes place just after eight, and given that we are poor teachers who don't want to have to go back to work on Monday, I'm also letting Branka know that she should be sure to buy our lottery ticket. In this way, our **utterances** do much more than is conveyed by their literal sentence meanings. I've tried to capture some of what they do here in my descriptions: 'an inquiry', 'an offer', 'a complaint', 'checking', 'accepting', 'excusing', 'slagging off', 'letting Branka know that she should be sure to'.

You already know something about speech acts from Chapter 1, where we saw how, depending on the context in which it was uttered, 'I'm here now' might be taken as a comforting reassurance, a stern warning or an apology. We also explored some of the speech acts accomplished by uttering 'I'm tired' and noticed how 'WELCOME TO POLITICS' could be a genuine welcome to a university department or a warning about the true nature of politics. This chapter explores the property that utterances have of counting as actions like welcoming or warning. The chapter contains three further sections, each of which includes several sub-sections:

- *Speech acts,* which explores the performative nature of utterances, or the way in which what we say to each other has 'force' as well as content.

- *Speech acts in the real world*, which describes a number of actual uses.
- *Use, usage and idiom*, which discusses some of the issues raised by the study of performative utterances.

4.2 Speech acts

4.2.1 Actions in words

Sunday evening at home, and I'm sitting at the kitchen table preparing for my pragmatics class. My then eighteen-year-old son is sitting at the top of the table turning the pages of the newspaper apparently looking for pictures. My then thirteen-year-old daughter is sitting opposite me with nothing better to do than think, and kick the underside of the table from time to time. All of a sudden, she speaks: 'Why don't we get a parrot?' My son and I ignore her. She speaks again: 'They're as intelligent as three-year-olds.' Looking up from my work, this time I reply: 'Some are as intelligent as eighteen-year-olds.' My son continues to turn pages as though he hasn't heard. Eleanor isn't only telling me something about parrots, she's trying to persuade me that we should get one. I understand both what she says and what she does, or tries to do, by saying it.

For my part, I'm not only telling her something (doubtful) about parrots, but I'm also turning down her suggestion and insulting my son in a typical father–daughter bonding exchange. She understands both what I say and what I do by saying it.

For his part, my son, who is partly the target but not the addressee of what I say, feigns deafness. My daughter and I both understand what he means by not saying anything. Even his silence is an action.

Later, I wish I'd said, 'Some eighteen-year-olds are as intelligent as three-year-olds.'

4.2.2 Language and action – understanding the phenomenon

Our butcher once asked why farmers have long ears and bald heads. When I obligingly said I didn't know, he took the lobe of one of his ears between thumb and forefinger and, pulling it downwards, said 'How much?' Next he ran his hand through his hair, saying 'Cor' as he did so. This neat joke shows how language (saying 'How much?') and action (pulling your ear-lobe downwards to indicate that you can't believe what you've just heard) can be co-incident. Of course there are times when actions are preferred to words, such as when flagging down a bus or a taxi; or times when either actions, or language, or both may be used, such as when greeting someone in the street; or times when both language and actions are required, as in the complicated ritual of introducing people to one another. These examples show that there is no clear-cut boundary between using actions to count as actions and using language to count as actions.

More than that, we usually realize that we are doing something with words when we talk. When my son was two years old he came into the bathroom one day when I was bent double scrubbing out the bath and said in a particularly jaunty and self-satisfied way

(2) It's me again

This struck me as a rather peculiar utterance. The sentence was an accurate description of a state of affairs in the world – indeed, it was a statement of the obvious. But when we use *It's me again* as an utterance, it's usually to apologize for troubling someone a second time. This didn't seem to be my son's intention on this occasion. I wasn't able to explain his utterance to myself until I recollected that on the previous occasion when he'd come into the bathroom as I was scrubbing the bath out, I'd turned to him in exasperation and said

(3) It's you again

He'd evidently understood the semantics but not the pragmatics of my utterance and had assumed that to get in first with 'It's me again' was the appropriate pragmatic strategy in the bath-scrubbing context we found ourselves in.

This simple example illustrates the difference between the literal meaning of sentences like *it's me again* and *it's you again* and the pragmatic meaning which results from the use of such sentences as utterances. Knowing the literal meaning of the sentences isn't enough to determine what they count as doing, what speech act is performed, when they are used.

Checking understanding (4.1)

1 Although *Sorry, I'm sorry* and *I am sorry* all express the same proposition and are therefore true under just the same conditions, they are each used to perform a range of different acts. Try to list some of the situations in which each might be used and decide what speech act would be effected in each case.

2 A former student once sent me an email beginning 'Remember me'. What speech act did she intend? What speech act did Hamlet's father's ghost intend when he said 'Remember me'?

3 Can you think of other examples of a single proposition being used for a variety of speech acts? Begin with my daughter's use of 'I'll never sell her' mentioned in Chapter 1.

4 One day my colleague, Hiroko, and I had lunch together in the staff restaurant. When it was time to pay, Hiroko found that she'd forgotten her purse. Our conversation went like this

(4) HIROKO: I haven't got any money
PETER: It's all right I've got money
HIROKO: I'll pay you back later
PETER: It's OK

Later I was surprised to find that Hiroko had put the cost of her lunch in my pigeonhole. What had gone wrong?

4.2.3 Locution, illocution and perlocution – what is said, what is done and the effect

I was once a passenger in a car travelling through Uzbekistan. At one stage in our journey, we passed a man standing by the roadside with his arms spread wide. Seeing my puzzled look, the driver explained that the man we had seen was selling fish (which made sense as we were passing a lake at the time). Notice that we can distinguish three aspects of this semiotic act:

1 its literal 'meaning': a man standing with his arms spread wide;
2 what it counts as doing (for those in the know): offering fish for sale;

3 the effect it has: presumably sometimes cars stop and a negotiation takes place (probably the intended effect); occasionally a foreigner is puzzled (presumably not an intended effect).

Notice that the same three aspects of meaning can also be distinguished in the utterance

(2) It's me again

1 *its literal meaning*: it conveys the proposition that the speaker has returned to a place he/she was in on a previous occasion. In saying this we are regarding 'It's me again' as a sentence with a **truth value**. (In fact, it's very difficult to think of any circumstances under which this sentence could be uttered without being true.)
2 *what it counts as doing*: when this sentence is used as an utterance, it usually has the force of, or counts as, an apology. Thought of in this way, it doesn't make any real sense to ask if the sentence is true or not – rather, the utterance represents the **intention** of the speaker to apologize for intruding.
3 *the effect it has*: the utterance will have effects or consequences that are not entirely foreseeable. Presumably, the speaker hopes it will mollify the addressee, but there will be occasions on which it has some other effect, such as making the addressee angry.

In *How to Do Things with Words* (1962) Austin called the first of these aspects of meaning – uttering a sentence with determinate 'sense' (i.e. non-ambiguous meaning) and reference, the **locution**. He called the second – performing an act by uttering a sentence, the **illocution**. And he called the third – the effect the utterance might have, the **perlocution**.

Checking understanding (4.2)

1 Thomas draws attention to *Interflora*'s neat slogan 'Say it with flowers!' (1995: 101). Can you determine the literal meaning of this slogan, the kinds of things giving someone flowers might count as doing, and the kinds of effects it might have?

2 Identify the locutionary, illocutionary and perlocutionary acts typically associated with saying

(3) It's you again

4.2.4 Language and action – Austin's theory of speech acts

The distinction between the meaning that sentences have as a result of our knowing whether they are true or false and the meaning that utterances have as a result of our understanding what they count as doing was first described in *How to Do Things with Words*. Austin draws attention to the **performative** or action accomplishing use of certain language formulas. A good example is

(5) Pass

When uttered by contestants in the television general knowledge contest, *Mastermind*, we call this use **explicitly performative** because the action of passing up the opportunity to offer an answer is accomplished just by saying 'Pass'. Moreover it's only felicitous to utter 'Pass' under narrowly defined circumstances, such as when asked a question to which one doesn't know the answer on *Mastermind* or at particular moments in the bidding sequence of a game of bridge. Try walking down the street nodding at people and saying 'Pass', and it won't be long before someone makes a telephone call and you get taken away in a van.

In the previous paragraph, we used the term 'explicitly performative' to denote the use of an expression that accomplishes an action merely by virtue of being uttered. Thus by uttering

(6) I call upon these persons here present to witness that I, AB, do take thee, CD, to be my lawful wedded wife (or husband) (UK *Marriage Act*, 1949)

the speaker both makes those present witnesses and marries the person addressed. Some years ago, this form of words was superseded by the less formal but no less performative

(7) I [name] take you [name] to be my wedded wife (or husband) (UK *Marriage Ceremony (Prescribed Words) Act*, 1996)

Checking understanding (4.3)

'I hereby pronounce you man and wife' counts as performing an action – we might say that it is explicitly performative. 'I sneeze' is not. Make a list of as many explicitly performative utterances as you can think of and in each case think through the conditions under which it would be appropriate to utter them.

As Austin points out, utterances do not need to contain an explicitly performative verb to be performative. For example, saying 'Pass' on a football field is not explicitly performative, although as a call for the ball it clearly performs an action.

Or take the case of promising. It would be distinctly odd for me to say to my wife

(8) I hereby promise to pick you up at eight o'clock

Even

(9) I promise to pick you up at eight

would only be felicitous if I'd failed to honour such an agreement on a previous occasion. It would be much more natural to say

(10) I'll pick you up at eight

Although the explicit performative *promise* does not occur in (10), the utterance certainly counts as promising. Or I can reassure my wife of the reliability of what I commit myself to by saying

(11) I'll pick you up at eight, don't worry

Or I can use pitch prominence

(12) I WILL pick you up at eight.

Even saying

(13) Shall I pick you up at eight

or

(14) Would you like me to pick you up at eight

commits me to the promised action in the event of my offer being accepted. Indeed, saying even (13) or (14) would be infelicitous or insincere, if my wife accepted and I then explained that I had a prior engagement. Yet only the first two of these seven ways of promising use the explicit performative verb *promise*. The last two examples are interrogative, and (14) even embeds what is promised within an interrogative sentence. Yet all of them count as making a promise. This is because they all share a common set of what Austin called **felicity conditions**, the conditions which make a speech act an appropriate utterance. Searle set out a taxonomy of conditions, or rules as he called them, on promising (1969: 63). Would you agree that the conditions on promising include minimally

- that I intend to deliver what I promise?
- that it's desirable to the person to whom I make the promise?
- that I wasn't going to do it anyway?

Thus we see that non-explicit, and even very implicit, ways of using language performatively are common. The implicit nature of many speech acts means that they are doubly pragmatic: they are pragmatic first because they convey meanings (**illocutionary force**) that are not entailments of the words actually used, and at the same time they are typical of other pragmatic phenomena in that these meanings are frequently conveyed indirectly in implicit ways. This is well illustrated by the case of

(2) It's me again

Typically this utterance counts as apologizing for an intrusion. Neither this nor

(3) It's you again

which expresses irritation, contains any explicit performative verb. One has the force of an apology, the other of an expression of annoyance, and both have literal meanings or entailments of a quite different kind.

Indeed, we might well ask how *It's me again* comes to be understood as an apology when, as my son demonstrated in understanding only its semantics and not its pragmatics, this is not a necessary assumption. Since the proposition conveyed in the utterance 'It's me again' is already obvious without being uttered, the speaker must have some further reasons for saying it. Like 'I'm a man' discussed in Chapter 1, if it was meant literally, it would lack felicity. It therefore conveys an implied meaning, perhaps in the case of 'It's me again' an implied meaning that it shares with 'It's you again', namely that the person indicated (me/you) is imposing on (the territory of) the other party in the exchange. One can't apologize for intruding unless one intrudes, so that intrusion is a felicity condition on apologizing for intruding. And one can't be irritated by someone intruding unless they intrude, so that, once again, someone's intrusion is a felicity condition on expressing irritation at an intrusion.

4.2.5 Proposition and force

At this stage we need to make some basic distinctions.

It's important to distinguish:	from:
• Sentences that describe states of affairs in the world	Doing things with words
Thus (3) It's you again describes a state of affairs in the world	and typically constitutes an expression of exasperation
• The truth or falsity of sentences	The felicity or infelicity of utterances
Thus (15) Some parrots are as intelligent as eighteen-year-olds is probably a false sentence	and felicitous as an utterance only under very particular conditions
• Truth as a way of determining meaning	Performative effect as a source of meaning
Thus the meaning of (2) It's me again consists less in knowing that it happens to be true	than in understanding the speaker's intention to apologize and so be forgiven for intruding
• The locution (uttering a sentence with determinate sense (= unambiguous meaning) sense and reference	The illocution (performing an act by uttering a sentence), and the perlocution (the effect the utterance might have)
Thus saying (16) I'm on holiday next week conveys the proposition that the speaker will be on holiday at the time indicated	and, when the addressee is the newsagent, instructs him to suspend paper deliveries; if overheard by a thief, one of the effects might be to cause the speaker's house to be burgled
• Propositional content	Force
Thus when saying (4) I've got money the speaker expresses the proposition that money is in his possession	the speaker reassures the addressee and undertakes to pay

The left-hand column in this list of distinctions treats meaning in the manner of truth-conditional semantics – if you know when a sentence is true or false, then you know what it means. Thus, to take Tarski's classic example,

(17) Schnee ist weiss

will be a true sentence if and only if 'snow is white'. (Note that I'm following the usual practice of using one language [here German] for the sentence and another [here 'English'] to describe the state of affairs the sentence purports to describe so as to avoid a confusion between sentence and state of affairs in the world.)

Working down the left-hand column above, 'Schnee ist weiss' is seen as a description of a state of affairs in the world whose meaning derives from recognizing the truth of the proposition it expresses. This way of understanding the meaning of (17) is to be contrasted with the speech act perspective set out in the right-hand column. Under this account 'Schnee ist weiss' would be uttered for some purpose, such as giving information to a child or confirming this strange fact to a Saudi who'd never seen snow. It would be felicitous in such contexts (only), would be meaningful as an act of informing or convincing, and would be likely to have effects that would be only partly predictable. Thus, from a speech act perspective, truth is beside the point – it makes no more sense to ask whether trying to convince is true than to ask about the conditions under which an imperative or an interrogative sentence is true. This point is well illustrated by the guest who says

(18) That was a wonderful meal

This is frequently false as a sentence, at least in Britain, but would typically be considered an appropriate utterance (and would be unlikely to have the effect of deceiving).

Checking understanding (4.4)

How does speech act theory help you to understand the following cartoon strip (Figure 4.1)?

Figure 4.1

4.2.6 Language and action – direct and indirect speech acts

We've already noticed that many speech acts are doubly pragmatic: they are pragmatic not only because they convey count-as-doing meanings that are not **entailments** but also because these meanings are frequently conveyed indirectly.

So when we say

(2) It's me again

we are being indirect. In fact, we are stating one of the felicity conditions (returning with a purpose that implies an imposition on someone else) that would make it appropriate to apologize. If I say to my wife

(14) Would you like me to pick you up at eight

I'm promising indirectly to pick her up by asking about one of the felicity conditions on doing it – that it is desirable to her. When I say to the newsagent

(16) I'm on holiday next week

I'm stating one of the felicity conditions on suspending the papers. And when Mr Logic asks whether one of the felicity conditions for buying stamps is in place with the utterance

(19) Do you sell postage stamps

he's assumed to be asking to buy a stamp.

These examples show that it's sufficient for a speaker to state or ask about a felicity condition on an action to imply that they are performing the action itself. This way of accomplishing a speech act, by stating one of the felicity conditions on the act rather than using an explicit formula has been usefully described as metonymic by Panther and Thornburg (1998).

Relatedly, it seems that a felicity condition on expressing exceptionally strong feelings is to lack the appropriate words. So that when we hear someone else's distressing news and want to express sympathy, we might say

(20) I don't know what to say

thus performing an illocutionary act by stating that we can't express the meaning we want to convey as a literal meaning or locutionary act. A witness to the Oklahoma bomb explosion in the USA said in a television interview

(21) There's got to be fatalities over there – I'm speechless – I've never seen anything like it

Bill Clinton, on being re-elected president of USA, expressed his thanks to those who had voted for him by saying

(22) I'm more grateful than I can say

The professor responsible for the launch of Beagle 2, a space probe to Mars, said to a BBC reporter

(23) I can't tell you how exciting it is to be involved in the whole thing

And a railway company in Britain placed a poster on stations headed

(24) We can't think of a word for people who abuse our staff (adding 'but here are some sentences', followed by a list of penalties imposed on yobs convicted of abusive behaviour).

4.2.7 Sentence types and direct and indirect speech acts

Imagine you had the misfortune to attend one of my pragmatics lectures and that after half-an-hour in which I had been particularly difficult to follow, I said

(25) I know this isn't very clear. Can anyone do any better

You might be very uncertain as to the illocutionary force associated with 'Can anyone do any better'.

If you were very bold, you might treat it as a genuine question and tell me that several of my colleagues had done better earlier in the week. Or if I held out a board-marker as I said it, you might take it as an invitation to come up and have a try yourself. Or if you thought I was being sarcastic, you might take it ironically as an assertion that no one else could do any better.

The bold reading takes my utterance as a direct speech act in which the interrogative form is used to ask a question. The board-marker reading takes it as an indirect speech act in which I ask about one of the felicity conditions that would need to be in place to make it worthwhile inviting someone else to come and have a try. I am thus understood to be implying that someone should come and do just that. The ironical reading takes it as an indirect way of asserting that no one can do any better, which is inferred if you assume that I am asking what appears to be an echoic *yes/no* question to which the only correct answer is no.

This example shows us how a sentence with interrogative form can be taken not only as a question, but also as an indirect request/order or as an indirect assertion.

English is fortunate in having one set of terms for sentence **form**:

- *declarative* (subject + verb order)
- *imperative* (no overt subject)
- *interrogative* (verb + subject order)

and another matching set for utterance **function**:

- *assertion*
- *order/request*
- *question.*

This metalanguage makes it easy to distinguish form and function. When form and function match, we call the effect a **direct speech act** as in

(26) I'll never sell her (declarative used to assert)
(27) Don't ever sell her (imperative used to give an order/issue a command)
(28) Will you ever sell her (interrogative used to ask a question)

In these cases, the mood, *declarative, imperative, interrogative,* gives an indication of the force, just as an explicit performative like *promise* functions as an **illocutionary force indicating device** (IFID).

When form and function don't match, the illocutionary effect is conveyed as an indirect speech act (Searle, 1975), as in the following examples:

(29) I wonder when the train leaves (declarative form functioning as a question = *do you know when the train leaves*, or as a request = *tell me when the train leaves*)
(30) (to a child) You'd better eat your dinner fast (declarative form functioning as an order)
(31) Can you open the door for me (interrogative form functioning as a request).

In fact, when we make a request or give an order, we almost always do it indirectly by using an interrogative sentence. This raises the question of whether it's appropriate to think of sentence forms as having prototypical functions, an issue to which we will return in the final section of the chapter.

Summary

In this section, we've seen that sentences are not only grammatical objects which describe potentially verifiable states of affairs in real or possible worlds. When used pragmatically as utterances, it's not so much the truth value of a sentence that determines its most salient meaning as what that sentence is used to do, its illocutionary force, and what perlocutionary effect it's expected to have. Speech acts are licensed not by considerations of truth, but by their felicity in the contexts in which they occur and by their ability to operate in those contexts.

Checking understanding (4.5)

What speech act is conveyed by each of the following and what effect is it likely to have?

(32) Have you seen that room of hers (My wife talking to me and referring to our daughter's bedroom.)
(33) You are on my right (Spoken by the chair of a meeting. He had just introduced two speakers and explained that the one on his left would speak first. The one on his right then began to speak.)
(34) ELEANOR: Dad, are you in a good mood today
PETER: Why, do you want to put me in a bad one
(35) You could get into a fight (A Newcastle United football fan in a pub when I asked if he thought the club's leading goal-scorer might be gay.)

4.3 Speech acts in the real world

Probably someone arranging/offering/promising to pick their partner up can choose the most felicitous formula from among the many options available without giving it a second thought. But imagine a slightly more problematic scenario. When you pick your partner up, they are with a friend to whom they've promised a lift – how do they give you this news? And imagine that the friend gets into your car and doesn't do her seat-belt up. How do you rectify the situation?

Although there are clearly many contextual variables to take into account in determining the most felicitous formula for conveying an illocution, we don't have a totally free hand in this because speech acts are to some extent formulaic. For example, if my neighbour at dinner is an overseas student studying in Britain, she may turn to me and say

(36) Can you give me the salt

I notice the slight difference between this and the UK formula

(36′) Can you pass the salt

Because speech acts are to some degree culturally institutionalized, we have expectations about preferred and dispreferred formulas. And as we cross cultures, we sometimes notice slight (and even not so slight) differences in the way that illocutionary force is conveyed.

The illocutionary force we read into the utterances addressed to us will also depend on our understanding of the context. I once stayed at a hotel in Bremen and on the first morning had to move twice at breakfast to get away from smokers. When I complained to the waitress, her response was

(37) It's very free in Germany

I took this as a rebuke intended to make me feel ashamed of my illiberal attitudes. I also took the abruptness of her response to be calculatedly insulting. However, at breakfast the following morning we got into conversation and she told me that she came from The Netherlands. In the light of this unexpected context, I revised my understanding of what she had said the day before. She was criticizing the local custom, and what I had taken as abruptness was an appropriately minimal way of expressing solidarity.

In the remainder of this section, I'm going to share a number of contexts where felicitous formulas were hard to arrive at and a number of contexts where misunderstandings occurred.

4.3.1 Being aggressive in the washroom

Let's start with a context where I had to think on my feet. I walk into the gentleman's lavatory in a Newcastle department store at 9.30 one weekday morning and find two sixteen-year-old boys in school uniform. One is washing his hair in a washbasin. As I enter, he turns to his friend, who's looking rather uncomfortable, and says 'Stop looking so English.' Then he turns to me and says 'Alright'. Both his utterances are formulaic. The first is a direct speech act, but it's the second, 'Alright' that I'm concerned about. Although formulaic, as an illocutionary act it may be located at any point on a continuum from greeting to threat. Given the dismissive command issued to his friend and the noticeably aggressive intonation he uses when addressing me, I'm slightly worried. But I decide to call his bluff:

(38) HAIRWASHER (to fellow student): Stop looking so English
HAIRWASHER (to Peter): Alright
PETER: More to the point are you alright

My use of 'more to the point' draws attention to the relative inappropriateness of his speech act in comparison to mine. I return his formula, which I intend him to determine as an inquiry as to his state of mental health. Fortunately for me, it has the perlocutionary effect for which I had hoped – he returns to washing his hair with a mumbled obscenity and his friend laughs.

4.3.2 Bullying in a university canteen

Another think-on-your feet situation, this time for a student. I'm in the canteen of a university where I'm an external examiner. The next table is occupied by several animated male lecturers. A female student approaches their table. She puts her hands on the back of an unoccupied chair.

(39) STUDENT: Is this a spare place
LECTURER: I'm sorry I don't think I know who you are do I
STUDENT: No I just wanted to take the chair

Again, the utterances are recognizable encodings of speech acts:

- By drawing attention to a felicity condition on the outcome the speaker desires, 'Is this a spare place' is a conventionally indirect way of requesting leave either to take a chair away or to occupy an empty place
- By stating a felicity condition on responding to a significant or a personal request, 'I don't think I know who you are' functions metonymically as a conventionally indirect way of not immediately acceding to a request
- By stating a desired perlocutionary effect, the speaker corrects an addressee misunderstanding of a previous utterance. Her use of the minimizer ('just') suggests that the addressee over-estimated the degree of imposition of the original request.

Watching this exchange, it seemed to me that the context in which the student carried no tray of food and placed her hands on the chair-back indicated to the lecturer that her request was to take a chair rather than to sit at the table. But the lecturer chose to respond as though her request was for a place at the table, which he treated as though it was a considerable imposition. The coercive 'do I' is calculated to oblige the student to respond to the literal meaning of 'I don't think I know who you are'. Although this is probably a true sentence, as a speech act, it's insincere, as is the use of formulaic 'I'm sorry'. For all these reasons, the perlocutionary effect the lecturer seems to intend is humiliation, as he takes advantage of being an older male in a senior position surrounded by other similar males.

After the student had taken the chair to another table, one of the lecturer's colleagues said 'That would have been even more effective if you hadn't had tomato ketchup all around your mouth.' The use of 'effective' suggests that they were well aware of what they were doing and of the performative properties of language and its perlocutionary effect. It's incidents such as this that demonstrate the validity of the language-as-action hypothesis that underlies speech act theory.

4.3.3 Literal meaning and illocutionary force at breakfast

An out-of-sorts couple sitting at the table next to me at breakfast in a guesthouse:

(40) HUSBAND (to waitress): Could we have some more coffee
<waitress goes away>
WIFE: You should say may we
HUSBAND: Why
WIFE: Because it could mean are you able
HUSBAND: That's what I meant
WIFE: Of course you didn't

In putting his conventionally indirect request to the waitress, the husband chooses 'could' from the politeness scale which includes *might* (most formal), *may, could* and *can* (least formal). The closer to the formal end of the scale, the greater the distance a speaker encodes between themselves and the addressee. The wife obviously felt that her husband wasn't sufficiently formal when addressing the waitress, as indicated by 'You should say may we'. When challenged, she tries to justify her objection to his use of 'could' by appealing to its literal meaning. But from a speech act perspective, the locutionary or literal sense of 'could' in her husband's request draws attention to a felicity condition on having more coffee. In this respect, her preferred replacement, 'may', which draws attention to another felicity condition, whether it is permitted to have more coffee, is no different. And although she is right to assert that he didn't mean 'could' literally, she seems to be overlooking the fact that in her previous utterance she objected to its use on the grounds that it would be understood literally rather than at the level of illocution.

It's fascinating to watch such 'folk' or natural attempts to unravel the distinction between propositional meaning and illocutionary force. Like the canteen encounter, this exchange also shows that people do know what they are doing when they use language, although, as with most language use, they find it difficult to provide accurate accounts of what they know.

And as with the canteen encounter, which I described as bullying, we might be tempted to describe what goes on here as a quarrel. This reminds us that speech acts sometimes play a role in the wider context of sequences of utterances and actions that, taken together, follow an expectable pattern and constitute a recognizable routine. These extended talk types are called **speech events** or, especially when they are goal-directed recognizable activities, **activity types**.

As we've already seen, sentence types such as interrogatives are frequently used to do things other than ask questions. Indeed, the list of interrogatives below, which we've already discussed in this or in earlier chapters, are exactly of this kind. As you read each of them again, you might like to recall the context in which it occurred and then consider its function in its wider speech event or activity-type context:

- what's your name by the way
- do you usually have this sort
- are we all here
- right, shall we begin
- may I speak English
- what's your name again
- is it tea or coffee
- have you got a plastic bag
- could you let me have a bit of paper by any chance
- why do farmers have long ears and bald heads
- shall I pick you up at eight
- do you sell postage stamps

What's important about all these indirect speech acts is that they play a recognizable role in a larger context. So 'why do farmers have long ears and bald heads', for example, is recognizable as the first turn in a joke inviting the standard response 'I don't know'. Spoken by a senior colleague when a meeting is due to start, the most appropriate response to 'are we all here' is non-verbal, as we saw – indeed to provide an answer such as 'no, we're not' would be accurate but useless. Because these utterances are open propositions, each invites some sort of response. Their functions and the nature of the responses that are appropriate depend on their roles in the speech events of which they are a part. In other words, they aren't only, or even in some cases principally, questions.

4.3.4 Propositional meaning and illocutionary force at the petrol station: the rude customer

I'm on my way home from work one evening and stop to fill up with petrol. When I go to pay, the person at the cash-desk says

(41) Do you know about our offer on oil

I understand the force of her utterance, which counts as a request to be allowed to explain what purports to be a bargain. How am I to respond? The preferred response is to accede to the request, which is conventionally accomplished by saying *no* with fall-rise intonation. But it's late, and I'm tired and thinking of the demanding family awaiting me at home. Why should I have heard of their miserable offer anyway? I'm ashamed to admit that I rather rudely said 'No' with falling intonation, like Mr Logic, attending to the literal rather than the illocutionary force, thus provoking the response 'I see I can't interest you'. This interesting example shows how the same lexical item, the same proposition, in this case *no*, can have quite opposite illocutionary forces and consequential perlocutionary effects depending on the intonation pattern assigned to it.

A week or two later I stopped again at the same petrol station. There was a different assistant this time, but she tried the same utterance as her colleague had done before. I didn't feel keen to go through the charade of fall-rise *no*, nor did I want to repeat the rudeness of falling *no*, so I decided to try 'Yes' instead. It had just the same perlocutionary effect as falling *no* and I avoided having to listen to an unwelcome offer. Why didn't I think of it the first time!

4.3.5 Trouble at the shops: the rude shop-assistant

One scenario anyone shopping in Britain will be familiar with is handing over a £10 note for a small purchase and being handed several heavy coins by way of change rather than a £5 note and correspondingly fewer coins. Quite often shop-assistants recognize that this counts as inconveniencing the customer and apologize as they hand you the coins. When they merely hand you the coins, I sometimes say

(42) You haven't got a £5 note

There seem to be two possible locutionary level interpretations of (42). One possibility is that this is a straight description of a situation of a kind that would be appropriate if I was checking my wife's wallet for her and had failed to find the £5 note that she needed for her train fare. But because the assistant already knows what I assert, this would be an unlikely reading here. Or at least, it could only be intended sarcastically and would be likely to give offence. The second, more likely, possibility is to interpret the *you haven't got x* formula as a pessimistic alternative to the default syntactic interrogative *Have you got x*. This locution would usually be signalled by interrogative intonation. The assistant then has to determine whether the illocutionary act performed is a request, a complaint, a demand for an apology or explanation, etc. The perlocutionary effect varies enormously in my experience – sometimes assistants offer explanations, sometimes they look in various tills for a £5 note, sometimes they ignore the utterance. This is what happened to me on one occasion when I was buying a sandwich at a high-street chemist turned general store and was given a handful of coins:

(43) PETER: You haven't got a £5 note
FEMALE ASSISTANT: I haven't. That's why I gave you coins

Notice that the assistant takes the locution to be a pessimistic interrogative, but like Mr Logic she responds at this level rather than to the illocution. The minimalist 'I haven't' and the redundant, obvious and therefore sarcastic reason she adds seem to me to compound the rudeness inherent in responding to the locutionary rather than the illocutionary act. The response, 'that's why I gave you coins', is sarcastic because it treats one of the felicity conditions underlying my utterance, that there's a slim possibility that they might have a £5 note, as one that I should have known better than to entertain. However, the looking-in-various-tills response you sometimes get shows that this is a felicity condition that can reasonably be entertained. Although the assistant's response looks like an explanation at the locutionary level, it seemed to me to have a quite different indirect force: although it might conceivably have been an explanation or indirect way of apologizing, I took it as a reprimand for the pessimistic inquiry that I should have known better than to make. What do you think? And would you buy a sandwich from her?

4.3.6 Addressees and illocutionary targets

I'm in the queue at our local post office and am wondering whether when my turn comes I'll be served by 'Dr Pragmatics', the postmaster who dealt so effectively with the complaint in Chapter 1, or by the young man at the counter next to him with the sign 'Training in Progress. Please be Patient.' It turns out to be the trainee:

(44) PETER (to trainee): How's the boss's training going
POSTMASTER: Ha ha ha
TRAINEE: Not too well actually
PETER: That shut him up he's usually got something to say

My first utterance is clearly not the intended perlocutionary effect of the sign. The conditions which make it a felicitous utterance include knowing that the postmaster enjoys banter of this sort. Moreover, although my utterance is addressed to the trainee, the illocutionary target appears to be the postmaster. By saying 'Ha ha ha' rather than actually laughing, the postmaster conveys indirectly that he thinks I've just made a feeble joke. At this point, the trainee could probably have avoided responding in a potentially tricky situation for him but he includes himself as an illocutionary target of my utterance by responding 'Not too well actually'. It seems that the illocutionary target is still the postmaster, as evidenced in his subtle choice of 'actually', suggesting that the poor performance entailed by 'not too well' is a surprise. By responding directly to my query, at the illocutionary level the trainee plays along with the joke. My final utterance contains two speech act descriptions, 'shut <him> up', the perlocutionary effect of the trainee's response to my query, and 'got something to say', a way of describing the kind of speech act at which Dr Pragmatics excels. The indexical 'that' is also interesting – does it index the locutionary act or the illocutionary force in the trainee's turn? If the latter, how interesting that a referent may be a psychological entity of this sort rather than an object in the physical environment or an item in the discourse context.

Checking understanding (4.6)

What interesting locutionary, illocutionary and perlocutionary features can you identify in the following real-world exchanges?

(45) CUSTOMER: Have you a biro I could borrow
POSTMASTER: Yes I have a biro and yes you can borrow it

Checking understanding (4.6) *cont.*

(46) CARETAKER: I'm going to get that key code off
PETER: So at the moment we're having the class with the door ajar
CARETAKER: ha ha ha when is a door not a door? when it's a jar

(47) I can apologize for the information that turned out to be wrong (British Prime Minister Blair referring to the intelligence used to justify the invasion of Iraq)

(48) PETER (at coffee point): Can I have coffee please
WAITRESS: Do you want it with milk
PETER: Is it easier black

4.4 Use, usage and idiom

At several points in this chapter, I've used the term 'formula', to describe the locutionary forms of sentences associated with particular illocutionary forces, sometimes claiming that these are conventional, expected, typical and even institutionalized. This final section of the chapter explores the balance between the apparently predictable aspect of speech act meaning and the kind of context-sensitive meaning that we call pragmatic. I'll be distinguishing between **use**, a term used to describe utterances which yield particular, context-sensitive meanings, and **usage**, a term used to describe regularities widely recognized as having particular pragmatic properties. Our discussion in the previous section of

(42) You haven't got a £5 note

explored both usage, the typical force associated with the formula, and use, what the speaker might be taken to be doing on the occasion when he used the formula.

4.4.1 Sentence forms and functions

Earlier in the chapter we talked about 'matching sets' of sentence forms and functions. But it isn't quite as simple as this because declarative sentences are used for many purposes other than asserting – stating, describing, claiming, to name just a few. And although imperatives are used when we give orders and make requests, we also use them to encourage people to work hard and to wish them a good journey. Similarly, interrogatives are used to inquire, to query, to express surprise and for a multitude of purposes. In fact, about the only thing one can say with confidence about interrogatives is that they call for a response of some kind from the addressee.

This prompts us to wonder about the borderline between 'direct' and 'indirect' use. At what point is the literal force overridden – how do we know when

(42) You haven't got a £5 note

is a request or a complaint rather than a statement of fact?

One way of dealing with this problem would be to categorize *You haven't got x* as an idiom, meaning <you owe me an explanation for not having *x*>. This was a favoured solution at one time and neatly bypasses the problem of worrying about the status of the literal meaning component of indirect speech acts. It also accounts for the institutionalized or formulaic property of speech acts. Thus *can you x*, as in 'can you pick me up at eight', is an idiomatic way of saying <do *x*>. One objection to this solution is that we expect idioms to be untranslatable, yet *can you x*, unlike a true idiom such as *kick the bucket* (= die), occurs widely across languages as an indirect way of making a request or giving an order. A further objection to the idiom account is raised by examples like

(25) Can anyone do any better

which may be used either as a direct or an indirect speech act. It's obviously unsatisfactory to have to claim that an expression is sometimes an idiom and sometimes not. For all these reasons the idiom theory, conventions of meaning, account of speech acts doesn't hold water. In attempting to account for the recognizability of speech act formulas, we are thrown back on a conventions of usage account (Morgan, 1978). This implies that a sufficient number of uses of a particular form or token comes over time to be understood as a typical convention of usage, as a speech act type.

When we come across an utterance like

(42) You haven't got a £5 note

we realize that it falls somewhere between type and token. Although there are typical illocutionary interpretations for each use of (42), there isn't a single typical interpretation. The various possible interpretations of (42) raise the problem at the heart of speech act theory, that of how the illocutionary force of an utterance is understood. Is it credible to suppose in the case of entirely unproblematic utterances like

(49) Can you pass the salt

that we begin by processing the literal meaning (I am being asked a question about my ability to pass the salt) which we realize is unlikely to be the intended meaning, so we then set about trying to infer what the speaker might have meant by what he said? Surely not. We all know that there is a convention of usage. (49) 'means' <you pass me the salt>. This is why Morgan argues that the indirect request in (49) is calculable but not calculated. If we accept that (49) has become so conventionalized as not to require an inferencing procedure like that required to determine the force of (42), and if we deny that speech acts are idioms, we are forced to the conclusion that there is little difference between the indirect speech act

(49) Can you pass the salt

and the direct speech act

(49′) Pass the salt

and that therefore the notion of literal meaning is to some degree problematic.

However logical this argument may be, we are obviously reluctant to abandon the notion of literal meaning as a stable, consistent component of sentences and utterances. Moreover, whatever its meaning status, there is clearly a difference between (49) and (49′), at least in terms of their politeness status.

Where does all this lead? For lots of reasons, a convention of meaning or idiom theory account of the non-literal meaning of idioms isn't a sensible solution. In fact, speech acts are formulas of varying degrees of typicality. Some, like (49), are instantly recognizable and, as Morgan put it, "short-circuit" the normal process of inference required to recover the illocutionary force of an utterance like (42) which is to some degree formulaic or type-like but still sufficiently token-like to require an inference to determine its force. In the case of (49), the convention of usage tells us that this is a request. This seems to be confirmed by the fact that the perlocutionary effect of (49) can be guaranteed. However, the varied and unpredictable perlocutionary effects of (42) tell us that each use is interpreted as particular to its context, as a token which, in combination with other contextually derived propositions (including felicity conditions and the encyclopedic knowledge of the addressee), enable that addressee to recover a context-sensitive meaning.

4.4.2 Guiding speech act interpretation

Because they are reflections of our intentions or psychological motivation, it's not surprising that speech act tokens are often hard to determine. And because they are context-dependent, pragmatic meanings will sometimes be liable to misinterpretation. In order to constrain the interpretation of locutionary acts so as to ensure that the addressee understands the illocutionary force we seek to convey, we will sometimes provide contextual cues to facilitate interpretation. When I say

(25) Can anyone do any better

I may hold out a board-marker to enrich the context or there may be an echoic quality to my intonation suggesting that this isn't my authentic voice and that the meaning is therefore ironic.

Another strategy where no explicit performative indicator of illocutionary force is used is to use an illocutionary force indicating device. Thus requests are often marked by the use of pre-verbal *please*, as in

(50) Please pick me up at eight

and

(51) Can you please pick me up at eight

Pre-verbal *please* is ungrammatical in non-request utterances such as

(52) *When do you please want to be picked up

and

(53) *I'll please pick you up at eight

Thus the grammaticality of pre-verbal *please* is determined by illocutionary force in both direct and indirect speech acts. What we are seeing is a syntactic reflex of a pragmatic phenomenon. In other words, what is grammatical is determined not within an autonomous syntax but in relation to the function of the utterance. The function of such devices is to constrain possible speech act determinations. We might call it procedural. Although they have some conceptual content, the principal use of IFIDs is to instruct the addressee in how to take the illocutionary force of what has been uttered in contexts where it might not be readily inferred. To the extent that speech acts are types more frequently than tokens, these constraining devices are relatively rare. As we shall see in the next two chapters, where token as well as type inferences are discussed, such constraining devices are very frequent in the field of implicature.

Summary

Speech acts might be seen as a prototypically pragmatic phenomenon in the sense that they challenge the notion that there is a one-to-one correspondence between a form and its function. It's simply not possible to argue that interrogative or declarative sentences have single predictable functions. In fact, the function of an interrogative sentence when used as an utterance crucially depends on an essentially pragmatic phenomenon, how the context assists the addressee in determining what is meant by what is said, whether the determination is typical, implying a convention of usage, or particular, as in uses that provoke inference.

Raising pragmatic awareness

1 You'll need a partner for this exercise. Working separately, you and your partner each choose one short extract from a contemporary play and copy it out without the original punctuation. The best extracts are those where two speakers are holding an emotional conversation over about ten turns and each of their turns is very short. Then exchange texts: you each invent your own punctuation using either conventional symbols or any new ones that you want to invent to capture illocutionary force. When you've completed the exercise, explain your suggested punctuation to your partner.

2 Working individually, either listen out for or recall occasions when a speaker responds to propositional content rather than illocutionary force. Television comedies and family arguments are good sources of data. Share and explain your examples in your tutorial group.

3 Collect a number of advertisements that contain spoken or written text and bring them to class. In your tutorial group, identify the locutionary, illocutionary and perlocutionary elements of these advertisements.

4 Choose an emotion such as anger or a behaviour such as showing tenderness or criticizing someone. During the next few days, see if you can provoke this emotion or behaviour in someone else. Report your strategies and your interlocutor's exact utterances to colleagues in your tutorial group.

5 Find a partner and together choose a picture of a couple from a colour magazine. Each of you should take the role of one of the people in the picture. Decide who will speak first and what proposition they will convey. The speaker should then try several different ways of conveying the agreed proposition – each time, the person addressed gives it a score out of ten for effectiveness.

6 What is the relationship between language and touch? Out of class, note the occasions when language accompanies touch. Note down what you observe and report it in your tutorial group.

Raising pragmatic awareness *cont.*

7 How do people express disagreement? Out of class, listen out for disagreements. Note down what you overhear and report it in your tutorial group.

8 Which of the features of talk identified as typically pragmatic in Chapter 1 play an important part in speech acts: accommodation, appropriateness, context, indeterminacy, indirect meaning, inference, reflexivity, relevance?

Discussions and essays

Based on what you already know about pragmatics, discuss the relative merits of each of the following views:

- Speech acts have the force they do because they are to some extent institutionalized uses of language.
- "A speech act typically consists of two major components: a content and a force. Some elements in the sentence indicate the force of the speech act which the sentence can be used to perform, while other elements give indications concerning the content of the speech act" (Recanati, 2004: 448).
- Their pragmatic properties come into existence only when sentences are uttered.
- "A distinction has to be drawn between the meaning expressed by an utterance and the way in which the utterance is used" (Verschueren *et al.*, 1995: 496).
- Meaning is use.
- Speech act theory reveals the strategic dimension of language use.

Further reading

Primary texts
Austin, 1962, 1971; Morgan, 1978; Searle, 1965, 1969, 1975.

Textbooks
Levinson, 1983: 226–83; Mey, 2001: 92–133; Schiffrin, 1994: 49–96; Thomas, 1995: 28–54; Yule, 1996: 47–56.

Handbooks
Sadock, 2004: 53–73; Sbisà, 1995: 495–505.

5 Implicit meaning

Words are like leaves; and where they most abound,
Much fruit of sense beneath is rarely found.
(Alexander Pope, An Essay on Criticism, *309–10)*

Keywords:

context, conventional meaning, cooperative principle, defeasibility, entailment, flout, generalized and particularized implicatures, hedge, heuristic, historical pragmatics, implicature, inference, maxim, principle, relevance, scalar implicature, truth value, utterance-token meaning, utterance-type meaning

5.1 Introduction

This chapter explores implicature. An implicature is a meaning that is conveyed but not explicitly stated. You only need to look at my response to my wife's question 'When will you be back' to see how prevalent such meanings are:

(1) I should be back by eight but you know what trains are like

Although I don't say that I won't be back by eight, I certainly imply that I probably won't. And given that I say that I 'should be' back by eight, how is it that my wife infers that I probably won't be? I also imply that trains are unreliable. You could hardly imagine anyone saying 'but you know what trains are like' in Japan where you can set your clock by them. Or at least, if anyone did say this, they certainly wouldn't imply that the trains were unreliable. As well as these implied meanings, I also intend my wife to infer that I'll be back too late to make the dinner and to buy the lottery ticket. As these implicatures are felicity conditions on Branka making dinner and buying the lottery ticket, this is why what I say counts as accepting her offer to have a meal on the table and letting her know that she should be sure to buy our lottery ticket, the speech acts identified in the previous chapter.

It's important to recognize that these implied meanings are of two kinds. For example, the implicature that I probably won't be back by eight seems to have more to do with the words I choose or the way I put things than with the context. But the implicature that I won't be able to buy a lottery ticket depends on the speaker and the hearer sharing a great deal of contextual knowledge. Because this implicature depends on contextual knowledge, the same implied meaning won't always arise when someone says

(1) I should be back by eight but you know what trains are like

Given some other context, the addressee is likely to infer different context-related implicatures. One more thought: which meaning do you think is more salient, the meaning I state, 'I should be back by eight', or the meanings I imply: <I probably won't be back by eight>, <I'll be back too late to make dinner>, <I'll be back too late to buy a lottery ticket>?

We already know something about implicature from Chapter 1, where we saw how, depending on the context in which it was uttered, 'I'm here now' might imply many different things, including <there's no need to worry any more>, <stop messing about and get on with your homework> and <I'm sorry I've held you up>. We also explored the implicature recovered from 'Are you two both together'. And we saw how someone could convey a meaning even by saying something patently false, such as 'I'm a man'.

The chapter contains four further sections, each of which includes several sub-sections:

- *Grice's theory of conversational implicature*, which identifies the issue of utterance interpretation to which Paul Grice sought a solution and works through his ideas on the 'logic' of conversation.
- *Neo-Gricean theories of implicature*, which shows some of the ways in which Grice's ideas have been developed and how we've come to see that lexical items as well as utterances have both literal and implied meanings.
- *Implicature in the real world*, which describes the contribution of implied meanings to actual instances of spoken, written and simultaneously spoken-and-written language use.
- *Implicature and conventionalization*, which discusses two areas in which neo-Gricean theories of implicature provide important insights into the way in which language change occurs.

Just to whet your appetite, pause and consider for a moment the implied meanings prompted by the following letter published in *The Times*:

(2) Sir, If drinking games really are the cause of declining academic performance [reports, October 30 and 31], perhaps Oxford should have considered banning them years ago

In fact, you might like to jot these implied meanings down, as we'll be returning to this letter later.

5.2 Grice's theory of conversational implicature

This section begins with a problem: how is it that we understand

(3) It's the taste

in the Coca-Cola advertisement to mean that the taste is good? By itself, 'It's the taste' means very little – in fact, we aren't even told what the taste is or whether it does anything. And yet we understand a meaning that isn't explicitly stated at all. And more puzzling still, 'It's the taste' was exactly what my daughter used to say when she started her destructive journey through the biscuit barrel on her return from school and was asked why she hadn't eaten her school dinner. I understood her to mean exactly the opposite of the Coca-Cola advertisement: that the taste wasn't good. How can the same sentence be understood to convey two meanings that are the opposite of one another and neither of which is explicitly stated by the speaker? This is the problem addressed in this chapter.

5.2.1 Implied meaning

You might at first think that there could be something special about the formula 'It's the taste'. But this isn't the case at all. Just the other day my wife was frying an egg and said all of a sudden

(4) This egg's very yellow

I knew as she said it that she didn't mean what I would have meant if I'd said it. So I asked her, 'Good or bad?' For her, 'very yellow' was at the top end of the colour range for yolks and hence good. For me, an orange yolk is good and a yellow one not so good: for me, 'very yellow' = very yukky! Or when I met our IT technician on the top floor of our building where the counselling service is located, I certainly didn't mean only what I said:

(5) I see you've been spending time in the part of the university most able to meet your needs

Or if we go back to an example from Chapter 1 and our entertaining postmaster when the customer complains about the notes he's been given:

(6) CUSTOMER: These aren't very clean – I gave you clean ones last time
POSTMASTER: Be careful you don't trip over the step on your way out

Notice that he didn't tell the customer that he was a fussy old fool, but he certainly conveyed it. And if the customer didn't get the message at the time, he would certainly have recovered it as he left and found that there isn't a step on the way out. One Saturday morning I went in just after the post-office had opened:

(7) POSTMASTER: It's a nice morning isn't it
PETER: Not bad
POSTMASTER: It'll be better at one o'clock

I understood him to mean that he'd be happier when the post-office had closed, but again, he never explicitly stated this.

The only time I heard anyone get the better of him was when an elderly lady, hardly as tall as the counter, went into a long description of what had happened the day before, which she found unsatisfactory. The conversation went like this:

(8) CUSTOMER: I gave you a pound yesterday, etc., etc.
POSTMASTER: My it's early in the morning isn't it
CUSTOMER: It's too early for you

Although the postmaster didn't actually tell the customer that he thought she was talking rubbish, he certainly conveyed it. And although the customer didn't actually tell the postmaster that he was stupid, he became unaccountably silent all of a sudden.

So the problem is this: how is it that in almost every utterance we can distinguish between what is said on the one hand and what is meant and not said on the other? By the end of this chapter, you should have a better idea of how to answer this question.

For the present, it's sufficient to notice that the context is often very important in determining what someone means by what they say. For example, the two contexts in which 'It's the taste' occurs help us to decide what the speaker means by saying it on each occasion. And knowing the speakers well enough would enable us to know what they each meant by saying 'This egg is very yellow'. And it's because of the physical location in which Archie and I meet that he's able to work out what I mean by 'spending time in the part of the university most able to meet your needs'. And whether or not there is a step to trip over makes a big difference to understanding what is meant by saying 'Be careful you don't trip over the step on your way out'. And knowing that the post-office closes at one o'clock on a Saturday enables us to understand what is meant by saying 'It'll be better at one o'clock'. And because it's part of the culture to believe that people find it hard to think properly in the morning, we understand why 'It's early in the morning isn't it' conveys that the postmaster couldn't follow his customer's line of reasoning and therefore it had to be tortuous. Given different contexts, we would have understood each of these utterances quite differently.

In order to solve the problem of how we understand speakers to mean things that they don't actually say, we need first to draw a distinction between what the linguistic philosopher Paul Grice (1967) called the 'natural' and the 'non-natural' meanings of utterances like

(9) Manchester United won

The natural meaning, discussed in Chapter 3, is that Manchester United scored at least one goal more than the team they were playing against. This is the **entailment**, a meaning present on every occasion when an expression occurs. Unlike entailments, non-natural meanings are variable so that on different occasions (9) could convey the meaning that Manchester United played particularly well or only rather modestly. Because non-natural meaning is only associated with the sentence from which it's inferred on particular occasions, it's not part of the entailment.

Grice argued that speakers intend to be cooperative when they talk. One way of being cooperative is for a speaker to give as much information as is expected. So an addressee who knew that Manchester United were playing the European Cup holders might be expecting the speaker to say that they had done reasonably well considering the opposition. Since 'Manchester United won' would be more than was expected, the speaker would imply that they had done brilliantly. Conversely, an addressee who knew that Manchester United were playing a non-league side might be expecting the speaker to say that they had scored several goals or that they had wiped the opposition out. Hearing only 'Manchester United won', less than might be expected, the addressee would draw the inference that they had played rather poorly. Because 'Manchester United won' is more than the addressee was expecting in the first context and less in the second, in each case it gives rise to a non-conventional meaning. This kind of meaning was called an 'implicature' by Grice. He deliberately chose this word of his own coinage to cover any meaning that is implied, i.e. conveyed indirectly or through hints, and understood as implicit in what's said without actually being explicitly stated.

5.2.2 Grice's Cooperative Principle

Grice formalized his observation that when we talk we try to be cooperative by elevating this notion into what he called the Cooperative Principle: "Make your conversational contribution such as is required, at the stage at which it occurs, by the accepted purpose or direction of the talk exchange in which you are engaged."

Within this Principle, he proposed four maxims (or "super maxims" as he termed them).

1. QUANTITY
1 "Make your contribution as informative as is required (for the current purposes of the exchange)."

Thus

(10) Some of the hijackers have been identified

being appropriately informative, gives rise to the implicature <not all the hijackers have been identified> by Quantity_1.
2 "Do not make your contribution more informative than is required."

Thus

(11) I don't drink

gives rise to the implicature <the speaker doesn't drink alcohol> by Quantity_2.

2. QUALITY
"Try to make your contribution one that is true.

1 Do not say what you believe to be false.
2 Do not say that for which you lack adequate evidence."

Thus

(12) Cigarettes are bad for you

being assumed to be well founded, gives rise to the implicature <the speaker believes or has evidence that cigarettes are bad for you>, and

(13) Are you married

being assumed to be a sincere question, gives rise to the implicatures <the speaker doesn't know> <the speaker wants to know> <the speaker thinks the addressee does know>

3. RELATION
"Be relevant."
Thus, the notice outside a pub I know which specializes in Sunday lunches

(14) Don't forget Mum on Mothers' Day

gives rise to the implicature <bring your mother here for Sunday lunch on Mothers' Day>

4. MANNER
"Be perspicuous.

1 Avoid obscurity of expression.
2 Avoid ambiguity.
3 Be brief (avoid unnecessary prolixity).
4 Be orderly."

Thus

(15) I went to the Conference and gave a talk

being an orderly representation of the world, gives rise to the implicature <in that order>, and the notice at Newcastle Airport

(16) Increased threat to your security – you can help by keeping your luggage and personal items with you at all times

is taken to convey the less obscure implicature that <by keeping their luggage with them passengers can help to reduce the security threat> (rather than increase it).

Taken together, the four maxims enjoin speakers to be informative to the expected degree (Quantity), to say things that are well founded (Quality), to be relevant (Relation) and to be clear (Manner). Because these maxims are mutually known to speakers and addressees, addressees infer meanings that are conveyed but not stated.

Checking understanding (5.1)

1 Grice observes that we are cooperative in other endeavours besides talk. Imagine two people working together on a single task such as cleaning a car, or building a wall, or changing a light-bulb. Can you think of any cooperative strategies they might use that are like those that apply in talk?

2 What implicatures do Grice's maxims enable you to recover from the following utterances?

QUANTITY$_1$

(17) The plumber made a reasonable job of fitting our new boiler
(18) If drinking games are the cause of declining academic standards . . .

QUANTITY$_2$

(19) Buy a mixed case and save a further 10% (Wine company advertisement)
(20) Oxford (should have considered . . .)

QUALITY

(21) INTERVIEWEE: The day's got a 'y' in it hasn't it

RELATION

(22) INTERVIEWER: Will the dealers be selling the dollar again today

MANNER

(23) No graffiti
Penalty $1000 (Sign on a bridge support in Hong Kong)

5.2.3 Flouting maxims

The implicatures that arise from examples (10)–(23) arise because the addressee assumes that the speaker is abiding by Grice's maxims, i.e. (10) is as informative as is possible, (12) is well founded, (14) is maximally relevant in its context and (16) is to be read in a way that assumes perspicuity. But the thought has probably already gone through your mind that speakers don't always abide so rigorously by these maxims. Take the headline of the fashion magazine feature article

(24) Brown is the new black as far as shoes are concerned

This clearly obscures and so flouts the maxim of Manner. However, we don't have any real difficulty in working out what is meant – we just have to provide a little more of the context ourselves and do a little more reasoning than would have been necessary had the speaker abided by the maxim.

As (24) shows, even when speakers flout maxims, there are still implicatures. These arise because the addressee assumes that the speaker is essentially cooperative, despite flouting a maxim, and must therefore be intending to convey an implied meaning. On one occasion I just stopped myself in time from responding to a complaining student with

(25) Well, it is a university

I cannot sensibly be intending to convey the entailment of 'Well, it is a University' since this meaning is already known to the addressee. In fact, whenever a maxim is flouted, there must be an implicature to save the utterance from simply appearing to be a faulty contribution to a conversation. In the case of (25), the addressee will try to work out what I am intending to convey in addition to the information that was already known to them (i.e. that we are in a university). A reasonable inference is that there's no point in complaining since what the student has noticed is to be expected. This then is the implicature, what is implicit in (25) but nowhere explicitly stated.

As we noted in Chapter 1, it's obvious that statements that are self-evidently true or self-evidently false must be uttered for some purpose other than to convey merely their stated meaning. Such utterances will be especially obvious invitations to look for an implicature. Spoken by a man

(26) I'm a man

is self-evidently true and therefore a flout on Quantity. Spoken by a woman, it's self-evidently false and therefore a flout on Quality. In each case, the utterance alerts the addressee/s to the need to infer an implied meaning.

Checking understanding (5.2)

1 Is it possible to flout all four of the maxims? Decide whether the following utterances are flouts, and, if so, of which maxims:

(27) He looks his age
(28) Have you seen that room of hers
(29) PETER: Have you done your homework
→ ELEANOR: Joanna had her ear pierced today
(30) Insults fly in aircraft toilets (Newspaper headline, *Metro*)

2 The following rhetorical strategies have been considered flouts of Gricean maxims. Which maxim do you think each flouts?

Checking understanding (5.2) *cont.*

- *Tautology*

(31) At the end of the day the Church can only afford to pay the number of people it can afford to pay (A bishop speaking on a radio programme when asked whether there would be job cuts in the Church)

- *Metaphor*

(32) Money doesn't grow on trees but it blossoms at our branches (Advertisement, *Lloyd's TSB*)

- *Overstatement*

(33) Now we've ALL been screwed by the Cabinet (Newspaper headline, *Sun*)

- *Understatement*

(34) BRANKA: (tasting a chilli potato dish in a tapas bar): This one is hot
→ PETER: (tasting another potato dish): This one is not so hot

- *Rhetorical question*

(35) How many divisions has the Pope (Attributed to Stalin)

- *Irony*

(36) PETER: (placing envelope on scales in post office): First class please
POST-OFFICE CLERK: Is there anything of value
→ PETER: No only the Yorkshire Post. Priceless

3 Advertisements often flout Manner. Can you say in which way each of the following advertisements does this?

(37) Ahead of current thinking (Advertisement, *National Power*)
(38) In cordless technology we have the lead (Advertisement, *Black and Decker* power-tools)
(39) The best 4 × 4 × far (Advertisement, *Land Rover*)
(40) First and fourmost (Advertisement, *Land Rover*)
(41) The Wafer happiness (on a billboard beside a main road with an arrow pointing ahead; *Wafer* is the brand name of an item of confectionary)
(42) We take the mega*hurts* out of buying a PC (Advertisement for computers)
(43) Walter Wall Carpeting (*Walter Wall* is the name of a chain of carpet stores)
(44) You just can't help yourself (Written message accompanying a television advertisement for *McCain* pizzas in which the cook takes a piece of pizza for herself. She then tries to make it look as though the pizza is still intact before serving her guests)
(45) BA better connected person (Advertisement, *British Airways*)
(46) Acts on the spot (Advertisement for an acne preparation).

Why do you think this sort of flout is so common in newspaper headlines and advertisements?

4 Are you now able to explain why 'It's the taste' gives rise to the implicatures suggested at the beginning of the chapter?

Summary

There are guiding principles which govern cooperative talk. Knowing these principles (maxims) enables an addressee to draw inferences as to the implied meanings (implicatures) of utterances. Every utterance, whether it abides by or flouts the maxims, has both 'natural' meaning (entailment) and 'non-natural' meaning (implicature). Flouting a maxim is a particularly salient way of getting an addressee to draw an inference and hence recover an implicature. Thus there's a trade-off between abiding by maxims (the prototypical way of conducting a conversation) and flouting maxims (an obvious way of alerting the addressee to an implicit meaning).

5.2.4 Hedging maxims

Sometimes when we talk we simply make assertions like

(12) Cigarettes are bad for you

But if you listen carefully when people talk, you notice that speakers are frequently reluctant to make bald statements. Often they prefer utterances like (47)

(47) All is I know is, cigarettes are bad for you

In this utterance, the speaker is making the assertion that 'cigarettes are bad for you'. But by prefacing it with 'all I know is', the speaker simultaneously advises the addressee that the quantity of information being conveyed is limited. So the speaker makes an assertion and simultaneously advises the addressee of the extent to which they are observing the maxims. Thus the maxim of Quantity is 'hedged' (Lakoff, 1972) – in the sense that we 'hedge' or lay off a bet which we feel commits us too far.

If the speaker had said

(48) They say cigarettes are bad for you

'they say' would be understood as a hedge on the maxim of Quality and would serve as a warning to the addressee that the speaker's information might not be as well founded as would normally be expected. So 'all I know' in (47) and 'they say' in (48) have a metalingual function, that is, they serve as glosses or comments on the extent to which the speaker is abiding by the conversational maxims.

I recently heard a journalist defend himself when being criticized for running a story about the sexuality of someone accused of a financial impropriety:

(49) I think we've got to move on from that. With the greatest respect by the way, I think that's rather an old-fashioned view

The journalist's use of 'by the way' advises his critic that the journalist's expression of respect is not fully relevant at the stage at which it occurs in the conversation.

When she was nine, my daughter went with a friend to see *Arsenic and Old Lace*, the play in which two sweet old ladies poison a string of male visitors. She described afterwards how, at one stage in the play, a character had said he thought it was his last glass of elderberry wine, making it clear by the way she related it that 'last' was meant to be ambiguous between 'last that evening' (the speaker's idea) and 'last because he was going to die' (how the audience took it). Then she added

(50) It was dead funny – if you see what I mean

'If you see what I mean' hedges the maxim of Manner. Having said 'It was dead funny', she realized she had produced a second, unintended pun, and so added 'if you see what I mean' to advise us of the obscurity of her utterance.

We've seen how conversational maxims can be hedged with metalingual glosses. Speakers can also use metalingual glosses to assure their addressees that the maxims are being scrupulously complied with, as the following examples show:

(51) Cigarettes are bad for you and that's all there is to it (*Quantity*)
(52) Cigarettes are bad for you for sure (*Quality*)
(53) The point is that cigarettes are bad for you (*Relation*)
(54) Put plainly, cigarettes are bad for you (*Manner*)

One important point about these maxim hedges and intensifiers is that none of them adds truth value to the utterances to which they are attached. Thus examples (47)–(54) are true under just the same circumstances as counterpart sentences without the maxim hedges would be. This confirms that the hedges and intensifiers are more a comment on the extent to which the speaker is abiding by the maxims which guide our conversational contributions than a part of what is said or conveyed. It seems then that when we talk, we not only convey messages, but frequently like to tell each other how informative, well founded, relevant and perspicuous these messages are.

Checking understanding (5.3)

1 List at least three hedges and three intensifiers for each conversational maxim.

2 Which parts of the utterance have truth value and which maxims do you think are being hedged or intensified by the clauses and phrases in the following answer provided by Sir Humphrey in the television comedy, *Yes Minister*:

(55) Well Minister, if you asked me for a straight answer, then I shall say that, as far as we can see, looking at it by and large, and taking one time with another, in terms of the averages of departments, then, in the final analysis, it is probably true to say that, at the end of the day, in general terms, you would probably find that, not to put too fine a point on it, there probably wasn't very much in it one way or the other, as far as one can see, at this stage.

Summary

Speakers frequently use highly grammaticalized hedges and intensifiers to inform their addressees of the extent to which they are abiding by the maxims. These hedges and intensifiers show that the guiding principles for talk suggested by Grice really do exist and that speakers orient reflexively to these principles as they communicate.

5.2.5 Implicature and entailment

So far we've demonstrated that one kind of meaning, implicature, arises as a result of interactants' mutual knowledge of the conversational maxims. The non-conventional status of this implicature is illustrated by utterances like 'It's the taste', which gives rise to different implicatures in different contexts of use. This is really another way of recognizing that an implicature is the result of an addressee drawing an inference as to the likeliest meaning in the given context. So if Coca-Cola is being promoted, 'It's the taste' will give rise to a quite different implicature from that invited in the context of school dinners.

In Grice's account, an implicature is an inductive inference, a probabilistic conclusion derived from a set of premises that include the utterance and such contextual information as appears relevant. Because inductive inferences are probabilistic, they may not always correspond to the meaning a speaker seeks to convey. And as they are inferences, they may be denied, even, on occasion by the speaker herself. Consider the following utterance

(56) We have a child

The obvious inference to draw is that we have one and not more, since the Quantity maxim enjoins us to provide as much information as is required. But if additional information inconsistent with the inference is adduced (such as the existence of a second child), then the original inference is no longer valid. So if I am asked when buying a Family Railcard whether we have a child, I can reasonably say

(57) Yes, we have a child, in fact we have two

But there are no circumstances under which I will ever be able to say

(58) *We have a child, in fact we have none

This tells us that (56) entails at least one child (the 'natural' meaning) and implies not more than one (the 'non-natural' meaning). Any attempt to deny the entailment, the conventional meaning, of (56) (at least one) must always result in a contradiction, since the speaker is simultaneously saying *x and not-x*. An implicature, on the other hand, is an inductive inference, a best guess as to the meaning being conveyed. Although this best guess will be valid on most occasions, it may be cancelled. Indeed, there are situations in which denying an implicature is appropriate, as (57) demonstrates.

Notice also that the direction of the entailment and the implicature cannot be derived algorithmically from example (56), but instead is determined by world knowledge. Hence

(59) I can swim a kilometre in twenty-five minutes (Implicature <not less than twenty-five>), in fact I can swim one in twenty-four on a good day

is grammatical, unlike the contradictory

(60) *I can swim a kilometre in twenty-five minutes (Entailment <not more than twenty-five>), in fact I can swim one in twenty-six on a good day

Summary

We began with Grice's hypothesis that there are agreed guidelines for talk. We've now been able to show two distinct kinds of meaning, one of which, implicature, arises as a direct consequence of interactants accepting these cooperative strategies. Thus what is conveyed in an utterance will typically consist of what is said or entailed on the one hand and what is implied on the other. This is represented in Figures 5.1, 5.2 and 5.3.

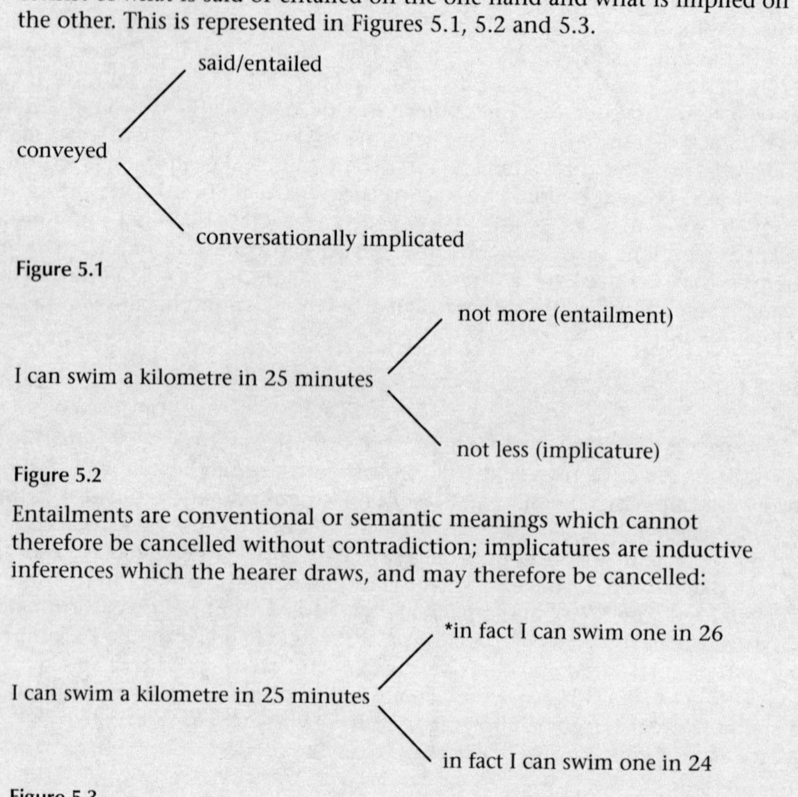

Figure 5.1

Figure 5.2

Entailments are conventional or semantic meanings which cannot therefore be cancelled without contradiction; implicatures are inductive inferences which the hearer draws, and may therefore be cancelled:

Figure 5.3

5.2.6 Generalized and particularized conversational implicature

Grice drew a distinction between what he termed **generalized** and what he termed **particularized** conversational implicature. Generalized conversational implicatures arise irrespective of the context in which the utterance occurs. So

(59) I can swim a kilometre in twenty-five minutes

always gives rise to the same generalized implicature <not less> whatever the context. This is clearly an implicature rather than an entailment since it can be denied by adding 'in fact I can swim one in twenty-four'. Similarly,

(61) Some people believe in God

always gives rise to the same generalized implicature <not all>, which can be denied by adding 'in fact everyone does'. In the case of generalized conversational implicatures such as those that arise in (59) and (61), the issue is not what is the most relevant way to take 'twenty-five' or 'some' – the same inferences, <not less> (for scales on which a short time is most valued) and <not all>, will always be drawn whatever the particular context.

Notice, however, that in particular contexts (59) might give rise to a whole range of other implicatures. For example, <I'm good at swimming>, <I'm not as good at swimming as you>, <I'll be back in half-an-hour>, <it shouldn't take you twenty-five minutes to do the shopping>, etc., etc. Equally (61) might be taken to imply <you believe in God>, <you don't believe in God>, <I believe in God>, <I don't believe in God>, <our parents believe in God>, etc., etc. Clearly there are as many implicatures as there are contexts for an utterance. Because each of these implicatures is context-bound, Grice called them 'particularized'. They are clearly different in kind from the context-free, generalized conversational implicatures associated with the use of words like *some*. Particularized implicatures are inferences that we need to draw if we are to understand how an utterance is relevant in some context. Thus the particularized implicatures that arise in the case of utterances like

(3) It's the taste

are derived, not from the utterance alone, but from the utterance in context.

The difference between generalized and particularized implicature will turn out to be a very important one for this reason: if all implicatures were particularized, one could reasonably argue that the single maxim of Relation, or Relevance, was sufficient to account for all implied meaning. The implicature would be what the addressee had to assume to render the utterance maximally relevant in its context. But generalized conversational implicature has little or nothing do with the most contextually relevant understanding of an utterance; it derives entirely from the maxims, typically from the maxims of Quantity and Manner. When a speaker uses the quantifier *some*, it's because they aren't in a position to use the quantifier *all*, and are therefore taken to be implying <not all> by the Quantity maxim.

We can now add this further distinction to Figure 5.1:

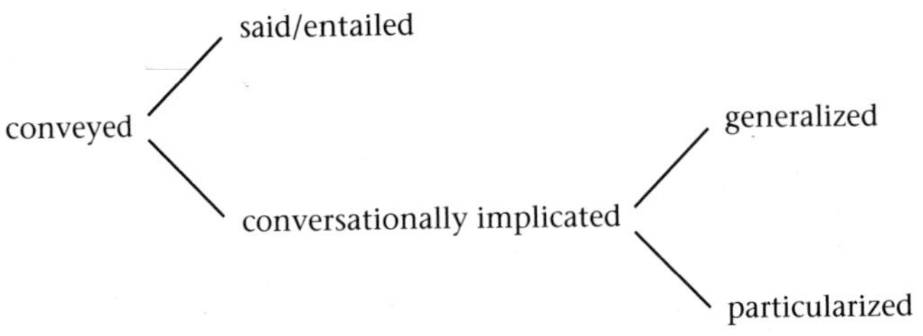

Figure 5.4

5.2.7 Scalar implicature

Several of the utterances discussed so far exhibit scalar properties. For example, 'should' in

(1) I should be back by eight

is a member of a scale which seems to include <*will, should, may, might . . .*>. 'Won' in

(9) Manchester United won

is a member of the scale <*win, draw, lose*>. 'Some' in

(10) Some of the hijackers have been identified

is a member of a scale which seems to include <*all, many, some, few, none*>. And when it comes to scales of approval for egg yolks, Branka's scale seems to be <*very yellow, yellow, not very yellow*> and my scale seems to span the orange/yellow continuum. Choosing any item on a scale will imply that the items above it (or below it if we're talking about times for swimming a kilometre or running 100m) do not obtain. This explains why we can resolve the problem of potential ambiguity that arose when I asked my knowledgeable friend at the race-course

(62) Would you recommend 8 or 9 (meaning horse number 8 or horse number 9)

By 'or', did I mean <either 8 or 9 but not both> or did I mean <either 8 or 9 or both>? This indeterminacy would be resolved if I added 'it has to be just one because I haven't enough money to back both'. Had I said that, I would clearly intend 'or' to mean <either 8 or 9 but not both>. Similarly, if I added 'I'm looking for a couple of possible horses for a dual forecast', I would clearly intend 'or' to mean <either 8 or 9 or both>. These two meanings can be explained by appealing to the notion of scalar implicature. Because *or* is on a scale below *and*, a speaker selecting *or* implies <not and>. Thus <either 8 or 9 or both> is an entailment and <either 8 or 9 but not both> is an implicature. This account of the meanings of *or* saves us having to say that there are two different *or*'s in the lexicon.

It's interesting to listen out for these scales when people talk. I was once at a meeting where I heard a student talked about in the following way:

(63) He wasn't a poor candidate, but he was a weak candidate

It occurred to me that one couldn't have switched these descriptions around to produce

(63′) *He wasn't a weak candidate, but he was a poor candidate

(although it's possible to use contrastive stress in a dramatic way and say:

(63″) He wasn't a WEAK candidate: he was a POOR candidate).

These examples show that when we are talking about candidates, there's a scale that includes <poor . . . weak>, with *poor* being a stronger condemnation than *weak*.

These scales also apply to clause structure, so that the use of conjunctions such as *if* and *or* enable us to draw the conclusions that speakers cannot commit themselves to asserting the proposition(s) within the clauses so introduced. Thus we only say

(18) If drinking games are the cause of declining academic standards

when we don't feel confident enough to assert

(18′) Drinking games are the cause of declining academic standards

'If drinking games . . .' therefore gives rise to the implicatures <possibly drinking games are the cause of declining academic standards>, <possibly drinking games aren't the cause of declining academic standards>. Usually, the wider context helps the addressee to understand which of the two possibilities is the likelier, as we shall see shortly when we return to this example. The role of context in helping us to decide whether the *possibly* or the *possibly not* proposition is intended is neatly illustrated by what happened on an occasion when I received information about how to get a conference. I ignored the sentence 'If you are staying at the Parliament Hotel, Lord Edward Street is shown on the map' because I had already been told that I would be staying at a different hotel. A colleague was less fortunate. Having forgotten that he had already been allocated a hotel, he assumed that he wouldn't have been informed about the Parliament Hotel unless he had been staying there, and presented himself at midnight after a night on the town, only to find he wasn't staying there and there were no rooms available!

5.2.8 Non-conversational implicature

Our children once chose a tube of toothpaste on the grounds that it had coloured stripes in it. The legend on the tube said

(64) Actually fights decay

'Actually fights decay' provides a perfect example of a conventional, or non-conversational, implicature. The lexical item 'actually' has a literal meaning or entailment – it means something like <in reality> or <in actuality>. But it also conveys a secondary, implied meaning, which is something like <although this is hard to credit>. This implicature is conventionally associated with *actually* but makes no contribution to truth-conditional meaning – it isn't part of the entailment of *actually*. Levinson defines conventional implicatures as "non-truth-conditional inferences that are *not* derived from superordinate pragmatic principles like the maxims, but are simply attached by convention to particular lexical items or expressions" (1983: 127). Unlike conversational implicatures, conventional implicatures are non-defeasible. In fact, conventional implicatures and implicative verbs share identical properties, although traditionally (and perhaps inappropriately) the latter, along with conventional cleft structure effects and factive predication, have been treated as presuppositions, as in the previous chapter.

Other examples of conventional implicatures include *but, even* and *still*, as in these examples taken from President Clinton's national TV address (18 August 1998) in the Monica Lewinsky affair:

(65) It constituted a critical lapse in judgement and a personal failure on my part for which I am solely and completely responsible. [New paragraph in written version] *But* I told the grand jury today and I say to you now that . . .

(Entailment <and>; conventional implicature <there's a contrast between the two conjoined propositions>.)

(66) *Even* Presidents have private lives

(Entailment <in addition/too/as well>; conventional implicature (loosely following Kay, 1990) <the attached proposition is at the end of a scale of expectability>.)

(67) I answered their questions truthfully, including questions about my private life, questions no American citizen would ever want to answer.

> [New paragraph in written version] *Still*, I must take full responsibility for all my actions . . .

(Entailment <in the continuing present>; conventional implicature <in spite of what has been said before, there is a further situation to consider>.)

We can now add conventional implicature to Figure 5.4:

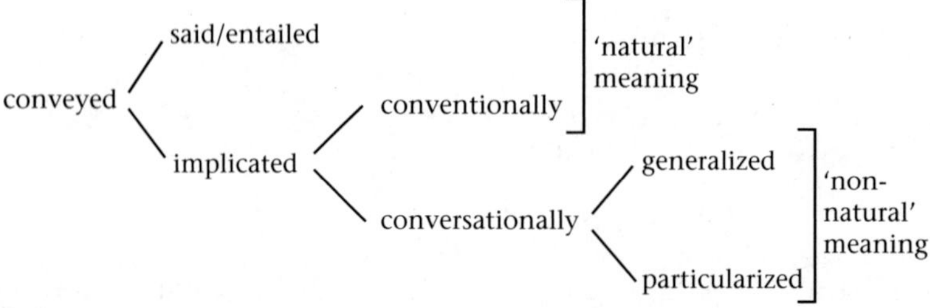

Figure 5.5

Summary

With Figure 5.5 in front of us, let's go back to the *Times* letter and the notes you may have made earlier:

(2) Sir, If drinking games really are the cause of declining academic performance [reports, October 30 and 31], perhaps Oxford should have considered banning them years ago

- Entailment: What's **said** is clear (although formalizing the entailments needs a bit of thinking through).
- Conventional implicature: Had the letter writer chosen to say 'If drinking games are actually the cause . . .' rather than '. . . really are the cause . . .', his scepticism as to whether drinking games are the cause of declining academic standards would have been **conventionally implicated.**
- GCI: The **generalized conversational implicature** <possibly drinking games are the cause of declining academic standards>, <possibly drinking games aren't the cause of declining academic standards> arises from the use of 'If'.
- PCI: The **particularized conversational implicature** is liable to vary with context. Context 1 invites what I'll call the 'Oxford interpretation': by using the intensifier 'really', the writer indicates his commitment to the proposition that the cause of declining academic performance has been identified. But this view seems incompatible with the **generalized implicature** resulting from the conditional environment, thereby casting doubt on the relationship of drinking games to academic performance. On this friendly-to-Oxford reading, one might infer that since Oxford didn't ban them years ago, drinking games aren't the cause of declining academic performance and that in any case academic performance isn't declining. In fact, drinking games are one of the glories of Oxford. Context 2: the author of the letter gives his address as 'Robinson College, Cambridge', thus providing a context for the 'Cambridge interpretation', that academic performance at Oxford declined a long time ago. Together with 'considered', the hedge 'perhaps' also hints at a *laissez-faire* attitude to academic management at Oxford.

5.2.9 Recognizing implicature

This section closes with a series of exercises containing examples of utterances and written texts which invite implicatures. These should enable you to check that you're able to identify the implicatures that arise, the maxims that are hedged and flouted and the means by which an addressee infers implicated meaning.

Checking understanding (5.4)

In August/September 1992 a WH Smith advertisement featuring various items of stationery appeared on hoardings in Britain together with the legend

(68) We don't sell uniforms

This advertisement was followed by a series of 'We don't sell . . .' posters, which included an advertisement shortly before Christmas featuring videos of romantic films bearing the legend

(69) We don't sell hankies

What are the implicatures in these two advertisements and how do they illustrate the non-conventional nature of conversational implicature?

Checking understanding (5.5)

Flouts: Which maxim is flouted by each of the following? How is the maxim flouted and what implicatures result?

(70) Am I seeing double (Question put by a potential customer standing in front of an optician's shop displaying a billboard 'Appointment not always neccessary')
(71) Standard – sub-standard I call them (Comment made after lighting a series of disappointing fireworks with the *Standard* brand-name)
(72) Also available in white (Comment scratched in the dirt on a white car)
(73) Just desserts (Menu heading in a restaurant)

Checking understanding (5.6)

Comment on the implicatures that arise in the following cases where the conventional axiology is reversed:

(74) England fail to lose (Headline in the *Sun* newspaper after England drew a cricket match with South Africa)
(75) Now worse than ever (Advertisement for the *London Dungeon*, a museum of horrors)
(76) The value of investments can go down as well as up (Statutory warning on advertisements for financial investments in UK)
(77) If you're as clever as Alister [our technician], you may be able to do it [download a printer file from the internet] for yourself. But if you're as clever as me, you'll ask Alister to do it for you.

Checking understanding (5.7)

Conventional and conversational implicatures: What is conveyed by the following statements?

(78) It's a humiliation to be sacked even from the Labour Party front bench (Comment by a Conservative member of Parliament on the sacking of a Labour spokesman)

(79) I have not even brought my wife into Horley Town Hall. That's what I think of Horley Town Hall (Leader of Horley Council speaking on BBC Radio 4)

Checking understanding (5.8)

Since an implicature is an inference, it must be calculable, in the sense that we can work out the steps that a hearer must follow to arrive at it. I once stood for election to a faculty post. When the nominations closed, the other candidate telephoned and left a message with our administrator, which she wrote down as follows (I've changed the name of the candidate):

(80) Hugh Martin called to say he sees you and he are rivals and he is sure the best person will win!

When I read the message, I said to our administrator

(81) I hope not

What implicatures can you recover from Hugh's message and my comment, and how are they arrived at?

5.3 Neo-Gricean theories of implicature

At the start of this chapter, I drew attention to the various implicatures arising from

(1) I should be back by eight but you know what trains are like

As our discussion developed, it became clear that some of these implicatures are generalized and some particularized. The generalized implicatures (<the speaker probably won't be back by eight>, <trains are unreliable>) are those not particular to the context. This differentiates them from the particularized implicatures, <the addressee should make dinner> and <the addressee should buy a lottery ticket>. These particularized interpretations are what make the utterance relevant in the context in which it occurs. But where do generalized implicatures come from?

You'll recall that at the start of the chapter I suggested that the implicature <the speaker probably won't be back by eight> seemed to have more to do with the words I chose than with context. And in due course we saw that this implicature was indeed scalar and arose because I chose to say 'should be' rather than 'will', thus causing my wife to infer that the will-be-back-by-eight situation did not obtain. Is it also possible that there's something about the way I put it when I say

'You know what trains are like' that invites the implicated meaning <trains are unreliable>? Could the formula *you know what x is like* carry the implicated meaning that the speaker takes a negative view of '*x*'? These are the ideas that we'll be exploring in this section of the chapter as we trace some of the neo-Gricean refinements of Grice's paradigm.

Checking understanding (5.9)

Do you think my use of "you know what trains are like" flouts Grice's first Quantity maxim, "Make your contribution as informative as is required"?

5.3.1 Horn's neo-Gricean pragmatics

One early piece of neo-Gricean work is Horn's work on lexical gaps (1972, 1989). Horn showed that Grice's first maxim of Quantity was capable of accounting for a gap in the inventory of lexical items which incorporate the negative particle: how is it that we have *none* (= not one) but not **nall* (= not all)? Consider the following:

- Natural language can represent the existential quantifier (∃) of formal language (the language of logic) with words such as *a* and its plural form *some*, so that any description containing 'a'/'some' refers to a single exemplar case/a number of exemplar cases.
- Natural language can represent the universal quantifier (∀) of formal language with words such as *all*, so that any description containing 'all' refers to all the members of the set described.
- Natural language can represent the negation of the existential quantifier (~∃) with words such as *none*, so that any description containing 'none' asserts that there are no cases (= not some) of what is described.
- But natural language cannot represent the negation of the universal quantifier (~∀) with words such as **nall*, to denote not-all cases of what is described.

Horn attributed the non-lexicalizability of **nall* to the fact that it was a Q1 inference of *some*, i.e. in natural language *not all* is implied by the use of *some*. And since it's already an implicature, it doesn't get lexicalized. And it turns out that incorporation of the negative particle is impossible in all cases where the meaning already exists as a Q1-inference. Thus we find

- *always, sometimes* (implying <not always>) and *never*, but not **nalways*
- *both, one* (implying <not both>) and *neither*, but not **noth*
- *and, or* (implying <not *x* and *y*>) and *neither x nor y*, but not **nand*
- *obligatory, permitted* (implying <not obligatory>) and *forbidden*, but not **nobligatory*.

The importance of these insights should not be overlooked for two reasons. What Horn showed was that the conversational maxim 'Make your contribution as informative as is required' determines what concepts can be lexicalized. Thus the explanation for this lexical gap is pragmatic. Second, Horn's work also opened up the possibility that a more extensive range of typical phenomena might be explained by the conversational principles that regulate the pragmatic use of language.

In his later work, Horn (1984) argues that Grice's maxims can be subsumed within two principles, the **Q Principle** and the **R Principle**.

The Q Principle reinterprets Grice's Quantity$_1$ maxim (Make your contribution as informative as is required): "Make your contribution sufficient. Say as much as you can." (Horn, 1984: 13).

The R Principle replaces Grice's Quantity$_2$ maxim (Do not make your contribution more informative than is required) and Grice's Relation and Manner maxims: "Make your contribution necessary. Say no more than you must." (Horn, 1984: 13).

When Branka understands me to mean that I probably won't be back by eight, this is a Q-based implicature – I've said as much as I can. The other three implicatures she recovers are R-based. The Q and R principles also account for the differences in the implicatures that are invited by

(82) I lost a dog this afternoon

and

(83) I broke a leg when I was sixteen

In (82), the addressee recovers as a Q-inference that the dog probably belonged to someone other than the speaker as a scalar implicature since the speaker did not say 'my dog'. In (83), the addressee recovers as an R-inference that the speaker probably broke one of their own legs, since breaking someone else's leg is highly improbable.

5.3.2 A theory of preferred interpretation: Levinson's neo-Gricean pragmatics

So far in this chapter we've distinguished what is said or entailed (what our words mean) from what is implicated (what we mean by our words). Following the Gricean account, we've represented these two categories of sentence meaning and speaker meaning as the superordinate distinction between levels of meaning, as in Figures 5.1–5.5. In this section, we'll explore Levinson's tripartite division of meaning (1995, 2000), which distinguishes **entailment**, which is context-free and non-inferential, **utterance-type meaning**, which is context-free and inferential, and **utterance-token meaning**, which is context-sensitive and inferential.

An utterance-type, as the name suggests, is a predictable type of utterance which has a regular inferred interpretation across a range of contexts. An utterance token is a single instance of an utterance whose one-off inferred interpretation depends upon its context. By contrast, utterance-types yield understandings whose meanings, unlike those of utterance-tokens, do not differ according to context. Utterance-type meaning resembles sentence meaning to the extent that it's expectable and thus, in one sense, conventional. But it's unlike sentence meaning in that it's inferred and therefore defeasible, as in

(1′) I should be back by eight, and indeed will be

Utterance-type meanings may result from a typical use such as 'should be' or an a-typical marked use such as 'fail to lose'. Utterance-type meaning is unlike entailment in that it's inferential and unlike utterance-token-meaning in that the inferential process doesn't take account of context.

As Levinson points out, the property of being to a degree conventional, which utterance-type meaning appears to share with sentence meaning, has made semanticists eager to view it as semantic. And because utterance-type meaning shares with utterance-token meaning the property of being a defeasible inference, pragmaticists too have been eager to claim it for themselves.

Utterance-type meaning results from Quantity, Informativeness and Manner-based **heuristics** or insights that govern the process of inferential enrichment. These heuristics then enable **principles** to be formulated. Levinson derives these three heuristics/principles from Grice's two Quantity maxims and the Manner maxim:

The Q-Principle
Quantity$_1$ (Make your contribution as informative as is required) → **Q heuristic**: "What isn't said, isn't" (2000: 35) → **Q-principle**:
For speaker – "Do not provide a statement that is informationally weaker than your knowledge of the world allows, unless providing an informationally stronger statement would contravene the I-principle. Specifically, select the informationally strongest paradigmatic alternative that is consistent with the facts."
For hearer – "Take it that the speaker made the strongest statement consistent with what he knows." (2000: 76).

What's said:	What's typically inferred:
(1) . . . should be back . . .	<won't be back>

The I-Principle
Quantity$_2$ (Do not make your contribution more informative than is required) → **I heuristic**: "What is expressed simply is stereotypically exemplified, i.e. minimal specifications get maximally informative or stereotypical interpretations" (2000: 37) → **I-Principle**:
For speaker – "Say as little as necessary."
For hearer – "Amplify the informational content of the speaker's utterance, by finding the most specific interpretation, up to the speaker's intended point." (2000: 114).

What's said:	What's typically inferred:
(84) Sperber and Wilson wrote about relevance	<Sperber and Wilson wrote about relevance together>

The M-Principle
Manner (Be perspicuous: avoid obscurity of expression; avoid prolixity) → **M heuristic**: "What's said in an abnormal way isn't normal" (2000: 38) → **M-Principle**:
For speaker – "Indicate an abnormal, non-stereotypical situation by using marked expressions that contrast with those you would use to describe the corresponding normal, stereotypical situation."
For hearer – "What is said in an abnormal way indicates an abnormal situation, or marked messages indicate marked situations." (2000: 136).

What's said:	What's typically inferred:
(85) Sperber and Wilson both wrote about relevance	<Sperber and Wilson wrote about relevance separately>

Let's look at examples of the way in which each of these principles enables us to get from what's said to what's typically inferred. For the sake of clarity, I'll be mixing utterances we've already discussed and adding new examples for variety.

Q-implicatures
Inferences resulting from applying the Q-Principle are essentially scalar, i.e. recovered because an item other than the most inclusive is chosen on a linguistic scale consisting of <a^1, a^2, a^3. . .a^n> where a^1 is the most inclusive. Thus

(86) Oxford don't get the same calibre of students as Cambridge

will imply <Oxford students aren't as good as Cambridge students> because 'Oxford get the same calibre of students as Cambridge' wasn't said;

(87) Chelsea won but Manchester United lost

invites the implicature <the speaker isn't a Chelsea supporter> because 'Chelsea won and Manchester United lost' wasn't said;

(88) He doesn't look his age

invites the implicature <the person described looks younger than they are> (rather than older) because 'He looks his age' (which entails that he looks at least his age, i.e. not younger) wasn't said;

(89) National calls now cost the same as local calls

will imply <national calls now cost less than previously> (rather than local calls now cost more than previously) because 'National calls now cost more than local calls' wasn't said.

I-implicatures
Inferences resulting from applying the I-Principle are based on principles of economy. Some of these are language-specific; others occur across languages. If you know a language other than English, you might like to test the extent to which the inferences suggested below hold in the languages you know.

(90) I wish I could teach/play football/cook like x

implies <*x* is a good teacher/football player/cook> because to supply the name of a poor teacher would be tantamount to a contradiction (cf. 'I wish I could tell the truth like Blair');

(91) If you've tried *x*, you won't like *y*

implies <*x* is superior to *y*>. It's worth noticing that if, contrary to the default, *x* is understood as not good, then nothing in the same category as *x* is even tolerable, as in

(92) Once you've experienced a meal at IBIS, you'll never want to eat anywhere else

The formula

(93) You don't know what it's like to be *x*

will usually imply <*x* is undesirable>, as in

(94) You don't know what it's like to be a student

The culture-bound nature of some I-inferences is readily illustrated by the formula *very x*, implying <good or bad because *very x*>. When Branka says

(4) This egg's very yellow

the evaluation is positive; when I say it, it's negative. When a barmaid says to two customers standing at a bar, one of whom is being served

(95) Are you together

she's offering to serve the other if they aren't in each other's company. This is the I-default.

M-implicatures
Inferences resulting from applying the M-Principle occur when an untypical form is used. Take the barmaid's utterance

(96) Are you two both together

'You two' and 'you . . . both' are inconsistent with the I-Principle and therefore provoke M-inferences. In a different context, 'you two' might be considered a stereotypical way for a parent to address children. We might speculate as to whether *you both* is always marked, even when used as a way of addressing a known couple.

Several utterances already considered in this and earlier chapters invite M-inferences, including

(28) Have you seen that room of hers

where 'that room of hers' rather than the unmarked 'her room' implies <there's something abnormal about the room>.

(42) We take the mega*hurts* out of buying a PC

where the abnormal 'hurts' is marked and implies <buying a PC is usually a painful experience>.

(76) The value of investments can go down as well as up

where the marked order in which 'go down' precedes 'go up' implies <the need to take care when making an investment decision>.

(97) Meanwhile, Peter Grundy has just told me of his long conversation with you earlier today

where 'long conversation' is marked and perhaps implies <the conversation was unsatisfactory in some way>.

Sometimes it's difficult to determine the boundary between an M-inference triggered by an abnormal form and a formulaic I-inference. For example, I first heard what is now a very common formula as recently as October 2001 when a series of Friday night television programmes were promoted in the following way:

(98) Make it [watching television] part of your Friday night – staying in is the new going out

Such ubiquitous examples as

(24) Brown is the new black as far as shoes are concerned
(99) Gay is the new straight
(100) White is the new red
(101) Staying at home is the new going abroad

suggest that the formula has become conventionalized and is now a maximally informative interpretation of a minimal specification. We might hypothesize that this process is especially likely to occur more rapidly when a new but abnormal formula allows a more economical expression of a meaning than its more transparent equivalent, as in this case. The same might be said of the once marked

(102) Your local company – nationwide

and

(103) The world's local bank

The point of these many examples is that the inferences which constitute the most salient meaning in each case arise from the way things are put rather than from the most relevant interpretation in some context. Although cultural knowledge may play some part in the determination of I- and M-inferences, because they are typical, i.e. stable over many different contexts of use, any context is broad rather than particularized. In a sense, such stereotypical inferences are cultural meanings and can therefore pose problems in intercultural communication, as we shall see in Chapter 12.

Checking understanding (5.10)

1 Earlier in the chapter, we suggested that

(11) I don't drink

invites the implicature <the speaker doesn't drink alcohol> by Quantity$_2$. How would it be treated in Levinson's neo-Gricean proposals? In a parallel Cantonese and English text taken from a public information leaflet distributed in Hong Kong, one of the speakers says

(104) I don't drink or smoke

The Cantonese version (translated) is

(105) Do not smoke, do not drink alcohol

Can you comment on the differences?

2 Under what circumstances would you say?

(106) I'm at university
(107) I'm at the university
(108) I'm at a university

Checking understanding (5.10) *cont.*

3 Conjunction reduction. How do Levinson's Principles help you to understand the differences between the (a) and (b) utterances?

(109a) They went to the Library and registered for a course
(109b) They went to the Library and they registered for a course
(110a) She took out her key and opened the door
(110b) She took out her key and she opened the door

4 I once heard the following 'joke' in an after-dinner speech:

(111) My father said it was time I went out and found a husband, so I went out and found Jane's

Can you explain how this joke works?

5 How does the notion of utterance-type meaning and utterance-token meaning help you to understand the following uses of language?:

(112) Now thicker than ever (Legend removed from a multi-roll packet of lavatory paper and blu-tacked to her brother's bedroom door by a younger sister)
(113) MORE HORNY THAN HORNBY (Advertisement, *Virgin Trains*)
(114) Wrong ticket? That's fine by us (Window sticker, Tyne and Wear metro train)
(115) See how the other half travelled (Advertisement for Royal Yacht, now a tourist attraction open to the public)

5.3.3 Optimality

In Chapter 1 we noticed that the meanings of *child actor* and *child psychiatrist* can't be determined algorithmically. It's clear that the structures and linguistic meanings of these two expressions under-determine the propositions they express. Without some process of strengthening or optimization, we cannot (fully) understand them. Let's assume (against reason) that this strengthening process is entirely syntactic and that the maximal interpretations, <child who acts> and <psychiatrist who treats children>, are underlying syntactic structures. If this were the case, *child actor* and *child who acts* would mean the same thing. As would *child psychiatrist* and *psychiatrist who treats children*. However, they clearly don't mean the same thing. I know very few child actors, but I've yet to meet a child who didn't act! And if you were to ask whether some particular person was a child psychiatrist, and you were told that she was a psychiatrist who treated children, you might draw the kind of conclusion that I drew when I asked the man at the publishers lunch if he was working that afternoon and he replied that he was going back to the office. So it's clear that we need an optimization process and that it has to be inferential.

The term **optimality** hasn't been introduced before because the chapter follows a historical trajectory and optimality theory has only recently spread from phonology, where it began in the early 1990s, to pragmatics. But it's clear that the chapter has in fact been about optimization, about the kind of pragmatic strengthening required to enable speakers and hearers to convey and recover meanings that aren't explicitly stated. Pragmaticists have been optimality theorists all along.

At the heart of optimality is the notion that for each meaning there must be an optimal form for which the speaker strives, and for each form there must be an optimal meaning for which the hearer strives. Optimality rather than grammaticalness is the metric which determines the well-formedness of utterances and utterance interpretations. These optimal forms/meanings are generated by applying Q and I/R Principles of the kind formulated by Horn and Levinson which act as constraints on possible optimal form/meaning pairings. Language is therefore a "set of pairs of meanings and forms such that for the given meaning, the form is optimal and for the given form, the meaning is optimal" (Beaver and Lee, 2004: 113) in some given common ground. The development of pragmatic optimality theory has focused especially on identifying and ordering constraints so as to find a principled way of generating optimal form:meaning pairs. Ordering constraints is necessary because some constraints clearly take precedence over others. This issue isn't new. For example, there's an obvious conflict between the speaker-favouring economy of the I-Principle and the addressee-favouring informativeness of the Q-Principle. And in the barmaid's offer to serve the customer, the I-inference arising from

(95) Are you together

is clearly blocked by the M-inference arising from

(96) Are you two both together

which takes precedence. The precedence of the M-inference and its unintended effect is then signalled by the barmaid by means of 'well you know what I mean' – what she meant was the blocked I-inference.

Once we have a full set of ordered constraints we expect to be able to predict the possible set of optimal forms and meanings. At present various proposals are being made as to the possible constraints and their ordering. These will presumably include economy-based constraints, perhaps something like <do not associate complex forms with simple meanings/simple meanings with complex forms>, and accommodation-oriented constraints perhaps such as <only accommodate new discourse referents as a last resort>. No doubt the principles and constraints that guide the inference process will be not only more delicately formulated but quite possibly differentially ordered or operative in different discourse and cross-linguistic environments.

Checking understanding (5.11)

1 Under what circumstances might you say to someone 'eat', 'please eat', 'you eat', 'do eat', 'do please eat'?

2 Can you decide whether the (a) or the (b) formula was used to advertise a medium-sized *Seat* car?

(116a) Supermini or sensible saloon
(116b) Sensible saloon or Supermini

And which of the two candidate formulas appeared in the public information television advertisement warning of the risk of getting drinks spiked in a bar?

(117a) Happens to men and women
(117b) Happens to women and men

Checking understanding (5.11) *cont.*

3 What sort of generating procedure/constraining functions would be required to account for the way the following are understood (or not understood)?

(118) Do you fit the bill? (Police leaflet appealing for identity parade volunteers)

(119) STEWARDESS: Something to drink Madam
FEMALE PASSENGER: Red wine
STEWARDESS: Red wine
→ MALE PASSENGER: Same again please
STEWARDESS: Sorry
→ MALE PASSENGER: Same again please
STEWARDESS: Red wine

5.3.4 Pragmatics and the lexicon

In the M-inferences discussed earlier, we can easily identify pairs of signifying expressions which provoke different implicatures:

- in (28), 'that room of hers' vs 'her room'
- in (42), 'mega*hurts*' vs 'megahertz'
- in (97), 'long conversation' vs 'conversation'.

The marked or abnormal expression to the left provokes a marked or less expected interpretation than the unmarked expression to the right. Having set out with Grice's theory of utterance interpretation, we now see that lexical items too contain both a residue of stable meaning and an implied element. A couple of years ago I was at a conference in Japan listening to a talk which distinguished between 'Japanese' pronunciation of English and 'Japanized' pronunciation of English. In each case, the speaker was describing the same object, the L2 English phonology of an L1 Japanese speaker, but viewed from two distinct perspectives. 'Japanese' pronunciation was a disapproving term indicating the extent to which the speaker's phonology fell short of a native speaker model; 'Japanized' pronunciation was a term of approval indicating the appropriateness of speaking a lingua franca in a way that allowed for the encoding of the speaker's own identity. In fact, none of this was explained explicitly by the speaker, but the implicated meaning was easy to infer in the context of his talk.

So it seems that it's not only utterances that are under-determined but that radical semantic under-specification is also a feature of the lexicon. As Blutner says, "The situated meanings of many words and simple phrases are combinations of their lexical meanings proper and some superimposed conversational implicatures" (2004: 56). Because these are 'situated meanings', the implicatures are 'conversational' rather than 'conventional'. In fact, as I write this chapter with the radio on in the background, I keep hearing the BBC encouraging me to buy a device which enables us to listen to programmes downloaded from the BBC website. Doing this will apparently

(120) Make the unmissable unmissable

I take the first 'unmissable' to be what I don't want to miss, and the second 'unmissable' what I won't miss if I do as I'm told. It stands to reason that we can't 'make *x x*', so that each '*x*' or use of 'unmissable' must contain different "superimposed conversational implicatures". A year or two ago I read Stephen Greenblatt's wonderful book *Will in the World*, which explores the interrelation of Shakespeare's life and writing. The book has a sub-title

(121) How Shakespeare became Shakespeare

It tells the story of how the 'Shakespeare' who was born one of six children to illiterate parents in a small provincial town in the English Midlands became the 'Shakespeare' we think of as the greatest writer in the English language. Perhaps one would be helped to this interpretation by regarding *how x became x* as a formula inviting the I-inference that the second instance of '*x*' was more valued that the first. And as you've been reading this sub-section, you'll have been reminded of 'WELCOME TO POLITICS' in Chapter 1 and the different conversational implicata associated with 'welcome' and 'politics' invited by the position of the sign in relation to the instructions for gaining entry to the building.

Checking understanding (5.12)

How does knowing that the situated meanings of words and simple phrases include conversational implicatures help you to understand my encounter with a colleague on the stairs when I'm dressed in blue?

(122) CHRIS: You're looking very blue
PETER: Oh
CHRIS: I don't mean blue in the depressed sense
PETER: You don't mean blue in one of its other senses
CHRIS: No no

and

(123) To go far you only need travel to Sunderland (Window sticker, Tyne and Wear Metro. The Metro network includes Sunderland.)

Summary

In this section we've traced out some of the most important work in neo-Gricean pragmatics. Horn's and Levinson's proposals include essentially the same phenomena, with Horn's Q Principle including Levinson's Q and M Principles and Horn's R Principle roughly equivalent to Levinson's I Principle. Levinson strictly delimits his proposals to utterance-type meaning or Grice's Generalized Conversational Implicature. This enables him to argue that there are three levels of meaning: the level of entailment, the level of stereotypical utterance-type meaning and the level of context-determined utterance-token meaning. As we saw, stereotypical meaning extends beyond utterances so that typical meanings are associated with typical lexical forms (e.g., *Japanese*) and atypical meanings with atypical or more marked lexical forms (e.g., *Japanized*). One of the most important

Summary *cont.*

observations that emerges from neo-Gricean approaches is that stereotypical implied meanings are inferred and not stated. Consider

(11) I don't drink

This gives rise to the stereotypically implied meaning <I don't drink alcohol>. But

(11′) I don't drink alcohol

being a marked or abnormal utterance, at least in my repertoire, gives rise to an abnormal meaning, which perhaps includes the notion that the speaker is encoding a degree of better-than-thou-ism. This is because it would have been enough to have said 'I don't drink' to have conveyed that the speaker didn't drink alcohol. As Levinson says, "The more explicit I try to be, the more unintended implicatures I will generate" (1997: 18).

5.4 Implicature in the real world

5.4.1 Implied meaning on the train

When I used to travel on Friday evenings and very often endured delayed trains, I took to carrying a letter published in *The Times* to share with fellow sufferers:

(124) Sir, I was moved almost to tears by the latest television commercial for Virgin trains, which ends with all the passengers rejoicing in the birth of a healthy baby boy.
Is it true that the mother wasn't even pregnant when she boarded the train?

And how about the bizarrely official notice on Birmingham New Street station

(125) You are reminded that New Street is a no-smoking area and you are requested to extinguish all smoking material

This is a clear candidate for a neo-Gricean M-inference unless you are charitable enough to take the Gricean view that the more likely reading of 'smoking material' is the one intended. Doncaster station is another of my favourites. Here passengers on the 7.23 to London regularly hear announcements like

(126) This is not the 7.30 this is the 7.23 service to London King's Cross. Please make sure you have the right type of ticket you may be on

and

(127) The 7.30 departs from Doncaster at 7.30

The relevance of (127) to passengers on the 7.23 isn't always immediately obvious, and in any case must be a flout on quality when it's already after 7.30. Less facetiously, notice that negative statements like 'This is not the 7.30' are by nature uninformative and often statements of the obvious or known, and so alert us to the likelihood of an implicature. The problem with (127) for passengers already on the train is that the illocutionary target is the small number of new passengers who boarded the train at Doncaster under the mistaken impression that it was the 7.30. For them, the implicature is that they should leave the train.

But I salute the 'train manager' who found a neat and marked way of acknowledging our arrival in London 45 minutes late:

(128) In a few minutes' time we shall be finally arriving in London King's Cross where this service will be terminating

On one occasion at King's Cross I'd no sooner occupied my reserved seat when an elderly gentleman approached, peered at the reservation slip above my seat and said

(129) I'm afraid these seats are reserved

This made me wonder whether a typical inference would be <reserved for us>, so that a preferred response might be something like 'I think this one's reserved for me' rather than 'Yes, you're right' (which would be rude for the additional reason that it ignores the IFID 'I'm afraid'). Had the speaker been a porter helping a passenger, the typical inference might be <reserved for the passenger I'm assisting>. I suppose the token inference in each of these cases is something like <you've got to move>. I say this is a token inference because if the person addressed was about to sit down, the inference would be <you may not sit in them>. Fortunately on the occasion when the elderly gentleman addressed me, he was accompanied by a lady with better eyesight who guided him to the correct seat.

5.4.2 Working in an institution

This is what I read at the bottom of a referees' form issued by the School of Education at Durham University:

(130) To assist in authentication please add an institutional stamp if you are in an institution

Earlier, I asked you to consider the stereotypical meaning of

(106) I'm at university

You probably concluded that (106) invites the I-inference that a person is 'at university' for a purpose stereotypically associated with being there, so that (106) would be an expectable thing for a student, but not for a non-student, to say. In the case of (130), 'in' seems to invite the stereotypical reading <a patient in> and 'an institution' to invite the stereotypical reading <a mental institution>. Notice that

(131) To assist in authentication please add an institutional stamp if you work in an institution

doesn't restrict the range of possible senses of institution in the same way. 'Work' too in (131) is much less specific with respect to likely stereotypical interpretations than the semantically emptier 'are' in (130). Although this might at first seem odd, when we read 'are in an institution' as a euphemism, we realize why semantic lightness is preferred over a more detailed description. Indeed euphemisms are a very expectable category of I-inference as they provide a rich interpretation of a minimal encoding. Perhaps 'drink' in

(11) I don't drink

should also be viewed as a euphemism. These arguments help us to see the social motivation for one category of I-inference at least.

Given that the conditional structure in (130) implies the possibility that the form filler might or might not be 'in an institution', knowing how to respond becomes problematic. If I obligingly stamp the form, will it be clear that I've taken the request in the most relevant way given the wider context and responded to a particularized rather than a generalized implicature? Or will I be confirming that I am 'in an institution'? And from a speech act perspective, how can I bring about the perlocutionary effect that seems to be desirable, that the form should be re-worded? Since the request came from another department in the same 'institution', it seemed felicitous to stamp the form and write in

(132) A happy description of what it is to work here

giving rise, I hope, to various implicatures, including <you might want to consider rewording the form>.

5.4.3 A challenge in the men's room

If you're a woman, you won't know that gentlemen's lavatories are a rich source of implicature. This is especially true on motorways, where it seems to be assumed that men have nothing (or almost nothing) better to do than read suggestive advertisements seemingly prompted by the immediate context. I plead forgiveness for sharing the following men's room message. I read it at the University of Edinburgh for one thing. And it has a public education element too. It's a poster intended to promote the use of condoms which reads

(133) Are you big enough to wear one?

As the word *condom* doesn't appear on the poster, the reader is left to infer that the 'antecedent' of the proform 'one' is an accompanying illustration depicting a condom. By providing an illustration and not asking

(134) Are you big enough to wear a condom

the poster seems to imply that condoms are out there already and not particular to the addressee. There may be an element of euphemism or deference present too, as the writer avoids a direct link between the addressee and the word *condom*. And perhaps also in the choice of 'wear', as in the euphemistic formula 'wear glasses'.

When we hear utterances, we hear them in the way chosen by the speaker. But in the case of written messages, we are both addressee and, as we read the message, addresser. How do I address myself on this occasion? Do I begin /'ɑ: jʊ/ or /ə 'ju:/? Do I I-infer that I'm being asked a *yes/no* question (/'ɑ: jʊ/) or do I M-infer from (/ə 'ju:/) the rather flattering proposition that although not everyone is big enough to wear one, I just might be? In distinguishing I- and M-inferences in this way, I'm assuming the same unmarked/marked distinction as would apply to an utterance. But could it be that /ə 'ju:/ has become the stereotypical *yes/no*-question interpretation of posters? I'm being asked to find the optimal form without knowing the meaning that I want to encode.

I need to think a bit about 'you' as well. There's the default inference in which 'you' picks me out as a person. But there's also the possibility of a metonymic reading in which 'you' refers to a male body part. The problem of interpretation isn't helped by 'big enough', where things are the other way round: the default reading seems to be related to a body part and the less expectable reading to the extent to which I might be a responsible or 'big enough' person. Notice how these inferences help me to determine what is radically under-determined in the proposition itself, a difficulty compounded by the written medium and the absence of a speaker who might, with various suggestive nods and winks, help me to understand which meaning is intended. All of these preliminary inferences need to made before I can work out the most salient message, the implicature that will assume a quite different propositional form from the one I'm currently struggling to flesh out. As we shall see in the next chapter, the distinction between levels of inference of this kind is very important. So, what is the most salient message of the poster, the implicature it conveys?

- Is your body part (untypically) large enough for you to be able to wear a condom, perhaps implying <you've no excuse for not wearing one>, <get on and wear one>, etc.?
- Are you a responsible enough person (unlike some others) to wear a condom, perhaps implying <use a condom and be proud of yourself>, etc.?

From the writer's perspective, the perlocutionary effect is all-important. One could imagine a fascinating research project in which one might test for significant associations between

- the *yes/no* question (/ˈɑː jʊ/) inference, the 'you' as a person inference and the <are you responsible enough> reading
  or between
- the flattering presupposition (/ə ˈjuː/) inference, the 'you' as a body part inference and the <you've no excuse for not wearing one> reading.

Imagine that two psycho-types of this sort could be identified. Assuming it was testable from a practicality perspective, in which cases would the intended perlocutionary effect be most likely to be achieved? Although these are slightly tongue-in-cheek questions, they do draw our attention to the importance of inferential communication in conveying meaning and the possibility of using it to bring about real-world effects.

5.4.4 Sub-titles – a costly economy

If you watch television with sub-titles, you'll have noticed how there are significant differences between what is said and what appears in the sub-title. For obvious reasons, it doesn't seem appropriate for a sub-titler to add to what is said, but it is common for the sub-titler to subtract from what is said by editing out. One motivation is clearly screen width, which often doesn't allow everything that's said to be represented on a single line or pair of lines. It's striking how often what's edited out has significant pragmatic function. The privileging of truth-conditional content over apparently expendable pragmatic marking is clearly seen in the (non-continuous) extracts examined in this sub-section. They're taken from a single broadcast interview involving an elderly person recalling aspects of her life. Pragmatic casualties include:

- Conventional implicatures. When these are edited out, the relationships between utterances which the speaker felt it necessary to encode have to be recovered as inferences:

(135) BUT sixty years ago the stigma of illegitimacy was strong

(In this and other examples discussed below, items printed in UPPER CASE – apart from 'I' – represent spoken text absent in the teletext sub-titles)

(136) OH yes YES
(137) but NEVERTHELESS one in which attitudes to illegitimacy

- Hedges – which the speaker uses to contextualize the way she puts things:

(138) I knew I wasn't their flesh and blood SORT OF THING
(139) and we didn't show it to that extent IF YOU KNOW WHAT I MEAN
(140) the WHOLE SORT OF end product REALLY

- Auxiliary assertion markers and auxiliary assertions. Without these, the relative importance of events cannot be determined:

(141) I remember a family THIS WAS when I was about nine I suppose
(142) and the friendship grew from that WHICH WAS LOVELY

Another editing strategy is to delete lexical items whose entailments can be recovered as implicatures, as in

(143) Her son and her daughter by her first marriage had BOTH left home
(144) at the same time it's ALSO frightening
(145) it's still hard FOR ME to believe that it's happened

In these cases, the M-inferences intended by the speaker are lost. In the case of multiple deletions, the audience can hardly hope to recover the many inferences required to make the kind of sense of what is said that the speaker intends:

(146) BECAUSE I MEAN they owned a car and everything
(147) and you could please yourself COULDN'T YOU SORT OF THING
(148) AND OF COURSE we used to get a few swear words IN BETWEEN

These data indicate how poorly served speakers are by the sub-titles that represent their utterances and how inadequate the representation in writing of spoken language can be for deaf and hard-of-hearing viewers. Looking at data such as these, it's difficult to avoid concluding that an injustice is being done. As speakers, we make decisions as to where to be explicit and where to convey meaning implicitly and about how to use hedges to represent propositional attitudes. By what right does someone else distort our indications of what we want to say and how we want it to be taken?

As well as showing the power of Gricean and neo-Gricean perspectives to explain actually occurring real-world data in an important communication context, the sub-title data also look forward to areas to be discussed in subsequent chapters. For example, the metalinguistic comment 'oddly enough', which is edited out of

(149) we felt as if we'd known each other for a long time ODDLY ENOUGH

has a metapragmatic function in that it shows the awareness of the speaker of the effect of her words. This is an area which we explore in detail in Chapter 7. In Chapter 11, we look in detail at interactive pragmatics or talk-in-interaction. Many metalinguistic formulas have a metasequential effect, that is to say they help to regulate talk. In the teletext data these are frequently edited out. For example, the topic shift marker is deleted in

(150) NOW when you eventually married you tried to find them again didn't you?

In (151), the sequential significance of the question is altered by the absence of 'so':

(151) SO did you get on with his mother

And in (152), the speaker's encoding of the degree of conversational (un)expectedness of the following proposition is lost when 'well' is edited out:

(152) and said WELL I was QUITE sure that's what families were for

5.5 Implicature and conventionalization

In this final section of the chapter we first examine the apparently puzzling phenomenon that we call tautology from the perspective of Gricean and neo-Gricean implicature. We then consider how Gricean and neo-Gricean pragmatics help us to understand historical language change.

5.5.1 Revisiting tautology

Lacking obvious informativeness, the utterance

(31) At the end of the day the Church can only afford to pay the number of people it can afford to pay

flouts Grice's first maxim of Quantity. Despite this, we assume a cooperative speaker and have little difficulty recovering an implicature. But how is (31) to be treated in a neo-Gricean framework? As marked, and thus provoking an M-inference? Or as scalar – a number not having been stated, (31) Q-implies <a restricted number>?

(31) is also an unusual utterance in the sense that it's infrequent. I don't think I'd heard it before and I'm pretty sure that I haven't heard it since. In this respect, it's very unlike formulaic tautologies which we hear often, such as

(153) Boys will be boys

(31) is also unlike (153) in another way. 'Can afford to pay' in (31) seems not to have different implicata in its two uses. This contrasts with (153) where the single signifying expression 'boys' provokes two different implicatures. The first 'boys' implies the semantically bare notion <male person> sometimes enriched by <of any age>; the second 'boys' implies something like <person who behaves in the way a boy behaves>. Thus the tautology in (153) is more apparent than real because pragmatic restrictions on 'boys' save us from saying something that might otherwise be vacuous. Once the implicata of 'boys' are determined, the meanings of formulas like (153) are liable to become conventionalized. According to this view, 'Boys will be boys' might be considered the most economical way of I-implying <male persons (including older ones) are likely to behave like boys>. On this account, (153) would be comparable to

(120) Make the unmissable unmissable

Or is the formula so entirely conventionalized that the I-inference has become an idiom conveying a non-inferred conventional meaning which then provokes a further contextually dependent, relevance-oriented implicature related to the occasion of use? As a conventionalized tautology turned idiom, it's unlike the one-off tautology (31) which, because of its infrequent occurrence, invites the type-inference <a restricted number>.

Frequently occurring tautologies like

(154) I'll see you when I see you

meaning/implying ?<I'll be late>/?<You'll be late>, and

(155) Enough is enough

implying/meaning ?<the speaker's patience is exhausted>, seem formulaic in the way that (153) is. Q-inferences for (154) and (155) might be motivated by scalar extrapolation along the lines of <I'll see you at *x* o'clock, I'll see you when I see you> and <*x* is enough, enough is enough>. But the unpredictable, idiomatic meanings of (154), <you'll be late>, and (155), <my patience is exhausted>, are hard to derive by this means. The conventional nature of (155) is also confirmed by the newspaper headline in the *Daily Mirror* during a period when lorry drivers were blockading oil refineries in protest against high petrol prices

(156) Enough is enough

This headline clearly invites the M-inference that an '*x* is *x*' formula that would typically be treated as an idiom is to be treated on this occasion as non-idiomatic, with the literal meaning seen as marked.

Another property of (154), (155) and, arguably, (153) is that they lack cultural content, a feature that would also make a conventionalized, idiomatic meaning more likely. One can't say quite the same thing about

(157) Football being football, there was only ever going to be one result

a sentence which I read in a newspaper account of particular game. 'One result' requires inferential elaboration <a result of a certain kind> and enrichment <the underdogs were going to win>, as the newspaper report confirmed. And the formula *x being x* does perhaps invite the I-inference that something bizarre is meant. But we need a degree of cultural knowledge to know that things often turn out unexpectedly in football to facilitate the inference <football is unpredictable>. The greater the degree of cultural knowledge required, the less likely a conventional meaning. This is well illustrated by

(158) John is John

Although there may be an I-inference invited by the economical formula *x is x* (where *x* is a person), perhaps something like <expect *x* to behave in character>, without the required cultural knowledge it would be impossible to know the characteristic of John being referred to. And without this knowledge, the utterance-token meaning of (158) cannot be inferred. In case you're curious, (158) was uttered by the then British Prime Minister, Tony Blair, in response to a question about the pugnacious Deputy Prime Minister, John Prescott, who punched a member of the public who had thrown an egg at him.

What these various examples of what we think of as a unitary phenomenon seem to show is that tautology covers a wide range of cases from single uses to frequently occurring established idioms. In addition, there seems to be a gradual process of conventionalization fed by various factors, which include frequency of use, the semantic emptiness of content, the degree of cultural knowledge implied and the extent to which inferences invite different meanings for repeated lexical items. So a tautology probably starts as a one-off, scalar-provoked Q-inference. As the Q-inferred meaning of the tautology becomes more frequent, the form in which the meaning is expressed may come over time to be seen as economical, thus becoming an I-inferred meaning. Over time, the component parts of the tautology, including its relatedness to a scale and its formulaic nature, may come to be associated with a meaning that becomes conventionalized or idiomatic. This is fed by frequency of use, which is also likely to increase as the meaning becomes more conventionalized and the expression as a whole becomes an ever more economical way of expressing a relatively complex meaning. As we know, clichés are useful, however dismissive we may be of those who say things in an unoriginal way.

So what of the future of

(127) The 7.30 departs from Doncaster at 7.30

It has some of the properties that might feed conventionalization. Although the two uses of '7.30' imply <the train scheduled to depart at 7.30> and <the time 7.30>, provided they are expectable, different implicatures of this kind don't necessarily prevent conventionalization, as 'Boys will be boys' shows. (127) also has an economical structure, although the semantically rich predicate 'departs' is against conventionalization. But the most obvious factor working against conventionalization is the wealth of cultural knowledge required to understand what is implied by the announcement. However, to those of us who have the requisite cultural knowledge and hear the announcement regularly, it's possible to imagine a process of conventionalization in which an idiomatic meaning becomes established, at least among ourselves. I'd give it a better chance than the M-inference provoking euphemism of a visitor from overseas whom we invited round for a meal and who asked

(159) May I explore the geography of your house

Notice, finally, that the pressure for the conventionalization in (159) is social. In the next section, we explore the process of conventionalization as a linguistically driven phenomenon.

5.5.2 Historical pragmatics

Imagine that over time

(127) The 7.30 departs from Doncaster at 7.30

acquires a conventional meaning. As we know, in its first use, it invites various inferences, including at least the particularized inference <if you are booked on the 7.30, leave this train>. The process of semanticization follows a path suggested by Levinson as typical in diachronic change: a linguistic form first invites a particularized inference, an utterance-token meaning. The more the form is used under circumstances in which the same utterance-token meaning arises, the more this meaning tends to be associated with the form, until eventually it comes to be seen as a typical meaning. Little by little 'The 7.30 departs from Doncaster at 7.30' comes to mean <leave this train>, especially as those who travel through Doncaster notice that several people do actually leave the train in response to the announcement. In due course, people who travel regularly through Doncaster begin to say 'The 7.30 departs from Doncaster at 7.30' when they meet in other places. Someone gets on the train at Peterborough with a smelly hamburger and I say to my travelling companion 'The 7.30 departs from Doncaster at 7.30', meaning, stereotypically, that the offending passenger should leave the train. Then, little by little, passengers with no experience of Doncaster begin to say 'The 7.30 departs from Doncaster at 7.30' to each other, often when intending to be helpful, as when advising a passenger unfamiliar with the route that the next station is the one they should get off at. During the long process of becoming conventionalized, the now stereotypical use of 'The 7.30 departs . . .' remains defeasible because it still invites an inferred meaning. The meaning is not yet conventional. But eventually the day comes when it's a contradiction to say

(128′) The 7.30 departs from Doncaster at 7.30 and you may stay on the train

The PCI → GCI → Semantic meaning process is complete. And then some clever person comes along and says

(128″) The 7.30 departs from Doncaster at 6.30

This invites a particularized inference, and the process starts all over again.

Of course, this is an imaginary journey through future time, but it does appear to be a journey that other linguistic expressions have made if we look back through the process of diachronic change.

Adjectives and the adverbs derived from nouns often exhibit semantic bleaching, or loss of meaning, in the process of acquiring a new function, as in *substance* → *substantial* → *substantially*. In this way, the adverbs derived from nouns like *general*, *nature* and *substance* have become a means of indicting the speaker's attitude to what they say. Similarly, the development of modal auxiliaries from full verbs in English involved both semantic as well as syntactic change. Once they were restricted to auxiliary function, these modals too gradually developed an epistemic meaning to reflect speaker belief or attitude as in

(160) She may be coming

alongside their original deontic one as in

(161) The law states that people under 18 may not buy cigarettes

Each of these functions is also restricted by syntactic co-occurrence constraints. For example, deontic meaning does not allow progressive aspect:

(161′) *The law states that people under 18 may not be buying cigarettes

The fact that epistemic *may* is found in different environments from deontic *may* suggests that a reanalysis resulting in a stable new meaning has occurred. In the case of deontic and epistemic modals, this is further confirmed by the behaviour of negation, which applies to the modal when the meaning is deontic (*may not buy* = <not permitted to buy>) and to the lexical verb when the meaning is epistemic (*may not come* = <possibly not come>).

From a pragmatic perspective, there's something suggestive about these historical changes – they seem to follow a pattern in which purely semantic items come to have a pragmatic function, including representing speaker attitude. Indeed, a syntactic structure such as a matrix sentence, which we would expect to convey propositional meaning, sometimes conveys propositional attitude with a function that mimics that of a sentence adverb. In (162), both the higher sentence and the embedded sentence have to be true for the sentence as a whole to be true, so that in this case the higher sentence contributes truth value:

(162) It is a truth universally acknowledged, that a married man in possession of a good fortune must be in want of a son and heir (Opening sentence of Emma Tenant's novel *Pemberley*)

By contrast, 'It's true that' in (163) reflects the commitment of the speaker to the quality of the proposition contained in the following part of the utterance and does not contribute truth value to the utterance as a whole:

(163) It's true that men want to be fathers

In fact, many pseudo-matrix sentences, such as *I think* and *they say*, hedge speaker commitment to maxims in this way. The question at issue is how forms used to convey propositional meaning come to have a pragmatic function.

Work began in the field known as **historical pragmatics** in the late 1980s/early 1990s. The purpose of historical pragmatics is to show the role of pragmatics in the process of syntactic and semantic language change. In particular, historical pragmaticists may take a **semasiological** approach, investigating the processes at work which enable a meaning to change while the form remains constant (as in the case of *may*), or an **onomasiological** approach, investigating the processes by which a form is recruited for a new function (for example, how epistemic meaning is expressed).

Following a semasiological approach, Traugott (1989, 1995) has studied a number of discourse particles and shown how their contemporary meanings and function are instances of a process of gradual 'subjectification'. By this, she means that certain lexical items gradually come to be used to reflect speaker perspective with a discourse marking function. In the case of *in fact*, for example, Traugott traces the appearance of the noun *fact* in the sixteenth century and its occurrence with the preposition *in* in phrases like *in fact and experience* in the seventeenth century. She shows how *in fact* began to be used in the eighteenth century to express an epistemic attitude, i.e. to reflect speaker belief. Soon thereafter, it acquired an adversative function as in *x but in fact y*, where the speaker advances *y* as a right way of viewing things over the earlier stated *x*. In the nineteenth century a further, not necessarily epistemic, additive function appears in which *in fact* is used metalinguistically as a discourse particle to promote a preferred proposition, as I did in the opening pages of this chapter:

(164) In fact, you might like to jot these implied meanings down

or

(165) By itself, 'It's the taste' means very little – in fact, we aren't even told what the taste is or what it does

Thus a lexical item, the noun *fact* first acquires an epistemic function when it occurs in the preposition phrase *in fact*, thus enabling a speaker to express a propositional attitude, and then acquires a further metalinguistic function, allowing a speaker to promote a preferred proposition over a preceding formulation.

In a Plenary address at the 1998 IPrA (International Pragmatics Association) conference, Traugott (1999) appealed to inference and the three levels of meaning discussed in the previous section as a way of accounting for semantic change. Taking *so long as/as long as* as an example, she argued that the original temporal meaning first invited one-off inferences, so that as early as Old English *as long as* sometimes conveys utterance-token conditionality alongside or as part of temporal duration. In Early Modern English, the use of *as long as* to introduce non-temporal propositions to do with cognition becomes more frequent. These utterance-token uses favour interpreting *as long as* conditionally. Through a process of preferred use, perhaps motivated by subjectification, these utterance-token uses gradually acquire a conventional status and the conditional meaning becomes an utterance-type I-inference. In the final stage, which we find first in the nineteenth century, the conditional meaning of *as long as* is no longer an inference but a new semantic meaning. Time reference is no longer required and adverb promotion within the sentence it introduces is allowed (in contradistinction to the temporal use). This new meaning allows a subjective conceptualization in the clause that *as soon as* introduces which is not possible in the original temporal meaning. If you know German, you can probably trace out this same process for *wenn* (= when), which first began to appear with a conditional meaning in Old High German (Lockwood, 1968).

Historical pragmatics is a very recent area of study which seems set to grow very rapidly. Obvious candidates for historical pragmatic analysis include the particles we've been dealing with in this chapter, *even, still, actually*, and many others that we haven't, like *just, surely* and *indeed*, where conventional semantic meaning appears to have been consolidated from first occasional and then typical inferred meanings.

Summary

The process of grammaticalization in which lexical items acquire new functions is especially obvious in the case of discourse particles like *in fact, even* and *indeed*. These new functions are inseparable from the semanticization process in which items acquire new or second meanings. Utterance-type inferences, particularly I-inferences and to a lesser extent M-inferences, are likely to contribute to this process. This is because I-inferences enrich, and M-inferences, being derived from marked expressions or utterance tokens, invite consolidation as unmarked interpretations.

5.5.3 Those who met him

Some years ago I met a philosopher whose PhD supervisor had been Paul Grice. I couldn't resist asking him if it was true, as I had read, that Grice had a very untidy office. "Not really," he said, and indicating a large window went on to describe how Grice had only enough books in his office to fill the space occupied by the window. From the way the story was told, it was obvious that the speaker had expected Grice to have more books in his office. "But," the philosopher added in a significant manner, "he'd read them all." We both laughed at the implicature.

I thought of that same implicature a year or two later when I was in the office of a professor who was telling me that you could always judge an academic by his library. As I surveyed the rows and rows of books that looked as though they'd been disturbed by nothing more intrusive than a duster, it was obvious that the person I was talking to had little in common with Paul Grice.

I can't resist sharing one more Grice story with you. Not long after Grice died, my father and I were having lunch in the Oxford College where Grice had been an undergraduate (and where Austin and Urmson had worked on speech acts and Searle had been a postgraduate). It occurred to me that my father must have been a contemporary of Grice. Our conversation went like this:

(166) PETER: Were you here with Grice
FATHER: <Looks quizzical>
PETER: Were you here with Paul Grice
FATHER: <Wrinkling his brow in an effort of concentration> Y-e-e-e-s <And then remembering all too clearly> He always struck me as rather a studious type

The implicature was unmistakable – Grice had not allocated his time at university as judiciously as he might have done!

Raising pragmatic awareness

1 This exercise works best with a partner or in a small group. Consider the way in which the likely interpretation of each of the utterances in List A would be altered by the insertion of each of the maxim hedges in List B:

List A	List B
I don't know	well
Do you know the way	anyway
She didn't say anything	honestly
It's a good idea	actually
Tomorrow's Saturday	so

Make up your own List A and List B in such a way as to provide better examples than these.

2 Working individually, cut four pictures out of a magazine and choose a different comment to attach to each. Each comment should flout a different maxim. Share your pictures and comments with friends or in your tutorial group.

3 Next time you attend a tutorial in a subject other than linguistics, take a sheet of paper and divide it down the middle. On the left-hand side, record what is said in a short conversation between the tutor and a student and on the right-hand side what is meant. Decide what implicatures arise and why. Bring this to your linguistics tutorial to share with colleagues.

4 Work with two friends. Each of you should spend a few days listening out for a different conventional implicatures such as *actually*, *even* and *but* in conversations. Share your findings.

5 Work with a television or radio interview. Copy down several utterances that contain maxim hedges. Bring them to your next tutorial and write them on the board without the hedges. Your colleagues should try to guess the original hedges. (Acknowledgement: this is Andrew Caink's idea.)

6 Choose a simple comic strip story and white out all the speech in the bubbles. Give it to the other members of your tutorial group and ask them to fill in the bubbles with maxim hedges only.

7 This exercise works best in a small group. Each member of the group takes one of the day's newspapers and identifies all the headlines which violate the Manner maxim. When you share your findings, try to arrange the violations on a cline from the most to the least extreme violation.

8 Each member of your tutorial group brings an utterance to the tutorial which they dictate. As each person dictates their utterance, everyone else writes down an imagined utterance spoken by the previous speaker which causes the dictated utterance to have an implicature. For example, you dictate 'The scissors are in the drawer' and I imagine the previous speaker might have said, 'Look at this new tie Roger's given me'. When the dictation is over, share the results. (Acknowledgement: this beautiful idea was thought up by Roger Maylor.)

9 Which of the features of talk identified as typically pragmatic in Chapter 1 play an important part in creating and recovering implicature: accommodation, appropriateness, context, indeterminacy, indirect meaning, inference, reflexivity, relevance?

Discussions and essays

Based on what you know about implicature, discuss the relative merits of each of the following views:

- We need a theory of implicature not because of the nature of language itself but because of the way we use it.
- The idea that we mean more than we say depends more on implicature than on any other phenomenon.
- Since what is said may be true while what is implicated may be false, implicature is not carried by "what is said", but only by "the saying of what is said". (Adapted from Grice's original.)
- Implicatures arise as much from 'what is said' as from the context in which an utterance occurs.
- Since conversational implicatures may arise either by comparing the way something is put with the way the same proposition might have been put, or by considering what is said in relation to the context in which it is said, they ought not to be regarded as a single phenomenon.
- "The central principle behind Grice's analysis is that there is . . . a system of mutual expectations, some sort of 'social contract', in operation between speaker and listener, knowledge of which allows discourse participants to draw certain inferences to do with rational communicative behaviour" (Seuren, 1998: 406).
- Most of the presupposition phenomena considered in Chapter 3 could be subsumed within a neo-Gricean account of implicature.

Further reading

Primary texts

Grice, 1967, in Grice, 1989 and in Davis, 1991; Horn, 1984; Levinson, 2000.

Textbooks

Levinson, 1983: 97–166; Thomas, 1995: 55–86; Yule, 1996: 35–46.

6 Relevance theory

'In apprehension, how like a god!'
(Hamlet, II.ii.320)

Keywords:

context, explicature, higher level explicature, implicature, indeterminacy, inference, procedural and conceptual encoding, propositional attitude, propositional form, relevance, salience

6.1 Introduction

In the previous chapter, we examined Grice's argument that contributions to talk are guided by the four maxims of Quantity, Quality, Relation and Manner. We then examined the ways in which utterance-type meanings are inferred in the work of the neo-Griceans. In this chapter, we examine the argument set out in Dan Sperber and Deirdre Wilson's major book, *Relevance: Communication and Cognition* ([1986] 1995), that a single principle of relevance is sufficient to explain the process of utterance understanding. While neo-Gricean thinking tends to focus on the relationship of utterance form to informativeness, Sperber and Wilson show how the cognitive notion of relevance rather than probabilistic induction is crucial in utterance understanding.

When Branka says

(1) When will you be back

I take into account that she already knows what I'm going to York to do and how long the journey takes. This enables me to work out that the most relevant way to understand her question is as an offer to make dinner. When I reply

(2) I should be back by eight but you know what trains are like

she takes into account the time at which we normally eat and the fact that it's a Saturday so we should buy a lottery ticket. Taken together with this contextual knowledge, what I say enables her to work out that the most relevant way to understand my reply is that she should make the dinner and buy a lottery ticket. We each know that what the other says will be an optimally relevant way of conveying the meanings we have in mind, given our awareness of each other's real-world knowledge and cognitive styles.

In Chapter 1, we saw that, depending on the context in which it was uttered, 'I'm here now' might imply many different things, including <there's no need to worry any more>, <stop messing about and get on with your homework> and <I'm sorry I've held you up>. Usually those we address have no difficulty working out the most relevant understanding of radically under-determined utterances such as this precisely because they take the context into account. Indeed, the greater the difficulty we have working out what someone means by what they say, the less relevant it will be. As we can see from this observation, **relevance** is used a technical sense to describe the degree of cognitive effort required for an addressee to achieve an understanding of what someone means by what they say.

In this chapter, we'll see that this effort isn't limited only to recovering implicatures of the kind Branka and I recover in our exchange in which the propositional form of the inference is entirely different from the propositional form of the original utterance. Relevance Theory also accounts for the kind of lexical enrichment needed in cases like that of 'finished' in an utterance like

(3) I've just finished a book

as discussed in Chapter 1, and for the inference that I wasn't sincere in saying

(4) I was wondering too

Although the inferences in these cases depend just as much on having access to context as in (1) and (2), they have different functions. In (3), the inference <finished reading> or <finished writing> elaborates the original proposition. And in (4) the inference applies to the proposition at a higher level – what sort of propositional attitude does the speaker take?

The chapter contains three further sections, each of which includes several sub-sections:

- *Determining relevance*, which explains Sperber and Wilson's theory.
- *Relevance in the real world*, which describes the way in which Relevance Theory enables us to make sense of actual instances of spoken interaction and written language.
- *Context and cognition*, which explores the relationship between what we understand from context and what we understand from utterances and how these perceptions relate to the cognitive notions of figure and ground.

Finally, to whet your appetite, consider the following letter published in *The Times*:

(5) Sir, I read that a dentist is alleged to have "grabbed a senior colleague by the genitals and tried to throttle him" (report, earlier editions, March 28).
They obviously don't teach anatomy as well today as they did when I was a dental student.

The letter writer invites us to enrich 'and' in the quoted proposition from the purely additive use presumably intended by the journalist who filed the 28 March report to something resultative like <and in that way> so that the grabbing and the throttling are associated stages in a single process. Our encyclopedic knowledge tells us that this isn't a legitimately relevant inference, although a letter inviting it may be witty enough to get published in *The Times*.

6.2 Determining relevance

Some years ago, I posted the following notice on my office door:

(6)

Office hours
Mondays
10–12

You can be sure of finding me in my office at this time

It was several weeks before I discovered that most students took this to be an instruction not to consult me at any other time. Whereas I had intended the literal meaning of 'You can be sure of finding me in my office at this time' to be an assurance of reliability, it had been widely interpreted as conveying the entirely different proposition <students should not come at any other time>. This tells us that the implicated premise I had assumed was readily recoverable, <Peter Grundy is willing to see students at any time>, wasn't recovered by those who read the notice. For them, the context <tutors don't like to see students outside office hours> was the implicated premise, leading to the implicated conclusion that I was willing to see students only in office hours. Thus, my notice had a quite different relevance from the one I had intended. This section of the chapter explores the procedures followed by addressees as they seek to determine optimally relevant interpretations of messages like (6).

6.2.1 Explicature and implicature – three examples

Recall the traffic sign discussed in Chapter 1:

(7) Angel parking

I asked whether passing motorists were being advised that an angel was parking, or that there was a parking place for angels. Or that they could park their angels there. But in fact you and I know that motorists are being advised that there is a parking place ahead for the vehicles of those who want to visit the sculpture known as the *Angel of the North*. So we see that even elaborating the syntactic relation of 'Angel' to 'parking' requires inferences involving a great deal of real-world knowledge about angels and what road signs are for. These I-inferences in the neo-Gricean account are called explicatures by Sperber and Wilson. An **explicature** is an enrichment of an original utterance, such as 'Angel parking', to a fully elaborated propositional form.

So in order to understand the road sign in an optimally relevant way, passing motorists needed to recover an explicature.

When I took up a new post in 1994, the course leader of one of the courses I was to teach left a file in my pigeon-hole containing papers relevant to the course. A note was attached to this file with four written instructions. The third instruction was

(8) Please attend course planning and examiners' meetings in future

My first reaction was one of panic – Oh no, I thought, I've missed some meeting I was supposed to attend. But as I reflected more carefully, it seemed to me that if I had missed a meeting, the written message I'd received would be a rather unfriendly way of communicating such information to a new member of staff and uncharacteristic of the course leader, who was obviously a very kind person.

What I was worrying about was determining the attitude of the writer of the message – her use of 'please' told me that I was being instructed, but was she reprimanding me or was she telling me that a new responsibility had come my way? What I was uncertain of was a speech act description for her utterance. The inference I needed to make would yield what Sperber and Wilson call a **higher level explicature** which would reveal the propositional attitude of the speaker to her utterance.

So in order to understand Alice's message in an optimally relevant way, I needed to recover a higher level explicature.

The third example: If someone said to you

(9) Have you seen my book

you'd need to take a lot of context into account in order to determine what the speaker meant by their utterance. If the speaker was your flat-mate and you had a habit of borrowing her property without permission, she might be asking you if you'd 'borrowed' the book she owned (explicature) and the utterance might be taken as a demand for its return. But if your tutor said it to you as she handed back an essay, you might take it to be a semi-rhetorical inquiry (higher level explicature) as to whether you had read the book she had written (explicature) implying that if you had, you'd have written a better essay. These inferences, <I want my book back> or <If you want to write a decent essay, you'd better read my book>, are **implicatures**. Unlike explicatures, an implicature is likely to have a propositional form different from that of the original utterance.

So in order to understand 'Have you seen my book' in an optimally relevant way, we need to recover an implicature.

In all three of these instances of written and spoken communication, there are explicatures, higher level explicatures and implicatures to be recovered. However, the most salient meanings are probably an explicature in (7), a higher level explicature in (8), and an implicature in (9). All are recovered as inferences. To put it another way, these inferred meanings are the most relevant ways of understanding what the originators of these messages meant by what they said (or wrote).

Checking understanding (6.1)

1 Recovering the higher level explicature in (8) was made more difficult because, as a new member of staff, I didn't know enough about the institution to enable me to recover even the explicatures. What problems do you think I faced in trying to recover these explicatures?

2 If (9) had been addressed to you, what indeterminacies would you have resolved by the explicatures and higher level explicatures mentioned above if the speaker had been (a) your flat-mate and (b) your tutor?

Summary

We might think of the process of understanding utterance meaning along these lines: an utterance like 'Have you seen my book' is an economical linguistic representation of an underlying logical form, *[seen], you, my book*. This linguistic form needs to be inferentially enriched by means of explicature to a full propositional form in which the reference of 'you' and the senses of 'seen' and 'my book' are fully determined. An addressee also needs to determine what sort of utterance this proposition is – an inquiry, a recommendation, an accusation, etc. We might think of this as a meta- or higher level representation, because it describes what the addressee infers the speaker does by uttering the sentence: <the speaker is asking if I've seen the book she owns>, <the speaker is asking if I've read the book she's written>, etc. This metarepresentation is, then, a higher level explicature. What the speaker seeks to convey is an implicature, <I want my book back>, <If you want to write a decent essay, you'd better read my book>, etc., which commonly takes a different propositional form from that of the original utterance.

6.2.2 Indeterminacy – the motivation for enrichment

Explicature, the inference or series of inferences that enrich the underdetermined form produced by the speaker to a full propositional form, is motivated by the indeterminacy of language. This indeterminacy is a consequence of the economy of expression which characterizes natural language. Thus determining even the contextualized meaning of items like *book* (physical object, contents, etc.) or *seen* (know the location of, have read, etc.) is far from straightforward. It requires an inferential process which provides an enriched interpretation consistent with the context of the utterance and the speaker's encyclopedic knowledge. And as we've seen, not only lexical items, but even apparently straightforward syntactic relations such as that between a possessive determiner and a noun, as in the phrase *my book*, represent a wide variety of semantic relations that have to be inferred on each occasion of use. If formerly, we had thought of the 'semantic' element of language as straightforward, we owe to Sperber and Wilson and to the neo-Griceans the insight that, when language is used for communication, inferences are required to determine even the sense of a lexical item.

Thus the title of a recently published cookery book

(10) How to eat

is presumably to be explicated as something like <How to eat well>. The original title is enriched by the addition of the conceptual constituent *well*. And

(11) SOCIOLOGY
PAPER ONLY

as written on the waste-bin beside the photocopier at the end of our corridor, is to be understood as conveying the meaning that the waste-bin is the property of the Sociology Department and that only paper which has been used and is to be recycled should be put in it. In this case, several conceptual constituents have been added, as has the description of a real-world object, the waste-bin, which was not included in the original written message. And the traffic-sign on the Durham University campus that reads

(12) Car park
Psychology

is to be explicated along the lines <This road leads to a car park and to the Psychology Department>. In this case, one of the processes of enrichment involves concept formation around the metonymic use of 'Psychology' to refer to a department. And the label of the package I saw in a supermarket (and couldn't resist buying as a visual aid to be displayed in pragmatics classes)

(13) No frills
Men's disposable briefs

is to be explicated along the lines <This package contains disposable briefs to be worn by men and is sold as an item in the 'no frills' range of basic goods>. And the following 'neckbill' on a bottle of Portuguese wine

(14) Buy 4 750ml bottles and get a short break for two in Portugal for the price of one!

is to be explicated so as to make it clear that the short break is not being offered for the price of a single bottle of wine.

As you can see, I've illustrated the point that explicature is necessary with examples where indeterminacy and economy of expression are so evident as to create potential ambiguity. But indeterminacy is present everywhere in language. Thus a Gricean account of what Bill Clinton meant by saying

(15) Even Presidents have private lives

would identify a conventional implicature associated with 'even' and enable us to recover an implicature. Relevance Theory will account for the implicature and will also explicate 'Presidents' (Presidents of countries, and particularly this President of the United States of America), 'have' (engage in) and 'private lives' (extra-marital relationships). In Clinton's utterance, enriching the single term 'Presidents' involves the addition of a conceptual constituent ('of countries') and conceptualizing an exemplar case in the form of a referential description. Notice that in another context, this same utterance could equally easily be explicated along the lines of <Presidents of multinational companies live away from the public gaze>.

Checking understanding (6.2)

What makes explicatures possible is encyclopedic knowledge and awareness of context. What knowledge would you need to take into account in order to explicate the following instances of language use so as to infer the meanings presumably intended by their authors?

(16) Avoidance of smoking and alcohol in moderation are also important factors in living a healthy lifestyle (From a University health and safety document)

(17) 'Mad sheep' fears prompt slaughter (headline, *The Times*)

(18) SHAREHOLDERS? COMMISSION?
NOT ON YOUR LIFE!
(Advertisement, *Equitable Life Assurance Society*)

(19) The mouse is buggered (spoken by a frustrated academic)

(20) Cave de Massé – sweet, medium, dry and red (on a menu)

(21) Cancellation
Second half only (Notice pinned to the door of a room in which two consecutive conference sessions had been timetabled)

Summary

Sperber and Wilson extend the inferential requirement in communication to

- explicature – an inference or series of inferences which enrich the under-determined form of the utterance to a full propositional form.
- higher level explicature – the inferred determination of speaker stance or propositional attitude.
- implicature – an inference which provides the addressee with the most relevant interpretation of the utterance.

Explicatures preserve and elaborate the form of the original utterance; implicatures are likely to be new propositional forms.

6.2.3 The essential principles of Relevance Theory

In this section, I'm going to list and briefly explain a number of the key principles of Relevance Theory. These are numbered for the sake of clarity.

1 Every utterance comes with a guarantee of its own particular relevance. Thus, to understand an utterance is to prove its relevance. Determining the relevance (of all phenomena to which our attention is drawn and not only of utterances) is our constant aim. As Sperber and Wilson say, "An individual's particular cognitive goal at a given moment is always an instance of a more general goal: maximising the relevance of the information processed" (1995: 49).

2 Because addressees cannot prove the relevance of the utterances they hear without taking context into account, "the speaker must make some assumptions about the hearer's cognitive abilities and contextual resources, which will necessarily be reflected in the way she communicates, and in particular in what she chooses to make explicit or what she chooses to leave implicit" (1995: 218).

3 However apparently grammaticalized linguistic structure may be, utterances are radically under-determined. So a single syntactic relation may represent a very wide range of logical and semantic relations. Even the determination of sense requires an inferential process.

4 Once the underlying logical form of an utterance has been fully elaborated, the utterance may be regarded as a premise, which, taken together with other, non-linguistic premises available to the hearer as contextual resources, enable her to deduce the relevant understanding. So in the case of

(9) Have you seen my book

the time referred to, the referents indicated by 'you' and 'my', the sense of 'book' and 'seen', the semantico-syntactic relation encoded in 'my book' and the speech act status of the utterance all require explicating. This explicated utterance and the addressee's encyclopedic entries triggered by it (such, perhaps, as whether she wears the speaker's clothes without asking permission, or has written a poor essay) enable an implicature to be recovered as a deductive inference. By that we mean that the implicature is the only **logical** conclusion that can be drawn from the premises. Of course, this description is slightly simplified because it suggests that all necessary explicating precedes the recovery of the implicature. In practice, the processes will often work in parallel and may involve recursion, i.e. going back over stages as understandings at different levels are confirmed. Indeed, sometimes we're aware of the recursive nature of the way we reach relevant interpretations. For example, I recently heard someone say, not very charitably, of someone they knew

(22) She's so ugly the tide wouldn't take her out

Although I'm ashamed to say that I laughed at the time, it was only later that I realized that I'd explicated 'out' in relation only to the tide washing her out to sea and not in relation to taking her out on a date.

5 The most accessible interpretation is the most relevant. This is an important notion because it enables us to discriminate in a principled way, i.e. by taking into account the degree of processing effort, between the various inferences which, time allowing, we might recover. Hence there's a trade-off between relevance and processing effort: "An assumption is relevant to an individual to the extent that the positive cognitive effects achieved when it is optimally processed are large" (Sperber and Wilson, 1995: 265). ("Positive cognitive effects" are changes in beliefs resulting from new information being added.) Thus the

greater the effect of an utterance, the more relevant it is. These effects need, therefore, to be economically achieved: "An assumption is relevant to an individual to the extent that the effort required to achieve these positive cognitive effects is small" (1995: 266). This means that the harder we have to try to understand something, the less relevant it is. This principle reflects a psychological reality with which we are all familiar, that of not being able to get the point, or at least not being able to get the point in the time available.

6 Context is not treated as given common ground, but rather as a set of more or less accessible items of information which are stored in short-term and encyclopedic memories or manifest in the physical environment: "people hope that the assumption being processed is relevant (or else they would not bother to process it at all), and they try to select a context which will justify that hope: a context which will maximize relevance. In verbal comprehension in particular, it is relevance which is treated as given and context which is treated as a variable" (1995: 142).

Let's see how the six principles outlined above apply to a particular instance of communication by reconsidering Alice's instruction

(8) Please attend course planning and examiners' meetings in future

I took her message as relevant and set out to prove its relevance (1).

But Alice had over-estimated my contextual resources (2) and (3). As a new member of staff I had trouble even recovering the explicatures.

One way of resolving 'in future' would lead me to recover the implicature that I had missed a meeting in the past and that Alice's message was a reprimand (4).

However, try as I may, even several years of processing effort later, I still haven't recovered the single accessible interpretation which satisfies my quest to establish the relevance of Alice's message beyond doubt (5).

I know that the relevance of the message is guaranteed, but the contexts are just too variable (6) for me to prove its relevance.

In Chapter 1, I said that one of the things you have to make up your mind about as you study pragmatics is whether the context determines the way we use language or whether the way we use language determines the context. As you can see, the relevance theoretic view is that an utterance is an instruction to find a context which optimizes its relevance. When we go into the doctor's surgery and the doctor says 'How are you?', we have to decide whether this is a greeting (to which we might reply 'Fine thanks! How are you?') or the beginning of the consultation (to which we might reply 'Not too good, I'm afraid').

Checking understanding (6.3)

In order to demonstrate how the most relevant interpretation is recovered, explain how the six principles of Relevance Theory outlined above might apply to

(23) She's taken ten years off my life

6.2.4 Procedural encoding

We owe to Blakemore, and particularly her 1987 book *Semantic Constraints on Relevance*, the significance of the crucial distinction between **procedural** and

conceptual encoding. Procedural encodings are processing instructions to be applied to conceptual encodings. Their effect is to make easier the recovery of the most relevant interpretation by constraining (i.e. limiting) the search for the contexts required to prove the relevance of the utterance. Although sentence adverbs like *fortunately* and *clearly* have some conceptual content, their function in helping the addressee to recover the **propositional attitude** of the speaker is procedural. Many procedurals lack truth value entirely. These include:

- disjuncts like *anyway* and *after all* and discourse particles like *so* and *therefore*, which constrain the search for a relevant interpretation by showing how the propositions to which they are attached relate to other propositions;
- adverbial particles like *even* and *only*, which speakers attach to propositions to constrain their interpretation;
- conjunctions like *but*, one of whose typical functions is to constrain an assumption otherwise warranted by the proposition that preceded it.

This distinction between conceptual encoding (for example, 'Presidents have private lives') and procedural encoding (for example, 'even') in

(15) Even Presidents have private lives

is the distinction between what Wilson and Sperber call "information about the representations to be manipulated, and information about how to manipulate them" (1993: 2).

This second, procedural or computational, type of encoding (i.e. information about how to manipulate representations), therefore, constrains the interpretation of conceptual meaning by limiting the available ground in relation to which it is to be interpreted. Let's look at some examples.

Recall that at the end of the last chapter, I said that the philosopher and I had both laughed at the implicature recovered from

(24) But he'd read them all

Merely saying 'he'd read them all' suggests to me that it is worth the processing effort of trying to determine how the philosopher's utterance is relevant, even though I might come to the conclusion that the entailment is actually the salient meaning the speaker intends to convey. However, his use of 'but' makes me reconsider the first part of what he had said and infer that he intends to convey that academics don't always read their books, an assumption that doesn't hold of Grice. The point is that the instruction to manipulate the representation in a particular way which 'but' provides makes (24) easier to understand, i.e. to find relevant, than the bald utterance 'he'd read them all'.

In our discussion of

(15) Even Presidents have private lives

in the previous chapter, we saw that 'even' conventionally implicates something like <the attached proposition is at the end of a scale of expectability> in the Gricean account of implicature. Conventional implicatures aren't recognized in Relevance Theory. Instead, items like *even* are regarded as procedural encodings. If the utterance 'Presidents have private lives' is true, then the utterance 'Even Presidents have private lives' is also true. Like most procedural encodings, *even* adds no truth value to the proposition to which it is attached. Rather, it advises us that the concept that Presidents have private lives is at the end of a scale of expectability and helps us to understand how it could be relevant. So if we infer that Clinton is claiming that he can do a good job despite his extra-marital relationship, it's because 'even' makes this inference easier to recover.

Consider again Alice's message which I failed to understand:

(8) Please attend course planning and examiners' meetings in future

Imagine that instead, Alice had written

(8′) So please attend course planning and examiners' meetings in future

Straight away I know that (8′) follows from what has gone before. And what has gone before? I've been told that I'm to take over responsibility for a course and a file of relevant papers has been left in my pigeonhole. I haven't been told that I missed a meeting. Thus Alice's instruction in (8/8′) is a consequence, not of a missed meeting, but of a new responsibility. I'm now to understand that attending course planning and examiners' meetings is part of this new responsibility. In fact, what's wrong with Alice's message is not just that she over-estimates my contextual resources, but the consequence of this over-estimate is that she fails to provide a procedural instruction sufficient to enable me to determine the context that would make the message relevant.

Checking understanding (6.4)

I was once sitting in a restaurant in Florence eavesdropping on the conversation at the next table, which was occupied by two married couples, one American and one British, who'd obviously been asked to share the table. At one stage in their conversation, the British woman said

(25) We're only about thirty miles from London

By an extraordinary co-incidence, the very next evening in a different restaurant I was eavesdropping on another conversation, this time involving two British couples, when I overheard one of the women say

(26) We're about thirty miles from Birmingham

Can you say how 'only' helps you to determine the relevance of (25)?

6.2.5 Salience and inference

At the beginning of this chapter we noticed that sometimes the most salient interpretation of what is said will be an explicature, sometimes a higher level explicature and sometimes an implicature. This realization suggests that we need to think a bit more about what determines whether the most salient assumption will be an explicature derived by inferential development of the logical form of the utterance to a full propositional form, or an implicature derived by inference alone.

The following exchange illustrates some of the difficulties in deciding the most salient meaning. It occurred when the owner of the second restaurant in Florence, the one where the couple from Birmingham were dining, approached my table and engaged me in conversation. He asked me if I knew Florence well:

(27) PETER: I was last here seventeen years ago
RESTAURANT OWNER: You were young then
PETER: Younger

Is the most salient meaning of my first utterance the explicated proposition that I had not visited Florence during the seventeen years preceding the time of utterance? Or am I, perhaps, implying that I remember it as a good time?

Under certain circumstances (which we won't go into here), his utterance, 'you were young then', might contrast with the apparent present reality. If it was intended as such a contrast, and particularly if he was responding to an implicature such as <the speaker remembers it as a good time>, the restaurant owner might intend his utterance to imply that I was romantic then – or even naïve, with the implicated conclusion that <Florence is not such a good place as you thought when you were younger>. This interpretation treats my first utterance as an implicit compliment to Florence and hence, indirectly, to the restaurant owner too. His response is intended as a modest demur.

Alternatively, 'you were young then' might imply that I am still young enough for it to be possible to assert that I was young seventeen years ago, and I'm being complimented on my youthfulness. In this case, the restaurant owner probably takes the explicated entailment of my first utterance, that I haven't visited Florence during the previous seventeen years, as the most salient meaning.

And what is the most salient meaning of his utterance for me? Is it the implicature that I am now old? If so, 'younger' might be explicated to yield <the speaker was even younger seventeen years ago than the speaker is at the time of speaking>. My utterance is then to be taken as a denial that I am now old and I imply that I am still young. Notice that in disagreeing with the restaurant owner, I try to minimize our disagreement by using the comparative form, 'younger', of the term he had used to describe me.

Or is the most salient meaning of the restaurant owner's utterance the entailment that I was young then, which I contradict politely by asserting that I was younger than I am now, thereby implying that I was not in fact truly young even then. In which case, there is a further implicated conclusion: that his implicature that my youth led me to take a too romantic view of Florence is ill-founded – my view is realistic rather than romantic.

Or do I recognize his contribution as a compliment, and, like he does when offered a compliment, demur modestly by implying that I wasn't young then? In this case, the speech act description recovered as a higher level explicature is the most salient meaning for me.

In this short, and necessarily complex, account of the possible ways in which the two parties understand each other's contributions to their three-utterance exchange, we see how salient meanings may be entailments, explicatures and implicatures. It's notably difficult to determine which were in fact the salient meanings in this exchange as we approach it as analysts after the event, although no doubt it was entirely clear at the time to the participants themselves. Superficially, it seems simple – three turns consisting of only twelve words in total. But as we have seen, determining how the contributions are intended to be relevant by the speakers and at which inferential levels they are taken as most relevant by the addressees is far from straightforward. The most salient meaning, whether an explicature or an implicature, is the meaning to which we respond in conversation.

6.2.6 Relevance Theory and degrees of understanding

Earlier in the chapter, I suggested that Relevance Theory was able to account for the understanding failures which occur when the processing load is too great for relevant assumptions to be recovered or when the addressee lacks sufficient contextual resources to infer the explicatures and implicatures which prove the relevance of the utterance. Relevance Theory is to be preferred over other accounts of utterance understanding to the extent that it recognizes and can account for the fact that not all utterances are successfully understood, and that a particular utterance may be understood in different ways and to different degrees by different addressees.

Accordingly, this section of the chapter concludes in *Checking Understanding* format with parts of a British text which posed real understanding problems for a group of non-native members of the British culture who were asked to work though it. I'll first describe the experiment I set up, and then ask you to identify the reasons why parts of the text posed understanding problems for this particular group. The idea is that relevance theoretic principles can be invoked to account for their understanding difficulties.

The understanding test was based on an extended joke-telling routine from a television programme, *The Two Ronnies*, in which one of the presenters, Ronnie Corbett, sits in a chair and tells the studio audience a joke. The sequence lasts for just over three minutes and contains a series of intermediate jokes as the joke-teller builds up to the main joke. According to Sacks, jokes exhibit "supposed supposable unknownness to recipients" (i.e. the audience should not have heard the joke before) and constitute an "understanding test" (1974: 341, 346). A joke is an understanding test in the sense that there's some supposed audience who wouldn't pass it (since if the test were failed by the real audience, the joke would lose its point). Jokes therefore confirm in-group solidarity by virtue of the expectation that they won't be understood by out-group members.

The group I selected to listen to Ronnie Corbett's joke were non-native-speaker university teachers of English from a single culture with near native-speaker competence in English but limited experience of the British culture. They could tell where the comic effects occurred because the studio audience indicated this with laughter whose intensity varied with the intensity of the effect. The informant group were left to work alone for an hour with a tape of the joke-telling sequence and twenty questions designed to determine the kinds of understanding difficulties encountered.

Checking understanding (6.5)

1 Can you explain why the participants were at a loss to know why the studio audience laughed after 'attic' in the following?

(28) tonight's story was actually handed down to me by my dear old grandfather (pause) the other night as he was clearing out our attic

2 Sperber and Wilson say "The speaker must make some assumptions about the hearer's cognitive abilities and contextual resources, which will necessarily be reflected in the way she communicates, and in particular in what she chooses to make explicit or what she chooses to leave implicit" (1995: 281) and "A speaker who intends an utterance to be interpreted in a particular way must also expect the hearer to be able to supply a context which allows that interpretation to be recovered" (1995: 16). Do these comments help us to explain why the participants

Checking understanding (6.5) *cont.*

were unable to understand why the studio audience laughed when they heard (29)?

(29) on with the joke which concerns these two Rugby players who were both spending the summer holidays at Scarborough (pause) for a bet

3 Sperber and Wilson remind us that pressure of time, complexity of structure, etc. limit our ability to recover contexts and that explicatures and implicatures may fail to be inferred for these reasons: "The organization of the individual's encyclopedic memory, and the mental activity in which he is engaged, limit the class of potential contexts from which an actual context can be chosen at any given time" (1995: 138). Does this help us to understand why the participants didn't find the following funny in the way that the studio audience did?

(30) I was watching the late-night film you know about Ivan the Terrible and his wife Blodwen the Extremely Disappointed

4 Sperber and Wilson say that the most accessible interpretation is the most relevant since "A phenomenon is relevant to an individual to the extent that the effort required to process it optimally is small" (1995: 153). In other words, there are degrees of accessibility, and the means chosen to convey meanings may have different accessibility properties for different addressees. Does this help to explain why the participants didn't see the joke in the following comment about a tooth that was causing the joke-teller problems?

(31) It was still plaguing me this morning at rehearsals so I thought it's no use I'll have to have it out so I went along to the BBC emergency dental service they have no appointment necessary you just go up to one of the scene boys and tell them to get a move on and that's the end of it

and in this comment on the joke-teller's *au pair*

(32) she's just come over to learn the language and she's doing very well (pause) this morning she said to me I hope you'll be forgiving me my extremely bad language but I'm afraid my grandmaster needs touching up

5 Sperber and Wilson say "The principle of relevance does not normally warrant the selection of more than one interpretation for a single ostensible stimulus" (1995: 167). Do you think this default could be a problem when we listen to a joke and might explain why the participants failed to laugh at each pause and at 'she's just come over to learn the language' when the joke-teller talks about his *au pair*?

(33) she's been doing a bit of work for us this weekend at home (pause) and (pause) no she's just come over it's true she's just come over to learn the language

Summary

Relevance Theory postulates a trade-off between processing effort and determining the relevance of an utterance. Like many advertisements and newspaper headlines, joke-telling routines also constitute an understanding test in which the processing effort is very great but worth engaging in because the understanding is correspondingly more rewarding. However, the processing overload that jokes may impose is easily demonstrated when the audience consists of non-native speakers or out-group members who lack the necessary contextual or linguistic resources. Relevance Theory provides an explanatory account of this phenomenon.

6.3 Relevance in the real world

In this section we discuss three real-world situations in which a relevance theoretic account of how meanings are understood helps to explain the complexity of communication.

6.3.1 Ostension and the plural audience

There are two obvious features of posters: they set out to grab your attention and they have a varied and unpredictable readership.

If you're a member of a British university, you may have seen the *Saneline* poster stating

(34) You don't have to be mentally ill to suffer mental illness

As an act of ostension, a way of attracting your attention, this poster is certainly spectacular. Ostension, drawing attention to a message likely to be relevant, is an important concept in Relevance Theory. Without ostension, phenomena pass us by. I was recently the target of a particularly spectacular act of ostension when the butcher recommended black pudding (a kind of sausage) on the grounds that it was 'just like the wife'. I was naturally curious to know how this description could be relevant to black pudding and obligingly responded to his ostensive stimulus with an inquiry. "Nice and spicy, no lumps of fat – just like the wife," he said.

The less captive the audience, the more prominent the act of ostension needs to be to attract attention. This is why academics often choose attention-grabbing titles for their conference papers. Or they may begin with an arresting opening. I admit to a shameless attempt to do this myself when I was giving a talk at a conference in Spain at the time of the deadly SARS epidemic in Hong Kong. I began my talk by explaining that I'd returned from Hong Kong two days earlier, and paused long enough for the relevance of this to be apparent before continuing "Don't worry I'm not ill." I then coughed twice in a contrived manner.

Posters and advertisements make use of arresting symbols and unexpected uses of language precisely because they lack a captive audience. Spectacular acts of ostension promise better rewards than less spectacular ones, so that the inferential effort to process them seems worthwhile. I guess the sign 'Blow up your Granny' in Newcastle market attracts customers to an otherwise modest stall where photographs are enlarged and framed.

Because it addresses a plural audience, a poster is very unlike an utterance, which, in Grice's words, should be "such as is required, at the stage at which it occurs, by the accepted purpose or direction of the talk exchange". Instead, in the case of posters, "the first hypothesis consistent with the principle of relevance" will depend on the different contextual resources each reader brings to the poster. Therefore posters, which necessarily address plural audiences, will be successful to the extent that they are able to provoke a wide range of relevant interpretations, each tailored to a particular (category of) reader. How does the *Saneline* poster meet these criteria?

On first seeing the poster, we're likely to wonder what the apparently contradictory, attention-grabbing ostension conveys. The reverse of a tautology (*x* is *x*), the apparently contradictory (not be *x* and be *x*) character of this ostension suggests that 'mentally ill' and 'mental illness' need to be differentiated at the level of explicature. And perhaps at the level of higher level explicature too: for example, 'mentally ill' may be understood by some as a 'scare quote' from which the poster writers disassociate themselves. These aren't the only explicatures required. The reader also needs to determine the sense and reference of several other items:

- whether 'you' is used deictically or non-deictically, with different readers perhaps expected to explicate 'you' in different ways depending on whether their knowledge of 'mental illness' is casual or at first hand;
- the sense of 'suffer' and whether <suffer from one's own illness> or <suffer from the illness of others known/not known to oneself> is understood;
- the time references associated with 'mentally ill' and 'mental illness' and whether both or either refer to present situations or future possibilities;
- the inferred sense of 'have to be' and whether it's understood to mean <it's not required> or <. . . but it helps>.

Depending on the choices made in determining these various senses and references, an implicature for the utterance as a whole can be derived: <call us if you need help>, <make a donation>, <seek help now>, <don't worry>, <you may be a victim of a misguided social policy>, etc., etc. Thus a poster likely to have a plural audience may provoke a wide range of different optimally relevant readings depending on the reader and the contextual resources they bring to the ostension.

As we see, the set of possible implicatures is very wide – no doubt a good deal wider than traced out here in fact. This perhaps indicates a successful poster.

6.3.2 Stranger danger

I'm sitting in a hospital waiting area. A small child and his mother are sitting opposite me. In due course, a nurse appears and this exchange ensues:

(35) NURSE: What's your name
CHILD: Jordan
NURSE: How old are you
CHILD: Three
NURSE: Three You're tall for three Do you go to nursery
CHILD: Yes
NURSE: Are you having a day off
CHILD: Yes
NURSE: Can I come with you

What goes through Jordan's mind as he decides how to answer? Perhaps something like this:

(a) The Nurse has sincerely requested "Can I come with you" where 'I' = *nurse* and 'you' = *me*. What does 'come with' entail?
[A partially explicated propositional form with pronominal referents assigned is embedded in a description of the Nurse's ostensive act.]

(b) The Nurse's utterance is optimally relevant.
[A default expectation given the ostension.]
(c) The relevance of the Nurse's request will be proved by working out why she wants to come with me.
(d) She wants to come with me to get away from the hospital.
[The first assumption Jordan entertains that's likely to satisfy (c).]
(e) Coming with me means having a nurse (= old, medically smelly person) tag along just so she can get away from the hospital.
[Inferred from (d).]
(f) Coming with me perhaps means <we go to together> so Mummy stays here.
[A further explicature enriching the propositional form and inviting a further inference.]
(g) A smelly old medical person wants to take me away from Mummy.
[An implicature that satisfies (b).]

You might like to consider how you'd set about proving the relevance of 'Can I come with you' if it had been addressed to you, given your age, gender, etc. Of course, we can only guess at what goes through Jordan's mind, but the entire conversation, including the intuitive understanding encoded in the Nurse's rephrased request, perhaps lends credence to what I've suggested:

(36) NURSE: What's your name
JORDAN: Jordan
NURSE: How old are you
JORDAN: Three
NURSE: Three You're tall for three Do you go to nursery
JORDAN: Yes
NURSE: Are you having a day off
JORDAN: Yes
NURSE: Can I come with you
JORDAN: No
NURSE: Can I have a day off too
JORDAN: <buries head in mother's lap>

Perhaps an indication that adults aren't always skilled at taking into account the cognitive abilities and contextual resources of children.

6.3.3 Getting from the airport to one's destination

What goes wrong when we intend one meaning to be inferred but our addressee infers another? This is the situation explored by Moeschler (2007), who describes sending an email to a fellow native speaker of French in another country who had invited him to present a paper there. In his message, Moeschler used the formula

(37) Pouvez-vous me dire comment aller de l'aéroport à X
'Can you tell me how to get from the airport to X'

This was understood literally (i.e. as a request for directions), and resulted in elaborate travel instructions. In fact, Moeschler had intended what he had written to be interpreted as a request to come and pick him up from the airport. According to Moeschler, the misunderstanding arose because the addressee didn't assign the intended higher level explicature to the proposition <([get] M, from airport, to X) how>. As a result, the message was treated, not as a request to be picked up, but as a conventionally indirect speech act (*pouvez-vous me dire/can you tell me*) requesting travel instructions (*comment aller de l'aéroport à X/how to get from the airport to X*), the optimally relevant interpretation from the addressee's point of view.

Moeschler suggests that this interpretation arose because it can be recovered at less cost to the addressee than the interpretation he intended since it doesn't require the addressee to interpret at the level of implicature in order to identify the intended illocutionary force, a process which would have necessitated several implicated premises, which Moeschler spells out in the following way:

(a) Someone arriving in a foreign country needs some help.
(b) To travel downtown alone from the airport at night is not a good idea.
(c) To ask how to go from A to B is to ask for some help to go from A to B.

These implicated premises then enable the addressee to recover as the most salient meaning the implicated conclusion that the speaker is making a request to be picked up. However, the addressee will not process beyond the most readily accessible higher level explicature to an implicature, if, as clearly happened on this occasion, he's able to recover an apparently salient meaning without taking this additional step. This is especially likely when the interpretation is consistent with the addressee's cultural expectations. In other words, the implicated premises that Moeschler assumed would be recovered were not of the same degree of relevance to the addressee when called upon to interpret the message. Either of two situations is therefore required for a pick-me-up-at-the-airport request to be successful:

(a) Moeschler's message will convey the intended meaning if the addressee shares the same cultural understanding (although gauging degrees of shared cultural understanding is difficult even in an apparently homogeneous culture).

or

(b) Moeschler needs to know enough about the differences between his and the addressee's cultures to adapt his default communication style appropriately – in this case, to be more explicit about his request for help (which may be difficult for him given the different effect such explicitness would be likely to have in his own culture).

According to the relevance theoretic account, the misunderstanding that occurs in this case is therefore not a matter of language understanding but, as in the previous example, a consequence of the differing contextual resources of the interactants.

We'll return to this misunderstanding in Chapter 12 when we discuss intercultural communication in more detail. Meanwhile, Moeschler's experience shows in a persuasive way how Relevance Theory is able to account for miscommunications of this kind.

Summary

The uses of language discussed in this section show that Relevance Theory provides a psychologically plausible model of utterance understanding involving a trade-off between processing effort and the recovery of relevant assumptions in contexts that license them. The theory provides a psychological generalization across the process of utterance understanding which predicts ease and difficulty of interpretation.

6.4 Context and cognition

We round this chapter off by considering, first, the economy that inferential pragmatics affords and, second, the importance of psychological plausibility in a theory of inferred meaning.

6.4.1 Why implicature?

When we discussed deixis in Chapter 2, we suggested that it was useful to have a small number of lexical items whose reference was determined in the contexts in which they occurred. When we look at explicature, we see a similar principle at work, this time at the propositional level. Think how uneconomical language would be if there was a different grammatical structure for each of the logical meanings encoded even in simple possessive structures like *my mother's son, my mother's mother, my mother's friend, my mother's car, my mother's cooking, my mother's politics, my mother's foot*, etc. Like deixis, explicature and, especially, implicature allow us to make use of context in the interpretation of what is said to us, and thus make possible an immensely more economical language than we would otherwise need. It's obvious that without inference, virtually every utterance would need to be formally unique – not a very practical proposition!

Implicature is like deixis in another way too. Because it allows us to communicate meanings as inferences rather than entailments, it's particularly attuned to face-to-face communication. Being defeasible, inferences are by nature more tentative than entailments. In fact, we often expect that our addressees won't concur with the inferences we calculate they will recover from our talk. If you study business negotiation closely, you'll often discover that entailments are preferred for less controversial and implicatures for more controversial suggestions.

But implicatures also make possible the very opposite of tentative talk. Because an implicature assumes that speaker and hearer can access a meaning that is conveyed but not stated, it reinforces solidarity between them. When friends are in our house, I often notice that implicatures pass between members of our family that our friends don't recover. We use implicature as a confirmation of our solidarity and common knowledge.

The availability of implicature as a means of conveying meaning also means that we can let context do more of the work for us. Thus, there will be occasions on which we favour explicit encoding of meaning, others on which we convey meaning implicitly, and yet others on which we allow context 'to speak for itself'. For example, if my wife and I take the car somewhere, we don't usually need to discuss who'll drive, who'll sit where, where we'll park, etc. We let context speak for itself. However, if we offer a lift to someone whose habits we know less well, we negotiate where they want to go to, whether it would be all right if we dropped so-and-so off first, whether they'd mind sitting in the back, etc. Similarly, my wife and I need far fewer words to advise each other on whether a particular clothes purchase would be wise than I would think appropriate if I were to accompany you on a shopping trip for the first time. So if I say to my wife that something she is trying on looks like the one Maja has, only she will recover the implicature, and the shop assistant will be in the dark as to whether I'm recommending a purchase or not.

It seems probable that it's not only individuals who vary in the degree to which they favour explicit encoding, implicit encoding or letting context do the work. Whole cultures too divide into what Hall (1976) has called 'high context' cultures (where the context does more of the work) and 'low context' cultures (where the relationships between people frequently need to be negotiated linguistically). We already had a tiny, relatively trivial glimpse of this possibility in the previous chapter when we compared a sentence in the Cantonese and English versions of a parallel text and saw how the English version required *alcohol* to be recovered as an explicature whereas in Cantonese there are two options, either imply *alcohol* or explicitly state it. Single examples like this mean little when taken alone, of course, but I think you could reasonably argue that different types of cultural organization favour different default degrees of explicitness for conveying meanings. For example, we might hypothesize that

- Societies in which individualism is a positive value will favour implicature because the understanding is recovered by the message receiver rather than explicitly stated by the message originator.
- Societies where no clear distinction is made between in-group and out-group members will need to take into account a more pluralistic audience in communication situations, and will thus allow for the more individualized understandings that implicatures, as context-dependent inferences, permit.
- Societies that are orderly and have strong in-group identity will favour explicatures in which inferences preserve and elaborate the propositional forms of utterances. Although inferred, the recovered meanings are more conventional than meanings that are recovered as implicatures, where a new logical form is inferred.
- Implicatures are more frequent in low context culture discourse. This is because the default setting for human behaviour is high context which, in its prototypical manifestation, exhibits the phenomenon of no talk. But because relatively little can be taken for granted in low context cultures, speakers frequently use implicature to test the ground in the negotiation of meaning. This is possible because inferred meanings, unlike entailed propositions, are not truth correspondent.

Of course, these are mere hypotheses and would be regarded by some as controversial. However, in a study of Chinese and English business correspondence in Hong Kong (Grundy, 1998), I was able to show that more explicit encoding has a more directive force and suggests that decision making is concentrated in relatively few hands rather than being more broadly shared. Thus each type of cultural organization favours a particular communication style. Or, put the other way round, the way in which we make meanings salient is one of the ways in which we create the cultures to which we belong.

6.4.2 Figure, ground and relevance

In discussing the conversation between the nurse and Jordan, I tried to model what might be going through Jordan's mind when the nurse asked him for a date. Relevance Theory is an attempt to show how cognition is involved in determining what someone means by what they say. The cognitive process triggered by an utterance begins, as we've seen, with the ostensive act which engages an addressee in cognitive processing. This ostension creates a figure which stands out against an immense background of information, verbal and non-verbal, most of which we ignore.

On two or three occasions in earlier chapters, I've also drawn attention to the figure/ground properties of language, including Talmy's figure/ground explanation of temporal clauses and presupposition in Chapter 3.

The figure/ground *gestalt* was first applied to visual perception by Rubin early in the twentieth century. It seems that human beings are cognitively wired to see objects as figures in a background. This accounts for our ability to recall the outline shape of a person or object with ease and for the immense difficulty we have in conceptualizing the background shape from which the figure is excised. You can try it now: picture the outline of the word you're going to read after the dash – easy! Now picture the outline of the page with the word 'easy' removed – impossible. It seems that the shape which distinguishes the words, the figure, from the background, the page, belongs to the words and not to the page. Of course, it's very fortunate that things are like this because otherwise we wouldn't be able to process relative salience, or, if you prefer, relevance, in the sea of stimuli that confront us.

It's easy to see why the figure/ground *gestalt* has interested cognitive linguists such as Talmy. It provides an explanatory account of the way language is and the way it needs to be to be useful to humans. Presuppositions are, then, part of the (back)ground against which assertions and other figures are foregrounded. Sometimes the ground is explicit (as in the case of 'semantic' presuppositions), sometimes implicit (as in the case of 'pragmatic' presuppositions).

As well as in stressing the importance of figure-creating ostension, Relevance Theory acknowledges a figure/ground understanding of information in a number of other ways. Saying that an utterance comes with a guarantee of its own relevance is another way of describing a figure, distinguishable once the ground or context which proves its relevance is identified.

Explicatures too are a ground we infer. Recall the dentist's letter in *The Times* and the understanding of 'and' as <and in that way> that the tongue-in-cheek reading requires. This piece of gapped information is recovered as an inference which, like explicatures in general, fill in the background implied by the lexical items that stand in relation to them as figures. In the same way, when I tell the restaurant owner in Florence that I was 'younger', I don't need to tell him what I was younger than because this is so self-evidently a part of the background – it's the figure, <that I was younger then>, that I want to draw his attention to. And notice how when I began my conference talk by explaining that I'd returned from Hong Kong two days earlier, I used each part of my utterance as first a figure and then a ground against which to evaluate the relevance of what I said next:

	What's said / figure	Context / ground
(38)	I returned from Hong Kong two days ago	SARS epidemic
(39)	Don't worry I'm not ill	SARS epidemic + (38)
(40)	<cough cough>	SARS epidemic + (38) + (39)

Sometimes, a speaker exploits the gapped ground for particular effect. I was recently on a train where the following exchange occurred:

(41) PASSENGER 1: Can you tell me what time it gets into Plymouth
GUARD: <looks in timetable book> Quarter to six
PASSENGER 2: Tomorrow

In the normal way, the gapped information, <today>, in the Guard's reply to the passenger's inquiry is part of the implicit ground in relation to which 'quarter to six' is a figure. Notice that this remains the ground in relation to which the sarcastic passenger's 'tomorrow' is understood.

As we see, Relevance Theory invites us to consider cognitive processes at a number of levels and in a way that the more rationalistic Gricean and neo-Gricean proposals do not.

Raising pragmatic awareness

1 This exercise works best in a small group. Each person should think up a sentence. Write all the sentences up in random order on the board. Try to see how each sentence could be relevant in the context provided by the previous sentences. As you do this, think about the problems anyone would have in working out the connections for themselves and what contextual resources are required. Try inserting additional sentences to reduce the processing effort required of the reader.

2 In your tutorial group, choose any of the keywords at the beginning of this chapter and write an entry for your chosen word for a Dictionary of Pragmatics. Compare your proposed entry with those of colleagues.

3 Record a short conversation between friends before your next tutorial. Choose three or four utterances and ask your colleagues to help you decide on the enrichment necessary to provide full propositional forms for them.

4 Working with the data collected in (3), try to identify utterances where the next speaker takes (a) the explicature, (b) the higher level explicature, and (c) the implicature as the most salient meaning.

5 Listen out for utterances whose relevance you could only determine with difficulty, or maybe couldn't determine at all. Report them to your tutorial group and explain why you think they were problematical for you.

6 Which of the features of talk identified as typically pragmatic in Chapter 1 play an important part in Relevance Theory: accommodation, appropriateness, context, indeterminacy, indirect meaning, inference, reflexivity, relevance?

Discussions and essays

Based on what you know about Relevance Theory, discuss the relative merits of each of the following views:

- Sperber and Wilson's account of implied meaning is to be preferred to Grice's because it has greater psychological plausibility.
- The postulation of explicatures and implicatures in Relevance Theory suggests that language is indeterminate in two quite different ways.
- "In verbal comprehension in particular, it is relevance which is treated as given and context which is treated as a variable." (Sperber and Wilson, 1995: 142)
- Grice's Cooperative Principle and the maxims capture a wider generalization about implied meaning than the work of either the neo-Griceans or Sperber and Wilson.
- The possibility of flouting maxims is a weakness in Grice's theory that both neo-Gricean approaches and Relevance Theory remedy.

Further reading

Primary texts

Sperber and Wilson, 1995; Carston, 1988, in Davis, 1991: 33–50; Wilson and Sperber, 1993.

Textbooks

Blakemore, 1992.

Handbook

Wilson and Sperber, 2004.

7 Metapragmatic awareness

'Well it's only if I mean you know if she's got a or if she needs the ground prepared as it were because obviously if she goes out she's got to succeed if it were whereas I can go out and just talk'.

British Prime Minister Blair discussing with President Bush the visit to the Middle East of American Secretary of State Condoleezza Rice

Keywords:

account, formulation, hedge, logical encoding, metalinguistic awareness, metapragmatic, metasequential, method, repair, troubles talk

7.1 Introduction

Because utterances serve different purposes in the different contexts in which they occur, their pragmatic interpretation will sometimes be effortful and even problematic. When speakers feel that this is likely, they typically use metapragmatic marking to guide addressees in the way they want what they say to be understood. So the pharmacist who wants to be sure that I understand 'they make you drowsy' as a warning adds the metapragmatic marker 'mind' to her utterance. And because I want to be sure that the colleague who reads my letter understands the relationship of what I write to the previous discourse, I say, 'There must *therefore* be a very good case for not allowing anyone to proceed to Year 3.' And when I answer Branka's question about the time of my return, I use 'but' to indicate that the second part of what I say is to be contrasted with the first part:

(1) BRANKA: When will you be back
PETER: I should be back by eight but you know what trains are like

I need to use 'but' because the unusual relationship between the first part of what I say and the second part isn't otherwise easy to recover, as (1′) shows:

(1′) BRANKA: When will you be back
PETER: I should be back by eight. You know what trains are like

'But' therefore functions as a processing instruction, constraining the possible interpretations that (1′) would invite and reducing the inferential effort required to recover the meaning I intend. As we might expect, this procedural instruction applies before the inferential process begins: in (1), 'but' indicates a relationship between 'I should be back by eight' and 'you know what trains are like', not between the Q-inferred 'I probably won't be back by eight' and 'you know what trains are like', as (1″) shows

(1″) BRANKA: When will you be back
PETER: I probably won't be back by eight but you know what trains are like

So it seems that the meta-function applies not only to the literal level but also to the pragmatic. That's to say, we can both ask what a particular expression means (a metalinguistic inquiry), and ask what someone means by using a particular expression (a metapragmatic inquiry). And we can use items like 'mind', 'therefore' and 'but' metapragmatically in a way that shows our awareness of the effects of language and its appropriate use. If we define pragmatics as the study of what we do with words in the contexts in which we use them to accomplish acts and to convey meanings beyond what is stated literally, then metapragmatics affords us ways of signalling our awareness of what we do with words to accomplish acts and to convey meanings beyond what is stated literally. This chapter explores the way this signalling is accomplished and the effects it has.

The chapter contains three further sections, each of which includes several sub-sections:

- *Metapragmatic and metasequential phenomena*, which explores the range of means available to language users of encoding their awareness of the pragmatic effects of what they say.
- *Metapragmatic marking in the real world*, in which three extended examples of metapragmatically marked talk are discussed in detail.
- *Intonation and metalinguistic awareness*, which discusses metapragmatic marking and the diacritic role of intonation as a means of conveying pragmatic and metapragmatic meaning.

7.2 Metapragmatic and metasequential phenomena

We begin this section with two folk views of metapragmatic phenomena, then present a more complete taxonomy before finally considering the way in which metapragmatic phenomena may also have a metasequential function.

7.2.1 Lay awareness and folk attitudes

Linguists tend to dismiss folk, or lay, attitudes to language because they are often value-laden and prescriptive rather than descriptive or explanatory. However, folk views provide insights into language users' conscious awareness. Because metapragmatic phenomena are so pervasive, it's not surprising that they sometimes attract lay comment, as these two letters in *The Times* show. The first was published on 2 June 1999:

(2) Sir, Please would you join me in a campaign to ban the words 'basically', 'essentially' and 'actually' from media and everyday speech?

Basically, if we could remove those words, it would actually add to the time that is essentially available for meaningful language by anything up to a third. And you would remove what is actually, basically and essentially an irritating substitute for 'um' – which at least has the virtue of brevity.

The second letter, from which I quote only a couple of sentences, was published on 25 March 2004:

(3) Why do speakers find it necessary to use 'you know what I mean' so frequently? Unnecessary, surely, if they have stated their thoughts clearly.

In Chapter 1, I used the term 'reflexive' to describe the way in which one part of what we say provides a comment on how a speaker wants to be understood or on how an utterance fits into the discourse as a whole. What the letter writers are objecting to is the (over-)use of language with this reflexive function. No doubt the second sentence of the first letter would be just as clear without the adverbs the writer uses ironically. But when used non-ironically, *basically* usually tells us that the writer is putting something economically and simply, *actually* tells us that what is said is trustworthy if unexpected, and *essentially* tells us that the proposition is perspicuous and relevant. And as we saw in Chapter 1 and again in our discussion of hedges in Chapter 5 and procedural encoding in Chapter 6, there are times when sentence adverbs have their uses. Indeed, there are times when they are essential, as we saw in the previous chapter when I failed to understand Alice's message for want of a *so*.

Much the same could be said about the second letter writer's pet hate, 'you know what I mean', which, as we saw in Chapter 1, I used to correct an unintended inference from 'my wife's very saucy' and which the barmaid used to correct an unintended inference from the form of words she chose when offering to serve a customer. In a sense, the letter writer is right to suggest that 'you know what I mean' repairs an unclear message. But think how much worse off we'd be if this option wasn't available.

And although the letter writers object to metapragmatic marking, they are rather hoist with their own petard: the first correspondent finds 'at least' a useful way of advising us of how to take 'which . . . has the virtue of brevity' and the second correspondent uses 'surely' to intensify the quality of 'unnecessary'.

As we'll see in the rest of this chapter, metapragmatic phenomena include a much wider range of items than those that displease *Times* correspondents. In many cases they are more closely integrated with conceptual meaning than the sentence adverbs and the corrective sentence considered above, and therefore (!) perhaps (!) less likely to attract folk attention of the kind displayed in the *Times* letters.

7.2.2 Metapragmatic awareness

As with most language use, and despite what was said in the previous sub-section, we tend to have relatively little conscious awareness of the metapragmatic dimension of our utterances. Just occasionally our awareness of the pragmatic dimension is conscious, as when the witness of the Oklahoma bomb describes himself as 'speechless' and the space probe professor says

(4) I can't tell you how exciting it is to be involved in the whole thing

However, this doesn't mean that we don't know what we're doing when we use language – just that our knowledge is tacit. In fact, metapragmatic use is much more pervasive than we usually notice. In a detailed paper exploring the extent of pragmatic metalanguage, Verschueren (2000) distinguishes explicit from implicit metalanguage. He argues that any item which reflects awareness of pragmatic effect has metapragmatic function. The explicit items he draws attention to include:

- **metapragmatic descriptions**, a category which includes both performative verbs and speech act descriptions. Recall my comment on the effect of the trainee's utterance on the postmaster in Chapter 4:

(5) That shut him up he's usually got something to say

Here the speech act descriptions <shut *x* up> and <got something to say> reflect my awareness of the pragmatic uses and effects of language. Or the use of 'rumours' by the man in the bar and the stallholder's inexplicit description 'the way you said it' in the market. In a paper on 'meta-talk', Schiffrin (1987) distinguishes three categories of what she calls 'metalinguistic verbs', verbs of saying (*say, tell, ask*, etc.), descriptions of talk functions (*clarify, define*, etc.) and speech event descriptions (*quarrel, joke*, etc.). In his account of 'reflexive language', Lucy (1993) covers the same ground as Schiffrin and Verschueren with the term 'metalinguistic use', defined as "a way of referring to events of speech". Similarly, what Lucy calls 'comments about language', such as *metapragmatic phenomena are pervasive*, show a similar kind of awareness. It's also worth noticing that speech act descriptions of this kind typically require inferential enrichment: for example, when my boss says 'I told you that', he doesn't describe the same speech act as I describe when I say it to him.

- **self-referential expressions** such as *this argument, my talk*, and *these perspectives*.
- **discourse markers** or **pragmatic particles** such as *anyway, undoubtedly* and *you know*. In my sentence in the previous sub-section

  (6) . . . and therefore perhaps less likely to attract folk attention

  'therefore' shows awareness of the relationship between the previous part of the sentence and the upcoming part, and 'perhaps' indicates my degree of commitment to the ontology of 'less likely to attract attention'.
- **sentence adverbs** such as *frankly, regrettably* and *obviously*. These sentence adverbs have a higher level function and indicate propositional attitude. Schiffrin draws attention to the comparable 'meta' function of higher level predicates such as *right, wrong* and *probable*. This awareness is shown in 'less likely to attract attention' in (6) and in Clinton's

  (7) Indeed I did have a relationship with Ms Lewinsky that was not appropriate. In fact, it was wrong.

  Here the higher level predicates 'not appropriate' and 'wrong' are used to make metalinguistic judgements about 'I did have a relationship with Ms Lewinsky'. And the sentence adverbs 'indeed' and 'in fact' encode propositional attitudes.
- **hedges** such as *sort of, in a sense* and *so far as I know*.
- **explicit intertextual links** such as *namely, for example* and *similarly*. Another kind of intertextual awareness is shown by what Schiffrin calls 'metalinguistic referents', such as *the former, the latter* and *the next point*.
- **quoted and reported speech**. You'll recall our discussion in Chapter 2 of the various extents to which quoted speech and encodings of reported speech reflect the deictic centres of the original and the reporting speaker. As well as these degrees of quotation/reportedness, glosses too may sometimes appear to be more like reported speech than speech act descriptions. Consider

  (8) A: The lecturer said he didn't know who I was
  B: I think he was pretending not to know you

  Here B glosses what the lecturer had said to A, using a metalinguistic description that shows metapragmatic awareness. This example and our Chapter 2 discussions give a small insight into the complexity of reported speech, which is discussed more fully by the contributors to Lucy's (1993) book *Reflexive Language: Reported Speech and Metapragmatics*.

- **mention**, an occurrence of an item with overt metalinguistic marking, as in:

  (9) The name 'Oxfam' is a contraction of 'Oxford Committee for Famine Relief'

  In written language, we often mark our metalinguistic awareness with quotation marks, as I did in (9). Sometimes the boundary between quotation and mention is hard to determine, as in the case of Mr Neale in Chapter 1 where what appears to be a quotation is also intended to be read metalinguistically:

  (10) People living nearby said Mr Neale would go away on 'lengthy business trips'

- **evidentials**, which mark the source/reliability of an utterance, such as 'I suppose' in

  (11) I suppose today it's especially important to be thinking carefully about what our students say to us

  Memory claims such as *(so far as) I recall, what I remember is*, etc. also make overt reference to the evidentiality of what is stated.

- **contextualization cues**, including control items such as *right, so, okay*, etc., and other overt indications of awareness of the effect of talk such as *oh, sorry* (= *I didn't expect you to say that*), etc.

Checking understanding (7.1)

1 How would you categorize the metalinguistic phenomena in the following?

(12) The word 'well' is a hedge
(13) Pragmatics, the module with four assignments
(14) Hedging is typical in lecturer-speak
(15) He said, 'You're nuts'
(16) She criticized me
(17) Let's put it this way
(18) I give you my word
(19) All the same
(20) Fortunately, it's unlikely
(21) By the way, the seminar was yesterday
(22) I guess this exercise has been challenging
(23) OK, enough's enough

2 Think up several examples of your own of mention, gloss, comment, quotation, and reference to events of speech.

3 Starting with *mind*, make a list of illocutionary force indicating devices and indicate their metapragmatic functions.

Among implicit metalinguistic phenomena, Verschueren lists:

- **deictics**, which are metapragmatic because, as Lucy says, they "reflexively take account of the ongoing event of speaking itself, in terms of which we can use and understand their referential and predicational value" (1993: 10). Deictics show metalinguistic awareness implicitly because they have a prior explicit function as demonstratives. But because understanding what is picked out and referred to by deictics depends on establishing a relation to the speech event in which they occur, they also implicitly refer to the speech event itself. Silverstein discusses indexicals as multifunctional because they combine 'semantico-referential' properties which are found in all the speech events in which they occur with indexical functions that are utterance specific and therefore reflexive (1976: 21,46).

- **aspect**, as in the case of English perfect which links an event to present time (present perfect) or to a past time (past perfect). Aspect may also affect our interpretation of the lexical verb, as in 'he was shot' (simple aspect) and 'he was being shot' (progressive aspect), which result in different mental representations of 'shot'.
- **mood and modality**. Because modality conveys the speaker's epistemic stance, his/her estimation of the degree of probability of an event, etc., it implicitly encodes metapragmatic awareness.
- **evidentials** such as *seems* and *likely*. These are implicit because they are fully integrated in the discourse, unlike explicit evidentials like *I guess*.
- **contextualization cues**, including prosody and intonation, code switching, fillers (such as *um*), hesitation markers (such as *er*) and pauses.
- **implicit voice**, or 'footing' (Levinson, 1988), i.e. the extent to which a speaker indicates self-ownership or other-ownership of content and commitment to it.

Checking understanding (7.2)

Identify the explicit and implicit metalanguage in

(24) INTERVIEWER: Can you tell us what the possible benefits of this new vaccine are
INTERVIEWEE: Well we desperately need a vaccine against this dreadful killer
(radio interview about a malaria vaccine)

(25) PETER: But they still get coffee made in Old Shire Hall
CARLA: But there is the seat of power
PETER: Well here is the receipt of power
(discussion about the withdrawal of the tea-lady from academic but not administrative departments)

(26) ASSISTANT: Is it for a sink or a bath
CUSTOMER: Haven't a clue mate I'd be guessing
ASSISTANT: My you're quick off the mark in Newcastle. Right on the ball like
(Service encounter in a builders merchant. The customer is wearing Newcastle Council uniform)

(27) BLAIR: Well it's only if I mean you know if she's got a or if she needs the ground prepared as it were because obviously if she goes out she's got to succeed if it were whereas I can go out and just talk

7.2.3 Metasequential awareness

Consider another utterance first discussed in Chapter 1:

(28) Right, shall we begin

Here, the contextualization cue 'right' has the metapragmatic function of advising us of the speaker's intention to be business-like. But it also tells us something about the place of the speaker's utterance in the wider discourse. It seems to be a conversational **method** for getting attention, prior to an act of ostension. As such, it's appropriate only when a (new) speaker wants to change the direction of the talk or to re-assert his or her hold on the floor, particularly when things need moving on. In other words, it tells us something about the place of the proposition in the wider talk or discourse context. I'm going to use the term **metasequential** to describe demonstrations by speakers of their metapragmatic awareness of the kinds of contributions they make to an ongoing piece of talk or, as the next example demonstrates, to a written discourse.

Keyword:

Method: a technical term used to describe the types of things we do when we talk. The most obvious method is turn taking.

If we reconsider

(29) There must therefore be a very good case for not allowing anyone to proceed to Year 3

we see that the function of 'therefore' isn't only metapragmatic. As well as its procedural function in helping us to interpret the proposition in an appropriate context, 'therefore' also marks a **formulation** consequent on what has gone before and as such has a metasequential function. We shouldn't be surprised to find that an expression has two functions – after all, speakers are simultaneously conveying pragmatic meanings and ensuring the procedural consequentiality of the talk exchanges or written discourse to which they are contributing.

Keyword:

Formulation: a method used in talk for indicating the significance or consequentiality of what's been said previously. Formulations are often signalled metasequentially by *so*.

'So' if we define sequentiality as the way in which contributions to talk construct the events of talk as movings-on, formulations, etc., then metasequentiality affords us ways of signalling our awareness of the way in which contributions to talk construct the events of talk as movings-on, formulations, etc. As we shall see shortly when we consider metapragmatic marking in the real world, metasequential awareness plays a very important role in talk. This is presumably because syntax, the binding principle within an utterance, doesn't apply across the separate utterances of a discourse. Because ongoing talk is essentially paratactic, procedural constraints help to ensure that the function of a contribution in a discourse is understood.

Checking understanding (7.3)

1 Metasequential references to the organization of talk occur frequently. For example, we say 'moving on' and 'let me explain that next'. Can you supply examples of any of the following?:

(a) metasequential descriptions;
(b) descriptions of talk events;
(c) conversational markers or particles.

2 Do you think any of the metapragmatic categories listed earlier also apply metasequentially: self-referential expressions, sentence adverbs, explicit intertextual links, gloss, contextualization cues?

7.2.4 From taxonomy to dimension

Levinson points out that Q- and M-inferences are metalinguistic because they make implicit reference to other, non-present members of a set (Q-inferences) or to unmarked but non-present expressions (M-inferences). In the same way, a speech act description like *claim* is metapragmatic not merely because it shows awareness of what is done when we make some 'claim' about *x*, but also because it implicitly relates what we say to other speech act descriptions that we didn't choose, such as *argue, contend, state,* etc. Could it be that the taxonomic approach we've been following in listing metapragmatic markers of various kinds misses the real point, that metalinguistic awareness is a dimension of language present in everything we say? This is Verschueren's 'claim':

> A second way of approaching 'Metalanguage' is to look at it as a dimension of language – to be found in *all* language use – rather than a collection of instances of Metalinguistic language use . . . it [this dimension] moves . . . into the realm of basic properties of any stretch of discourse. (2000: 440)

He continues:

> There is a constant interaction between pragmatic and metapragmatic functioning. This observation definitely lifts metapragmatics or Metalanguage (seen as a dimension rather than an object) from the merely interesting and useful to the absolutely necessary if we want to understand language use. (ibid.: 442)

While work on the explicit ways in which we mark our pragmatic awareness, for example, by means of discourse particles and hedges, attracted early researchers, in fact, the implicit nature of our metapragmatic and metasequential understanding is in many ways more remarkable. We monitor everything we say for intelligibility and appropriateness. At the level of the utterance, we are likely to be most concerned with constraining or assisting pragmatic interpretation. In ongoing talk, we are also concerned to make clear the nature of each contribution as a talk type or method. In the following section we see how pervasive both metapragmatic and metasequential marking are in real-world language use.

7.3 Metapragmatic marking in the real world

In this section we show the role of metalinguistic awareness in three real-world speech events, examining both extended single speaker contributions to talk and multi-speaker interaction.

7.3.1 Giving evidence

In this sub-section I discuss evidence given by the then Pro-Vice-Chancellor for Academic and Student Affairs at Hong Kong University to an Investigation Panel set up to investigate a case of alleged interference with academic freedom. In his testimony, the PVC, Professor Wong, describes two meetings he arranged with Robert Chung, a PhD student he was supervising. At these meetings, the Professor Wong relayed the displeasure of the then Hong Kong Chief Executive at the monthly opinion polls conducted by Robert Chung into the Chief Executive's perceived performance, and suggested that they should be abandoned. Robert Chung also gave evidence to the Panel. The significant differences in the way each witness gives evidence are particularly evident in the metapragmatic awareness each displays.

7.3.1.1 Speech event descriptions

Wong describes the speech event variously as a 'conversation'

(30) In the conversation, I also realised

and a 'meeting'

(31) part of the purpose of the meeting

Overall he uses the description 'meeting' or 'meet' twenty-five times and the term 'conversation' four times in his evidence. Chung uses the term 'conversation' seventeen times and 'meeting' or 'meet' twelve. This suggests that Wong conceptualizes the event as a more formal encounter. But Chung uses one or the other of these descriptive terms four times as frequently as Wong in relation to the first of their two 'meetings', perhaps suggesting that the event itself is psychologically prominent.

Here is the wide context in which Wong refers to the event as a 'meeting' and a 'conversation'. The data are set out as in the Investigation Panel's final report, except that I've italicized metalinguistic phenomena:

(32)
Page 71
In the *conversation*, I *also* realised that there might be
misperceptions, *therefore*, I *clarified* right at the
beginning that I *was relating to him views expressed by*
other people that I had heard, and *I thought he should*
take note of them. I did not necessary share those
views, *therefore* I *made it very clear* that part of the
purpose of the *meeting* was for him to be aware of the
concerns that I gathered from different sources.
But then I *said* my main *concern* for the *meeting*

Page 72
was not to find out *who said what. So* I never went back
to *say* whether we had double-checked whether a certain

person really *said* such things. I *was concerned about*
the substance of the *comments*, and I *think* there was
the real substance being *mentioned.*

(Evidence given on 11 August 2000 by Wong Siu-Lun relating to a meeting held with Robert Chung on 29 January 1999.)

7.3.1.2 Speech act descriptions

Speech act descriptions are chosen from a wide set of possible alternatives. Because speakers choose descriptions that encode their belief systems, they are ways of encoding ideology. In this light, we may find the ideological encoding of Wong's speech act descriptions revealing: 'clarified' (71/18), 'was relating to him views expressed by other people that I had heard' (71/19–20), 'I thought he should take note of' (71/20–1), 'made it very clear' (71/22), 'said my main concern' (71/25), 'say' (72/2), 'was concerned about' (72/3). In this way, Wong interprets his own speech acts to Chung. Such interpretations of the speaker's own speech acts occur three-and-a-half times as frequently in Wong's testimony as in Chung's. Wong also provides speech act descriptions of third party linguistic acts, as in 'concerns that I gathered from different sources' (71/24), 'who said what' (72/1), 'said such things' (72/3), 'comments' (72/4) and 'the real substance being mentioned' (72/5). He does this more than twice as frequently as Chung, perhaps suggesting that he is pulling rank.

7.3.1.3 Logical encoding

Wong's evidence shows attention to logical encoding as he tries to show the coherence of each of his actions. In this extract, he uses 'also' (71/17), 'therefore' (71/18, 71/22), 'but then' (71/25) and 'so' (72/1). In the entire testimony, Wong uses a much wider range of connectives than Chung. Wong's connectives occur at the rate of 1 in every 4.9 lines of testimony, Chung's at the rate of 1 in every 16.5 lines. The commonest connective type is causal (*so, because*, etc.), accounting for 70 per cent of Wong's and 53 per cent of Chung's logical encodings. Causal connectives frequently have metasequential as well as metapragmatic function. For example, *so* invites us to assume a deductive relationship in the organization of talk between what follows and what has preceded the connective. In this way, witnesses seek to justify their actions and to guide the formulations of consequentiality that the Panel will see in their actions. This is especially clear in the following uses of 'so' (italicized by me) in Wong's data:

(33)
I divided my working day
Page 70
into the morning working in the PVC's office and in the
afternoon at the Centre of Asian Studies.
→ *So* on that day, one of the reasons the meeting was
held in my PVC's office was that I could only meet him
→ in the morning, *so* that was the first reason. Then
secondly, I also knew that Robert would be having his
oral examination for his PhD thesis in a few days' time,
→ that was on 2nd February 1999, *so* I did not want him to
have any misconceptions, because I was not supposed to
→ talk about his exams before the examination. *So*
I deliberately avoided asking him to meet me at the
Centre of Asian Studies, where we generally discuss his

→ PhD work. *So* those were the two main reasons why we met
at the PVC's office.
→ *So* at the start if the conversation, I mentioned
to him that I wanted to keep the conversation private,

The importance of logical encodings of this sort is that they seek to constrain interpretations and, frequently, to establish logical relations that might not otherwise be inferred.

Summary

As we see, these encodings of metalinguistic awareness and their intended metapragmatic and metasequential effects differ between the two principal witnesses. The metapragmatic dimension of their evidence isn't adequately represented by a taxonomic inventory of categories of item because it pervades all that is said. It's an integral dimension of their talk and a means of encoding ideology.

Did his attempts to constrain the Panel's interpretation help Professor Wong? After hearing evidence for eleven days, the Panel concluded that undue pressure was put on Chung with the intention of restricting his academic freedom. Subsequently, the Vice-Chancellor and Pro-Vice-Chancellor Wong resigned.

For a fuller discussion of these data, see Grundy and Jiang, 2005.

Checking understanding (7.4)

Try and identify indications of metalinguistic awareness in the following extract from Professor Wong's testimony relating to his 1 November meeting with Robert Chung.

(34)

So that comment I heard from the vice-chancellor
reminded me –
THE CHAIRMAN: You have not told us what that comment was,
nor to whom it was made. Could you please say what it
was – say it in English or in Cantonese – and say who
else was there at the time.

Page 108

W. Mr Chairman, I cannot recall exactly the wording. It
was in Cantonese, but I cannot recall exactly the
phrasing of it. I can only remember the gist, that
because the name of the University was involved, and he
did not want the University to be involved in political
debates.
THE CHAIRMAN: To whom was that comment made?
W. I remember it was in the open area of the
vice-chancellor's office, where the newspapers were
put. So it was in the general area. There are

Checking understanding (7.4) *cont.*

secretaries around.

THE CHAIRMAN: To whom was the vice-chancellor speaking?

W. I think the vice-chancellor was reading the newspaper. I just came in, if I remember, to the general office. His secretary was there. I do not remember whether other people were there. But he mentioned that, and I heard that comment. Therefore, when I went back to my office, I took that copy of the Morning Post and read it myself.

7.3.2 Metalinguistic awareness in talk

In this section, we examine an encounter between the warden of a student hostel, known as 'The Doctor' on account of his having recently been awarded a PhD, and two students, Nicole and Susie, on the staircase one evening. This is how the conversation opens:

(35) DOCTOR: how's it doing
SUSIE: yeah no erm Nicole wants to no we need a word with you
DOCTOR: [oh right]
NICOLE: [no]

> Transcription key
> The deep brackets indicate that the Doctor's 'right' and Nicole's 'no' overlap, i.e. they're spoken simultaneously

Susie's response to the Doctor's opening greeting 'how's it doing' is not the preferred greeting. Instead she begins with three metasequential particles, 'yeah' (= I hear your greeting), 'no' (= but we have business to transact), 'erm' (= how to begin?). (My interpretations are obviously challengeable, so do feel free to think through your own both here and in the continuing analysis.) Susie's second use of 'no' signals a **repair** from the relatively informal 'Nicole wants to' to the official trouble-reporting register 'we need a word with you'. The Doctor acknowledges this turn with the metapragmatic 'oh' (= a surprise) and the metasequential 'right' (= I understand it's to be **troubles talk**).

Keywords:

Repair: a method used in talk in which a speaker rephrases what has just been said in order to make it clearer. Sometimes repairs occur before an utterance is complete, so that a speaker appears to change direction as they talk.
Troubles talk: a type of talk in which a problem that needs to be resolved is discussed.

As Susie's opening turn selects Nicole as next speaker after the Doctor, Nicole now continues with a metasequential 'no' (= it's not small talk). She then reports 'someone's been nicking stuff out the fridge':

(36) DOCTOR: oh [right]
NICOLE: [no] someone's been nicking stuff out the fridge (2.0) so

> Transcription key
> (2.0) indicates a two-second pause.

At the end of this brief **account** there's a long pause, but the expected next speaker, the Doctor, doesn't self-select, so Nicole provides the metasequential marker of an upcoming formulation, 'so', and then stops again. Typically the speaker who provides an account of an event also provides a formulation in which the consequence of what's just been said is stated. But in some talk-types, including seemingly this one, the authority to whom the trouble is reported is expected to decide the outcome.

> **Keyword:**
>
> **Account**: a method used in talk for describing a series of events. Accounts are often followed by formulations.

However, the Doctor seeks more information before determining what should be done:

(37) DOCTOR: which one
NICOLE: ours (.) well Susie's butter's gone and my cheese has gone as well

> Transcription key
> (.) indicates a micro-pause roughly equivalent to the time it takes to utter a single syllable.

The Doctor asks 'which one'. Nicole gives the minimal response 'ours' (= which did you expect?). She then pauses before signalling metapragmatically, and maybe metasequentially, ('well'), that the upcoming contribution is to be slightly unexpected. In fact, the agentless description 'Susie's butter's gone and my cheese has gone as well' is a 'more polite' way of conveying the proposition already conveyed by 'someone's been nicking', in her previous turn. The effect of this rephrasing is to slightly enlarge the distance between herself and the Doctor, and therefore to stress the official nature of the talk.

The Doctor's metasequential 'right yeah' acknowledges Nicole's turn and invites her to continue:

(38) DOCTOR: right [yeah]
NICOLE: [like] I opened new packets and stuff so=
DOCTOR: =right the whole lot
NICOLE: yeah

> Transcription key
> = at the end of Nicole's turn and the beginning of the Doctor's indicate that their turns are 'latched', i.e. there's no discernible pause between them.

Nicole continues with a metalinguistic and implicitly metapragmatic 'like' (= does what comes next match your expectation), followed by another element in her account of the event, 'I opened new packets and stuff'. Her turn ends with an invitation to the Doctor to formulate, 'so', which he appears to anticipate. Being unwilling to formulate, in his next turn he confirms that he has understood (metasequential 'right'), adding a supplementary inquiry, 'the whole lot', which Nicole confirms with a minimal 'yeah'.

You may wish to quarrel in places with my suggested analysis, but the general point is clear – that speakers use a wide range of metasequential markers to help them to make clear to each other what the status of each of their contributions to the talk is and what they expect by way of contributions from each other. If you listen in an aware way to the conversations that go on around you, you'll notice how prevalent such metasequential markers are and how they usually pass without notice.

One way of looking at the talk exchange up to the moment (which has not yet come) at which the Doctor agrees to determine an outcome is to regard the troubles reporting as a preliminary stage in the conversation. The Doctor seems keen to extend this part of the exchange as far as possible, as his next question, prefaced by the metapragmatic/metasequential 'well' (= don't expect the contribution you hoped for), shows:

(39) DOCTOR: well do you actually know when it happened
NICOLE: erm (.) right it was there on Friday and we went to get it yesterday and it wasn't there so
SUSIE: yeah

Although Nicole stops short of formulating what is readily inferred as an explicature, the metasequential marker of the upcoming formulation, 'so', still occurs. Susie's confirmation of Nicole's account, 'yeah', invites the Doctor to self-select and proceed to a determination of what's to be done.

In the next phase of the conversation, the Doctor proposes an outcome:

(40) DOCTOR: right erm (2.0) there not a lot (.) can do about it I can sort of like .hh (2.0) have a word with people if you want
(1.5)
DOCTOR: erm .hh (3.0) I mean (.) do you do you want to sort of like have a word with everyone or just (.) do you want us to put a sign up or
(1.5)

Transcription key
.hh indicates an audible in-drawn breath.

The Doctor's proposed outcome is signalled metasequentially with 'right', which acknowledges the students' previous turns and projects his own upcoming contribution, and with 'erm' and a pause, which signals a shift to a new method, which involves determining a consequent course of action. This is followed by a metalinguistic comment on the courses of action open to him, 'there not a lot (.) can do about it'. The first two of the three suggested options are also metalinguistically hedged and the last two tail off with suggestions that there might be alternatives, although these are not explicitly stated and cannot be recovered as explicatures:

(40a) I can sort of like .hh (2.0) have a word with people if you want (1.5)
(40b) erm .hh (3.0) I mean (.) do you do you want to sort of like have a word with everyone or just (.)
(40c) do you want us to put a sign up or

The first suggestion, that the Doctor should 'have a word with people', is framed as an offer. The 1.5-second pause that follows it invites a response, but neither of the students wishes to accept this offer. Rather than explicitly reject it, a strongly dispreferred strategy especially given the authority status of the warden, they remain silent.

The second proposed course of action, (40b), begins with a metasequential pause ('erm'), an in-drawn breath ('.hh'), a further pause, and the Doctor's metasequential signal of a formulation unlikely to be received positively ('I mean'). This formulation is the least 'official' of the three courses of action proposed, hence the signal 'I mean'. It's also the least attractive to the students because they could already have taken this course of action without the Doctor's help. He orients to this least-attractive status of his suggestion by the very short micro-pause before his third suggestion

(40c) do you want us to put a sign up or

Although all three suggestions orient to the official nature of the proposed courses of action in their register ('have a word with people', 'have a word with everyone' and 'put a sign up'), only this third suggestion encodes the Doctor's status with the use of institutional 'us' to refer to himself.

There is a further significant pause at this point, but this time the Doctor doesn't take up the turn, and Nicole then accepts his third, and, because third, presumably his least favoured, suggestion. She orients to the unsatisfactory nature even of this third proposal with the predicate 'do' and the metapragmatic tag 'won't it':

(41) NICOLE: yeah a sign'll do won't it
DOCTOR: on near the fridge
NICOLE: yeah
DOCTOR: (. .) and on the pantry door it's just the one upstairs isn't it next to the showers

It seems that conversational preference conventions oblige her to accept a third suggestion even if she isn't happy with it, as she signals metapragmatically. Having got Nicole's reluctant agreement, the Doctor is then quick to confirm the places where the notices are to be placed, and orients to his relative unfamiliarity with the location of fridges by asking for confirmation that 'it's just the one upstairs' with the metapragmatic tag, 'isn't it'.

So far we've said nothing about the distal (i.e. non-immediate) context, the Doctor's responsibility for dealing with problems of the kind being reported to him. Early in the conversation this was oriented to by the troubles reporting and by the register chosen for it, and latterly in the register chosen for the outcomes suggested by the Doctor. There's also another interesting element of the distal context of which the Doctor must be aware, student solidarity. Although students bring complaints to him, there's another code which forbids them to name peers who may be responsible for the anti-social behaviour complained of. In this context, Nicole's use of 'someone' in 'someone's been nicking stuff out the fridge' is likely to be an attributive rather than a referential description, i.e. 'someone' doesn't refer to an identifiable person. However, there's always the possibility that 'someone' is a referential description and that the identity of the thief is known to or suspected by Nicole and Susie – it's just that student solidarity prevents them from substituting a name for the description 'someone'.

Having determined a course of action, and with this aspect of the distal context in mind, the Doctor's next task is to make a token attempt to discover the identity of the person responsible for the theft. I say 'a token attempt' because if the identity of the thief was really to be discovered, it wouldn't be necessary to put a sign up. Had the Police been called, one could hardly imagine their suggesting putting up a sign and then turning to the task of identifying the culprit. So in the order in which the Doctor turns from one topic to another, he implicitly orients to the distal context, and particularly to student solidarity which obtains even in a situation where the students themselves are victims.

This is how the next phase begins:

(42) DOCTOR: (..) and on the pantry door it's just the one upstairs isn't it next to the showers (2.0) so I mean it's likely [it's] to be someone (1.0) around that area you would've thought wouldn't you (1.5) there's only about one fridge on that floor in't there

> Transcription key
> The square brackets [it's] indicate an uncertain transcription, i.e. the analyst can't be absolutely sure that 'it's' is what was said.

Having asked for confirmation that there's a single fridge on the floor above, the Doctor signals a change of talk method, first by the significant two-second pause, then by signalling an upcoming formulation ('so'), then by repairing this to a self-made suggestion or formulation ('I mean'). The reason for the repair to a self-formulation, or at least to signal metasequentially that it's to be a self-formulation, is that a self-formulation implies less speaker commitment than a 'logical' formulation. It's therefore more appropriate to a context in which accusations, however implicit, threaten the students' face by virtue of being invitations to abandon the principle of solidarity. Thus when the self-formulation appears, it's metapragmatically hedged by 'likely', by the hypothetical 'you would've thought' and by the tag 'wouldn't you'. In this way, the Doctor invites Nicole and Susie to treat 'someone around that area' as a referential description. The 1.5 second pause that follows 'someone around that area' provides an opportunity for the students to name a likely culprit. But when this opportunity isn't taken up, he continues his turn by re-cycling the query about the number of fridges on the floor. Thus his invitation to the students to break ranks and name the thief is inserted between two versions of the same inquiry, an inquiry which is relevant to the agreed course of action of posting a sign.

Nicole ('yeah') and Susie ('mm') both confirm that there's a single fridge on the floor:

(43) NICOLE: yeah
SUSIE: mm
NICOLE: yeah somebody with a cheese toastie machine

Nicole then signals her willingness to pursue the investigation a stage further with metasequential 'yeah', and provides a more particular description, 'somebody with a cheese toastie machine'. This description appears to be a strong candidate for a referential reading i.e. 'someone with a cheese toastie machine' (= Mary Smith) rather than an attributive reading (= someone with a cheese toastie machine whose identity is unknown). And this candidate determination appears to be validated when Susie laughs and confirms the description:

(44) SUSIE: <laughs> yeah
DOCTOR: ay er do you know anyone who's got one (2.0)
NICOLE: Wo I've got one but I'm not going to nick my own cheese am I
<laughs> so
SUSIE: mm no

The Doctor also confirms the description ('ay'), signals metapragmatically and metasequentially with the hesitation marker 'er' that what comes next is significant, and then invites the students to name the thief: 'do you know anyone who's got one'. After a pause, Nicole rejects this context by taking 'anyone' in a marked way to include herself. She invites a formulation by another speaker ('so'), metasequentially excuses her contribution with 'Wo' (?=well) and metapragmatically appeals for solidarity with the tag 'am I'. Susie obligingly provides ('mm no').

Having failed to get Nicole to name a culprit, the Doctor then turns to Susie and the theft of her butter:

(45) DOCTOR: and they've taken your butter as well
SUSIE: yeah
DOCTOR: what type of butter was it
SUSIE: Flora light

In doing this, his metasequential use of 'and' indicates that the direction of his talk is still directed to identifying the thief.

Checking understanding (7.5)

The rest of the conversation follows below. Try to identify the function of the metalinguistic, metapragmatic and metasequential markers in lines 3–12 and 41–2 for yourself, concentrating on items that I've italicized.

(46) SUSIE: Flora light
(3.0)
DOCTOR: you can go round and have a look *if you want to*
SUSIE: yeah
(3.0)
NICOLE: it's not *like* it'd still be there *is it*
(1.5)
SUSIE: dunno it's *virtually* a full packet
NICOLE: *yeah* mine as well *actually* I know it was
<Vicky approaches>
DOCTOR: *yeah* just seeing people using your cheese again
and you cannot really accuse someone cos they
might have bought (.) bought it themselves
NICOLE: I know
SUSIE: mm
DOCTOR: I'll stick a notice up (.) and if it keeps
happening then [(1.0)]
VICKY: [what's happened]

Checking understanding (7.5) *cont.*

DOCTOR: we'll call a
meeting [and so forth]
SUSIE: [getting stuff]
VICKY: nicked
NICOLE: somebody keeps nicking stuff from the fridge
SUSIE: uh
(2.0)
VICKY: what in terms of what milk or (.)
NICOLE: cheese
VICKY: cheese
DOCTOR: cheese is quite expensive
VICKY: yeah
SUSIE: Flora
(3.0)
VICKY: it's annoying
(1.0)
SUSIE: mm
(4.0)
VICKY: Susie
SUSIE: yeah
VICKY: will you help me with my [linguistics work] <laughs>
DOCTOR: [*right* I'm off]
SUSIE: *all right then* Doctor
NICOLE: I'll just go and get a load of [my washing]
SUSIE: [see you later] pet
(1.0) yeah yeah that's fine [yeah]
VICKY: [are you] about to call
somebody
SUSIE: no no no no

7.3.3 Providing an explanation

In this section we see how a non-native speaker of English uses metapragmatic marking to cope with the challenges of explaining a situation in a second language. The speaker, Erich, is a middle-aged businessman in an advanced language class. He thinks that he was given the wrong change in a bookshop the previous day and is explaining to his fellow students why he thinks this. Consider the opening of his explanation:

(47) as far as I- as I remember (.) I am accustomed to check my money every day because of er (. .) I have to (.) make an invoice for my company (0.8) and I every day I er

Transcription key
a - attached to an item, e.g. I-, indicates a self-check by the speaker, typically signalled by a glottal stop

The metapragmatic self-check signals the speaker's search for a suitable next item after 'as far as I-'. That next item, 'as I remember', consists of an evidential memory claim functioning as a hedge on the degree of well-foundedness of what comes next. The micro pause after 'remember' is a metapragmatic indication of the speaker's search for a next item. 'Because of' signals an upcoming evidential whose somewhat personal status is signalled by the hesitation marker 'er'. However, the speaker then decides to change direction, an upcoming repair signalled by a micro pause. The further micro pause after 'I have to' signals the upcoming chunk 'make an invoice for my company'. The extended pause that follows signals the end of the explanatory phase and the beginning of a new phase in which the speaker gives an account of his regular practice. This begins with a repair from 'I' to 'every day I'. Repairs are important evidence of metapragmatic awareness and of the speaker's monitoring of speech in progress. This is followed by a hesitation marker, 'er', as the speaker signals his search for a suitable next item. This hesitation marker is then taken as an invitation by a fellow student to anticipate Erich's completion.

When Erich recommences, his continuing talk shows a similar level of metalinguistic awareness:

(48) and that day (0.5) and and (2.0) I missed er five pounds (.) er

The significant pause after 'that day' functions as a metapragmatic call for attention to an upcoming item which, as the two 'and's tell us, will be an account. This is because 'and' is the standard additive marker in an account and, as here, frequently precedes accounts too, indicating the method that is to follow. The second long pause, two seconds long in fact, is a further call for attention before the significant piece of evidence 'I missed er five pounds', with the hesitation marker drawing attention to the importance of the following item (and inviting confirmation of it by a fellow student). This is followed by a micro pause and a further hesitation marker indicating a possible change of method. However, the speaker decides to continue with his account, as 'and' confirms:

(49) and er (. .) and I knew (0.8) that I had three fifty pounds notes (0.8) in the (0.5) on the wallet

The hesitation marker and the paused utterances show the care the speaker takes in choosing next items, while the half-second pause after 'in the' marks a self-check prior to the repair 'on the', as it happens, a repair away from the native speaker norm.

Erich's explanation is notable for the constant metapragmatic monitoring it contains and the prevalence of contextualization cues in the form of pauses and hesitation markers. We might speculate that the importance of a topic in which his integrity is at stake (the bookshop denied that he'd been short-changed) together with the difficulty of finding optimal forms in a second language provide a psychological motivation for close self-monitoring. But whatever the motivation, these data strongly support Verschueren's claim that metalinguistic awareness is a dimension of language and not just a set of markers deployed on occasion as constraints that help the addressee to determine an intended meaning.

For a pedagogic perspective on these data, see Grundy, 2002.

Checking understanding (7.6)

Try and identify indications of metalinguistic awareness in Erich's continuing account. (Ignore teacher and student contributions.)

(50) ERICH: on the wallet and one ten pound and one one pound
STUDENT: and the ten pound one's gone
ERICH: (1.5) but I think it it was my fault (0.5) I had to clarify the situation immediately
STUDENTS: <vocalized agreement>
ERICH: and there are several reasons because I was unable to do this (.) um (. .) maybe of my poor English (. .) or maybe of (. .) some other
TEACHER: I er I said he was too nice a man he says his English is not good enough I say he's too nice a man
ERICH: and I think um (1.0) therefore (.) I (1.8) I suggest (. .) to forget about it

7.4 Intonation and metalinguistic awareness

In the first section of this chapter, I said that this final section would discuss metapragmatic marking and the role of intonation as a means of conveying pragmatic and metapragmatic meaning. In choosing the term 'marking', I was treating indications of metapragmatic awareness as a kind of diacritic telling us how to take the propositional content of utterances. One very obvious contextualization cue that hasn't had more than a few passing mentions so far is intonation. Indeed, our neglect of this area, which isn't untypical in the pragmatic literature, is often commented on by phoneticians and phonologists. Pragmatic meaning, they argue, is frequently signalled phonetically and so pragmaticists can't afford to ignore this dimension. The kind of data that make this view hard to resist are examples like

(10) People living nearby said Mr Neale would go away on 'lengthy business trips'

It's precisely the unusual intonation suggested by the quotation marks that tells us not to take 'lengthy business trips' at face value and therefore invites the inference that Mr Neale had been to prison on a number of occasions. Notice also that an oral performance of this written message would require a pause before 'lengthy business trips', exactly the kind of contextualization cue that informed our understanding of Erich's metalinguistic awareness in the previous section.

So is the phonetic dimension a means of encoding metalinguistic awareness and guiding addressees in the intended interpretation of utterances? Or does the contribution of phonology to pragmatic meaning go beyond this meta-function?

There's a local television presenter in the region where I live with the same family name as me. Occasionally I'm asked if we're related. This was how one such conversation went the other day:

(51) ACQUAINTANCE: Are you related to the other Grundy
PETER: Which 'other Grundy' do you mean

If I hadn't known of another Grundy and had used an unmarked intonation contour, the most relevant way to interpret what I said would be something along the lines of <tell me who the description the 'other Grundy' refers to>. But when I pick 'other' or 'other Grundy' out with an intonation contour indicating that I treat it as a (non-legitimate) mention, a very different implicature arises: <there's no 'other Grundy' worthy of mention>. This example seems to confirm that intonation can be used in an abnormal way to provoke an abnormal inference.

One example of intonation discussed earlier was the 'Are you big enough . . .' poster in Chapter 5. I suggested that /ˈɑː jʊ/ is the default way of asking a *yes/no*-question and that the abnormal /ə ˈjuː/ invites an M-inference. But then I went to on speculate that perhaps /ə ˈjuː/ has become the poster default. This makes us wonder about the point at which a default and a marked realization might be considered unmarked alternatives.

Consider

(52) You see I was slim then

This utterance occurred in a family discussion recorded for analysis by a student. As I studied the transcribed data, I realized that where the main stress fell was crucial in deciding the significance of this contribution in the discussion. To understand what was meant, I needed to go to the recording to discover whether the speaker had said

(52′) You see I / ˈwɒz slɪm/ then

or

(52″) You see I /wəz ˈslɪm/ then

It seems that in this case, the speaker uses stress assignment to draw attention to the semantic focus of her utterance. While there are pragmatic consequences of the decision she takes, the phonetic ambiguity of (52) is surely more semantic than pragmatic.

The same argument might apply to some of the data discussed in Chapter 4. The two possible realizations of

(53) You haven't got a £5 note

are conventionally associated with interpreting the utterance as an assertion or a pessimistic way of asking a *yes/no*-question. And in

(54) CASHIER: Do you know about our offer on oil
CUSTOMER: No

fall-rise 'no' conventionally invites the cashier to explain about the offer, and falling intonation conventionally marks a response to the literal force of the question. Of course, the effects of whichever intonation pattern is chosen in (53) and (54) are pragmatic. This is because there's a preferred choice given the context so that a dispreferred choice has a marked effect. So it's not that intonation of this kind is intrinsically pragmatic, but rather that, like any aspect of an utterance, what is said needs to be reconciled with the context in which it's said. It is, in my opinion, plain wrong to claim that because there are different interpretations of utterances depending on their intonational realization, intonation is intrinsically pragmatic. If each realization matches some context in a conventional way, the phonetic realization is as much a part of the conventional meaning as any other truth-conditional element. Just as lexical items have entailments, invariable meanings across all contexts in which they occur, so intonation is for the most part a conventional diacritic aspect of utterances. Only on those occasions when intonation functions as a contextualization cue, as in (10) and (51), is an unusual inference invited. This is the reason why pragmaticists have on the whole not been too bothered about intonation.

Summary

Metapragmatic marking shows the awareness speakers have of the effects of what they say and of the need to constrain the interpretation of utterances so that their optimal relevance is more readily grasped. The need for metapragmatic and metasequential marking is a fall-out of the general indeterminacy, and hence economy, of language and of the one-to-many property of forms to functions.

The pragmatic categories that we studied in the earlier chapters – deixis, presupposition, speech acts, implicature – were for the most part first drawn to linguists' attention by philosophers of language offering rationalistic explanations of linguistic phenomena. But now we see that indexicals, illocutionary force indicating devices, maxim hedges, Gricean conventional implicatures, speech act descriptions, and procedural encoding generally share a common reflexive function that prompts our understanding of what is meant by what is said. It almost tempts us to begin our study of pragmatics from a different perspective – with naturally occurring data and its 'dimensions'.

Acknowledgement: The troubles reporting data were collected by Susan Millington, who conducted a preliminary analysis. I'm very grateful to her for permission to use these data here.

Raising pragmatic awareness

1 Position yourself somewhere where you expect purposeful talk to occur – perhaps your Departmental office. Try to identify any ways in which metasequential phenomena are used to make the nature of the contributions clear.

2 Eavesdrop on a conversation and make a list of some of the metalinguistic, metapragmatic and metasequential phenomena you overhear. Bring them to your next tutorial and share them with your colleagues.

3 Listen to or record a conversation and select a number of metalinguistic items. Do they also have a metapragmatic function?

4 Make a close study of the metapragmatic phenomena a member of your family or a close friend displays and report your findings to your tutorial group.

5 Think up two or three new procedural constraints and explain to your tutorial group what their function is and why you chose the particular linguistic items to mark them.

6 How does the reflexive nature of the language we use relate to the other features of talk identified as typically pragmatic in Chapter 1: accommodation, appropriateness, context, indeterminacy, indirect meaning, inference, relevance?

Discussions and essays

Based on what you know about metapragmatic awareness, discuss the relative merits of each of the following views:

- "Speech is permeated by reflexive activity as speakers remark on language, report utterances, index and describe aspects of the speech event . . . and guide listeners in the proper interpretation of their utterances" (Lucy, 1993: 11).
- The metalinguistic function occurs when a linguistic form is used to describe the act of speaking itself, or to represent, gloss or refer to another linguistic form.
- The metapragmatic function occurs when a linguistic form is used to guide the hearer's pragmatic interpretation.
- The metasequential function occurs when a linguistic form is used to guide the hearer's understanding of the way a turn contributes to a conversation.
- Discourse markers have conventional meaning and yet typically resist truth-conditional characterization.

Further reading

Primary texts

Blakemore, 1987; Lucy, 1993: 9–32; Schiffrin, 1987; Verschueren, 2000.

Textbooks

Mey, 2001: 173–205; Verschueren, 1998: 187–95.

8 Pragmatic inference and language evolution

'The primates on the other side of the fence seemed to have completed several thousand years of evolution within a couple of hours and had now developed a rudimentary language and pointing system, consisting of the phrase "toooonullyergoingdown" and projecting their two inner fingers up to the sky.'

Description of Birmingham City football fans circulated on the internet by a disgruntled supporter of a rival team

Keywords:

coincident context, complementary context, constraint, hearer meaning, iterated learning, language evolution, pragmatic strengthening, sentence meaning, speaker meaning

8.1 Introduction

When you think about it, it's really odd that what we mean by our words is more important than what our words mean. We spend for ever trying to understand the inferential process at the heart of pragmatic meaning, but it rarely occurs to us to ask why language is like this: why do we use words to convey what we don't say? How has language got to a situation when we don't say what we mean and we mean what we don't say? How have we got to a situation where anything can mean anything? So that when Branka wants to know if she should make dinner, she says

(1) When will you be back

And when I want her to make dinner and buy a lottery ticket, I say

(2) I should be back by eight but you know what trains are like

If you were the Master (or Mistress) of the Universe, is this how you'd design human language?

In the two sections of this brief chapter that follow we'll try and work out how pragmatic inference has come about and how an account of language evolution is incomplete without taking **pragmatic strengthening** into account. By 'pragmatic strengthening' I mean every kind of enrichment, from assigning a referent to 'you' and 'I' and accommodating the background belief that I will 'be back' in (1) and (2) to drawing the type and token inferences discussed in Chapters 5 and 6. Specifically, we'll focus on:

- *Pragmatic meaning,* including a review of the kinds of contribution pragmatics makes to language understanding as discussed in previous chapters.
- *Pragmatic meaning and language evolution,* in which I'll argue that the inferential dimension of language is what makes language evolution possible.

8.2 Pragmatic meaning

The chapters you've read so far aren't in a random order. Nor are they in the same order as in either of the previous editions of this book. In the second edition, the discussion of presupposition was delayed until Chapter 6 because the style checker confirmed my hunch that the chapter was relatively inaccessible. In this edition, I had a more linguistically principled, if less reader-friendly, motive: with each chapter, the degree of pragmatic strengthening required to accommodate the speaker's intended meaning increases.

In Chapter 2, the only assumption needed to determine a deictic reference is the ability to link a linguistic expression to what is indexed by its use in the immediate context. Sometimes we can even use gesture as a supplementary means of making the ostension manifest. In Chapter 3, we went a step further. I argued that whereas an indexical was an instruction to look for a referent in the immediate context, in the case of presupposition the addressee was content to take the existence of a proposition on trust, i.e. without the need to locate it in the immediate context. In both instances, the existence of what is indexed is non-controversial – in the case of a deictic because it can be readily verified in context, and in the case of a presupposition because the speaker assumes the addressee's willingness to accommodate what is presupposed. Perhaps this is why Silverstein writes about "the extreme of presupposition displayed by deictics" (1976: 35), and why presuppositions are *quasi*-indexical in the sense that they also index a (non-present) context.

In Chapter 4, we took another short step when we recognized that holistic formulas like 'I'm tired' may function as different acts in different contexts, depending on the speaker's intention. In doing this, we differentiated propositional meaning (what is said) from force (what is done by saying).

In discussing presupposition, we'd separated the semantic notion of a presupposition as a precondition for truth and the pragmatic notion of a presupposition as a precondition for appropriateness. When we got to speech acts in Chapter 4, the semantic meaning (the locutionary act) was seen to be less salient than the pragmatic meaning (the illocutionary act). And in Chapter 4, we also began to see the conventionalization of pragmatic meaning in formulas like 'Can you *x*' where an 'indirect' formula becomes the preferred way of performing a speech act. Thus a formula like 'would you mind' in

(3) Would you mind opening the window

isn't an invitation to an addressee to discuss their philosophical attitude to window opening.

From this point, it's a further short step to Chapters 5 and 6 and implicature, where utterances go beyond the type expectations associated with 'Can you *x*' to being tokens whose meaning will always be context-sensitive. With implicature, we see several developments:

- The importance of inference in the recovery of optimal meaning and especially the role of the addressee in determining relevance. This contrasts with the speaker-centred origo implicit in a deictic reference, and the speaker's presumption of what is non-controversial for the addressee in a presupposition, and the speaker's notion of an optimal form for a meaning in a speech act.
- A developed notion of context. The **coincident** context indexed by deictics, absent but assumed in a presupposition and treated as a determinant of the value of a speech act, is supplemented by what we might call a **complementary context** – a context which is never coincident and has to be supplied by the

addressee in order to find relevance in the otherwise non-relevant nature of what is said. Whereas deictics point to/are instructions to locate a context in the here and now, utterances that give rise to implicatures are instructions to locate a context not in the here and now.

- A further reduction of the role of the semantic element as pragmatic strengthening applies to lexical items as well as to utterances.
- The (strong) possibility that the most salient meaning of an utterance will take an entirely different propositional form (and represent an entirely different underlying logical form) from those of the original utterance, so that the most salient meaning is conveyed but not stated.
- The appearance of procedural constraints. One consequence of relying on complementary context to determine meaning is that understanding utterances becomes problematic because they are no longer linked indexically to the here and now. It's not, therefore, surprising that constraints are required to help addressees to recover optimal meanings and that speakers need to have sufficient metalinguistic awareness to monitor the extent to which the meanings they intend are recoverable.

Chapters 2–7 chart a progression from speaker-controlled strategic use of language to addressee-determined meaning. '**Speaker meaning**' is a term commonly used to distinguish pragmatics from semantics, with the latter seen as the study of '**sentence meaning**'. However, as we see, **hearer meaning** also lies at the heart of pragmatics.

Silverstein distinguishes two functions of signs: the first is *semantico-referential* and denotes the propositional element of speech events where "sign tokens preserve their reference in all the speech events in which they occur" and are sentence bound and context independent (1976: 21); the second is *pragmatic*, where meanings are defined relative to their communicative function as utterance-bound, context-dependent types. As we've being 'doing pragmatics', chapter by chapter the balance has been shifting away from semantico-referential salience to a situation where the semantico-referential meaning counts for relatively little in our understanding of what is meant by what is said.

8.3 Pragmatic meaning and language evolution

This chapter began with a folk view of first use of human language by *Homo Brumiens*:

(4) The primates on the other side of the fence seemed to have completed several thousand years of evolution within a couple of hours and had now developed a rudimentary language and pointing system, consisting of the phrase "toooonullyergoingdown" and projecting their two inner fingers up to the sky

We know that primates don't point. Linguists would probably also concur that in the early stages, human language makes use of pointing and is holistic, with complex meanings expressed by non-compositional vocalizations. And although it may not be the most plausible, ritual abuse isn't the daftest among the long list of suggested motivations for human language.

8.3.1 Language evolution and language change

How then does language evolve in places other than football grounds? One persuasive proposal is Kirby's (2001) iterated learning theory (ILT). Kirby's argument is that a language can only evolve if it's learnable, thus enabling it to be transmitted from one generation of users to the next in a process of **iterated learning**. In each cycle of learning, what gets learnt has been partly determined in the previous cycle, so that each time learning is repeated by a succeeding generation, what is learnt changes or evolves. This opens up the possibility of tracking language evolution from historical sources, as in historical pragmatics.

ILT is a theory in which the language (rather than the user) adapts in the direction of further learnability as a result of its transmission from one generation to the next. How then does the language adapt?

To be readily learnable, language has to be componential, with a single form able to combine with many other forms. In other words, language has to develop syntax, a system in which a limited number of rules permits the combination of a restricted set of items into a potentially infinite number of sentences. According to the ILT account, language evolution is therefore a progression from the expression of propositions holistically (i.e. a-syntactically) to the expression of propositions componentially (i.e. syntactically). Furthermore, Kirby is able to show by means of computer simulations that communication systems that are compositional and recursive do get generated from holistic communication systems as a result of iterated learning over sufficient numbers of generations (2002). ILT also accounts for the semi-systematic nature of irregularity. For example, Kirby and Christiansen point out that "the top ten verbs in English by frequency are all irregular in the past tense" (2003: 289). It's precisely the frequency of *gave, made, went*, etc. that allows them to remain irregular, and thus unlearnable by the general rule <add -ED>.

8.3.2 The evolution of pragmatic meaning

It's striking how little mention there is of pragmatics in the considerable language evolution literature that's appeared in recent years. ILT, for example, is typical in being a theory of the evolution of linguistic form rather than of linguistic function.

If the evolution literature rarely mentions pragmatics, equally the pragmatics literature rarely mentions evolution. One exception is Levinson, who notes that animal cries that warn of danger take for granted that the danger is in the here and now. He continues, "The question naturally arises, then, whether in studying indexicality in natural languages we are studying archaic, perhaps primitive, aspects of human communication, which can perhaps even give us clues to the evolution of human language" (2004: 98). Later in the same paper, he suggests that "Indexicality probably played a crucial part in the evolution of language, prior to the full-scale, recursive, symbolic system characteristic of modern human language" (ibid.: 121).

At some point, it seems that our ancestors learned to point to the danger of which they were warning, so that indexicality is no longer taken for granted but overtly signalled by means of a gesture that indexes the source of danger in relation to a deictic origo. Over time, one supposes, the animal cry conventionally associated with the gesture becomes a way of referring to the danger itself. We have a pragmatic inference linking an indexical sign to an entity in the immediate context. Now it's only a matter of time before we begin to point and say 'YOU and YOU and YOU'.

But danger may come from a variety of sources. If each of these sources of danger is indicated by the same gesture and proto-linguistic vocalization, the semantic value of the vocalization, the sign, necessarily varies from occurrence to occurrence. We have pragmatic meaning. On one occasion "toooonullyergoingdown" is linked to an entity dressed in red, on another to an entity dressed in blue. On one occasion what is meant by saying "toooonullyergoingdown" is <toooonullredyergoingdown>, and on another <toooonullblueyergoingdown>. Now it's only a matter of time before we say

'I'm tired' in the evening and again the next morning and mean quite different things on each occasion.

But "toooonullyergoingdown" is not yet decomposable. Although he has context-sensitive pragmatic meaning, Homo Brumiens still lacks syntax. However, as the process of iterative learning picks up pace, it occurs to Homo Brumiens that "wunnnnullyergoingdown", which he uses to index one context, and "toooonullyergoingdown", which he uses to index another, share a common element, *yergoingdown*. All of a sudden there are five words in the language, *toooonullyergoingdown, wunnnnullyergoingdown, yergoingdown, toooonull* and *wunnnnull*. We have componentiality. Because the components of language exist as concepts which are potentially combinable in new ways and can even be tried out in the mind (e.g., *yergoingdowntoooonull??*), meaning is freed from the one-to-one association with an immediate context on which it had depended. Over time, our ancestors came to rely on pragmatic strengthening to interpret uses of language in relation to complementary as well as coincident contexts.

Thus a plausible theory of pragmatic inference is also evolutionary. Deixis, and then presupposition, and then speech acts represent early stages of accommodation made necessary by an increasingly componential, and therefore under-determined, syntax. Finally, the addressee learns to infer meanings that depend on supplying a complementary context.

As language develops a componential syntax, the components themselves become ever more symbolic and ever less indexical. They even become delexical as derivational morphology turns *nature* to *natural* to *naturally*. And whole utterances no longer need a coincident context to be interpretable so long as the loss of transparency that results is remedied by pragmatic strengthening. Language also becomes more economical as linguistic formulas license an ever increasing number of interpretations. These formulas are relevant, not because they are indexical and convey some message equally recoverable from the coincident context, but as a result of the addressee's ability to supply a complementary context.

The following schemata are adapted from Grundy (2007a) and summarize the process by which inferred meaning evolves:

LANGUAGE

In the beginning
Language is holistic and not readily learnable.

Later
Language begins to exhibit componentiality and learnability.

Later still
Language is both componential (learnable) and formulaic (frequent).

Eventually
Language is predominantly componential and readily learnable.

USE OF LANGUAGE

In the beginning
Language is used indexically.

Later
Language is used to presuppose.

Later still
Language is used with illocutionary force.

Eventually
Language is used to mean things that are not said.

ACCOMMODATION

In the beginning

Addressees accommodate a link between an entity in the here and now and an accompanying linguistic demonstration directed to it.

Later

Addressees accommodate the existence of propositions not demonstrably verifiable in the here and now.

Later still

Addressees accommodate the variable semantic value of the same formula across a range of contexts.

Eventually

Addressees accommodate the role of non-coincident complementary contexts in the interpretation of utterances.

8.3.3 Language learning stages

In first language acquisition theory, it's long been known that phonemes that are rare in the languages of the world tend to be acquired later than those that are common. Put another way, in the process of acquisition, the behaviour of each new human being reflects the fundamental nature of human language.

If, like me, you're interested in instructed second language learning, or even if your interest extends no further than your classroom experience, you might wonder whether the way we teach languages also mirrors in some intuitive way the fundamental stages of language evolution. Does each language learner in a few months or years follow the same inferential trail that has taken the human species tens, or perhaps hundreds, of thousands of years?

Seems unlikely perhaps, but I wonder whether you recognize this process from your experience:

SECOND LANGUAGE INSTRUCTION

In the beginning

Second language instruction tends to proceed through demonstrations in which learners are encouraged to associate spoken and sometimes written second language with realia (real objects) and visuals (pictures of objects and situations) and, in traditional teaching, with first language spoken and written equivalents.

Later

Learners are encouraged to make interlingual identifications within the second language. In order for this important stage to be accomplished effectively, learners have to exercise a principle of goodwill, accepting that new vocabulary items will often share category membership (e.g., *dog, cat*) or be in a superordinate/hyponymic relationship with items whose meanings they already know (e.g., *dog, animal*). Thus new words are learnt as non-controversial interpretations by extension from known interpretations (e.g., *I like fruit, especially apples, oranges and pears*, when *pears* is a previously unknown vocabulary item). A similar accommodation is necessary for the paradigmatic properties of the language, so that if a plural or a past form exhibits particular componential properties in a few cases, it may be presupposed that these properties will apply across a wider field.

Later still

Learners are encouraged to recognize that form, meaning and context are not in an invariant relationship, so that particular contexts license different interpretations of the same form and different forms may have the same communicative value.

> *Eventually*
> As the learners' knowledge approximates to that of native speakers, they encounter second language utterances whose pragmatic meanings are more salient than their literal meanings and can only be determined by recourse to a recoverable complementary context.

One further observation. In language teaching theory, perhaps the most fundamental distinction is between methods that follow a learn-in-order-to-use approach and methods that follow a use-in-order-to-learn approach. Learn-in-order-to-use approaches typically privilege the production of optimal forms for meanings, corresponding to an early coincident context stage in language evolution. Use-in-order-to-learn approaches typically privilege the recovery of optimal meanings from forms, corresponding to a later complementary context stage.

Summary

In this brief chapter, I've tried to show that the pragmatic dimension of language has been present from the beginning and that human language could not have evolved without pragmatics. Not only that, but the various stages of language evolution each require a further accommodation of inferred meaning. Pragmatics, or at least pragmatics of the kind we've been studying, is at heart the study of inferred meaning. In this chapter and in the ordering of the chapters in this book, we've tried to trace out an evolutionary account of the application of reasoning and inference to language use.

In *Knowledge of Language*, Chomsky wrote of his account of human language:

> We must distinguish between the literal meaning of the linguistic expression produced by S and what S meant by producing this expression . . . The first notion is the one to be explained in a theory of language. The second has nothing particular to do with language; I can just as well ask, in the same sense of 'meaning', what S meant by slamming the door. (1976: 76)

In this chapter, we've shown that this view of pragmatics as an epiphenomenon, a feature of language that isn't intrinsic but a mere consequence of the availability of a system of syntactic rules and semantic tokens, is fundamentally wrong.

Raising pragmatic awareness

1 Think of an animal you know well – dog, cat, horse. Prepare answers to the following questions and bring them to class for discussion: Does this animal have any understanding of the relationship of language and context? If this animal understands some of the things you say, is it only the literal meaning that's understood, or is there an element of pragmatic meaning that's conveyed? When you communicate with this animal, how do you make use of extra-linguistic signs?

2 Think of two or three things that you've used language to do today that wouldn't be possible if your addressees couldn't access complementary contexts. Discuss these with your colleagues.

Raising pragmatic awareness *cont.*

3 In your tutorial group, try and brainstorm pragmatic functions you might want language to perform and that can't be performed at present. (It may help if you think of the terms discussed in Chapter 1 as functions of language, i.e. we want to be appropriate, relevant, etc. It may also help to consider this problem from both a speaker's and a hearer's perspective.)

4 Do you think computers will ever be able to know what you can accommodate and to take your encyclopedic knowledge into full account in communicating with you?

5 To what extent does the computer software you're familiar with match and to what extent does it fall short of your friends in inviting you to infer meanings from the messages it sends you?

Discussions and essays

- We shouldn't be surprised to find that as the indexicality of language reduces and the number of deictic forms shrinks, we find a corresponding development of metapragmatic markers indicating propositional attitudes and of procedurals that enable a speaker to indicate the way they would like a hearer to understand what they mean by what they say.
- If you'd read only Chapter 2 of this book and were asked to frame a hypothesis about pragmatic meaning in general, you might wonder whether all pragmatic meaning might be indexical. Each of the statements below is a generalization about pragmatic meaning arising from a particular chapter. Discuss the relative merits of each:
  - All pragmatic understanding is ultimately indexical (Chapter 2).
  - All pragmatic understanding is ultimately a matter of accommodation (Chapter 3).
  - All pragmatic use is ultimately performative (Chapter 4).
  - All pragmatic meaning is ultimately inferred (Chapter 5).
  - All pragmatic meanings are enrichments of under-determined linguistic forms (Chapter 6).
  - Metapragmatic awareness is an intrinsic property of language use (Chapter 7).

Further reading

Grundy, 2007a; For language evolution background: Christiansen and Kirby (2003); Tallerman (2005).

9 Politeness phenomena

PHYLLIS: He's a very polite-spoke man aren't you
PETER: It's not what they say at home

Keywords:

distance, etiquette, (positive and negative) face, face threat, imposition, model person, (positive and negative) politeness, power, redress, redundancy, universal, usage

9.1 Introduction

Imagine that I've just given a talk at your university and afterwards we're chatting over a drink. In the course of our conversation I tell you that I'll be visiting another university a hundred kilometres away the following morning and then I'll be returning to your university in the evening. Do you think you'd be likely to say

(1) When will you be back

I guess probably you wouldn't, because we don't know each other well enough to ask such questions so directly. But when my wife asks, it's a natural enough question and I don't feel threatened by it – in fact it's positively friendly.

Imagine also that you're kind enough to be thinking of asking me to join you for a meal the following evening and need to know when I'm going to be back. Perhaps you'll find a formula like

(2) I don't know if you're likely to be back in time for dinner, but if you are, I'd be delighted to take you to a local restaurant

Given the fact that we only met ten minutes before, this would be a well-judged way of offering me dinner. But had my wife said it to me, I'd be visiting a lawyer on the way home. The point is simple: you are 'polite', my wife is 'polite', but you and she are 'polite' in different ways. This is because the distance between my wife and me on the one hand and between you and me on the other is not the same, and whereas there's nothing imposing in my wife asking about my return plans and dinner arrangements, there is something imposing when a relative stranger does this.

Let's imagine for a moment that you aren't so aware of social niceties as I supposed before, and instead of your well-judged inquiry, you plunge in and say 'When will you be back?' Given that we barely know one another, I don't think I'd risk the relatively intimate 'you know' and say

(3) I should be back by eight but you know what trains are like

Perhaps I'd say something like

(4) Not too late I hope – maybe around eight if I'm lucky

This is because it's not appropriate to talk to someone we've only just met in the same way as we talk to people we know well.

We each have expectations as to how we should be addressed by the various people we meet in the various contexts in which we meet them. The study of politeness is the study of the ways in which these expectations are met (or not, as the case may be).

The chapter contains three further sections, each of which includes several subsections:

- *Politeness phenomena and Brown and Levinson's theory*, which first familiarizes you with the parameters within which politeness is usually discussed and then explores the most comprehensive account we have of the systematic nature of politeness.
- *Politeness phenomena in the real world*, in which several real world politeness challenges are explored.
- *The universal character of politeness*, in which the claim that Brown and Levinson's schema captures universal properties of politeness is discussed.

9.2 Politeness phenomena and Brown and Levinson's theory

In their classic book on politeness, which we'll be discussing later in this section, Brown and Levinson note a growing interest in "the linguistic expression of social relationships" ([1978] 1987: 49), of which politeness phenomena are an obvious and pervasive example. Politeness principles have long been considered to have wide descriptive power in respect of language use (Lakoff, 1972, 1973), to be major determinants of linguistic behaviour (Leech, 1983), and to have universal status (Brown and Levinson, [1978] 1987). Politeness phenomena also extend the notion of indexicality because they show that every utterance is uniquely designed for its context. Needless to say, not all of these claims have gone unchallenged, but they make good starting points for our study.

Seen as the exercise of language choice to create a context intended to match the addressee's notion of how he or she should be addressed, politeness phenomena are a paradigm example of pragmatic usage. Among the aspects of context that are particularly determinate of language choice in the domain of politeness are the power–distance relationship of the interactants and the extent to which a speaker imposes on or requires something of their addressee. In being 'polite', a speaker is attempting to create an implicated context (the speaker stands in relation *x* to the addressee in respect of act *y*) that matches the one assumed by the addressee. Politeness phenomena are thus one manifestation of the wider concept of etiquette, or appropriate behaviour.

In the rest of this section, we'll first look at the parameters that determine politeness phenomena, such as the power–distance relationship of interactants and the extent to which a speaker imposes on an addressee. We'll then see how Brown and Levinson build their theory around these parameters.

9.2.1 Face

I was walking in the park recently when out of the blue (literally) I became the victim of a bird with a heavy payload. Fortunately I was wearing a coat and had a packet of paper handkerchiefs in my pocket. I was alternately dabbing my head and trying not very successfully to remove bird dirt from the shoulder of my coat when all of a sudden a jogger appeared. He was clearly heading my way. As you can imagine, I felt (and probably looked) pretty foolish. I had the humiliating feeling that I was about to be laughed at. In fact, my sense of self-esteem, or, to use a folk term, my **face**, was so threatened that I felt obliged to speak and explain my already obvious predicament:

(5) PETER: I've been attacked by a bird
JOGGER: Not the kind of bird you were hoping for

In his brilliantly judged reply, the jogger made me feel good about myself all over again: I suppose he could tell that under different circumstances I'm just the kind of suave chap who might have a chance of being attacked by the right kind of 'bird'!

Recently on the London Underground it was my turn to see someone else lose face. I was waiting with a suitcase to be let through the staff-operated barrier. In front of me, the member of staff on duty was trying to explain to two deliberately obtuse visitors to Britain that the Circle Line wasn't operating and they'd need to use the Metropolitan Line. The more patience she showed, the more unpleasant they became, before eventually striding off in a self-righteous way as though everything was her fault. I'd seen her humiliation, which, like my bird problem, no doubt prompted her to speak:

(6) BARRIER OPERATIVE: I'm going to scream
PETER: Then I'll scream too
BARRIER OPERATIVE: Thank you

I was quite moved. I thought I was just making a small joke, but my gesture of solidarity obviously went further than I'd calculated in restoring her damaged self-esteem.

At one time, we had a make of car with a poor reputation for reliability. On one occasion, I went to the garage in a tearing rage when the repair attempt the day before had once again proved ineffective. All the way there I was rehearsing how I was going to tear a strip off the service manager. When I got to the garage, there were two customers in front of me, each of whom did to the service manager exactly what I had been planning to do. When my turn came, he looked up at me with big sad eyes and, running the back of his hand across his forehead, said

(7) I need a cup of tea after that

I felt so sorry for him that my complaint collapsed into

(8) You'll need a cup of coffee after me

We both had a good laugh. I expressed my displeasure but, by making a joke of it, minimized the extent to which he lost face.

Conclusion: Face matters. Considerate people take into account the addressee's need to be well regarded and their right not to be humiliated.

Checking understanding (9.1)

To what extent do you think the following exchanges take into account the addressee's face?

(9) SNACK-BAR OPERATIVE ON TRAIN: It's quite slow at the moment (referring to coffee machine)
PETER: Because
OPERATIVE: I don't know – it just is – perhaps it's having a rest

(10) PETER (to stranger in corridor): You're looking lost
STRANGER: I am lost

(11) I think bullet points would be better here (supervisor's marginal gloss in draft chapter of PhD student's thesis)

9.2.2 The effects of politeness

Being on the receiving end of politeness affects each of us differently because polite utterances encode the relationship between the speaker and ourselves as addressee. Thus we might expect someone who happened to be sitting next to us in a lecture and who we didn't know all that well to ask for a piece of paper with a formula like

(12) You couldn't let me have a bit of paper by any chance could you

And we'd expect a different person, perhaps an older brother, to put the request in the more direct way:

(13) Give me a sheet of paper fathead

If we don't see the relationship between ourselves and the person who addresses us as they do, we'll be upset by the strategies they employ, since these strategies imply the nature of our relationship as they see it. This function of language, to imply the most appropriate speaker–addressee relationship, is at the heart of linguistic politeness.

I once had an appointment with the doctor. When I got to the surgery, the following written message was prominently displayed in the waiting room:

(14) Owing to unforeseen circumstances, one of our Doctors has not been able to attend morning surgery. Consequently, the other partners are running late. We apologize for any inconvenience this may cause you, and assure you that all patients will be seen as quickly as possible.

As the minutes ticked by, I began to get more frustrated. And I began to think about the message and how annoying it was. What 'unforeseen circumstances', I thought? Why 'our' doctors, and why the capital 'D'? Why 'has not' rather than *hasn't*? Any why 'any' inconvenience? And why 'may'? Why not simply *apologize for the inconvenience*, or even *apologize that you're having to wait*? And is 'assure you' really necessary? And what does 'as quickly as possible' really mean? And then I began to imagine a nightmare scenario in which I eventually got to see Dr Moore and he started to talk like his notice.

But when I eventually did get to see him, we had a normal, jokey conversation. What a difference between our relaxed chat about my stiff neck and the formal, distance encoding message in the waiting room. So after I'd seen the doctor, I popped back into the waiting room and wrote the message down to share with you.

Checking understanding (9.2)

1 It's difficult to imagine a doctor talking in the register used for the message in the waiting room. If you're like me and feel that the way the message is written is inappropriate, can you rewrite it in a more appropriate way? What sort of person would find the original message appropriate do you think?

2 You can test my claim that the purpose of linguistic politeness is to imply the most appropriate speaker–addressee relationship by ranking the following texts on a scale from the one you'd be happiest to be on the receiving end of yourself to the one you'd be least happy about. You might like to try this with a friend or colleague in your class: you should each read the texts and rank them for acceptability, and then share your reasons.

(15) Text A – a letter from a colleague in another department:
Dear Peter,
Thank you very much for agreeing to register our students on Tuesday. I know it must have made a very difficult day even more fraught but it was very helpful to me. I appreciate what you did and I feel indebted to you.

(16) Text B – notice in a classroom at University of Portsmouth:
In order to promote a better learning environment please do not bring food or drink into this teaching room and remember to switch off your mobile telephone.
Thank you.

(17) Text C – the opening paragraph of a letter about home insulation:
Dear Mr Grundy
Your home qualifies for free insulation
Following your recent energy assessment by Newcastle Warm Zone, I am pleased to inform you that, subject to the information you provided, you will qualify for free insulation measures.

3 When our water supply is interrupted for repairs, the water company puts a postcard through our letter box the week before. The company keeps revising the text of this postcard. Study the four versions below – the first is the earliest version (1990) and the fourth the latest (2008). Which do you like the best, what changes can you identify, and why do you think the company keeps revising the text? A good way of doing this task is to work with a partner and study two of the texts. Then find another team who choose a different pair of texts and discuss your findings.

(18a) INTERRUPTION OF WATER SUPPLY
Please note that your Water Supply will be
turned OFF on
Sunday 11th November 1990
From 4.00am for up to 7 hours
During this period it would be inadvisable to draw hot water or to use any mechanical appliances connected to the supply. It is essential to

Checking understanding (9.2) *cont.*

ensure that all taps remain shut to avoid the risk of flooding when the supply is restored.

For further advice please telephone 091 – 2654144

(18b) WATER OFF

Please note that your water supply will be
TURNED OFF
WEDNESDAY 28TH FEB
FROM 9AM TO 1PM

During this time please minimize the use of hot water and ensure that all taps remain shut to prevent the risk of flooding when the supply is restored.

We regret any inconvenience this may cause you.

For help and advice contact Customer Services on the telephone number overleaf.

(18c) ESSENTIAL MAINTENANCE

In order to carry out work to the water mains your
WATER SUPPLY
will be temporarily
TURNED OFF
Friday 9th July
from 10:00hrs to 14:00hrs

We apologize for any inconvenience and we will work as quickly as possible to restore your supply. During this time you should not use hot water or any mechanical devices connected to the supply such as washing machines and dishwashers. Please ensure that all your taps are turned off so that the water does not run when the supply is restored. Conventional heating systems may be operated but if you have a combined central heating/hot water system the hot water should not be used. Do not use instantaneous water heaters during the interruption.

For help and advice contact Customer Services on the telephone number overleaf.

(18d) ESSENTIAL MAINTENANCE

In order to carry out work to the water mains your
WATER SUPPLY
will be temporarily
TURNED OFF
Friday 15 February between 09:00hrs to 13:00hrs

We apologize for any inconvenience and we will work as quickly as possible to restore your supply. During this time you should not use hot water or any mechanical devices connected to the supply such as washing machines and dishwashers. Please ensure that all your taps are turned off so that the water does not run when the supply is restored. Central heating may be used **but do not run off any hot water** from the system.

For help and advice contact Customer Services on the telephone number overleaf.

In ranking the texts in the Checking Understanding (9.2) exercises for acceptability, you were making decisions about the way that propositions were conveyed. Take

(16) In order to promote a better learning environment please do not bring food or drink into this teaching room and remember to switch off your mobile telephone.
Thank you.

The notice gives a reason ('in order to promote a better learning environment') for the request, which is redressed to some degree by the IFID 'please'. The redundant 'remember' is deferential and conventionally implies that the action is something you'd want to do. 'Your' personalizes the message, and the elaborate formula 'mobile telephone' treats you as important.

In ranking this text in relation to the others, you were making decisions about these encodings and their effect on you – whether you prefer this message or the more economical

(16′) Do not bring food or drink into this room. Switch off mobile phones

or something between the two. Or perhaps you prefer the conventional iconic symbols for food and drink and mobile phones with prohibition encoding diagonal lines through them.

Conclusion: The way we say things to each other has real effect. This is because it encodes not only propositional content but also our understanding of the relationship between us. This insight suggests that every instance of communicated language exhibits politeness.

9.2.3 Redress and redundancy

We've just compared various ways in which a classroom notice might remind us about classroom etiquette. In the comparison, I said that 'remember to' in the University of Portsmouth notice was redundant. But in fact, as we saw, the redundancy was a good deal more extensive than this. Unlike presupposition, and pragmatic presupposition in particular, which encourage economical communication by allowing shared propositions to be taken for granted without being stated, politeness phenomena frequently go in the opposite direction. The politeness phenomena in

(12) You couldn't let me have a bit of paper by any chance could you

are obviously extensive. Even in (13), 'fathead' is a departure from maximal economy, and as a ritual insult has politeness status.

In fact, most utterances exhibit a trade-off between economy and the speaker's preference for a more elaborate linguistic strategy than is strictly needed to communicate the proposition he/she has in mind. Of course, there will be situations when the strategy most likely to enable speakers to satisfy their needs will be to utter (13) without even the endearing 'fathead', but these will be relatively rare.

One very obvious feature of (12) and (13) (and of (1) and (2) as well) is that the more economical utterances are used when the speaker knows the addressee well, and the more elaborate when the speaker knows the addressee less well. Asking someone for a sheet of paper isn't much of an imposition if it's a brother or sister we're asking. But asking a relative stranger we happen to be sitting next to in a lecture is a bit more tricky. It's as though the extra language we use is a kind of redress for the imposition.

Conclusion: We're more likely to use redressive, and hence less economical, linguistic formulas when we place demands on those we address, especially when we don't know them well.

Checking understanding (9.3)

1 Imagine you're in a café and there's an umbrella under the seat of the person at the next table, who gets up to leave without picking it up. What would you say (or not say) if they were (a) a good friend, (b) a stranger the same age as yourself, (c) a stranger much older than you?

2 What do you make of the redressive language in this fragment of a telephone conversation where I'm giving an address to someone (female) I've never met

(19) PETER: Oxon
A: Oxon?
PETER: Yeah I suppose that's Oxfordshire
A: Oh Oxfordshire

and in what was said when a young man came into a pub and approached the barman, who was about the same age as him and who he obviously knew slightly

(20) BARMAN: Bad news I'm afraid – Kel's injury isn't so serious as was at first thought so we won't be needing you – sorry

9.2.4 Power, distance and imposition

In the previous sub-section, we noticed the relationship between the degree of imposition of a request, say, for a sheet of paper, and the nature of the relationship between speaker and addressee. These are the areas that we explore below.

Scenario 1

I'm standing at the bar enjoying a quiet drink. Two men come in and the one in front says to the barman

(21) A pint of Bass please

He then consults his friend, who also wants a pint of Bass. The first man then says to the barman

(22) Can you make it two please

If the first man had consulted his friend before ordering, he would of course have said 'Two pints of Bass please' in the first place. But because he gives his order in two parts and because each part is for the same drink, he acknowledges this little extra imposition with 'Can you make it . . .', a *yes/no*-question at the locutionary level to which it's technically possible to answer 'no' if you happen to be Mr Logic.

In (21) and (22), the social distance and power relationship remains constant since the two utterances involve the same two speakers, so the only variable is the degree of imposition of the request.

Scenario 2
I'm standing in the corridor outside my office and I see a workman in blue dungarees approach a female colleague, to whom he says:

(23) Excuse me you couldn't tell me where Room 253 is possibly could you

It makes me think of all the times students ask to be directed to rooms and why none of them ever uses such elaborate redressive formulas. Of course, the blue-collar male and the white-collar female aren't in a relative power relationship (probably both are employed by the university) and the imposition *per se* is identical to that when a student asks to be directed to a room, so the strikingly redressive utterance seems to encode a perceived social distance.

Scenario 3
I'm chairing a session at a conference. One of my tasks is to make sure the speaker finishes her talk on time. I have a set of cards to hold up, one to warn the speaker when there are five minutes left, another to warn her when there are three and a final card which says 'Please stop'. When her time's up, I hold up the 'Please stop' sign, which she ignores. After another couple of minutes I hold it up again. She continues droning on as though I don't exist. As she's eating into the time needed for delegates to get from one room to another, I hold the sign up for a third time, this time with my hand obscuring 'please'. And this does the trick.

If you compare the contexts in which I hold up 'Please stop' and 'Stop', the imposition hasn't changed and nor has the social distance between us. But the longer the speaker goes on for, the more powerful I become as my right to end the session increases with time, hence my choice of a less redressive formula. (As the topic of the speaker's talk was the relative absence of redressive formulas in Finnish, I felt especially pleased with myself and couldn't resist making a poor joke about having found the best way to finish a talk.)

Conclusion: In deciding on the redressive language needed when performing a speech act, we take into account the degree of imposition of what we seek to accomplish by our utterance and any social distance or power differential between ourselves and those we address.

Checking understanding (9.4)

1 This example is taken from Brown and Levinson ([1978] 1987: 80): imagine you are on a station platform and two people approach you one after the other. The first says

(24) Got the time, mate?

and the second says

(25) Excuse me, would you by any chance have the time?

What assumptions would you make if you were addressed in these two ways and why would you make them?

2 Imagine a parent says to a young child

(26) Just eat it up

and the child says to the parent

(27) Aren't you going to eat it

Checking understanding (9.4) *cont.*

Each intends to get the other to eat their dinner. Why would they use different strategies to achieve the same effect?

3 Imagine you have a five-year-old daughter called Honey with a personality to match her name and you want to spend a morning shopping without a small child in tow. How would you ask Honey's best friend's mother to look after Honey for the morning?

Now imagine you have a five-month-old baby called Howler, also with a personality to match her name. You've been invited to stay with a friend who hates babies so you want to dump Howler on your elderly neighbour overnight. How would you ask your neighbour to look after her?

What are the differences between the way you would make the two requests and what reasons can you suggest for these differences?

9.2.5 Brown and Levinson's model of politeness strategies

By way of preparation for this sub-section, in the previous sub-sections, I've already introduced some of the key notions brought together by Brown and Levinson in their account of politeness phenomena.

9.2.5.1 Face wants and face-threatening acts

The most fully elaborated work on linguistic politeness is Brown and Levinson's *Universals in Language Usage: Politeness Phenomena* (1978), re-issued with a new introduction and revised bibliography as *Politeness: Some Universals in Language Usage* (1987). Working with data gathered from Tamil speakers in southern India, Tzeltal speakers in Mexico and speakers of American and British English, they provide a systematic description of cross-linguistic politeness phenomena which is used to support an explanatory model capable of accounting for any instance of politeness. Their claim is that broadly comparable linguistic strategies are available in each language but that there are local cultural differences in what triggers their use.

Brown and Levinson (B&L) work with Goffman's notion of 'face', a property that all human beings have and that's broadly comparable to self-esteem. In most encounters, our face is put at risk. Asking someone for a sheet of paper, or telling them they have to wait to see the doctor, or complaining about the quality of their repair on our car, or trying to get them to bring their conference talk to a conclusion, or even asking someone the time, these all threaten the face of the person to whom they are directed. So when we perform such actions, they're typically accompanied with redressive language designed to compensate the threat to face and thus to satisfy the face wants of our interlocutors. So we may ask someone just to 'let us' have 'a bit' of paper, or apologize for the inconvenience caused by having to wait to see the doctor, or make a joke of our complaint, or add 'please' to our request, or ask the time in a way that either stresses our solidarity with the addressee or acknowledges the trouble we are causing. These are all examples of politeness, the use of redressive language designed to compensate for face-threatening behaviour.

B&L assume a 'Model Person' with two kinds of face, **positive face** and **negative face**. Positive face is a person's wish to be well thought of. Its manifestations may include the desire to have others admire what we value, the desire to be understood by others, and the desire to be treated as a friend and confidant. Thus a complaint about the quality of someone's work threatens their positive face. Negative face is our wish not to be imposed on by others and to be allowed to go about our business unimpeded and with our rights to free and self-determined action intact. Thus telling someone they cannot see the doctor at the time they expected to is a threat to their negative face.

In dealing with each other, our utterances may be oriented to the positive or to the negative face of those we interact with. In

(24) Got the time mate

the kinship claiming 'mate' and the informality of elliptical 'Got' show that the utterance is oriented to the positive face of the addressee, who's being treated as a friend and an equal. It's therefore an example of **positive politeness**. But in

(12) You couldn't let me have a bit of paper by any chance could you

the remote 'could', the pessimistic negative and 'by any chance', the minimizing 'a bit', and the tag are all oriented to the addressee's negative face and seek to compensate for and play down the imposition and potential loss of face that having to give someone a piece of your own paper involves. It's an example of **negative politeness.**

Checking understanding (9.5)

Recall the train announcement examples in Chapter 2

(28) The next station is Kowloon Tong. Passengers may change there for MTR trains
(29) The next station is Kowloon Tong. Passengers should change here for KCR trains
(30) The next station is Newcastle. Passengers for Sunderland, Middlesbrough, Carlisle and the Newcastle Metro should change here
(31) The next station is Kowloon Tong. Passengers please change to MTR trains at Kowloon Tong

Do you think there's a difference in the extent to which the announcements address positive and negative face?

9.2.5.2 Positive, negative and off-record politeness

When he/she has a face-threatening act to perform, B&L's Model Person chooses from three superordinate strategies. They are do the act on-record, do the act off-record and don't do the act at all. By 'on-record', B&L mean without attempting to hide what we are doing, and by 'off-record' they mean in such a way as to pretend to hide it. Thus if I were to say

(32) I don't know what's wrong with my mobile – it doesn't seem to be charged

this might well be an off-record way of hinting that I'd like you to let me use yours. In theory, you could ask if I was hinting that I wanted to use your mobile and I could deny that I was and claim that I was merely making an observation – it's in this sense that I'm acting off-record.

Of the three superordinate strategies, the first, perform the face-threatening act on-record, is the most usual. In fact, there are three subordinate on-record strategies, making a total of five available strategies when we have a face-threatening act to perform:

Do the act on-record – baldly, without redress
– with positive politeness redress
– with negative politeness redress
Do the act off-record
Don't do the act

An illustration may help. If you live in Britain, you've almost certainly had the experience of someone asking you for a pound coin to release a trolley at the supermarket. When it happened to me the other day in the car park at our local supermarket, this is how the exchange went

(33) SHOPPER: Excuse me you haven't got a pound coin have you
PETER: Probably <produces coin from pocket>
SHOPPER: There you are there's your two fifties

As you can see, the shopper chooses to go on record (she names what she needs, 'a pound coin'). And she decides to appeal to my negative face – 'excuse me' indicating that she's impeding my right to go about daily business uninterrupted. The negative declarative and the tag encode that she doesn't necessarily expect me (to be able) to satisfy her face wants. I suppose my 'probably' reflects the modality of her utterance. But once I've produced a coin, her next utterance addresses my positive face wants as she ascribes ownership of the 'two fifties' to me.

Theoretically she had other options when she asked if I had a pound coin. Her utterance might have been on-record and bald

(34) I need a pound coin

or on-record and oriented to my positive face

(35) Give us a pound for the trolley, love

Or she might have gone off-record and said loudly to herself as I passed

(36) You can never find a pound coin when you need one, can you

Or she might have decided that it was just too face-threatening to her and/or me to ask for a pound coin and said nothing. Had I been the Prime Minister, this might perhaps have been her likeliest strategy.

In picking one of these five strategies, speakers work with an equation in which any distance differential, any power differential and any imposition are computed:

Social Distance (D) + Power Differential (P) + Ratio of Imposition (R) =
degree of face-threat to be redressed by appropriate linguistic strategy

In Checking Understanding (9.4), you worked on politeness strategies which were the result of each of these three factors being particularly strong. When the shopper approaches me in the supermarket car park, there's no power relationship between us since we're strangers and more or less the same age. The speaker may infer some distance differential from our physical appearance and dress style, although it seems unlikely that perceived social status counts for much in a supermarket car park. Thus in dealing with her need, the most important factor in the equation that adds up to x degrees of face threat is imposition: how face-threatening is it to be approached by a total stranger and asked for a pound in exchange for two fifty-pence pieces in a supermarket car park? Once this is computed, then the appropriate redressive language is selected. Had the shopper had a handful of heavy change amounting to a pound rather than two fifty pence coins, perhaps she'd have computed the imposition differently. As she might have done had the encounter occurred in a park nowhere near a supermarket.

Notice also that the shopper's strategy according to this model is rationalistic (i.e. she works out what she wants to achieve by reasoning) and teleological (i.e. she has an end in mind). She then decides on the means of achieving it – by saying 'Excuse me you haven't got a pound coin have you'.

An important point about B&L's five strategies is that they are ranked from *Do the act on record baldly*, which has no linguistically encoded redress, through a sequence of escalating politeness strategies to *Don't do the act*, where the face threat is too great to be redressed by any language formula so that the most appropriate politeness strategy is not to do the act. A speaker will only choose a highly ranked strategy where the face threat is felt to be high, since being 'too polite' implies that one is asking a lot of someone and/or that there's a significant power or social distance differential between those involved.

Checking understanding (9.6)

1 I 'collect' a certain kind of notice from hotel rooms. Here are a couple from the collection. Read them carefully and decide on the writer's purpose and the politeness strategies intended to achieve this purpose:

(37) Dear Guest,
The items in this room have been provided for your convenience and remain the property of the Room Attendant in charge. Should you be interested to collect any of the guestroom items as souvenirs of your stay at the Petaling Jaya Hilton, you may purchase them from our Executive Business Centre at the Main Lobby.
Thank you.

(38) Soft, fluppy and enveloping, this bathrobe will bring you moments of pure tenderness. If you can't leave without it, don't hesitate to acquire one for Euro 50 at the reception desk.

2 Can you identify examples of

- agentless passives
- deference strategies
- impersonal statements of general rules
- institutional first person plural pronoun
- reason/explanation

in this notice from our doctor's waiting room and say what their effects are:

(39) Please note
Patients who are required to provide samples for analysis, are reminded that they may only be accepted if they are presented in the appropriate specimen bottle.

Checking understanding (9.6) *cont.*

These are available on request from reception or the practice nurse. Samples which are presented in non-sterile containers present a health and safety hazard to our staff and therefore cannot be accepted.

Why do you think doctors communicate with patients in this way?

3 Imagine you're sitting opposite someone on a train and their personal stereo is leaking noise and preventing you concentrating on the book you're reading. Make a list of several different ways of asking them to deal with the problem. Then try and match each of these to B&L's five superordinate politeness strategies.

9.2.5.3 Positive and negative politeness strategies

In discussing redressive use earlier in this chapter, we commented on a number of politeness strategies. For example, in

(16) In order to promote a better learning environment please do not bring food or drink into this teaching room and remember to switch off your mobile telephone.
Thank you.

we identified giving a reason ('in order to promote a better learning environment'), the deferential use of 'please', 'remember' and the elaborate 'mobile telephone', and the use of 'your' to personalize the message. We might also have commented on the nominalization 'a better learning environment' and the use of 'Thank you' to acknowledge the addressee's assumed cooperation. And in

(33) SHOPPER: Excuse me you haven't got a pound coin have you

we noticed the shopper's apology ('excuse me') and her pessimism.

B&L (1987: 102, 131) list the positive and negative politeness strategies available to their Model Person, which, as you'll see, include those identified in (16) and (33):

Positive politeness
Notice/attend to hearer's wants
Exaggerate interest/approval
Intensify interest
Use in-group identity markers
Seek agreement
Avoid disagreement
Presuppose/assert common ground
Joke
Assert knowledge of hearer's wants
Offer, promise
Be optimistic
Include speaker and hearer in the activity
Give (or ask for) reasons
Assume/assert reciprocity
Give gifts to hearer (goods, sympathy, etc.)

Negative politeness
Be conventionally indirect
Question, hedge
Be pessimistic
Minimize imposition
Give deference
Apologize
Impersonalize
State the imposition as a general rule
Nominalize
Go on record as incurring a debt

Looking back, we can also see these strategies in some of the data discussed earlier. Among the positive politeness strategies are the jogger's assumption of my *want* of the right kind of 'bird', my *presupposing of common ground* with the barrier operative, the *joke* with the service manager at the garage, and my asking the snack-bar operative for *a reason*. Among the negative politeness strategies, there are my *hedges* in 'I think bullet points . . .' and 'I suppose that's Oxfordshire'.

Among B&L's list of positive politeness strategies not exemplified in our previous discussion, you'll have noticed how we try to find agreement and to avoid disagreement wherever possible, as in this exchange I overheard on a train

(40) PASSENGER A: I thought it was dead patronizing
PASSENGER B: Did you

Or in this exchange when I saw the Dean using the new photocopier

(41) PETER: It's brilliant this machine isn't it
DEAN: Yes it has a mind of its own
PETER: That's also true

I begin with a positive or exaggerated view of the world ('It's brilliant this machine'). However, my tag, 'isn't it', allows for the possibility of a second point of view, a respectful strategy given that I'm talking to the Dean. This was fortunate, as he was finding the complexities of the machine more apparent than its brilliance, and he did indeed have a second point of view. Although superficially agreeing with me at the level of literal meaning, and signalling this with the overt agreement marker 'Yes', his 'it has a mind of its own' implies something rather different: that he did not think it was so brilliant, presumably because he couldn't get it to do what he wanted it to do. 'That's also true' confirms this implicature and continues the fiction that we are in agreement, matching the Dean's 'Yes' with my 'also'. So although I represent the machine as brilliant and he has another opinion, our politeness strategies minimize our disagreement. I'm able to agree with the Dean (and hopefully curry a little favour), and we all find life easier when unity prevails.

One last point about this exchange: notice how I assumed that, as the less important person, I should speak first when I met the Dean in the corridor. Gu (1990) says that an inferior always speaks first in an encounter in China. Do you think there's a politeness norm in this area in the culture of which you are a native member?

Among negative politeness strategies not exemplified in our previous discussion, you'll have noticed how frequently we avoid interfering with the freedom of others by impersonalizing, as in the question I heard a student ask in the corridor

(42) Are there any toilets around

Sometimes a speaker goes half-way down the impersonalization road, as in the following multi-directed question asked by one of a group of four students walking in front of me in the street:

(43) Does anyone know which room we're supposed to be in

B&L's list probably isn't exhaustive. You can also challenge their categorization of particular strategies as positive or negative if you wish. And of course most utterances combine attending to both the positive and the negative face wants of those we address. But I guess you agree that their treatment of politeness phenomena is comprehensive and convincing.

Checking understanding (9.7)

1 Recall two or three occasions when the politeness behaviour you observed was particularly striking and try to work out why this was, referring where appropriate to strategies listed by B&L.

2 Return to the three texts (15), (16) and (17) that you listed in order of acceptability in Checking Understanding (9.2). Can you identify any of B&L's politeness strategies in them and say how the politeness strategies contributed to your ranking?

One way to test B&L's schema is to see what happens when speakers don't compute power (P), distance (D) and imposition (R) in expectable ways. Not surprisingly, this is a typical source of humour in television sit-coms. Although this doesn't happen often in real life, when it does the results can be entertaining. I remember a wonderful occasion in my first teaching post when the Headmaster and I took a group of twenty-five boys camping. This was a very rare event for the Headmaster, who was perhaps trying to re-live his own youth and whose memories of camping dated mainly from the Second World War. To the great amusement of the boys, he began by setting a working party to digging a latrine (of which he was destined to be the sole user). Another working party was sent scavenging for timber to make a camp-fire. A third group assisted in the preparation of the evening meal, a monster stew into which the Headmaster threw everything he could lay his hands on, including, towards the end of the preparation period, several rather earthy potatoes that he couldn't be bothered to peel.

When the meal was eventually served, there was an apprehensive circle of boys with enamel plates swimming in doubtful stew watching to see what the Headmaster would do. The Headmaster served himself last, by which time all the cutlery had been taken. "Have any of you chaps seen a fork?" he asked, whereupon a cheeky thirteen-year-old chimed in with "I'd try a spade if I were you sir." I can't say that the Headmaster smiled. The humour resulted from the very great power differential which was being ignored in the positive-face oriented joke, and the implicit ridiculing of hours of painstaking cooking which threatened the Headmaster's negative face. Laughter, on this occasion, and frequently in sitcoms, is one way of marking the incongruous politeness status of an utterance.

9.2.6 Folk beliefs and pragmatic insight

You may recall that in Chapter 7 I used quotation marks when I said that the agentless description

(44) Susie's butter's gone and my cheese has gone as well

was a 'more polite' way of conveying the proposition already conveyed by

(45) Someone's been nicking stuff out the fridge

in Nicole's previous turn.

Having got to this point, we're now able to say more about how the two utterances differ. The informal in-group colloquialism 'nicking', the use of the delexical noun 'stuff' and the reduced 'out the fridge' in (45) address the Doctor's positive face, treating him as an equal and a friend. This contrasts with the agentless (44) in which 'been nicking' has been replaced with the less accusatory 'gone', a description repeated in a rhetorical structure that contrasts with the non-prestige use of 'out the fridge'. We're now able to see that (44) isn't strictly 'more polite' than (45). They have different politeness statuses, that's for sure, with (45) exhibiting a range of positively polite phenomena absent in (44). However, the judgement that (44) is 'more polite' than (45) isn't a linguistic judgement at all, it's a folk judgement. This is why at the beginning of this chapter I was careful to avoid a value judgement and simply made the point that you and my wife are both 'polite' but in different ways.

In fact, much of our everyday thinking about politeness is bedevilled by the fact that 'politeness' is a folk term used in the kind of value-laden way that I was guilty of in Chapter 7. In Britain 'politeness' is typically used to describe negative politeness, which is presumed to be 'a good thing', hence the folk view of (44) as 'more polite' than (45).

A typical folk view of politeness is implied in Phyllis's use of 'very polite-spoke' in the exchange with which this chapter begins. I guess a strong connotation of 'very polite-spoke' is standard or RP speech. Such a folk view of politeness as the speech style of the middle classes is clearly value-laden. Thus the value-neutral way in which 'politeness' is used as a term of pragmatic description applicable to all communicative instances of language use is easily confused with the quite different, but widely held, ideological attitude to politeness in society at large. From a pragmaticist's point of view, as we said earlier, 'politeness' is the term we use to describe the relationship between how something is said to an addressee and that addressee's judgement as to how it should be said. This has nothing at all to do with prescriptive approaches to linguistic etiquette.

The difference between the folk view and the linguist's view is perhaps the difference between treating a variety such as RP or Standard American as a marker of politeness and noticing the real subtleties of the face-aware use of language in the exchange between Phyllis and myself that occurred one afternoon at work. I was pouring myself a cup of tea in the kitchen when Phyllis, our tea-lady, said to someone else in the kitchen, but about me

(46) He's a very polite-spoke man aren't you

to which I replied

(47) It's not what they say at home

Of particular interest in this exchange are Phyllis's switch to me as addressee ('aren't you'), and the choice of 'it's' in my response. Phyllis was talking about me to a third party in my presence, and therefore politeness required that I should be included in the conversation. Phyllis does this with the tag 'aren't you', which, strictly speaking, renders her utterance ungrammatical. Since her utterance was a compliment, I felt obliged out of modesty to demur in some way, and chose

(47) It's not what they say at home

rather than

(47′) That's not what they say at home

The cleft structure of both (47) and (47′) gives rise to the presupposition that they do say something else at home. But 'that' would have been taken to refer to the proposition that the person described is a very polite-spoke man and I would have implied that they say something different at home, thus implicitly contradicting Phyllis's opinion. But in saying 'it', I merely imply that at home they don't say what she says, and thus convey that she's kinder than my family. This example illustrates the pervasive nature of politeness: even the choice between seemingly semantically empty categories such as anaphoric 'it' and 'that' is politeness driven.

Checking understanding (9.8)

Do you think the folk view that politeness is a thing of the past and that everyone's rude nowadays makes any sense?

9.3 Politeness phenomena in the real world

In this section we first explore a context in which positive and negative politeness are blended, and then consider speaker- and addressee-oriented face-saving strategies, before finally exploring a hotel guest who'd had enough and resorted to rudeness.

9.3.1 Service encounters and identity

If you're a regular rail traveller in Britain, you'll know that the various train companies claim to view passengers as customers. In other words, they think of the relationship as a service encounter. Here's a typical on-board announcement:

(48) Any customer requiring breakfast please make your way to the restaurant car now

Notice how the more nominal 'any customer requiring breakfast' and 'make your way' are preferred to the more verbal 'if you want breakfast' and 'go to', marking this as a service encounter in which the customer is shown deference.

One aspect of (48) familiar to rail travellers in Britain is the switch from the description 'any customer requiring breakfast' to 'your way', the latter implying either a spoken or understood second person pronominal antecedent. It's as though 'any customer' is the formal member of the *tu/vous* set and the anaphoric 'your way' the familiar. Here are several more examples of the same phenomenon:

(49) If we have any people on board not wishing to travel I would advise you to step back on to the platform now
(50) Will anyone not intending to travel please make your way back to the platform
(51) Would anyone not intending to travel please make your way back to the platform
(52) Will anyone leaving us in York please make sure you take all your personal belongings with you
(53) Passengers who are leaving the train at York please make sure you have all your luggage with you

Of course, it's usual to address both positive as well as negative face wants even in a service encounter that encodes the fundamentally unequal status of customer and service provider. Thus, in (52) we find plain and friendly 'make sure' immediately after an impersonal ('anyone'), nominalized ('anyone leaving'), power-encoding ('us'), and the redressive IFID ('please'). But the dissonance evident in (48)–(53) with their lower order grammaticalness is very striking. Without a formal member of a *tu/vous* pronominal set, these service encounter obsessed companies have invented one. How long till they either see sense and say

(48′) If you want breakfast please make your way to the restaurant car now

or have the courage of their convictions and say

(48″) Would any customer requiring breakfast please make his or her way to the restaurant car now

9.3.2 Face-saving formulas for the speaker: a long day

I'm having dinner in a hotel when the head waiter approaches my table. This is what happens next

(54) HEAD WAITER: Are you having dessert sir
PETER: I might have yes. See how I go
HEAD WAITER: After your main course. It's been a long day sir
PETER: Yes see how I go

As you've probably worked out, I've finished my starter and am waiting for the main course but the head waiter thinks I've finished my main course and am waiting to be offered a dessert. The way he puts the question 'Are you having dessert' (rather than 'Would you like a dessert') seemed to me to imply that he supposed an ordinary waiter was looking after me and that if this wasn't the case then I was privileged to have attracted the attention of the head waiter. As head waiters in restaurants in Britain are much more important than guests, his loss of face was very great. I was struck by the face-saving formula 'It's been a long day', which he chose to excuse his mistake. And then shortly afterwards I heard someone else do it when he'd got something wrong. I then realized that this phrase has become a conventional way of excusing yourself for a mistake and doing at least something to restore your dignity. The following exchange confirms that the formula is conventionalized and used by people whatever the time of day.

I'm in the airport departure lounge at 8.45 a.m. waiting for the call to go to the gate. There's a passenger in a wheelchair nearby. In due course, a member of staff appears and asks the passenger if he needs assistance getting to the gate. The passenger points out that the member of staff has already offered him assistance, and rather ungraciously adds

(55) PASSENGER: . . . You're getting confused
STAFF MEMBER: It's been a long day
PASSENGER: And it hasn't even started yet

If you see anyone in a wheelchair at Newcastle airport, my advice is to leave them to it!

Although we usually think of the face of the addressee being threatened, we should also remember that speakers too can easily lose face.

9.3.3 Maintaining addressee face when wants aren't met

It's quarter to twelve at night and I'm in a hotel in Beijing. I'm just getting ready for bed when I hear the guest in the room across the corridor arriving. From the exchange I overhear, I guess he's accompanied by a bellboy:

(56) GUEST: Do you have any nice girls in the hotel tonight
BELLBOY: Oh no I'm afraid not. But you may go across the road

I'm sure you've noticed that when you make a request which the person you address can't satisfy, they tend to try and minimize your face loss. Sometimes there's an alternative suggestion, as on this occasion when the bellboy's 'but' encodes his metapragmatic awareness of making a next-best suggestion.

This is what happened to me on a plane when I was offered Worcester sauce by an airline that I knew from previous experience specialized in sachets of imitation Worcester sauce:

(57) STEWARDESS: Would you like a drink sir
PETER: Tomato juice <offers pre-distributed cardboard beaker>
STEWARDESS: Would you like Worcester sauce
PETER: Is it real Worcester sauce
STEWARDESS: It's a sachet
PETER: <Shakes head and smiles>
STEWARDESS: Actually I can give you a glass

Isn't that wonderful! A gift even!

And this is what happened in two different bookshops on the same street when I approached an assistant holding the first edition of a well-known textbook and asked, with a pessimistic hedge, if they had the second edition in stock:

(58) PETER: Have you got the second edition of this – it doesn't seem to be on the shelves
SHOP 1 (after consulting the computer): No it's not in stock. We can order it for you

(59) PETER: Have you got the second edition of this – it doesn't seem to be on the shelves
SHOP 2 (after consulting the computer): No we did have it but it's sold out.

In the first shop, the assistant makes an offer which is personalized ('for you') and in the second the assistant's reply avoids saying directly that the book isn't in stock, instead inviting this as an inference, before explaining why my request can't be met.

In the following example, notice the use of 'only'. This is a sandwich shop where I sometimes buy a lunchtime bun:

(60) PETER: Are there any bacon buns
ASSISTANT: Only sausage

Both the sausage offer and the implicit apology conveyed by 'only' help to minimize my face loss.

On another occasion, I watch a couple scrutinize a pub menu for several minutes before one of them approaches the bar:

(61) CUSTOMER: Have you got any salady things
BARMAN: Not really

The customer knew his request was unlikely to be met, hence 'salady things', and the barman minimized the customer's loss of face by hedging his confirmation.

So we see that when we find ourselves with no option but to disappoint an addressee because we can't meet their request, we generally take care to do it in a way that preserves face.

9.3.4 A hotel breakfast

I don't know about you, but one of things I find most face threatening when I stay in a hotel is finding it's one of those hotels where you aren't allowed to have breakfast until you've been checked off at the dining room entrance. At a hotel I once stayed in, the waiter asked my name and then couldn't find it on his list. So he then asked my room number, and couldn't find that on his list either. He kept me standing there looking (more than ever) like an idiot despite the fact that I had a room key in my hand. He then asked me if I'd had breakfast in the hotel before. I took this to be a continuation of the checking procedure, of which I'd already had enough. This how the exchange went:

(62) WAITER: Have you had breakfast here before
PETER: Sorry
WAITER: Have you had breakfast here before
PETER: I only arrived here yesterday

Rather than responding to the first 'Have you had breakfast here before' with 'No I haven't', I felt it was time to challenge the interrogation mode with 'Sorry'. When the question was repeated, I decided to let him infer that I obviously hadn't had breakfast before from 'I only arrived here yesterday'. It was rude. And it turned out that the waiter had decided not to bother about the fact that I didn't exist on his list: 'Have you had breakfast here before' turned out to be the conventional formula preparatory to explaining how the self-service system worked rather than a further step in the interrogation. So I looked even more foolish.

One conclusion we can draw from this misunderstanding is that politeness phenomena, because of their redressive function, enable civilized exchanges to occur. When politeness is left behind, as here, things can go wrong very quickly. A couple more questions from the waiter and I might have resorted to striding past him and risking fisticuffs.

9.4 The universal character of politeness

In the key to Checking Understanding (9.4), I made the point that over-classes tend to favour distance encoding negative politeness strategies so as to maintain their social status and under-classes tend to favour solidarity encoding positive politeness strategies as part of their struggle for equality. I also stated at the beginning of Section 9.2 that B&L argue that politeness phenomena are universal. If this is right, we should be able to extrapolate the intra-societal politeness behaviour we noted in over- and under-class communication to whole societies. Thus in hierarchical societies with strong class distinctions, the over-classes will see to it that the under-classes employ more negative politeness strategies when addressing their 'elders and betters' as a way of encoding and thus maintaining the distance between socially stratified groups who acquire face status through birth. More egalitarian societies, on the other hand, will employ positive politeness strategies as a way of encoding and thus confirming a less territorial view of face. In such societies, face is said to be 'ascribed' on merit rather than 'acquired' by birth.

With this in mind, we turn to one challenging line of criticism of B&L's model, that the politeness usage they describe is not universal. Thus Matsumoto (1988) argues that in Japanese the structures associated with negative politeness strategies in B&L's model do not have a negative politeness function but instead constitute a social register. Gu (1990) argues that the model is unsuited to Chinese usage in which politeness phenomena still reflect to some degree the etymology of the word for politeness, one of whose constituent morphemes (*li*) denotes social order. Like Matsumoto's and Gu's, most other criticisms of the B&L model on these grounds post-date the 1987 re-issue of their book.

Of course, we wouldn't expect identical computations of appropriate politeness formulas across cultures any more than we would across varying situations in a single culture. Just as we employ different strategies to get different people to do things for us, so asking for assistance when, for example, your car breaks down will impose to different degrees in different societies (Nwoye, 1992). It's important therefore to separate culturally variable estimates of power, distance and imposition, which we would expect to occur, from the strategies and linguistic manifestations of strategies which a universal account of politeness would need to capture.

Much of Matsumoto's criticism centres on the way that deference is manifested in Japanese honorifics. She claims, in my opinion rightly, that B&L's formulation doesn't account for such data. But her perspective seems to me to raise the issue, not of whether politeness phenomena are universal, but rather of whether B&L are right to treat deference as a politeness strategy. As she says, "It is far from clear that deference can be equated with the speaker's respecting an individual's right to non-imposition" (1988: 409). In fact, we probably need to distinguish situations where deference is given unexceptionally as an automatic acknowledgement of relative social status from situations where it's given exceptionally in a particular situation as a redressive strategy. In the first case, the use of honorifics reinforces an existing culture and isn't a chosen politeness strategy at all since the speaker attempts to produce a context-reflecting utterance acceptable to the addressee as addressee. In the second, the speaker uses deference to produce a context-creating utterance acceptable to the addressee in the situation shared by the speaker and himself. The problem of course is how to distinguish between situations where speakers have little or no option in their choice of *tu/vous* type alternatives and situations where they do, and can thus use honorifics as politeness markers to invoke new contexts. Perhaps an illustration will help.

I once took part in a debate with a Conservative member of the British Parliament many years my senior in which I probably said some hard things about his speech. After the debate I bought a round of drinks. When it came to asking him what he'd like to drink, this is how the exchange went:

(63) PETER: And for you sir
MP: Oh so it's sir now is it

Mine was clearly a politeness strategy that misfired as I tried to create a context to match my addressee's perception of how he should be addressed. Matsumoto (1988) gives examples of four ways that you might ask someone in Japan if they were going to have lunch, each displaying deference at an appropriate level. One could hardly imagine a Japanese professor addressed with the elaborate deference that professors customarily receive in Japan challenging the speaker in the way that the Member of Parliament challenged me:

(64) Oh so it's o-yuuhan mesiagari-masu now is it (Oh so it's honorific-dinner eat(subject honorific)-polite now is it)

This shows that we need to distinguish between language which is reflective of presumptive context (the Japanese professor) and genuine politeness phenomena which are used to bring a context into being (as I attempted to do unsuccessfully with the Member of Parliament).

In fact, objectors to B&L's account frequently cite exotic examples of apparent deference which are claimed as evidence that some notion of social order or societal interdependence rather than positive and negative face underlies politeness. A typical example is provided by Gu (1990) who cites the etymology of *bai* (to prostrate oneself at the foot of another) as in *baidu* (to read) as evidence that knowing one's place underlies Chinese politeness. Without being a native member of Chinese society, it's difficult to say anything definitive about this claim, but I rather doubt that it's right. To my mind, it would be like claiming that the Greek word *polis*, meaning *city*, from which *politeness* (and *police*) are derived somehow determines the principles of politeness in the societies whose word for politeness is derived from a common ancestor. Or take the case of

(65) Can you give me the salt

mentioned in Chapter 4. Surely making the request in this way doesn't mean that deference is a motivating principle in the cultures where this is the default. What I'm suggesting is that the prostrating oneself element of *baidu* is as conventional and inert as a politeness strategy as the notion that a salt-giver is a powerful person invited to dispense a valued commodity to others of inferior status.

Whether B&L have proposed a model that is universal is always open to discussion. But what's important about their work is their observation that politeness is not equally distributed. As they say: "It is not as if there were some basic modicum of politeness owed by each to all" (1987: 5). Rather what's owed depends on the calculation of what's expected in each social and situational context that arises.

Raising pragmatic awareness

1 Working individually, eavesdrop on two or three conversations and write down what people say when they smile. Try to identify the politeness status of what is said. Share your findings with friends or other members of your tutorial group. Finally, invent a further eavesdropping task with a politeness dimension for members of your tutorial group to try.

2 Devise and carry out a simple rapid anonymous sampling experiment such as mine in the two bookshops described in Section 9.3.3. Report your findings to your colleagues in your next tutorial.

3 Cut a picture out of a colour magazine which contains two people who are clearly together. Write down five or six different ways in which one of the people might

- invite the other out
- ask the other the time
- accuse the other of telling a lie
- tell the other he/she smells.

Bring your picture and possible utterances to the tutorial and ask your colleagues to decide which way of accomplishing the face-threatening act would be most appropriate for the people concerned.

Raising pragmatic awareness *cont.*

4 This exercise works best in a small group. Pick a nation and decide how that nation is stereotypically seen by yourselves. Then try to associate this stereotype with typical politeness strategies. If you can get this exercise to work, do the same thing with an intra-cultural group such as the young or the old within your own culture or with some ethnically or gender constituted group. If possible, follow this up by careful observation of a representative of the group you were stereotyping to see whether your stereotype is at all reflected in the person you observe. To what extent do you think stereotyping is one person's view of another person's pragmatics? (Acknowledgement: this is Kelly Glover's idea.)

5 Listen out for the way people reflect their own status in talk. Make a careful note of what you hear and report it to your next tutorial group.

6 Think about the politeness strategies of people in another country you've visited and compare it with the strategies with which you're familiar. What conclusions do you draw about power–distance differentials or perspectives on imposition in the two societies?

7 Which of the features of talk identified as typically pragmatic in Chapter 1 play an important part in a speaker's choice of politeness phenomena: accommodation, appropriateness, context, indeterminacy, indirect meaning, inference, reflexivity, relevance?

Discussions and essays

Based on what you know about politeness, discuss the relative merits of each of the following views:

- Different individuals value positive and negative face to different extents so there can be no one-size-fits-all approach to politeness. There are no model persons.
- A world without politeness phenomena would be a very scary place.
- Politeness phenomena are an obvious means of constructing and maintaining social class.
- A rationalistic explanation for politeness phenomena in terms of means–ends reasoning overlooks the fact that politeness is a dimension of language that reflects the identity of the speaker.
- "To be polite, speakers attempt to give options, avoid intrusion, and make their interlocutor feel good" (*Encyclopedic Dictionary of Applied Linguistics*, 1998: 248).
- Folk or lay uses of the term 'polite' often capture facts about the use of language that Brown and Levinson's theory doesn't account for.

Discussions and essays *cont.*

- Politeness is "a battery of social skills whose goal is to ensure that everyone feels affirmed in a social interaction" (Foley, 1997: 270).
- Our naïve understanding of politeness phenomena focuses more or less exclusively on what Brown and Levinson call negative politeness.

Further reading

Classic text

Brown and Levinson, 1978/1987 (especially the 1987 introduction). Key passages reprinted in Jaworski and Coupland, 1999: 321–35. Position summarized in Foley, 1997: 270–5.

Politeness as a principle of pragmatics

Leech, 1983, especially 79–84.

Journal articles

Matsumoto, 1988, 1989.

Special issues

Journal of Pragmatics 14/2 (especially papers by Gu and Kasper); *Journal of Pragmatics* 21/5 (politeness across cultures).

10 Empirical pragmatics, interactive pragmatics, talk-in-interaction

I have only one eye, – I have a right to be blind sometimes . . . I really do not see the signal.
(Horatio Nelson)
(This reported utterance when Nelson put the telescope to his blind eye at the battle of Copenhagen is very wittily used by Jacob Mey in his review of Horn and Ward)

Keywords:

account, adjacency pair, *aizuchi*, conversation analysis, empirical pragmatics, ethnomethodology, formulation, latching, macro/micro contexts, members' method, overlap, pause, (dis)preferred contribution, rationalistic pragmatics, repair, talk-in-interaction, transition-relevance place, turn (constructional unit)

10.1 Introduction

In this chapter, we explore the extent to which the kind of pragmatics we've been doing privileges a **rationalistic**, theory-driven attitude to pragmatic meaning over an approach that takes into account the social and psychological contexts in which utterances occur. We also consider whether pragmaticists might have something to learn from the ethnomethodological approach to language taken in conversation analysis.

You may have noticed as you've been reading this book that the rationalistic/psychological motivation fence is one on which I've been sitting a little uncomfortably. In the introductory section of each chapter (Chapter 8 apart), I've used a simple example to draw attention to an area in which pragmaticists have made a good deal of progress. In the second section, I've approached the area from an explanatory perspective. Typically, this explanatory approach has been rationalistic – we've assumed that speakers are rational beings with ends in mind and that they use language so as to bring those ends about. And then in the third section of each chapter I've shared more extensive real world data in a way that I hope has helped to set the rationalistic account in a wider social context. Sometimes you may have felt that this more **empirical** approach shows up the limitations of the rationalistic assumptions we've been exploring. So what does rationalistic pragmatics overlook?

Take the exchange

(1) BRANKA: When will you be back
PETER: I should be back by eight but you know what trains are like

Knowing that the person indexed by Branka's use of 'you' and my use of 'I' can only be determined by someone present at the time of the utterance doesn't really capture anything of the social or psychological reality of the way Branka and I talk to each other. The same point could be made about knowing that Branka's question presupposes that I will be back. When we come to speech acts, it's a little more interesting. For example, Branka may be expressing exasperation (another Saturday and you aren't around) or she may have an ulterior motive in asking when I'll be back. However, we've had little opportunity to explore such psychological dimensions of her utterance in the way we've been doing pragmatics. We've assumed that even psychological motivations of this kind can be subsumed within a means–ends, rationalistic account of language use. Much the same might be said about our approach to implicature – we've been interested more in the reasoning process by which implicatures are recovered than in the rather striking fact that social meanings to do with meals, household obligations and lottery tickets are conveyed so very implicitly.

When I asked at the end of Chapter 7 whether we might have started to study pragmatics in the wrong place, this is partly what I was getting at. Is it appropriate to set out with categories like *deixis, presupposition, speech acts* and *implicature* already in mind? If 'back' in (1) is a shorthand for a place known to both Branka and me, then it functions as a way of encoding membership, principally a social and psychological notion. Similarly with the formula 'you know what *x* are like': depending on the '*x*' that fills the slot, I encode the extent to which our membership is of a closed group consisting just of us or of a wider social group. Perhaps my use of 'but' is a way of encoding my care for the person I speak to rather than simply a device that constrains her interpretation of what I say. Do I constrain the interpretation only because I'm rational or might I also have feelings for the person I talk to?

As well as evaluating the adequacy of the rationalistic approach of mainstream inferential pragmatics, we'll also outline the approach to talk followed in **conversation analysis** (CA). CA approaches language without a pre-existing explanatory theory. The idea is that by studying use, we establish usage principles. For example, when we talk, my wife and I take turns. This may seem obvious, but even in our short exchange, you'll notice that I know when Branka's turn is about to end so that I'm able to respond the moment she finishes speaking. I also know what a preferred response should look like in both form and content. This is why I orient to the dispreferred content of my response with the use of 'should', by this means acknowledging that I can't deliver maximally expected next turn content in response to the question 'when will you be back'.

In this chapter, then, we're going to scratch the surface of a more empirical approach to talk. The chapter contains four further sections:

- *Decontextualized pragmatics,* which explains Kopytko's critique of rationalistic pragmatics.
- *Personal context in the real world,* which explores a real-world encounter in which psychological and social factors appear to be the prime motivation for the interactant's behaviour.
- *Talk-in-interaction,* which examines the extent to which conversation analysis might serve as the basis for understanding interactive pragmatics.
- *Approaches to pragmatics,* which discusses some of the issues motivating the approach to pragmatics taken in this book.

10.2 Decontextualized pragmatics

In this section, we first outline Kopytko's argument that rationalistic pragmatics is highly reductive and then consider his specific criticisms of Brown and Levinson's account of politeness phenomena.

10.2.1 Rationalistic pragmatics

In a paper which appeared in the *Journal of Pragmatics* in 1995, Roman Kopytko drew a distinction between what he called 'rationalistic' and 'empirical' pragmatics, arguing that we're in danger of the ultimate paradox, a decontextualized pragmatics. But how could the study of the relationship between language and the contexts in which it's used ever be decontextualized?

According to Kopytko, much of our theorizing is based on rationalistic assumption rather than empirical findings. We tend to place our faith in the predictability of pragmatic meaning and to use only one of our faculties, reason, when trying to work out what someone means by what they say. Nor do we take into account the possibility that there may be degrees of reason. We also take an extremely reductive view of language, simplifying real-world data and inventing model or idealized examples to illustrate our assumptions. Thus we promote reason and overlook the various psychological and affective factors that might explain why what I do today I don't necessarily do tomorrow. Our goal is a deterministic theory of action in which past experience enables us to predict the outcomes of the future situations we are to encounter. This, then, is decontextualized pragmatics – an algorithm into which I can feed an utterance and determine its function or meaning on the basis of previous experience.

This reductive approach is motivated by our belief in the purposefulness of our use of language. Our actions, including our linguistic actions, are assumed to be teleological, i.e. we have a goal in view and we make use of language to bring that goal about. Sequences of talk aren't unscripted outcomes, but, according to this view, calculated.

Rather than this highly reductive approach to data, which we match with highly reductive categories to which we ascribe it, we should learn to recognize and seek to explain the "unexpected emergent properties which come to light in the course of a speech encounter due to the presence of 'specific' participants in the group" (Kopytko, 1995: 485) and "unexpected contextual intrusion (e.g. *faux pas*, excitement, anger, emergent group properties, etc.)" (ibid.: 486). Thus we overlook the importance of "attitudes, personality, emotions, irrationality, ignorance, values, contradictory goals, unpredictable reactions, etc." (ibid.: 487) in motivating utterances and understanding them. We ignore such features of interaction in favour of "an 'ideal type' " of pragmatics, "a prescriptive model . . . more concerned with the question of how 'rational agents' should use their language to meet the standards of rationality and predictiveness than with describing how language is actually used by the speakers" (ibid.: 489).

Shall we take a step back and draw breath?

When we study syntax, and especially the generative model, we try to provide an account of data that is both explanatory and predictive, i.e. capable of accounting for all and only the grammatical structures of a language in a highly deterministic way. This is what syntax is. Kopytko's objection, it seems to me, is to a generative pragmatics of this sort. Such a pragmatics, if it existed, would try to apply to context-sensitive functional data an explanatory method designed to predict the rule-bound nature of context-free formal data. My guess is that it's precisely Chomsky's claim discussed in Chapter 8 that what a speaker means by their words "has nothing particular to do with language" that encourages rationalistic pragmatics: we seek to prove Chomsky wrong by following generative syntax down the extremely attractive path towards an explanatory, predictive theory of pragmatic meaning. However, as I suggested in Chapter 8, this isn't the way to prove Chomsky wrong about pragmatics. Nor is it easy to account for context-sensitive data with a deterministic methodology of this kind.

10.2.2 Kopytko on Brown and Levinson

Kopytko criticizes Brown and Levinson's theory in particular as a classic example of a rationalistic approach (1995, 2001). Kopytko's position is that, like generative linguistics, the kind of pragmatics whose roots lie in linguistic philosophy applies a reductively 'Cartesian' perspective (i.e. reason-based, after the seventeenth-century French philosopher René Descartes) to the study of language. Such a narrowly understood notion of cognition takes little or no account of the truly situated context of language use. While B&L aren't pure Cartesians in Kopytko's judgement, their Model Person calculates the politeness strategies required to achieve some outcome in a rational, goal-oriented way which reduces complex variables to simple calculations. Thus, "methodological reductionism in pragmatics (e.g. politeness theory in terms of models (MP) and reduced social variables (P,D,R)) leads directly to a pragmatic paradox – that of a 'decontextualized pragmatics' " (1995: 487). At issue is whether the social context and personal variables such as affect and emotion are adequately taken into account in B&L's rationalistic proposals. Or have we been studying just those aspects of the human condition that we can easily model in a rationalistic pragmatics? Kopytko makes one more telling point, which resonates with our mention of pragmatics as the study of 'hearer meaning' in Chapter 8, pointing out that "it is the hearer who assigns politeness to any utterance within the situation in which it was heard" (ibid.: 488).

10.3 Personal context in the real world

As you read the first half of the following exchange between a student (S) and a university librarian (L), notice the pauses between turns and at places where the turn might have been passed from one speaker to the other. These are highlighted with arrows:

(2) S: right (1.5) tsuh I'm tempted to say one two three testing
[but I don't suppose] I should should I .hh I left a (. .) I left
L: [<laughs>]
S: a folder here on Friday I think an orange folder (.) I wonder if
→ it[d] been handed in (0.7) I was at the inter-library loan desk
→ (1.0)
L: oh right
→ (0.5)
S: I think it was sort of orangey coloured
→ (1.0)
L: it's not this one there?
S: (1.0) dunno I hope so (1.0) no
[ ]
→ (2.0)
L: it's OK
<L types>
<L looks around for folder>
(28.0)
L: no I'm sorry
→ (1.0)
S: .hh oh dear (1.0) OK
→ (3.0)
S: alright (.) you don't happen to know if [anyone handed]
L: [if we] find
it to who
→ (1.5)

S: [yeah]
L: [your] name is

These pauses show the dysfunctional nature of the exchange. Rather than a typical trajectory in which each speaker takes up the next turn immediately the other speaker completes the previous turn, this exchange is punctuated by pauses between turns, indicating the difficulty the speakers experience continuing the talk.

There are a number of other features of their exchange worth commenting on:

- S begins by orienting to the start of business between himself and Librarian ('right (1.5)'). This follows his initial (unrecorded) dealings with the researcher who asks his permission to record the inquiry he's about to make. His click-like vocalization ('tsuh') precedes a reference to being recorded ('I'm tempted to say one two three testing'). This is followed by a comment on the inappropriateness of that reference ('but I don't suppose I should should I'). The real business then begins with the indrawn breath ('.hh').
- the pause after 'I left a (..)' is striking. The exchange takes place on a Monday and S has had the three days since the previous Friday to rehearse his opening utterance, and yet he can't get beyond three words. One consequence of choosing 'a' rather than either 'my' or 'an' is that he can no longer mention the folder's colour (orange).
- S's description of the folder is hedged ('I think an orange folder', 'I think it was sort of orangey coloured'), suggesting the encoding of distance between himself and L.
- S's use of 'it[d]' rather than *it's* (the square brackets indicate that 'd' isn't a 100 per cent certain transcription) is striking: by infringing sequence of tense expectations, S seems to distance himself psychologically from the event of losing his folder.
- a default assumption arising from 'I was at the inter-library loan desk' is that this isn't where he is now since, had he been, he would have used the deictic 'here'. But in fact the recording does take place at the inter-library loan desk. This also supports the hypothesis that S places psychological distance between himself and what appears to be a traumatic event as he fails to link his present location indexically with the Friday location.
- L's 'oh right', the pause, and her not taking up the next turn perhaps encode her surprise at the anomalous 'I was at the inter-library loan desk'. She must be wondering what kind of person she's talking to, or at least about his present state of mind.
- S's '.hh oh dear (1.0) OK' indicate that he accepts that his inquiry has come to end. However, he can't bring himself fully to accept this and so after a three-second pause he tries again ('alright (.) you don't happen to know'). L then interrupts him with an offer to take his name in an attempt to bring the encounter to a conclusion. S reluctantly accepts this as the necessary outcome ('yeah').

S then gives his name and college. However, he continues beyond this, and the encounter takes a new direction. When you read the first half of the exchange, I suggested that you should look out for the pauses. As you read the final part following on from the point at which he's given his name, notice both overlaps, which I've highlighted with arrows in the left margin, and latched turns, which I've highlighted with arrows in the right margin:

(3) S: (2.0) and er
→ (.) it's my dissertation so it's – so [it's slightly]
L: → [oh God (.) no]
S: → important (.) it's OK it's [not] not as impor[tant as]
L: → [no] [<laughs>]
S: → it seems (.) because I (.) you know [I haven't written]
L: → [you haven't]
S: as much as I should have done
S: <laughs>
L: <laughs> [ ]
S: → [so]
L: → [for] once you have to be thankful= ←
S: =yeah yeah that's true yeah (.) ye ←
L: OK
S: OK
L: um ye- we'll get in touch with you= ←
S: =grand thank you that's great (.) thank you very much= ←
L: =is there a telephone number ←
S: (. .) um (. .) well my telepho- my home num-= ←
L: =you you have e-mail have you ←
S: → yeah [yeah]
L: → [ye] we can send it you [if we find it]
S: → [great thank you] that's great (.)
→ [thanks] a lot
L: → [bye]

If you hadn't been told, you'd find it hard to believe that the two halves of this encounter involve the same two interactants. This second part of the exchange is characterized not by the pauses and hesitations of the first part, but by overlap and latched utterances as S and L co-construct their dialogue. Notable features include:

- L's five uses of the back-channel to support S in his opening turn: 'oh God (.) no', 'no', 'you haven't' and two sets of laughter.
- S's care not to up the consequences for L of his loss: 'it's slightly important (.) it's OK it's not not as important as it seems (.) because I (.) you know I haven't written as much as I should have done'.
- L's anticipatory contributions as she seeks to co-construct S's discourse: it's remarkable that she's able to anticipate both the negation and the present perfect of 'you haven't' as she and S speak simultaneously at this point. She also responds to S's metasequential signal of an upcoming formulation ('so') by suggesting a formulation for him ('for once you have to be thankful').
- the stage-by-stage process by which L withdraws from empathetic back-channelling and anticipatory contributions as she slowly reasserts her official status. This is a three-stage process:
  - first, there's the institution encoding 'we' in an otherwise informal utterance ('we'll get in touch with you') following the metasequential self-check on 'ye-'
  - then, there's the impersonalized 'is there a telephone number'
  - finally, there's an offer made on behalf of the institution, 'we can send it you if we find it'.
  - L's sensitivity in picking up the problem with the telephone number. Perhaps S lives in university accommodation without a dedicated personal line and he doesn't want a potentially face threatening call coming through to someone else. His concern is shown in '(. .) um (. .) well my telepho- my home num-', which L immediately responds to with 'you you have e-mail have you'.

It seems clear from the two parts of this conversation that much more is going on between these two people than is easily accounted for with the kind of rationalistic accounts of pragmatic meaning studied in earlier chapters. The psychological motivation (using both terms in a non-technical way) for the first half of the exchange seems to be the difficulty S has in mentioning the contents of the folder: the face loss involved in losing your dissertation is obviously very great and the face threat to the person expected to find it for you is also considerable, especially if it turns out that she isn't able to produce it. As a result, S seeks to prolong the encounter and L to curtail it. In the second half of the exchange, the mention of the dissertation seems to be the motivation for L's transformation of a service encounter into a notably empathetic human encounter.

As a motivation, the shaming loss of the dissertation for S, the obligation on L and the unexpected context in which S's rehearsed visit to the library finds itself being recorded for research purposes – all these illustrate how we need to take into account not only the rationality of human beings, but their emotional state and the emergent properties of the discourse if we hope to understand the way pragmatic meaning is conveyed. Had S met a different librarian, or had he gone to a different library desk, or had the folder been waiting for him – we can only speculate about the way things might have been.

10.4 Talk-in-interaction

The study of talk, or **talk-in-interaction** as conversation analysts call it, adopts an ethnomethodological approach. **Ethnomethodology** is a way of studying behaviour developed in sociology. Ethnomethodologists begin without *a priori* assumptions. They observe (the *-ology* of ethnomethodology) methodical patterns (the *-method-* of ethnomethodology) which are recognized by group members who share a common culture (the *ethno-* of ethnomethodology). These methodical patterns are then called **members' methods** because they are recognized by all those who share the common culture (members) and are expectable routines (methods). We noticed some of these methods – **account**, **formulation**, **repair**, etc. – in Chapter 7 when studying Nicole and Susie's discussion with the Doctor.

10.4.1 Members' methods

Consider the opening of what will turn out to be a six-and-a-half-minute conversation involving a university student and the head porter of the College where she lives:

(4) P: hello young lady=
S: =hiya (1.5) em I was round yesterday I've had some CDs
nicked (.) [from Yoko]
P: [so they] tell me (.) and I put (1.0) in your
pigeonhole (.)
S: right
P: [you know] (.) a little parcel like that
S: that's what Magda said [she saw it yeah]
P: [and it was a little] bit torn mind
(.) but I put it [in] (.) and when Robin phoned me last
S: [well]
P: night (.) I said I remember (.) I can't remember which name
it was but I knew it was in the first pigeonhole
[A B] C or D
S: [yeah]

S: yeah that's what me and Magda had looked in [to see our
P: [that's right
S: mail]
P: and] it was there

The conversation begins with an exchange of greetings

(5) P: hello young lady=
S: =hiya

The first thing to notice is that these two greetings occur sequentially, i.e. one of the two parties greets the other first. If you knew nothing about the organization of talk, you might expect both parties to greet each other simultaneously. But it turns out that overlaps are rare in talk, and even exchanges such as greetings typically occur as distinct **turn constructional units**, or, more simply, **turns.**

Greetings are a special kind of turn known as an **adjacency pair**, adjacent utterances produced by different speakers and ordered so that the first member of the pair (**first pair part**) requires an appropriate second member (**second pair part**) of a relevant type to be produced as a response. Typical examples of adjacency pairs are greeting–greeting, invitation–acceptance/refusal, apology–acceptance/rejection (Schegloff and Sacks, 1973). Notice also the transcription convention, the equal signs at the end of one turn and the beginning of the next indicating **latching.** Latching isn't a particular property of adjacency pairs – it may occur in this case because the address term 'young lady' isn't part of the greeting and the student is therefore encouraged to complete the adjacency pair rapidly.

After her greeting which completes the adjacency pair, there's a significant 1.5 second **pause**, before the student cites the motivation for her visit:

(6) S: =hiya (1.5) em I was round yesterday I've had some CDs
nicked (.) [from Yoko]
P: [so they] tell me (.) and I put (1.0) in your pigeonhole (.)
S: right
P: [you know] (.) a little parcel like that
S: that's what Magda said [she saw it yeah]

The micro pause after 'nicked' provides an opportunity for the porter to begin speaking. Places at which turns are offered are called **transition-relevance places** (TRP) and are typically intonationally marked. But the porter doesn't immediately start a new turn at this point, so the student continues her turn by mentioning the place from which they had been nicked, 'from Yoko'. However, 'from Yoko' is redundant since it is readily inferred as an explicature and since, as the conversation reveals, the porter had been telephoned by a colleague the evening before, presumably on the prompting of the student. This redundant coda finally obliges the porter to begin a new turn.

In fact, the porter begins his new turn as an **overlap.** Overlapped material may be harder to hear and, perhaps for that reason, typically contains propositionally less important material, as is the case here, with the student's redundant 'from Yoko' and the porter's proform 'so' standing for the proposition already expressed by the student. Then after a micro pause, the porter commences an **account** with the use of 'and': however, this 'conjunction' doesn't link 'so they tell me' and 'I put it in your pigeonhole' – rather it advises us that an account is upcoming.

Accounts are typical features of talk exchanges. Sometimes their function is remedial – for example, the preferred second pair part in an invitation is an acceptance. Often a refusal, the dispreferred second pair part, takes the form of an account which explains why the invitation cannot be accepted. In this exchange, the porter's account is notable for its deliberate delivery, frequent pauses and marked word order. Obviously enough, accounts should be truthful representations of events that both parties can agree, hence the pause after 'pigeonhole' which prompts the student's 'right', the porter's overlapped appeal for understanding '[you know]', and the student's confirmation that the porter's account squares with her own understanding of the situation, indicated by 'that's what Magda said' and by 'she saw it yeah'.

The porter's use of 'and' as he continues his account orients to a significant item in the account, that the parcel was damaged:

```
(7)   S:   that's what Magda said [she saw it yeah   ]
      P:                          [and it was a little] bit torn mind
           (.) but I put it [in  ] (.) and when Robin phoned me last
      S:                    [well]
      P:   night (.) I said I remember (.) I can't remember which
           name it was but I knew it was in the first pigeonhole
           [A B] C or D
```

The state of the parcel is also oriented to by 'mind' and by 'but': despite its being 'a little bit torn' he put it in the pigeonhole. The student then attempts to interrupt with 'well', which signals her wish to re-base the discussion – perhaps to ask why a damaged parcel was put in the pigeonhole. But the porter refuses to give up the turn and continues his account with 'and', again signalling a further development.

The porter's switch from reported speech 'I said . . . I can't remember which name it was' to direct speech 'I knew it was in the first pigeonhole' reinforces the veracity of his account.

The porter's turn also contains a **repair**, in which an intended sequence is replaced by a new one: 'I said I remember (.) I can't remember which name it was.' Perhaps he was going to say that he remembered putting it in the first pigeonhole, but then repaired his account to make it more particular and thus convincing. Most repairs are of this kind, self-initiated and self-completed. Occasionally, a repair is other-initiated, for example, when you ask the speaker to clarify something that was unclear to you. Very occasionally, repairs are other-initiated and other-completed, but this sort of correction of what someone else says is obviously rare and distinctly face threatening.

In (8) below, we can distinguish the student's first 'yeah' as a back-channel confirmation of what the porter says. It has the function of encouraging him to continue. Presumably the student, whose family name begins with 'B', is confirming that the first pigeonhole is the right one. This encouraging use of the back-channel is known as **aizuchi**. As there is no single word for this conversational strategy in English, we borrow the word *aizuchi* from Japanese. Her second 'yeah' confirms that she had 'looked in' the appropriate pigeonhole.

```
(8)   P:   night (.) I said I remember (.) I can't remember which
           name it was but I knew it was in the first pigeonhole
           [A B ] C or D
      S:   [yeah]
      S:   yeah that's what me and Magda had looked in [to see our  ]
      P:                                               [that's right]
      S:   mail]
      P:   and ] it was there
```

The porter then completes his account by asserting that the parcel was indeed in the appropriate pigeonhole.

(9) P: and⌋ it was there (. .) so after this (.) I mean it's (. .) it's Durham students going in the bloody place (1.0) I caught two yesterday (. .)
S: doing [what] (1.0) doing what=
P: [afternoon]
P: =just walking about (. .) [they] don't live there (1.0) definitely English students (2.0)
S: wh wha what hh
P: in Yoko Hall (1.5)

Accounts are typically followed by **formulations** in which the significance of the account and its consequence are formulated. As we've already seen, upcoming formulations are often signalled by *so*, as occurs here in 'so after this'. However, the expected formulation doesn't occur directly because the porter repairs his strategy and instead signals with 'I mean' that a more personal formulation is upcoming. This formulation consists of a causal explanation or attribution of blame, 'it's Durham students going in the bloody place'. In this way, he decides that it's more important to attribute blame at this stage in the talk exchange than to explain what measures will be taken in the future.

The causal explanation is immediately followed by the account of another incident which, although not directly related to the disappearance of the parcel, is intended to support the causal explanation. The student's reaction, 'wh wha what hh', shows that she is wrong-footed by the appearance so early in the exchange of a causal explanation.

Although we've examined only the very short opening sequence of a talk exchange, and although we started with no *a priori* theoretical assumptions or categories, we noticed several 'methods' which were highlighted in bold – turn, adjacency pair, latched utterance, pause, transition-relevance place, overlap, account, repair, *aizuchi*, formulation.

10.4.2 Talk-in-interaction structure

In a series of papers written between 1968 and 1980, Schegloff and a number of co-researchers established the basic methods underlying talk-in-interaction.

In their seminal paper 'A simplest systematics for the organization of turn-taking in conversation' (1974), Sacks, Schegloff and Jefferson (hence SS&J) discuss the way that turns are allocated in conversation. The four paragraphs and *Checking Understanding* tasks that follow are based closely on this paper.

SS&J show that a turn projects its own end, or transition-relevance place, and that the speaker may select next speaker or allow self-selection of next speaker to take place in a way that minimizes gaps and overlaps. Because a turn's end is projected, next speakers have an opportunity to prepare their contributions.

Checking understanding (10.1)

Turn to the interaction between Susie, Nicole and the Doctor in Chapter 7 and find examples of

1 a turn whose end is projected and explain how this is effected;
2 a place where the speaker selects the next speaker;
3 a place where next speaker self-selects;
4 a place where there's a gap, and account for it;
5 a place where there's an overlap and account for it.

SS&J also describe a range of ways in which a next speaker is selected. These include the use of adjacency first pair parts, an address term such as the name of the intended next speaker, repair techniques such as one-word clarificatory questions and repetitions of parts of a prior utterance with question intonation. Tags may also serve as an exit technique for a turn. Sometimes a next speaker is selected as the natural next speaker by virtue of being the understood recipient of some request, comment or suggestion without any overt selection procedure.

Checking understanding (10.2)

Working with the Doctor data, find examples of

1 a first-pair part in an adjacency pair;
2 the use of an address term;
3 a one-word or a short *wh*-phrase clarification request;
4 a clarification request involving repetition;
5 a tag used as an exit technique;
6 a place where there's a natural next-turn taker.

SS&J show how turn size may vary either because units such as sentences naturally vary in length or because a speaker may have a turn more than one unit long if no other speaker self-selects at a TRP. They show how, in a conversation involving four or more participants, schism may occur so that more than one conversation occurs simultaneously. And they show how conversation can become discontinuous so that lapses occur, although in the case where a next speaker has been selected only pauses, rather than gaps or lapses, are possible.

Checking understanding (10.3)

Working with the Doctor data, find examples of

1 an example of a long single-unit turn;
2 an example of a short single-unit turn;
3 an example of a long turn resulting from lack of next speaker self-selection;
4 a pause or a lapse.

SS&J also show how turns regularly have a three-part structure, consisting of orientation to preceding turn, business of present turn and orientation to next turn.

Checking understanding (10.4)

Find an example of a three-part turn in the Doctor data.

Obviously enough, this is only a beginning, but a beginning that shows the systematic nature of conversation and provides a detailed metalanguage to supplement the surprisingly small number of metasequential folk terms, such as *topic* and *interruption*. In fact, metapragmatic folk terms are by no means universal, which seems to indicate different cross-cultural awarenesses. In Japanese, for example, there's no single word for *interruption* but, as we saw in the previous section, there is the word *aizuchi*, meaning to use the listener channel in ways that are supportive of the speaker by interjecting expressions like 'I see', 'yeah', etc. In English, it's the other way round. There are some languages in which the verb form *interrupt* is in regular use but the nominal *interruption*, although feasible, is felt to be awkward – this is generally the case in Slavonic languages, for example.

Even when two languages appear to have a common metasequential folk term, it's not necessarily used to describe the same phenomenon in an identical way. So that what a member of another culture understands by *pause* or *topic* may not be the same as your understanding.

10.4.3 Talk and context

In CA, a distinction is often drawn between '**macro**' and '**micro' contexts**. Macro contexts are said to be 'distal' in the sense that they exist outside the talk exchange. Thus in Chapter 7 I described as distal contexts student solidarity and the Doctor's responsibility for sorting out student problems referred to him. Although I didn't use the term 'distal' in Chapter 9, we can now see that Matsumoto's argument that deference characterizes Japanese interactions is an argument for the recognition of social hierarchy, an important distal context. In contrast, micro contexts are created within the micro domain of the talk exchange. The question is whether talk is determined or constrained by distal contexts, with context seen as presumptive, or whether it's talk which creates context.

Until the late 1980s there was no real challenge to the received view, summarized (but not accepted) by Zimmerman and Boden, that "since social structure forms the presumptive context of activities of lesser scale, such as social interaction, it is ultimately the fundamental explanatory resource" (1991: 5). In other words, the received view was that context constrains talk. But by 1992, Duranti and Goodwin were writing, "context and talk are now argued to stand in a mutually reflexive relationship to each other, with talk, and the interpretive work it generates, shaping context as much as context shapes talk" (1992: 31).

Schegloff (1992) has a more radical perspective. He argues that a distal context can only influence a talk exchange to the extent that it's made relevant in it. Therefore, there's no such thing as a distal context: if macro contexts aren't relevant, we can discount them; and if they are relevant, they'll appear as micro contexts oriented to in the talk itself. Recall the situation when you walk into the doctor's surgery mentioned in Chapter 6 and you have to decide on whether 'how are you' is a social greeting or a professional inquiry. Although the existence of extra-interactional phenomena such as professional status and setting is not in doubt, demonstrating that such aspects of context are being oriented to is much more problematical.

However you choose to resolve the macro/micro issue yourself, there can be no doubt that we all bring a potentially infinite number of contexts to conversations: our age, sex, ethnicity, social class, occupational background, family status, etc. And of course, each of these contexts is made up of many parts, several of them apparently incompatible. Thus students may be intelligent, young, irresponsible, serious-minded, rebellious, radical, uninitiated, poor, etc.

With these thoughts about the role of context in mind, recall the porter's opening turn in the conversation we studied earlier in the chapter:

(5) P: hello young lady=
S: =hiya

Notice how the porter encodes elements of the macro context, that the student is female, of a certain social class (perhaps not the same class as he is), and that he is older than her. The question for the analyst is why the porter chooses to orient to these aspects of the distal context in the opening turn of an interaction. Why is it relevant that the speakers are of different sexes, ages and classes? Or to ask the question from a political correctness perspective, is it legitimate to treat their different sexes, ages and classes as relevant? These questions become all the more interesting when we know another element of the distal context, that the porter is responsible for the security of parcels and that the person to whom he is speaking has come to talk to him precisely because he has this role and a package addressed to her has gone missing. Thus the porter sees to it that the conversation is not just between a porter and a student, but between an older male and a younger female. Perhaps now the student's latching of the second pair part of her greeting is more explainable and makes known her exasperation with the context being created.

If we recall our discussion of 'high-context' and 'low-context' cultures in Chapter 6, we might hypothesize that distal contexts are likely to be invoked especially in high-context cultures, where what Hofstede has called "status consistency" is valued over "overall equality" (1980: 94). In the encounter we've been studying in this section of the chapter, the porter invokes status consistency elements of context such as age and gender in an overall equality culture as part of his bid to determine the relevant events that occurred and to attribute blame in a way that is favourable to his position.

As we can see, this discussion takes us beyond essentially rationalistic explanations and into the area of social structure and psychological motivation. Reason alone is insufficient to account for the student's exasperation as revealed in her latched response to the porter's greeting.

10.4.4 Interactive pragmatics

As we've seen, the study of conversation reveals orderly patterns of turn taking in which accounts precede formulations and in which there are **preferred** and **dispreferred contributions**. These methodic patterns are recognizable to members of a common group and frame sequential communication. CA thus captures the principles of **talk-in-interaction**. However, we need to ask whether a similar kind of criticism to that which Kopytko levels at rationalistic pragmatics might also be levelled at CA: the success of CA lies principally in its ability to describe methodic structure. In rigorously denying the existence of contexts that aren't relevantly oriented to in talk, is it possible that only a very narrow context is ever considered? Is a focus on methodic action, however empirical, any more likely to capture motivation than a rationalistic account of inferential meaning?

In a brief paper in *Pragmatics*, the journal of the *International Pragmatics Association*, Briggs criticizes CA for identifying abstract patterns which are applied across a range of cases and for pursuing the everyday in a strictly local context which excludes the historical, social and cultural circumstances in which talk occurs. Briggs claims that those who identify orderly behaviour such as cooperation, rationality, relevance, politeness and turn-taking are ideologically motivated. Such concepts are reductionist generalizations which deny the broader political context in favour of a narrowly adjacent micro context in which society is stable and orderly. Think for a moment of all the occasions when speakers try to shout each other down or parties use violence, either individual or collective, and you get the point.

Even the short opening of the porter/student dialogue is open to a quite different kind of analysis from the one suggested above. This different, post-methodic analysis sees not order but underlying chaos and political struggle in the roles of the parties. They are divided by age, sex and class and will use their respective political identities to attribute blame. Truth, and in particular what circumstance, immediate or distal, is responsible for the security and subsequent disappearance of the student's parcel, will be determined in the talk by the exercise of power.

Is it too irreverent to suppose that, if we were to pursue Briggs's critique, we might in due course end up, like the rationalists and empiricists before us, not with an account of what we took to be language use but instead with an account of a small area of language usage. When we studied *How to Do Things with Words*, we began brightly with the notion that a sentence in a context of use is an utterance, but now we see that we have ended up knowing only what an utterance is. Might we pursue the attractive postmodern notion that talk is fundamentally disorderly, and end up knowing only what disorderly talk is?

Summary

Our understanding of utterances as speech acts and of meaning as conveyed in the form of implicature rather than stated literally seems insufficient to account for the meaning of utterances arranged sequentially as accounts and formulations, as preferred and dispreferred contributions, each of which is more or less procedurally consequential, i.e. shaping of the outcome. Utterances occur in the wider context of talk and their meaning is sensitive to this context. However, the study of talk within the CA tradition is largely a study of the members' methods that talkers use rather than of the meanings they convey.

A more sequentially aware pragmatics enables us to study the way in which pragmatic meaning is related not only to propositions but also to the containing methods of talk. An empirical pragmatics looks beyond utterances to the conversational context in which social meaning is conveyed and to which interactants bring not only reason but personal history, emotion and psychological motivation generally. An interactive pragmatics thus goes beyond the rationalistic approach to pragmatic meaning on the one hand and the CA account of sequential methods which takes no account of meaning on the other. In Chapter 12, I'll make some further suggestions about how to 'do interactive pragmatics'.

10.5 Approaches to pragmatics

This book began with a quotation: "We all know what light is; but it is not easy to tell what it is." Of course, physicists now know exactly how to 'tell what light is', and no doubt one day we'll have an equally developed understanding of language and of the usage principles that we study when we study pragmatics. But our present situation with respect to pragmatics is a bit like Dr Johnson's with respect to light: we know what pragmatics is, but it's not easy to tell what it is. This is why, rather than starting out with a bold definition, in Chapter 1, I made several comments about what pragmaticists are interested in.

Most pragmatics textbooks follow a different strategy and typically begin with a definition of pragmatics. Levinson, for example, begins by describing the historical origin of the term *pragmatics* before rehearsing a number of candidate definitions (1983: 5–35). These include:

- the study of language from a functional perspective;
- the study of the context-dependent nature of language use and language understanding;
- the study of the effects of language use on the grammar of language;
- the study of non-conventional, or, more narrowly perhaps, non-truth conditional meaning, possibly to be understood as speaker- or utterance-meaning rather than sentence-meaning.

In a similar way, Green begins by defining pragmatics as "the study of understanding intentional human action" (1996: 2), and Mey as "the science of language as it is used by real, live people for their own purposes and within their limitations and affordances" (1993: 5), a definition that he abandons in the second edition of his book.

Although it may seem odd to begin a book as we did without defining its subject, the fact of the matter is that the wide range of phenomena we've been investigating do not fit neatly under a single definition. And that's not the end of the problem. More difficult even than defining pragmatics is the task of delimiting its domain. Broadly, we've been distinguishing between what we might call conventional sentence and pragmatic speaker and hearer meaning, taking conventional sentence meaning to be a meaning associated with linguistic expressions whenever they are used, and pragmatic speaker and hearer meaning to be the meaning associated with sentences as they are used in particular contexts.

In deciding what to include in this book, I've had to draw lines in ways that are to some degree arbitrary. For example, although we've discussed deixis as a relation between a point of origin and a referent, we skated very rapidly over the actual process of reference assignment – surely a pragmatic phenomenon, and one which Green, for example, discusses in some detail.

Pragmaticists are interested not only in the actual use of language, but also in usage principles, in trying to find a 'grammar' that accounts for the way language is put to use, on the assumption that language would not be as it is if it were not used for communication. In this chapter, we've critiqued proposals for usage principles which appear to be too narrowly rationalistic or too narrowly methodic. Yet if we were to achieve not merely a description of pragmatic phenomena as they occur when language is used but a proper 'grammar' of pragmatics, we'd expect such a usage theory to have explanatory power and to be able to predict future use. In arguing for an empirical pragmatics, we aren't necessarily giving up on an explanatory account of the way language is used – rather we're arguing for a better understanding of our data and a wider view of context as necessary preliminaries to theory building.

At the beginning of this chapter, I drew attention to the way I'd been trying to ride two horses simultaneously in following a theory-driven account in the second section of each chapter and then switching to a data-driven account in the third section. I hope you'll agree that a turning point came in Chapter 7 where we considered first Susie and Nicole's meeting with the Doctor and then Erich's explanation of his predicament to his colleagues. At this point, we began to use new terms to describe the emerging data: account, formulation, repair, for example. And our transcription conventions changed from something close to the way we might represent everyday talk to a less interpretative style without punctuation and able to represent behaviour like simultaneous speech.

Pragmatics is a broad church – much broader in fact than appears in the thumbnail sketch in this section. You'll need to decide how sectarian you want to be and what kind, or kinds, of pragmatics you wish to do yourself.

(Acknowledgement: the Library data were recorded and transcribed by Charlotte Harper, who conducted a preliminary analysis, and the student/porter conversation was recorded and transcribed by Joanne Burdon, who carried out a preliminary analysis. I'm grateful to both of them for allowing me to reproduce their data.)

Raising pragmatic awareness

1 Working as an individual, listen out for two consecutive utterances which are paired but where the second utterance is a slightly surprising rejoinder to the first. Bring your adjacency pair to your tutorial. Read only the first utterance of the pair and invite your colleagues to guess the second. Discuss the expected and the actual illocutionary forces associated with each pair part.

2 While you are involved in a conversation, watch out for interruptions. Note who interrupts, how they interrupt and how the other speakers react. Report your observations in your tutorial group.

3 While you're part of a conversation, listen out for clarification requests and repairs. Are repairs usually self- or other-initiated and self- or other-completed? Why do these repairs occur? Report your observations in your tutorial group.

4 Observe two people who are deeply involved in a conversation. Record any moments of their interaction that are striking so that you can describe the para-linguistic features of talk-in-interaction which you observed to your tutorial group.

5 Decide in advance that you will eavesdrop on five seconds of a conversation from some predetermined moment (such as when someone next puts food in their mouth). Record exactly what is said, paying special attention to its sequential properties, and report your findings in your tutorial group.

6 Each member of your tutorial group should eavesdrop on the beginning of a talk sequence where the first speaker has a reason for talking. Does the speaker introduce the reason immediately or not? Compare your different observations in your tutorial group.

7 Work with a partner and together eavesdrop on a two-speaker conversation. You should take one speaker and your partner the other: each listen carefully for the occurrence of fillers, hesitations and pauses. Compare your observations.

8 How are conversations closed? Is the gist formulated? What sort of agreements are made? How are topics closed? Are they recycled? Do the same systems occur at the end of conversations as apply at the end of topics within conversations? Report your observations in your tutorial group.

9 Which of the features of talk identified as typically pragmatic in Chapter 1 better serve the purposes of rationalistic and which of empirical approaches to the study of pragmatics: accommodation, appropriateness, context, indeterminacy, indirect meaning, inference, reflexivity, relevance?

10 How, if at all, do the features of talk identified as typically pragmatic in Chapter 1 contribute to (a) conversation analysis, and (b) the study of interactive pragmatics: accommodation, appropriateness, context, indeterminacy, indirect meaning, inference, reflexivity, relevance?

Discussions and essays

Discuss the relative merits of each of the following views:

- Rationalistic approaches to pragmatic meaning are more likely to enable us to understand utterances than the close study of particular instances of use.
- The fundamental flaw in pragmatic approaches to language understanding is that they're driven by a means–ends view of human behaviour.
- Any scientist has to choose between the close analysis of a single case whose findings cannot be generalized to other cases and a more reductive approach which enables findings to be generalized over many cases. So it is with pragmatics.
- Pragmaticists interested in cognitive motivation and pragmaticists interested in social motivation need to talk to each other more.
- There's every reason to suppose that Austin, Grice, and Brown & Levinson all thought that they were revealing fundamental empirical facts about the way talk works.

Further reading

Rationalistic and empirical pragmatics: Kopytko, 1995, 2001.
CA, primary texts: Sacks, Schegloff and Jefferson, 1974; Schegloff, 1992.
CA textbooks: Duranti, 1997: 245–79; Hutchby and Wooffitt, 2008: 41–65; Mey, 2001, Ch. 6; Schiffrin, 1994: 232–81; ten Have, 2007, Chs 1–3; Yule, 1996: 71–82.

11 Intercultural pragmatics

In language there are only differences.
(Ferdinand de Saussure)

Keywords:

cross-cultural communication, intercultural communication, intracultural communication, pragmalinguistics, socio-pragmatics, trans-cultural communication

11.1 Introduction

You wouldn't expect to find a chapter about intercultural communication in a book on syntax or semantics. Even in a book on phonology, it would be unlikely. But because pragmatic meanings are context-sensitive and therefore culturally situated, as pragmaticists we're naturally interested in what happens when meanings are exchanged between people who don't share a common culture. Take speech acts, for example. Given that speech acts are to a degree culturally institutionalized routines, we might expect the pragmatic phenomena used in intercultural encounters to differ from those used in the intracultural encounters we've been examining so far.

My wife and I aren't communicating across cultures (except in the trivial sense that no one ever fully shares the culture even of those they know most closely), so it's not surprising that our exchange appeals to cultural knowledge:

(1) BRANKA: When will you be back
PETER: I should be back by eight but you know what trains are like

I assert, correctly, that Branka does indeed 'know what trains are like'. And while the formula *you know what x is like* typically implies a negative evaluation, I probably wouldn't have used this formula if I'd been talking to someone who didn't share the same cultural knowledge of trains as myself. This is because in a different culture, 'you know what trains are like' might imply any number of different negative evaluations: that they're dirty, slow, inconvenient, cold, hot, crowded, dangerous, populated by thieves, etc. So that even if the formula *you know what x is like* implies a negative evaluation universally, i.e. in every language (which, by the way, I'm not claiming), the nature of the relevant negative evaluation would still be culturally conditioned.

Unlike *you know what x is like,* most formulas don't have stereotypical interpretations: recall my misunderstanding of the Dutch waitress in Chapter 1 when she intended 'very free' to imply <too free>, an implicature that I didn't recover until I discovered that she wasn't German.

If you think back to Chapter 1, you'll also recall that I discussed the cultural knowledge required to understand the newspaper headline

(2) All systems go as Eriksson enters unknown territory

The headline writer used a formula, 'all systems go', whose most salient meaning for most people is <everything ready and working>. But because Eriksson, the then England football manager, had until that point been experimenting with various formations (or systems), the headline writer was able to invite an unusual, more literal interpretation, <all systems are abandoned>. This headline appeared on the sports pages of the newspaper and was thus addressed to readers who belonged to a particular sub-culture. No doubt there were many readers of the newspaper for whom the sports pages held little interest and who might have misinterpreted the headline had they read it. This then raises the issue of whether intercultural communication is qualitatively any different from any other communication: for meanings to be successfully conveyed, as Sperber and Wilson say, "the speaker must make some assumptions about the hearer's cognitive abilities and contextual resources" (1995: 218). You don't need to have travelled much to know that distal contexts vary from culture to culture. But you might nevertheless take the view that successful intercultural communication, like successful **intracultural communication**, orients only to micro contexts that are readily accommodated by addressees. So although the pragmatic phenomena, including speech act forms, may differ from those found in intracultural communication, intercultural communication is equally relevance oriented. It may not, therefore, be essentially different from interaction involving native members. These are the issues explored in this chapter.

The chapter contains three further sections, each of which includes several sub-sections:

- *Issues in intercultural communication*, which explores the ways in which culture-specific knowledge is encoded in utterances, considers the problems that arise in cross-cultural communication and speculates about the role of inference in intercultural communication.
- *Intercultural pragmatics in the real world*, which shows how speakers make sense of each other's utterances in situations where they don't share a common context.
- *Lingua franca pragmatics*, which discusses the status of English as a global lingua franca and the kinds of accommodation speakers of lingua francas make. We also discuss the special problem of lingua francas and written language.

11.2 Issues in intercultural communication

Scenario 1: I'm in Nanjing with a rather rudimentary map. I'm trying to work out how to get to the park. But I mis-read the map and instead wander into a military barracks. As neither the guard on duty nor I share a language in common, he has the bright idea of telephoning the university to find an English speaker. Once it's clear that I'm a mere tourist, there are smiles all round. The man from the university proceeds to give me directions to the park over the telephone: "Go south till you get to the end of the barracks and then go east. When you see the park, go south again and enter through the north gate." As I'm used to relative direction giving (left, right, straight on – in relation to me, the deictic centre), these absolute instructions are a surprise. They remind me that space is conceptualized in different ways in different cultures.

Scenario 2: I'm on a flight from Amsterdam to Istanbul. The Dutch stewardess uses the public address system to make an announcement about the time difference between Amsterdam and Istanbul

(3) It's one hour later than in the Netherlands

I wonder why she doesn't say that Istanbul is 'an hour ahead'. I wonder about the linguistic resources of Dutch and English and whether saying that one place is *ahead* of another has the same unmarked status in Dutch as the English expression. I wonder whether the extent of the time difference might have an influence on the linguistic formula too: if we were flying to Beijing, surely it would be 'seven hours ahead of the Netherlands' and not 'seven hours later than in the Netherlands'?

Three days later, I'm on the return flight and listening carefully for any announcements about time differences. There are two:

(4) Amsterdam is one hour earlier as in Istanbul

and

(5) And please keep in mind that it's one hour earlier as in Istanbul for your transfer connection

I wonder why she doesn't keep it simple and say that it's 'five to six' in Amsterdam. As I'm used to conceptualizing time in spatial terms (ahead, behind, etc.), I find 'later' and 'earlier' confusing (the sun rises earlier in Istanbul so it's later there!). The stewardess's descriptions are a surprise. They remind me that relative time is conceptualized in different ways in different cultures.

The question to explore in this section, then, is whether, despite the oddness of someone else's way of doing things in their own culture, we can puzzle out what someone means by what they say in intercultural encounters.

11.2.1 Cultural membership

In the first chapter of the first edition of this book, I cited as an example of indirectness a conversation between our tea-lady, Phyllis, and myself. This is what I wrote:

> It is also remarkable that we're so clever at interpreting indirectness. Take the following conversation which Phyllis, our tea-lady, and I had recently:
> PHYLLIS: Wasn't the wind dreadful in the night
> PETER: I didn't hear it
> PHYLLIS: Ee it was dreadful
> PETER: You know what they say
> And she did: she understood the indirectness perfectly, and continued with
> PHYLLIS: I must have a guilty conscience

I thought I'd made it clear that my utterance 'you know what they say' implied that Phyllis had a guilty conscience, although, as it was the first chapter, I didn't spell out in detail how this inference was arrived at, viz:

> *Original utterance:* You know what they say
> *Implicated premise:* <if you heard the wind, it was because you were awake>
> *Explicated utterance:* You know what they say about people who lie awake in the night
> *Implicated conclusion:* <you must have a guilty conscience>.

In her final turn, Phyllis confirmed what I had implied, that she must have a guilty conscience. Despite this, what I meant by saying 'You know what they say' wasn't clear to readers. In fact, approximately half the questions I received about the book were about this example. I even had a telephone call from an academic in the middle of a tutorial at a British university who wanted elucidation. He and the students in his tutorial group were all at a loss to know how to understand what I meant by what I'd said.

What this tells us is that <you must have a guilty conscience> is recovered as an I-inference by Phyllis, myself and anyone else (+/– you?) who belongs to the culture which regards 'you know what they say [about sleeplessness]' as the stereotypical way of conveying that meaning. However, this certainly isn't a universal utterance-type meaning. A Japanese academic who wrote to me explained that his English native speaker colleagues also found the example puzzling. He'd been thinking about the utterance and had recovered the implicated premise <if you heard the wind, it was because you were awake>. But he'd recovered a quite different implicated conclusion, and wanted to know whether I'd been making a suggestive comment about what Phyllis got up to between the sheets! Good guess, but wrong!

Although I removed this example from the second edition, I've reinstated it in this edition (but no longer in the first chapter) because it illustrates very neatly how I-inferences can be extremely problematic for those who don't share the speaker's cultural membership. It also illustrates how wrong you can be in assuming that native speakers who live in the same society as yourself share an identical cultural knowledge. 'You know *x*' ('you know what trains are like'; 'you know what they say', etc.) is the formula we use to show meta-cultural awareness and to pragmatically presuppose that there are others who don't have this knowledge. However, we need to be aware that these others may be many and unexpected. And they may not recover meanings that are stereotypical for in-group members.

11.2.2 Culture-specific knowledge

Let's consider briefly the difficulties someone might have if they didn't share the cultural knowledge of participants in some of the situations discussed in previous chapters:

Chapter 1

(6) Are you two both together

An addressee or an overhearer unfamiliar with British culture might assume that an M-inference was invited by the abnormal way of putting things. Although this assumption might be confirmed by the speaker's metapragmatic comment 'you know what I mean', a non-native addressee still might be uncertain as to the appropriate M-inference to draw. And presumably the (unintended) M-inference associated with the barmaid's question wouldn't be recovered by native members of a culture where homosexuality or any mention of it was proscribed.

Chapter 3

(7) I don't know why National Express give you three tickets

The pragmatic presuppositions that make my utterance appropriate require detailed cultural knowledge. In fact, it turns out that even the ticket inspector doesn't know that National Express is a (rival) train company.

Chapter 4

(8a) Sorry
(8b) I'm sorry
(8c) I am sorry

In my experience, the speech acts stereotypically associated with each of these formulas aren't known to many proficient speakers of English as a second language.

In contrast to the previous example, I might expect *OK* and *It's OK* to be used across languages/cultures in the same way as in my conversation with Hiroko:

(9) HIROKO: I haven't got any money
PETER: It's all right I've got money
HIROKO: I'll pay you back later
PETER: It's OK

This is because the more economical formula, *OK*, is associated with the preferred option, the acceptance of an offer, whereas the marked formula, *It's OK*, is associated with the dispreferred option, the rejection of an offer (although, exceptionally in this case, rejecting the offer is the friendlier action). But I doubt that this *OK/It's OK* alternation is universal. There are presumably languages/cultures in which only either *OK* or *It's OK* is sayable, and languages/cultures in which an *OK* formula is used for one function (i.e. accepting or rejecting) and a different formula not involving *OK* for the other.

Chapter 6

As we saw, the relevance of several parts of the joke about the two rugby players was not apparent to the non-native member group who listened to it.

Chapter 9

(10) A pint of Bass please
(11) Can you make it two please

As we've seen, different cultures make use of broadly the same linguistic strategies for politeness purposes, but the circumstances in which these linguistic strategies are used vary across cultures. Who's to say that (11) would have been the redress formula chosen by someone unfamiliar with the culture-specific imposition constituted by ordering a further unit of a drink that had just been ordered?

Leech coined the terms **pragmalinguistics** and **socio-pragmatics** to describe the kinds of pragmatic knowledge native members have. Pragmalinguistic knowledge is knowledge of the "particular resources which a given language provides for conveying particular illocutions" (1983: 11), such as the redressive formula 'Can you make it two please'. The judgement that a redressive formula of this kind is necessary is a matter of socio-pragmatic knowledge. Leech calls this 'local' knowledge because it varies from culture to culture.

While it's obvious that this sort of local knowledge is useful in cross-cultural situations, it's not at all clear that it's relevant in intercultural communication. This is because **cross-cultural communication** occurs when a non-native member operates in someone else's culture. **Intercultural communication** occurs when interactants communicate outside their own cultures, often using a lingua franca that isn't the first language of either. This is an important distinction that isn't always scrupulously maintained in the literature, where the terms are sometimes used interchangeably. This may be because there are situations where speakers in cross-cultural and in intercultural situations find themselves faced by identical problems. For this reason, in the rest of this chapter, I'm going to use four terms to describe the relationship of communication and cultural membership:

- *intracultural communication* = communication involving interactants who share a common culture. A typical situation is when compatriots communicate in their own language, making use of each other's knowledge of their shared culture as a contextual resource.

- *cross-cultural communication* = communication where a non-native member interacts with a native member of a particular culture. A typical situation is when someone travels to another country and communicates with native members of the local culture in their language.
- *intercultural communication* = communication when the interactants don't share a common culture. A typical situation is when someone from one culture meets someone from another culture on neutral ground and communicates in a lingua franca. So if someone from Brazil and someone from China meet at a conference in Addis Ababa and use English as a lingua franca, this is a case of intercultural communication.
- *trans-cultural communication* = any communication that isn't intracultural. This is a term which I've invented. The motivation is that frequently we don't need to discriminate between the issues that arise in cross-cultural and intercultural situations so that an umbrella term which covers both is useful. Another motivation is that the distinction between cross-cultural and intercultural communication isn't always easy to draw. Imagine the Brazilian and the Chinese attend a conference in the United States and are joined by an American. Describing the ensuing three-way communication as trans-cultural saves us attempting neat distinctions that it's hard to be certain about.

The following *Checking Understanding* section invites you to explore the difficulty of arriving at such neat distinctions.

Checking understanding (11.1)

Imagine you're a French national who works as a steward(ess) on Air France. You speak French and English. You're looking after four passengers, one from France, one from Korea, one from Morocco and one from the UK. Which language would you use to speak to each of them and to what extent would you regard the communicative contexts as cross-cultural, intracultural or intercultural?

The *Checking Understanding* activity will have helped you to appreciate the complexity of encounters where distal contexts may be relevant to one interactant and not to another. Not long ago on a flight from Hong Kong to Amsterdam, I opened my cutlery package and found a seriously dirty fork lurking there. I called the stewardess and showed it to her. She explained that it was impossible for the airline to tell whether the fork was washed because the cutlery came pre-wrapped. Feeling aggrieved that the threat to my face hadn't been redressed with an apology and that no clean fork was offered, I asked if what had happened could be noted so that a similar situation could be avoided in the future. Later the stewardess returned and said that the incident had been noted. She then added that it was a rare event, only happening once a month. Again, there was no apology.

Socio-pragmatically, she and I had entirely different views of appropriate conduct – indeed, each of her actions (or inactions) struck me as inappropriate, and I thought (not for the first time) of giving the airline for which she worked a miss on future occasions.

This sort of situation reminds us that although we can often find pragmalinguistic formulas that work well enough in intercultural encounters, it's more difficult to recognize that the socio-pragmatic expectations of those we interact with may be very different from our own. Nor is this problem readily resolvable: imagine the knowledge an airline steward/ess would need to have to take into account every passenger's socio-pragmatic expectations, even assuming that their native cultures or sub-cultures were known.

11.2.3 Trans-cultural communication and high and low contexts

In Chapter 6 and in Chapter 10, I briefly mentioned Hall's view of cultures as 'high-context' and 'low-context'. In high-context cultures, according to Hall, the context does more of the work and language is used to reinforce externally perceived social structure (Hofstede's "status consistency"). Thus, 'you know what trains are like' and 'you know what they say' appeal to distal contexts and so are status-consistent, high-context references. In low-context cultures, language is used to create new social structure for the purposes at hand (Hofstede's "overall equality") and relationships between people frequently need to be negotiated linguistically. As exchanges such as that between Phyllis and myself show, we often mix high- and low-context utterances:

(12) PHYLLIS: Wasn't the wind dreadful in the night (Low)
PETER: I didn't hear it (Low)
PHYLLIS: Ee it was dreadful (Low)
PETER: You know what they say (High)
PHYLLIS: I must have a guilty conscience (Low)

It's sometimes claimed that there is a set of properties which go with each cultural polarity: according to this account, high-context cultures are shame driven because an individual's status-consistent behaviour is conditioned by the opinions of others. Such societies are characterized by deference and the maintenance of relative position. Low-context cultures are said to be guilt driven because individuals are accountable to themselves for their behaviour, and to be characterized by courtesy and the possibility of social mobility. This helps to explain why I used the formula 'a suggestive comment about what Phyllis got up to between the sheets' when I related the story of the Japanese academic who wrote to me to ask about 'you know what they say'. I was too ashamed to mention *sex*, settling instead for a euphemism, although in fact the Japanese writer had used the term 'sexual activity' in his message. If you live in Britain you'll have noticed that many of the formulas in use for referring to sexual behaviour are high-context and shame driven. Typical examples include

(13) Would you like to come back to my place for coffee
(14) We're just good friends

and

(15) Are they sleeping together

Again, this suggests that we not only mix and high- and low-context utterances (as in the Phyllis/Peter conversation) but also tend to favour high-context formulas in one situation and low-context formulas in another.

In the wider field of pragmatics that we've been exploring in this book, meaning is conveyed by drawing an inference from two kinds of premise, the utterance we hear and our encyclopedic knowledge of the world. The question that then arises is whether, in different cultures, utterances (language) and knowledge of the world (context) have the same weight in determining what meanings are conveyed, or whether in some cultures either language or context plays a more deciding role than in others. More particularly, within any particular society we may expect the relative roles of language and context to vary with situations and their culture-specific evaluation.

As intercultural communication is necessarily less context-rich than intracultural communication, we expect the role of (non-formulaic) language to be relatively greater in intercultural encounters. In the two sub-sections that follow, we explore first speech acts and then implicated meaning in **trans-cultural communication**.

11.2.4 Speech acts in trans-cultural communication

Over the years, researchers have attempted to determine the socio-pragmatic and pragmalinguistic expectations of various cultural groups. The first large-scale research project of this kind was Blum-Kulka, House and Kasper's (1989) *Cross-cultural Speech Act Realization Project* (CCSARP). Blum-Kulka and her colleagues constructed a series of Discourse Completion Tests, or Tasks (DCTs), designed to find out how participants would react in scripted situations which tested apologies and requests. The results enabled the researchers to compare the reactions of different participants representing different cultures.

The CCSARP has been widely imitated in thousands of subsequent studies. We might even construct a DCT of our own to be administered in the airline industry, perhaps including an item such as the following:

> You're an airline stewardess and a male passenger some years older than yourself calls you and explains that he's found a dirty fork in his cutlery package. Complete the following dialogue:
> PASSENGER: Excuse me, I'm afraid I've got a dirty fork
> STEWARDESS: ....

Such a DCT might then be expected to reveal similarities and/or differences in the socio-pragmatic behaviour and pragmalinguistic formulas used by the employees of various airlines.

There are a number of points to be made about this approach to research in pragmatics:

- It would obviously be impractical to collect this kind of data opportunistically. Dirty forks only occur once a month and presumably not on occasions that the researcher can predict and therefore arrange to observe. Unfortunately, the alternative of planting dirty forks on unsuspecting passengers raises ethical issues.
- We can never be sure that participants asked to estimate how they would behave do in fact self-report accurately. So we can't be sure that the data we collect are valid.
- The absence of a real-world social and psychological context lays this approach to data collection open to the kind of criticisms of rationalistic pragmatics discussed in the previous chapter.
- DCTs focus on identifying speech acts, which are usually understood in terms of reductive taxonomies. For example, for our DCT, we might be expecting to find apologies, explanations for the occurrence of the phenomenon, offers to replace the dirty item, etc.

- Speech acts are a way of describing speaker meaning, i.e. optimal form, not hearer meaning.
- The aim is to identify typical behaviour across large populations rather than to investigate emergent, unpredictable, token utterances, which, in this sort of research, are disregarded.
- The findings are likely to have practical application in cross-cultural encounters where not only socio-pragmatic knowledge but also pragmalinguistic formulas assist non-native members to communicate effectively and appropriately. Because intercultural communication typically occurs in a lingua franca, the pragmalinguistic formulas are less likely to have transfer value in this situation.

11.2.5 Implicated meaning in trans-cultural communication

In this sub-section, we consider the categories of pragmatic inference explored in Chapters 5 and 6 and the implications for communication.

Utterance-token meaning

At the beginning of the chapter, I suggested that intercultural communication isn't essentially different from intracultural communication, at least to the extent that in both the speaker takes into account the cognitive abilities and contextual resources of the addressee/s. Since utterance-token meanings are particular to the contexts in which they arise, they won't be problematic in intercultural communication provided that a speaker makes sound judgements as to the encyclopedic knowledge of an addressee.

Utterance-type meaning – M-inference

Recovering utterance-type meaning is more likely to be problematic in trans-cultural communication. This is because non-native members aren't always aware of the culture-specific nature of what's stereotypically conveyed by the formulas they hear. Imagine that I'd been accompanied by a non-native visitor when I had the encounter with the small boy described right at the beginning of this book:

(16) SMALL BOY: Man
ME: Is that your brother
SMALL GIRL: Yes
ME: It takes all sorts
MOTHER: It certainly does

I suggested in Chapter 1 that the use of the distal demonstrative in 'Is that your brother' might have encoded my wish to take revenge on the small boy who'd embarrassed me. Since the formula 'Is that your brother' is only minimally more marked than 'Is he your brother', the markedness of my M-inference inviting utterance might easily have gone unnoticed by the visitor. But if the visitor's mother tongue used a more distinctly marked structure to encode 'Is that your brother' than to encode 'Is he your brother', with a correspondingly marked meaning, perhaps my utterance might have been understood as more accusatory than I intended.

Utterance-type meaning – I-inference

In Chapter 1, I described 'It takes all sorts' as an idiomatic way of suggesting that the small girl's brother was a character. This is because the formulaic, non-specifying, minimal nature of 'It takes all sorts' ('all sorts' of what? to do what?) suggests a high-context stereotypical meaning. But how is our non-native visitor to know which of several possible candidate meanings is stereotypically associated with the formula I use? A further difficulty is that my utterance is socio-pragmatically conditioned. How is the visitor to know what kind of contribution is socio-pragmatically licensed in such a situation?

Fortunately for trans-cultural communicators, not all I-inferences are so idiomatic (and thus unpredictable) or so dependent on culture-specific socio-pragmatic licence. As we noted earlier, formulas like *you know what x is like* invite a negative interpretation of '*x*'. Although the invitation to view '*x*' negatively probably isn't universal, we might nevertheless expect a similar interpretation across many cultures. The same might be said about structures discussed in Chapter 5 like

(17) You don't know what it's like to be an *x*

and

(18) If you've tried *x*, you won't like *y*

Utterance-type meaning – Q-inference

Because Q-inferences are based on scalar phenomena, we'd expect them to be universal across languages where the same categories exist. Thus *some* will imply <not all> and *should be* will imply <probably won't be> and

(19) *x* don't get the same calibre of students as *y*

will imply <the students at *x* aren't as good as the students at *y*> as cross-linguistic universals.

Lexical implicata

I recently gave a talk at a language teachers' conference whose theme was *Finding My Voice*. Clearly the implicata associated with 'Finding' and 'Voice' were sensitive to the context, and particularly to the accompanying conference information which drew attention to the challenges teachers face in the early stages of their careers. The title of my talk was

(20) Finding My Voice: Reconciling me to me

The semantically empty proform 'me' and the apparent tautology invite enrichment. As the title of a talk at an international conference attended by delegates from many different cultures, I hoped the formula I chose was intriguing but not opaque. Nevertheless, at the beginning of my talk, I glossed the two uses of 'me' as <me the professional teacher> and <me the individual with personal values>. However, if we reflect for a moment, we see that even these explicatures fall short of being fully informative. Imagine I'd been an investment banker addressing a bankers' conference and had chosen the same title for my talk. And imagine I'd explicated the two uses of 'me' as <me the investment banker> and <me the individual with personal values>. I don't suppose the personal values that I'd have gone on to talk about would have been the same as the values I talked about at the teachers' conference.

In the case of (20), the semantically empty item 'me' invites the addressee to supply self-generated context to enrich the lexical meaning. In the case of semantically replete items, the enrichment is likely to come from encyclopedic knowledge of a more culturally conditioned kind, as in the example discussed in Chapter 5

(21) How Shakespeare became Shakespeare

Summary

Utterance-token meaning: Because of the production conditions on utterance-token meaning, token inference presents no particular problems in either cross-cultural or intercultural communication.

M-inference: It's possible for an abnormal utterance to go unrecognised in trans-cultural communication; equally, even when the invitation to recover an M-inference is recognized, a different inference from that intended may sometimes be recovered.

I-inference: The cross-cultural communicator is likely to have difficulties recovering stereotypical interpretations of idiomatic formulas. In a situation where what's socio-pragmatically appropriate isn't obvious, recovering I-inferences is more problematic still. Formulaic structures which have wider cross-cultural currency and which invite stereotypical interpretations are less problematic. In intercultural communication, we might expect culture-specific I-inferences to be rarely invited because idiomatic native member formulas are unlikely to be known to non-native member, lingua franca users.

Q-inference: Q-inferences are usually unproblematic in trans-cultural communication.

Lexical implicata: Because native members have a culturally conditioned sense of the implicata conventionally associated with particular lexical items, the cross-cultural communicator will often be at a disadvantage. In intercultural communication, where culturally conditioned implicata are less 'local' and don't advantage one interactant over another, we might expect lexical enrichment to be more dependent on the immediate context and therefore to veer more towards 'token' than 'type' interpretations.

Checking understanding (11.2)

1 Which of the following native-member utterances discussed in Chapter 1 would you expect to pose problems for the cross-cultural communicator? Explain your decisions.

(22) Where's the ladies' room
(23) Are we all here
(24) Right, shall we begin
(25) What's your name again
(26) He's from Barcelona
(27) Radion removes dirt AND odours
(28) The campaign group called the Freedom Association
(29) Meanwhile, Peter Grundy has just told me of his long conversation with you earlier today
(30) We have designs on your man
(31) I've just finished a book

Checking understanding (11.2) *cont.*

(32) I'm tired
(33) I'll never sell her
(34) People living nearby said Mr Neale would go away on 'lengthy business trips'

2 If you were an interpreter translating the utterances (22)–(34) into another language, which would you expect to be problematic and how would you represent them in the second language?

11.3 Intercultural pragmatics in the real world

In this section, we first explore a brief intercultural service encounter. Then we reconsider the problem Moeschler encountered when he hoped to be met at the airport, this time analysing his email from a neo-Gricean rather than a relevance theoretic viewpoint. Finally, we consider a trans-cultural encounter involving three interactants, each a native member of a different culture.

11.3.1 Requesting a drink in lingua franca English

We're on our way to Warsaw. The Polish passenger across the aisle from me wants another drink and calls out to the Dutch stewardess:

(35) PASSENGER: Excuse me lady can I have a drink
STEWARDESS: One moment while I come back
PASSENGER: Sure

I notice how the passenger's form of address ('lady') is intended to be deferential and at the same time constructs his own identity as a male person. From my large collection of airline data, I know that it's usual for stewards/stewardesses to use honorifics and very rare for passengers to do this. The term 'lady' seems to be a little off-key. It isn't used as an address term in British English and I doubt it has the same honorific status in American English as I guess the speaker intends.

I notice the stewardess's idiosyncratic use of 'while' with the deictic 'come back'. I suppose 'until I come back' would have just about passed the native speaker expectation test. Probably 'I'll be back in a moment' would have been more expectable still.

I wonder about 'sure'. It's not in my variety of English so I can't be certain, but I sense that in American English 'sure' usually indicates that a request is readily granted. But is the stewardess's utterance a request? Surely not.

You get the point. From a native speaker/native member perspective, the English used in this exchange doesn't conform to the stereotype. If you wanted to be judgemental, each of these utterances exhibits elements of pragmatic anomaly. Yet the speakers don't have any difficulty conveying the meanings they intend and constructing an intercultural context that enables them to do business. In intercultural communication we don't expect stereotypical native member optimal form/optimal meaning pairings. In fact, stereotypical form/meaning pairings reinforce high-context culture and so are irrelevant in communicating meanings interculturally except to the extent that they may be economical.

11.3.2 Getting from the airport to one's destination revisited

In Chapter 6, we saw how Moeschler's request

(36) Pouvez-vous me dire comment aller de l'aéroport à X

was understood as a request for information rather than a request to be picked up. Moeschler's relevance theoretic explanation for this failure in trans-cultural communication appealed to context. In particular, Moeschler cited three contexts as implicated premises:

1 Someone arriving in a foreign country needs some help.
2 To travel downtown alone from the airport at night is not a good idea.
3 To ask how to go from A to B is to ask for some help to go from A to B.

Without first accommodating these implicated premises, the implicated conclusion <M wants to be picked up at the airport> can't be recovered. Appealing to the relevance theoretic notion of effort, Moeschler argued that the implicated premises weren't recovered because the processing effort wasn't warranted, it being less costly to explicate (36) as a request for information.

I want now to consider Moeschler's request from a neo-Gricean perspective. One reason for doing this is that Moeschler's relevance theoretic explanation seems to privilege the recovery of context ("contextual resources") over the processing of form ("cognitive abilities"). Arguably, the neo-Gricean approach pays more attention to form than to context. The question to be asked, then, is how cognitive abilities and contextual resources are balanced in trans-cultural communication and whether the linguistic form by means of which Moeschler makes his request might trigger the inference that he is asking to be picked up from the airport.

- *Q-implicature*. For (36) to Q-imply <M wants to be picked up at the airport>, the addressee must suppose a scale: a^1, a^2, a^3 (= *comment va-t-on de l'aéroport à X*), a^4 (= *pouvez-vous me dire comment aller de l'aéroport à X*), a^5,... a^n. The addressee processes a^4 as an invitation to infer something other than the straightforward request for travel instructions that a^3 invites.
- *I-implicature*. For (36) to I-imply <M wants to be picked up at the airport>, the addressee must understand 'pouvez-vous me dire comment aller de l'aéroport à X' as the stereotypical way of making a request to be picked up.
- *M-implicature*. For (36) to M-imply <M wants to be picked up at the airport>, the addressee must understand 'pouvez-vous me dire comment aller de l'aéroport à X' as an abnormal way of asking for instructions and therefore as having an abnormal meaning.

It seems that what actually happened was that the addressee understood (36) as the stereotypical way of asking for directions, as many French speakers tell me they'd have done. End of story. I leave it to you to decide whether Moeschler's relevance theoretic account or the neo-Gricean explanation is more persuasive.

We can perhaps speculate about trans-cultural requests of this kind a little further within the neo-Gricean framework. What follows is entirely suppositional because it explores Moeschler's request not in the language in which it was made, French, but in the two English representations of it that Moeschler provides. One representation is the translation provided in his 2007 paper cited in Chapter 6

(37) Can you tell me how to get from the airport to X

The other is taken from a paper he wrote in 2004, where, as well as (37), he provided a second translation

(38) How should I go from the airport to Rabat

As neo-Griceans, we know that the formula in which a request is made plays a part in determining how the addressee understands the nature of that request.

Let's imagine that you are a French speaker living in Rabat and receive emails from two English-speaking visitors who'll shortly be arriving at Casablanca airport and need to get to Rabat where you'll be looking after them. Imagine your English is so limited that you have to use a dictionary to understand their emails. However, you're a pragmaticist, and once you've translated the messages, you expect to be able to puzzle out what your visitors mean by what they say. Jack asks

(39) Can you tell me how to get from the airport to Rabat

and Jill asks

(40) How should I go from the airport to Rabat

Since their messages differ, you suppose that the pragmatic meanings also differ. What then are the optimal meanings for each of these forms?

Jack's 'Can you tell me' is a conventionally indirect request, a more face-aware equivalent of *tell me*. Like *pouvez-vous me dire* in your mother tongue, (39) seems to be a request for travel instructions, given its conventional indirection. (Although technically, yes, the matrix sentence, 'Can you tell me', is more costly than Jill's more direct formula.)

Jill's 'How should I go' appears to be marked in two ways. First, the past tense of the modal 'should' suggests that her self-directed journey is to occur in a world less likely to come about than would have been the case if *shall* had been chosen. (Or does 'should' encode not remote possibility but a deferential attitude? Perhaps ask an English native speaker about this.) Second, unlike *get*, Jill's use of 'go' encodes deictic directionality, with the deictic centre the location of the speaker at the airport. (Although wouldn't we use *aller*? And isn't *go* more salient lexically than *get*? Perhaps ask an English native speaker about this too.)

All things considered, (40) seems to you simultaneously to convey two pragmatically contradictory perspectives, that Jill doesn't see herself making the journey (conveyed by the past form 'should') and that she does see herself making the journey (conveyed by the deictic 'go'). It appears to be marked, so probably she isn't simply asking for travel instructions, given that asking for travel instructions is the expectable norm. So what can Jill mean? Perhaps she wants to be picked up at the airport. (If so, she obviously doesn't know how far Casablanca is from Rabat.)

As you can see, this is all speculative. But it does illustrate that cognitive abilities, and particularly the ability to infer meaning from language forms, are important in trans-cultural communication. Indeed, they may be especially important given the reduced contextual resources that interactants share.

11.3.3 Intercultural diplomacy

In his book *An Intercultural Approach to English Language Teaching*, Corbett discusses the need for lingua franca English learners to be comfortable in a range of cultural and linguistic environments, arguing that today's learner needs to be a cultural diplomat with the ability to mediate between language varieties and culturally constituted groups. In this sub-section, we examine a trans-cultural encounter involving the mother in a British host family (HM), a Hong Kong Chinese student whose first language is Mandarin (CS) and whose higher education in Hong Kong and the UK is conducted in English, and a Japanese student in the UK to learn English (JS).

The following exchange shows how consciously aware each of the participants is of the medium in which they communicate:

(41) HM: but the old lady at Chester-le-Street (. .) I think I said to you bad chest (.)
<demonstrates by coughing>=
CS: =oh yes=
JS: =yes <laughs>
HM: I – think – she – will – go – to – her

HM's opening turn follows a long off-topic insertion sequence. Her use of 'but' signals that the insertion sequence is complete and that her upcoming contribution will return to the topic, which host family one of JS's friends is likely to be allocated to. 'But' is followed by 'the old lady at Chester-le-Street' and a micro pause. This pause marks the noun phrase off as a topic rather than a grammatical subject. HM's topic-comment structure mimics a preferred Mandarin and Japanese discourse style and shows how the native English speaker adapts to the trans-cultural context. HM then continues with an elliptical pidgin-structure 'I think I said to you bad chest'. She demonstrates the meaning of 'bad chest' by simulating coughing. CS's 'oh yes' acknowledges the reference to 'the old lady at Chester-le-Street' and her health problem. JS's 'yes' and her laughter acknowledge her understanding of the meaning of 'bad chest' and her appreciation of the demonstration. HM then continues: 'I – think – she [= one of JS's friends] – will – go – to – her [= the old lady]. As the transcription indicates, this turn is uttered in a deliberate, word-by-word style. This is because the illocutionary target is JS, who has difficulty understanding rapid, native speaker English.

This short extract shows how HM takes into account the trans-cultural context and how each of CS and JS show understanding at the level expected of them.

Later in the same conversation, JS describes the food provided by another host mother for one of her friends:

(42) JS: and also she use many (1.5) er [hh
HM: [<laughs>]
(2.0)
JS: flour food?
CS: flour [food?]
JS: [oh] (. .) powder (.) food
CS: ah (. .) the [powder oh]
JS: [can you] understand
CS: [oh]
HM: [um]
(1.0)
CS: use a lot of powder
JS: use [a lot] (.) make mashed potato
CS: [yeah]
CS: yeah
JS: potato powder
HM: oh (.) artificial
JS: yeah (1.0) so (. .) very very <laughs> (1.0) easy

HM laughs when JS has difficulty finding a description of the food (l.2). However, when JS produces the obscure 'flour food', it falls to CS to clarify the meaning. CS's expression of surprise ('oh', l.7) is a reaction to the use of artificial food and shows her immediate comprehension. This contrasts with her use of 'oh' in l.9 where she realizes that it'll fall to her to try and explain to HM what JS means and that this may not be easy. CS and JS then co-construct an explanation directed at HM (l.12–16). Only when HM has finally understood what's meant by 'flour food' is JS's account complete. She then moves to a formulation 'so (. .) very very <laughs> (1.0) easy'.

This extract also shows the awareness speakers have of the trans-cultural nature of their communication and of the pragmatic and sequential implications of the context. Strikingly, it also shows that being a native speaker of a lingua franca isn't always an advantage as non-stereotypical interpretations are likely to be more problematic than they would be for a non-native lingua franca speaker expecting more token unpredictability.

Who then is more comfortable in the linguistic environment in which CS, HM and JS operate? We might measure the extent to which speakers fail to adapt to trans-cultural contexts by noting instances of laughter, assuming laughter to be evidence of a speaker's feeling of their own displacement and/or the incongruity of the conversational contributions of themselves or others. By this (admittedly naïve) criterion, CS appears to be the most at ease and JS the least at ease. All three interactants show 'diplomacy' and the ability to mediate between varieties. They also indicate which other is the appropriate illocutionary target, as they work collaboratively to achieve intercultural understanding.

Summary

In this section, we've explored some of the pragmatic and sequential features of three instances of trans-cultural communication. The first brief exchange showed that non-typical form-meaning pairings are often unproblematic in intercultural communication where stereotypical native member optimal form-meaning pairings don't apply. In the second case, the perlocutionary effect wasn't the one the sender of the message intended. This could be because the sender had a cultural expectation which wasn't shared by the person who received the email. On this analysis, the sender failed to find a sufficiently marked means of communicating what for his host was an abnormal request. Finally, the three-way trans-cultural conversation shows the contextual awareness of interactants and how they try to find remedial strategies for situations where the cognitive abilities and contextual resources of any of them may be inadequate to the demands of the situation.

(Acknowledgement: the host family data were collected by Zhang Lin (Lindy), who together with Huang Jaixin (Beryl), Qi Wenting (Winnie) and Qi Yuan (Eileen) carried out the preliminary analysis and kindly agreed to the reproduction of the data here.)

11.4 Lingua franca pragmatics

In this section we first speculate about pragmatic meaning in a lingua franca and then consider the special case of written language.

11.4.1 Pragmatic meaning in a lingua franca

A lingua franca is a language in which people with different first languages communicate. More often than not, the lingua franca isn't the mother tongue of any of those who use it. Although there's no empirical evidence to support the claim, it's widely believed that on most of the occasions when non-native speakers use English as a lingua franca, they use it to communicate with other non-native speakers, i.e. in intercultural encounters. A typical example of such use would be an international academic conference in which English was the working language, even though only a minority of delegates spoke it as a first language. To the extent that English is a global lingua franca, it's become deterritorialized. To some extent, therefore, it's become the cultural property of all its users and not only of those who speak it as a first language.

Some languages are closely associated with distinct cultural groups; others belong to anyone who chooses to use them. There are many examples of the close relationship of language and culture, particularly in Europe, where national borders and language use frequently coincide. Virtually everyone who speaks Polish is a Pole, for example. Equally, it's rare for someone to consider themselves a Pole unless they speak the language. There's a good reason for this close association of language and nation: from the late eighteenth century to the end of the First World War, Poland's territory was appropriated by greedy neighbours. It existed as a nation without territory, a nation defined as a population who spoke Polish.

English is clearly at the opposite end of the continuum from Polish. For more than three centuries, there have been communities of English speakers who aren't British. Today only a minority of those who speak English as a first language are British. There are also significant numbers of people who are British by nationality but who don't speak English as a first language. As everyone knows, the deterritorialization of English has been accelerating rapidly. In fact, according to Graddol, there have been more non-native than native speakers of English since the 1970s. In the twenty-first century, linguistic migration no longer depends only on the movement of people. Today, lingua francas spread through cyberspace as citizens of the virtual world communicate.

The deterritorialization of English and its widespread use as a lingua franca by second language speakers in intercultural interactions have several implications for pragmatics. For a start, English is no longer learnt as a second language principally because it provides non-native members with access to the culture of native members. Although English is still an access language, for example, in the natural sciences, it's also a language of representation. If I learn English in Brazil or in China, I intend to use it interculturally to represent myself. I may use it actively in intercultural encounters. Or I may use it passively, on my website, where I represent myself to the world beyond the community of speakers who share my mother tongue.

Since the ownership of English now includes many second language speakers, we may expect its new owners to make changes. As Seidlhofer says, "English is being shaped at least as much by its non-native speakers as by its native speakers" (2005: 339). In order to prove this thesis, Seidlhofer and her colleagues are assembling a corpus of lingua franca English structures which differ from native speaker norms. In the field of phonology, where, for obvious reasons, data are easier to collect, Jenkins (2000) has proposed a 'core' phonology for English lingua franca communication. This core isn't based solely on native speaker norms but also takes into account English lingua franca use. To give one example, Jenkins suggests that the core phonology shouldn't include, for example, interdental fricatives, segments which are hard to produce and which are found only in a very small number of languages, including, as it happens, English.

Although we might agree that some I-implicatures and some M-implicatures are the interdental fricatives of pragmatics and that aware English native speakers might try to avoid them in intercultural communication, pragmatics is not so easily reduced to a core as phonology. This is because pragmatic meanings are essentially negotiated accommodations. They are also typically instantial, i.e. context-sensitive, and only institutionalized to a limited degree. This is why in our study of intercultural communication in this chapter, we've been exploring the ways in which speakers take account of the cognitive abilities and contextual resources of each other. And this is why we've concluded that utterance-token meaning is favoured over utterance-type meaning in low-context intercultural encounters where both stereotypical and abnormal formulas aren't readily recognized as such.

Under these circumstances, being an English native speaker in an English lingua franca communication isn't necessarily an advantage, as the data examined in 11.3.3 show. In terms of production, the optimal form HM uses to encode her meaning is quite unlike her native repertoire: it includes topic-comment discourse structure, a pidgin structure in which 'bad chest' represents <she has a bad chest>, a paralinguistic demonstration of the meaning of 'bad chest' and a deliberate word-by-word realization of 'I think she will go to her'. However, she makes use of procedural 'but' and twice hedges propositions with 'I think', indicating the importance of procedural encoding in intercultural communication. And in terms of comprehension, HM is at a notable disadvantage when compared to CS in assigning an optimal meaning to the form 'powder food' and the explanation 'use a lot (.) make mashed potato'.

11.4.2 Lingua francas and written language

We shouldn't overlook the importance of writing in discussing lingua francas, having discussed lingua franca English as a means of self-representation on the internet and having noted how migration is now a virtual phenomenon. In both these contexts, the lingua franca is almost always written English. Earlier in this chapter, we also reconsidered Moeschler's failed email communication, again an instance of written language. Indeed, it may have occurred to you to wonder whether the negatively polite formula '*pouvez-vous me dire . . .*' is well suited to the email context in which it's used. This raises the possibility that the conventional way of asking for travel instructions in the spoken medium might possibly have a different illocutionary force when employed in the written medium. In fact, we speculated about form:meaning pairings in writing in Chapter 5 in relation to the realization of 'are you' in the context of a poster.

Writing as a cultural phenomenon

There are a number of aspects of written communication to consider:

- Written language is obviously not dialogic in the same way as spoken interaction. For this reason, it doesn't allow the kind of comprehension checking process available to HM, CS and JS. Because it transcends time, and because the context in which it's interpreted is often unknowable in advance, writing doesn't rely to such an extent on context as spoken language does. Token inference isn't, therefore, so pervasive.
- Some cultures have no written language. In others, the written form is notably orality-oriented, i.e. it closely mirrors the spoken form. In English, the difference between the spoken and written forms is very marked: whereas the spoken language favours a Germanic lexis and is often highly elliptical, the written form favours Romance lexis and more elaborate structures.
- Writing is used for a wide variety of purposes. At its most basic, we use writing to represent what we might otherwise convey in spoken form. Every time we make a shopping list or leave a written message for a friend, this is what we do.

However, there's also another sense in which writing is the most creative and original way of using language available to us. Careful, calculated and literary, this mode of writing carries a culture across time from one generation to the next. Perhaps it's worth considering how this comes about.

The 'careful' nature of writing

For a start, writing has to be codified (i.e. a representational system has to be devised) and standardized (the system and its implementation for every lexical item has to be accepted across a wide community of users). Going beyond lexis, a more sophisticated kind of standardization involves developing broad agreement about genres, the forms used for the various written functions – letters, academic papers, company reports, etc. These are obviously to some degree culture-specific, as studies in contrastive rhetoric have shown. The fact that we 'learn' to write (and that at this apprentice stage we're willing to accept corrective advice from experts) tells us that, when it comes to writing, there are degrees of skill. Skilled writing needs care and is very time-consuming compared to speaking: this is because it involves a process of recursive drafting as we attempt to satisfy standard ways of conveying the meanings we have in mind. This in turn presupposes that there are agreed ways of putting things across a wide community of language users and generalized interpretations across many cases.

At this point, as pragmaticists, we prick our ears up. Writing, it seems, has typical qualities which we might expect to be problematic in lingua franca use. Indeed, even in an intracultural context, different writers have different levels of skill, and degrees of literacy are often used as a means of rationing resources like continuing education. This in turn reminds us of the institutional nature of writing and the power of the discourse community which determines whether any particular piece of writing has readers.

While intercultural users of English may more or less speak as they wish provided that they take the cognitive abilities and contextual resources of their addressee/s into account, it's not yet clear whether writing requires intercultural users to conform to norms that have a long cultural history and that extend in a natural way out of the basic notions that written languages are codified and standardized. But to the extent that writing relies on typical formulas learned over a long apprenticeship, we might expect lingua franca writing to remain at the orality-oriented end of the writing spectrum. If you're a native speaker of English, you'll know from experience that more ambitious English lingua franca writing often feels slightly 'other'. It may be that this is because the conversational implicata typically associated with lexical items are especially important in the collocations we make use of when we write. And we might suppose that these implicata are not always available to non-native members. Although native members have only the haziest ideas of these implicata at the conscious level, when we function as native writers at the 'careful' end of the continuum, we have an intuitive sense of how they contribute to the readability of the text we create. So if I had to place a bet, I'd hazard a guess that lingua franca writing will extend orality-oriented writing into areas in which writing in English was once 'careful' only.

Pragmaticists haven't traditionally paid much attention to writing. Perhaps it's time for a change. If I really wanted to know how apologies and requests are made in intracultural, cross-cultural and intercultural contexts, I have a ready source of valid data in the masses of emails sent that encode just such acts.

Raising pragmatic awareness

1 Imagine you've had a minor accident and hurt your wrist. You need to go to hospital to check whether a bone's broken. If you're used to western medicine, imagine the hospital is in Beijing. If you're used to Chinese or some other non-western medicine, imagine the hospital is in New York. First of all, a clerk checks to see whether you might be entitled to free treatment or whether you need to pay. Then you describe your symptoms to a nurse. She tells you to wait for the doctor, to whom you again describe your symptoms. Then you're sent for an X-ray where you meet a radiologist. You return to the doctor, who discusses treatment options with you. You then receive treatment from the nurse. Finally, an orderly gives you medication and explains the circumstances under which you should return to hospital. With colleagues in your tutorial group discuss whether you and those who treat you would regard your conversations as cross-cultural or intercultural.

2 Plan a situation for a fellow member of your tutorial group in which they would be expected to perform various socio-pragmatic acts. Explain the situation to your colleague and ask whether they would perform all the acts and what pragmalinguistic formulas they would consider using.

3 Design a small set of DCTs for other members of your tutorial group to complete. Compare results.

4 Focus on a group you know well who belong to a different sub-culture from yourself. Talk through the typical ways in which they use language that identify them as members of the sub-culture.

5 Discuss with other members of your tutorial group any occasions on which you felt culturally ill-at-ease and the linguistic strategies that you felt were appropriate or inappropriate in the situation you found yourself in.

6 A distinction is sometimes drawn between the 'modernist' spread of English to speakers of other languages by native English speakers and the 'postmodern' effect that second language users have on English. First, distinguish modernist and postmodern aspects of the exchanges between CS, HM and JS and then talk through the extent to which your experience of English in trans-cultural contexts is modernist or postmodern.

7 Which of the features of talk identified as typically pragmatic in Chapter 1 play an important part in trans-cultural communication: accommodation, appropriateness, context, indeterminacy, indirect meaning, inference, reflexivity, relevance?

Discussions and essays

Discuss the relative merits of each of the following views:

- "Although 'intercultural' and 'cross-cultural' are often used interchangeably, they do not have the same meaning. While cross-cultural communication is usually considered a study of a particular idea(s) or concept(s) within several cultures that compares one culture to another on the aspect of interest, intercultural communication focuses on interactions among people from different cultures" (Kecskes, 2004: 1–2).
- The study of pragmatics is the study of culture-conditioned use and meaning.
- Since contexts vary cross-culturally, intercultural communication isn't all that cultural.
- If "pragmatics is essentially about the users of language in a real life situation, and about the conditions that enable those users to employ linguistic techniques and materials effectively and appropriately" (Mey, 2004: 42), trans-cultural users are pragmatically disadvantaged.
- Utterance-token meaning is a more appropriate focus in preparing second language users for intercultural communication than utterance-type meaning.
- As English is no longer a foreign language for anyone, non-native users may legitimately expect their own particular stereotypical inferences to be drawn by those they address as they use English ideologically to encode their own identity.
- Intercultural communication depends to a greater extent on non-reductive token-inference than intracultural communication, which also accommodates the more reductive, type-inference.
- Globalization generally leads to homogenization. So it is with language.

Further reading

Scollen and Scollen, 2000; for studies of cross-cultural and intercultural issues, the journal *Intercultural Pragmatics*.

12 Doing project work in pragmatics

Keywords:

analysis, data, data collection, ethical issues, experiment, findings, generalizability, hypothesis, participant, pilot, population, qualitative, quantitative, sample, transcription, validity, variables

This chapter contains suggestions for project work with a pragmatic orientation. It discusses the types of project which are viable and the issues involved in successful data collection and transcription.

12.1 The nature of pragmatic investigation

Many linguists, although not by any means all pragmaticists, view their subject as a science. They see the purpose of linguistics as bringing order to the apparently untidy set of data that we call language. Rather as an astronomer might observe the revolution of known planets around a star and form the hypothesis that their motion suggested the presence of a further, as yet undiscovered planet, and then set out to test this hypothesis, so in linguistic investigation too, a favoured method is to frame and then test hypotheses. To take an arbitrary example, I once overheard someone say to a two-year-old

(1) Why don't you use your spoon

whereupon the two-year-old obligingly picked up her spoon and tried to feed herself with it. If two-year-olds can understand indirect speech acts, it seemed reasonable to hypothesize that my then fifteen-year-old son shouldn't have any trouble with them either. And so when I next saw him eating with his fingers, I said, trying to capture the intonation pattern of the original utterance:

(2) Why don't you use your knife and fork

Unfortunately the perlocutionary effect was not as I had intended – he responded to the propositional content rather than to the illocutionary force of my utterance.

We can easily imagine potentially investigable topics in this area that might well, given a little thought, be turned into testable hypotheses. These topics might include

- whether family members show that they are displeased with one another by responding to the propositional content rather than the illocutionary force of each other's utterances, typically treating indirect speech acts as though they were direct speech acts;
- the extent of any association between compliance with indirect parental requests and age of child, gender of child, gender of parent, time of day, subject of request, etc.;

- whether the compliance/non-compliance of two-year-olds with indirect requests is a matter of choice rather than degree of pragmatic understanding;
- whether indirect requests in parent-to-child communication are more commonly associated with money talk than with personal hygiene and bedroom tidying talk.

Each of these topics is potentially investigable. A typical way to proceed would be to try and frame a testable hypothesis. For example, we might hypothesize that two-year-olds respond equally (un)cooperatively to indirect and to direct requests. And then we might set out to test this hypothesis by designing an experiment in which a sample of two-year-olds was selected, either randomly or according to some criterion, and stimulated to action by a series of requests, some expressed directly and some expressed indirectly. Or we might wish to compare two samples of two-year-olds, perhaps one consisting of kindergarten attenders and one of non-kindergarten attenders. The data resulting from such an experiment might be best collected on videotape. Once the data had been collected, they could be analysed and a finding would emerge, either that the hypothesis was proved or that it failed, or that the different samples yielded different results. If it turned out that the sample of two-year-olds complied more readily with direct than with indirect requests, this finding would presumably have implications for the way adults should talk to two-year-olds on occasions when they wanted to get them to do things. And the finding that two-year-olds respond more readily to direct requests might suggest follow-up experiments: for example, it might be useful to try and design an experiment to determine whether two-year-olds failed to respond to indirect requests because they were failing to understand their pragmatics or because they didn't like being talked to indirectly.

This kind of research is usually called 'empirical' because it studies real, observable phenomena, in this case the reactions of two-year-olds to a series of direct and indirect requests. The research method outlined above is typical:

- Frame a testable hypothesis (or series of hypotheses) suggested by some observation about the way the world appears to work.
- Design an experiment which will enable you to collect data from an appropriate population which test this hypothesis.
- Collect the data under experimental conditions.
- Quantify the data in order to determine whether or not the hypothesis is proved.
- Consider the implications of the findings and whether follow-up experiments would be useful.

Very often empirical research of this sort tries to determine whether there is a significant, as opposed to a chance, association between two variables. So that, for example, you might try to establish whether there is a significant association between kindergarten attendance or age and understanding of indirect speech acts as demonstrated by compliance with indirect requests.

Recognizing the scientific basis of linguistics has important consequences for the way we investigate language. But this doesn't mean that all pragmaticists think of the area of linguistics they are interested in as essentially scientific. Nor does it mean that every aspect of pragmatics readily lends itself to such methods of investigation. In fact, precisely because pragmatic meaning depends so much on inference, which isn't a directly observable phenomenon, there are lots of ways of investigating language use that aren't designed as experiments of the kind suggested for the investigation of two-year-old responses to indirect requests.

If you were interested in interactive pragmatics, for example, you'd rarely want to design an experiment to elicit sets of **data** that would be easily comparable. In fact, you could argue that we got further in our analysis of the interactions in the library or between the warden and the students by trying to understand them in terms of the occasion-specific sequential and metasequential properties of interaction rather than by investigating how frequently the speakers made use of particular pragmatic strategies. These interactions weren't collected as part of a controlled experiment at all. And unlike the purposes for which most elicited data are collected, i.e. checking for the presence/absence of some predetermined property, these data challenge us to provide an exhaustive analysis of all the contexts oriented to in the interactions.

Obviously very different techniques are involved in researching two-year-old talk by means of hypothesis testing as suggested above and researching the structure of interaction in the ways demonstrated in Chapters 7 and 10. The first approach is often called '**quantitative**' because it requires a substantial quantity of data whose regularities can be determined, often by detailed statistical means. The second approach is often called '**qualitative**' because its results rely more on the interpretative insight of the researcher than on objectively measured associations between sets of **variables**. Quantitative results can often be generalized to other populations – so we might expect our findings to apply to other two-year-olds as well. However, we wouldn't expect other warden/student encounters to follow the same course as the one we studied qualitatively in Chapter 7. The lack of generalizability of qualitative studies is often compensated for by the deep understanding they provide of the case we study.

Pragmatic research makes use of both qualitative and quantitative methods. When you identify the area you wish to research, it's usually fairly clear which method is likely to give the better result.

12.2 Collecting data

You may be collecting your data because you wish to test a hypothesis. In this case, your data will usually be elicited, as in the hypothetical two-year-old project discussed above. If this is the case, you'll need to design elicitation **experiments** very carefully to make sure that you're collecting valid data, i.e. data that enable you to measure what you seek to measure rather than some other phenomenon. This means that all the non-relevant variables need to be eliminated. It wouldn't be very useful, for example, if a linguist set out to measure the cognitive skills of two-year-olds as demonstrated in responses to indirect requests only to realize afterwards that the results reflected the extent to which the requests themselves were palatable.

More often in your own work, you'll probably collect your data first and have only a fairly general idea of what you hope they will show before you've collected them. The researcher who obtained the library data, for example, never imagined that she'd end up investigating how speaker and addressee face-threats are managed at the inter-library loan desk.

There are some fairly well-established *dos* and *don'ts* when it comes to data collection. One of the most obvious relates to the so-called 'Observer's Paradox', the effect that the observer or collector has on the nature of the data itself. In fact, we saw this effect at the beginning of the library interaction when the student oriented to the context of being recorded. If you tell someone you'd like to ask them a number of questions, they'll provide you with data that reflect this situation and are therefore unlikely to represent their natural speech style. So it's important to find a means of collecting data which isn't influenced by the collection procedure itself.

Similarly, if you tell your friends to have a natural conversation while you record it on tape, you'll get anything but a natural conversation. I'm not saying that it isn't interesting to analyse data in which speakers orient to their situation as data providers, and maybe even to a supposed overhearing audience such as a tutor to whom you may eventually submit your work. However, in most situations you're unlikely to be able to collect representative data if your informants know that they're being recorded. On the other hand, there's an ethical issue: it's widely agreed that we ought not to make use of data provided by informants without their consent. Rather than work with informants (or even 'subjects' as they're sometimes termed), we aim to work with willing **participants**. After all, strictly speaking, the data belong to those who provide it, so wherever possible, they should participate in our research and have access to the results we obtain from our analysis.

We also need to take care that our participants aren't damaged by our use of the data they provide. Usually, it's enough to ensure that the data can't be traced back to its source. This is why I omitted the sequence in the library data in which the student reveals his name and address, although from an analyst's perspective this is an exceptionally interesting exchange owing to the student's having an exotic family name which the librarian has trouble hearing accurately.

More practically, we often need to know things about our participants (such as their ages or nationalities or status in an organization) that may well not be directly revealed in the data they provide, so we need to talk to them anyway. Therefore we have to decide whether

- to obtain the prior written consent of our informants before we collect data from them (the gold standard);
- to ask permission to use the data after they've been collected;
- not to ask permission at all.

The decision we make will typically depend on the circumstances in which the data are collected and the kind of talk that's expected to occur.

- *Asking permission before collecting data:* We obviously need to ask permission before collecting data if we're hoping to record our own job interview, or if we're recording a business meeting or a doctor–patient encounter.
- *Asking permission once the data has been collected:* Some years ago a colleague and I conducted a small-scale research project in which we decided that valid data could only be obtained if permission wasn't sought until after the data had been obtained and the nature of the project and the transaction involved were such as to justify this. Every afternoon for four weeks we recorded every transaction that occurred between 4 and 5 p.m. in a tourist information office. We were hoping to find out whether native and non-native speakers and native and non-native members of the culture used the same pragmatic strategies to achieve the same ends, such as finding overnight accommodation in the local area. Although the staff of the tourist information office knew they were being recorded, if we'd told the clients as they walked through the door that they were going to be recorded, the data would obviously have been distorted. So the transactions were recorded covertly.

  As each informant left the counter, they were approached by a research assistant who explained to them that they'd been recorded as part of a research project whose purpose was to study the ways in which people make requests, with the ultimate aim of developing teaching materials that would help non-native speaker visitors in the future. They were asked whether they would agree to the conversation they had just had being analysed or whether they would prefer the recording to be erased. As it happened, only two informants asked for their conversations to be erased. Both were non-native speakers who said that if they'd known they were being recorded they'd have spoken better English! In the case of all the rest who gave their consent, we were then able to ask about their native/non-native speaker status, their language learning backgrounds, ages, etc.

- *Recording without asking permission:* Many researchers would consider it acceptable to record short anonymous bursts of talk without obtaining the speaker's consent under certain conditions. For example, I might pretend to be an innocent bystander if I happened to be fortunate enough to be passing with my pinhead microphone and concealed recorder and saw a motorist returning to their car just as a traffic warden was attaching a parking ticket. Because this material is in the public domain and might equally be recorded by a passing television crew, and since the identities of the participants will remain unknown and therefore no one can be damaged by the analysis of the data, this might be considered the type of situation that it would be ethical to record without the consent of the informants. Recording short talk episodes under circumstances such as this is really only a small extension of the rapid anonymous observation I conduct when I write down utterances of the kind that have been the principal source for much of the data cited in this book. Unlike the other situations discussed, it's also uncertain that data being obtained in this way are going to be used at all – pragmaticists collect masses of data rather as tourists take masses of photographs, but only a small part of all the data we record in this way will ever be transcribed, let alone analysed.

You may be wondering about how the extended interactions analysed in this book were obtained. The library data discussed in Chapter 10 were collected with the full prior consent of all the participants. The warden/student data discussed in Chapter 7 were obtained by a student collecting data for her pragmatics project by simply allowing the recorder to run as she went about her business. She obtained the consent of the three other people involved when she decided to use the data for her project. The classroom data discussed in Chapter 7 were recorded with the full prior consent of all the participants because they were to be used subsequently for pedagogic purposes. The student/porter data studied in Chapter 10 were recorded entirely by chance. The researcher had a recorder in her bag and was on the way to the station to collect data according to a pre-arranged plan. She didn't realize that her recorder was running until she reached the station and found that she'd collected gold on her way there. Subsequently I asked the porter for permission to use the data in this book.

There are a number of other points to keep in mind when you collect data. These include:

- *Whenever possible, do a* ***pilot*** *collection exercise first.* This will enable you to see whether the data you're collecting are (a) audible and therefore transcribable, and (b) useful for the purposes you have in mind. I know of one researcher who had the brilliant idea of comparing what a hospital doctor told an outpatient during a consultation with the way the patient relayed that information to friends and family after the consultation. Fortunately, she hadn't invested too much time before she discovered that the experimental design was impractical. A willing consultant was found who could see the benefit to himself of participating in such a project. The researcher's idea was to approach only patients who came to the hospital with a friend or family member. If they were willing to participate, the consultation was recorded. After the consultation, they were given a recorder and simply told to let it run for the next thirty minutes. Unfortunately most of the vital data from this phase was drowned out by the roar of passing traffic as the patients joined the queue at the bus stop!

- *Give some thought as to whether you need to use all the data or just some part.* There are circumstances when excluding any of the data you collect would render them an incomplete record of a speech event and therefore of limited value. There are other occasions on which some random sample, such as the second ten minutes of a classroom interaction, might be preferred just because it's a random sample and directly comparable with other samples selected according to the same criterion. There are still other occasions when you're looking for particular types of data, such as inserted sequences between a question and the eventual answer, which probably means that you'll have to transcribe all the data collected and then select your target data from the whole. If you've thought these issues through before you begin your data collection exercise, you'll probably be able to collect your data more economically and are likely to collect only data that are genuinely useful.
- *Don't be too ambitious:* an hour of conversation involving several speakers can take many days or even weeks to transcribe accurately. So limit the amount of data you set out to collect to what you can practically transcribe and usefully analyse – two or three minutes of talk will keep you occupied for many hours.
- If you collect data featuring more that two or three speakers, when you come to transcribe it, you're guaranteed to have *problems in some places determining who the speaker is.* These can sometimes (but not always) be overcome by recording your data on video, but this is usually impractical. Another option is to be present during the speech event and to note down the opening words of each speaker. To do this, you'll need to number the speakers, perhaps according to their locations around a table. But even this method is far from foolproof, as you'll quickly discover. There are also practical problems associated with recording a many-speaker event: inevitably some speakers will be nearer the microphone than others, so some will be harder to transcribe. And the **transcription** will be harder still in the sections where several speakers talk at the same time, such as at points of agreement or when schism occurs, i.e. when a larger group becomes two smaller groups for a number of exchanges so that two or more conversations run concurrently.

Once you've tried to collect your own data, you'll become aware of the need to plan carefully – nothing is more frustrating than to have data which don't really reveal what you'd hoped they would or which are so difficult to hear that you can never get an accurate enough transcription to work with.

12.3 Transcription conventions

When you make a transcription, you'll need to make decisions about the notation conventions you employ and about how to set the transcription out on the page.

12.3.1 Notation

Conventional transcriptions of conversations use standard orthographic script rather than phonemic transcription. This is fortunate since the task of transcription would be overwhelming otherwise. (Of course, you're always able to give a phonetic representation of an item in your subsequent analytic discussion if you need to.) Most standard orthographic transcriptions are adapted to show how items like *and* and *your* are actually spoken since their realization may vary in obvious ways. So you might expect to use representations like *n* and *yer*. You also need to indicate hesitations like *er* and *um*, other fillers and uptake signals like *uh*, *uh-huh* and *yeah*, and audible breathing (*hh*) and indrawn breath (*.hh*). You may also decide to indicate any particularly marked representation of a lexical item, such as Nicole's odd use of 'wo'.

A more difficult issue is whether and how to represent intonation and pitch. The easiest solution is only to indicate very marked examples, so that distinctive pitch prominence might be marked by capitalizing the appropriate segments (e.g., you WHAT) and the louder of two simultaneous utterances where the speakers compete for the floor by underlining. There are more elaborate systems for marking intonation contours such as the one worked out by Crystal and Davy (1969: 24–40), but they're very laborious to employ and require a degree of skill to interpret too. Many transcribers also avoid standard punctuation marks altogether because they can only represent broad interpretations of the functions of utterances and are often ambiguous.

More important in many ways than marking intonation is marking features of conversational sequencing. For example, you'll almost always need to mark pauses in talk. The most widely used convention is parentheses, as we saw in Chapter 7, with the length of pause indicated in tenths of a second, so that '(2.5)' represents a pause of two-and-a-half seconds. Micro pauses can also be marked with parentheses and points, with '(.)' roughly equal to a one-syllable length pause, and '(. .)' roughly equal to a two-syllable length pause, again as we saw in Chapter 7. Sometimes the micro-pause that we expect at transition relevance places (TRP) doesn't occur, so that the utterances of the two speakers are latched, a phenomenon usually indicated by an '=' sign.

Another sequencing phenomenon that needs to be marked is the overlap of two speakers. The start of an overlap may be marked by a double slash '//' and the end of the overlap by an asterisk '*', which may be indicated in both speakers' utterances. An alternative is to use deep brackets, as I've been doing in this book:

(3) S: yeah [yeah]
L: [ye] we can send it you [if we find it]
S: [great thank you] that's great (.)
[thanks] a lot
L: [bye]

Notice how double slashes and asterisks have different implications for the appearance of the transcription on the page:

(4) S: yeah //yeah*
L: //ye* we can send it you //if we find it*
S: //great thank you* that's great (.)
//thanks* a lot
L: //bye*

As you see, using different symbols to mark the start and the end of an overlap (such as slashes and asterisks or right- and left-facing brackets) makes a transcription clearer.

You'll also need a convention to indicate that the transcription is uncertain or that there's a contribution which you are unable to transcribe. This may be done with single or double parentheses or with square brackets. As you'll have noticed, I've been using square brackets, as I did for the crucial but not 100 per cent certain past tense in the student's explanation:

(5) S: a folder here on Friday I think an orange folder (.) I wonder if
it[d] been handed in

You may also want to indicate an important non-linguistic feature. This may be done with square or angled brackets as in

(6) L: it's OK
<L types>
<L looks around for folder>

You'll have noticed that I've also used this convention for laughter, although some researchers use the '@@@' symbol. The advantage is that this makes it possible to indicate the length of the laughter.

Although these are relatively widely agreed conventions, there's considerable minor variation in the way that different linguists use and adapt them to their own purposes. There's nothing to prevent you using conventions that are especially suited to your own data as long as you provide a key indicating how the conventions are to be understood.

Before you begin your own transcription, you'd be well advised to study two or three examples. The *Handbook of Pragmatics* (1995: 646–54) provides a useful summary of transcription principles and Schiffrin (1994: 422–33) provides a comprehensive summary of the conventions used by Jefferson, Tannen and others. Another useful source is Atkinson and Heritage (1984: ix–xvii), reprinted in Jaworski and Coupland (1999: 158–66). Hutchby and Wooffitt (2008) also have an informative chapter on transcription. However, remember that transcription techniques have been developed within the CA tradition with its close focus on members' methods: the resulting transcription may, therefore, be more detailed than you need for an empirical pragmatics analysis.

Checking understanding (12.1)

Transcription is a tricky matter. The following examples compare an early stage transcription of the library data with the transcription in Chapter 10. Study the places where I've inserted downward arrows (↓) in the two transcriptions and comment on the differences between the transcriptions and their effects.

1 Early stage

(7) S: right (2.0) ↓I'm tempted to say one two three testing
[but I don't] suppose I should should I .hh I left ↓um (. .) I left
L: [<laughs>]
S: a folder here on Friday I think an orange folder (.)

Final

(7′) S: right (1.5) ↓tsuh I'm tempted to say one two three testing
[but I don't suppose] I should should I .hh I left ↓a (. .) I
L: [<laughs>]
S: left a folder here on Friday I think an orange folder (.)

2 Early stage

(8) S: a folder here on Friday I think an orange folder (.) I wonder if
↓it's been handed in (. .) I was at the inter-library loan desk
(1.0)
L: oh right
(1.0)
S: I think ↓it's sort of orangey coloured

Checking understanding (12.1) *cont.*

Final

(8′) S: a folder here on Friday I think an orange folder (.) I wonder if ↓it['d] been handed in (0.7) I was at the inter-library loan desk
(1.0)
L: oh right
(0.5)
S: I think ↓it was sort of orangey coloured

3 Early stage

(9) L: no I'm sorry
(.)
S: .hh oh dear
↓(1.0)
S: OK
(5.0)
S: right ↓[you don't know if anyone]
L: ↓[if we find it to who]

Final

(9′) L: no I'm sorry
(1.0)
S: .hh oh dear ↓(1.0) OK
(3.0)
S: alright ↓(.) you don't happen to know if [anyone handed]
L: [if we] find it to who

4 Early stage

(10) L: =is there a telephone number
S: (..) um (..) well my ↓telephone my home [↓number]
L: ↓[you you] have e-mails have you?
S: (..) yeah [yeah ↓great thank you that's great thanks] a lot
L: [yeah we can send it you if we find it]

Final

(10′) L: =is there a telephone number
S: (. .) um (. .) well my ↓telepho- my home ↓num-=
L: ↓=you you have e-mail have you
S: yeah [yeah]
L: [ye] we can send it you [if we find it]
S: ↓[great thank you] that's great (.) [thanks] a lot
L: [bye]

12.3.2 Setting the transcription out on the page

This is a more problematic area than it might appear to be. You only realize the complexities of the problem and the effects of the decisions you make once you've tried a few ways. A number of possibilities are discussed below:

1 Start each new speaker at the left-hand margin. If you have an adequate way of indicating latched utterances and overlaps, in theory, a transcription in which all new speakers begin at the left-hand margin, even when overlapping the previous speaker, will be transparent. However, as soon as you have more than two speakers, this becomes problematical, as the following example shows:

(11) TRAVEL AGENT: we're not British Rail //agents*
CUSTOMER: //you're* not a//gents I see*
MANAGER: //but I'll*give you a rough idea

This is not only difficult to follow, but might also give the false impression that the customer and the manager simultaneously overlap the travel agent.

2 Wherever there's a TRP, start the new turn at the left-hand margin. This convention not only solves the problem highlighted in (11), it also shows where TRPs occur. Notice how this means that a speaker who self-selects at a TRP will also start a new line at this point. When Nicole tries to get the Doctor to take the turn and eventually has to continue herself, the data were represented as follows:

(12) DOCTOR: how's it doing
SUSIE: yeah no erm Nicole wants to no we need a word with you
DOCTOR: oh [right]
NICOLE: [no] someone's been nicking stuff out the fridge
(2.0) so

I chose this method of representing the data in Chapter 7 when you first encountered an extended interaction because data are easy to read in this form when you're unfamiliar with transcription conventions. But a more accurate representation perhaps would have been

(12′) DOCTOR: how's it doing
SUSIE: yeah no erm Nicole wants to no we need a word with you
DOCTOR: oh [right]
NICOLE: [no] someone's been nicking stuff out the fridge
(2.0)
NICOLE: so

This convention also enables a transcriber to distinguish a TRP such as that between Nicole's two turns from a genuine in-turn pause such as occurs in Nicole's continuation:

(13) DOCTOR: which one
NICOLE: ours (.) well Susie's butter's gone and my cheese has
gone as well

Some transcriptions that start a new line at each TRP also employ a capital letter at the start of each turn.

3 Start the next speaker at the point in the line where the previous speaker terminates. This method has the advantage of capturing the notion that talk

continues naturally but has the disadvantage that it doesn't enable TRPs to be unambiguously transcribed. Both this and the first method may be suitable for very short examples of data but are not as satisfactory for longer conversations as [2], which is likely to be the best method for you.

4 Use columns for each speaker. This is an uncommon method of transcription but can be used quite effectively where the encounter is very unequal. For example, a teacher–pupil exchange which followed a question–answer format might lend itself to this method of representation. One advantage of the method is that utterance or speech act types as well as data can be represented in this format. So if we'd transcribed the opening of the encounter between the porter and the student whose parcel had gone missing in this way, we'd be able to use the same format to categorize the contributions of each speaker

(14)	P: hello young lady=	S: =hiya (1.5) em I was round yesterday I've had some CDs nicked (.) //from Yoko*
	P: //so they* tell me (.) and I put (1.0) in your pigeonhole (.)	S: right
	P: [you know] (.) a little parcel like that	S: that's what Magda said //she saw it yeah*
(14′)	P: Greeting	S: Greeting + account + statement of problem
	P: Confirmation + account	S: Confirmation
	P: Account	S: Confirmation

Notice that this transcription begins to be overtly interpretative, not only in the (questionable) labels I attach to each contribution but in even in the way I allocate the left-hand column to one speaker and the right-hand to another. All transcription is to a degree interpretative, as the *Checking Understanding* exercise you've just worked on shows. However, we usually favour as neutral a way of setting out the data as possible so as to distinguish data collection and display on the one hand and analysis on the other.

5 One interpretative method occasionally used is based on Chafe's distinction between *fragmentary*, *substantive* and *regulatory* intonational units, unit types which Chafe believes indicate consciousness and meaning processing (1994: 63). Using underlining to mark fragments, regular script to mark substantive units and italics to mark regulatory units, and with each unit marked off by slashes, the student's opening turn in her exchange with the porter might look like this:

(15) STUDENT: / hiya / *(1.5) em* / I was round yesterday / I've had some CDs nicked / <u>(.) from Yoko</u> /

Because regulatory units have either a metapragmatic or a metasequential function, this form of transcription enables us to distinguish ways of directing the understanding of interaction from the conceptual content it contains.

Whichever method you choose for transcribing your data and however you adapt it to your own needs, you'll quickly discover how time-consuming making a good transcription is. Unfortunately, we're still many years away from having a computer programme with voice recognition capable of turning multi-speaker natural talk into a transcription for us, so meanwhile we have to rely on careful and repeated listening. A further time-consuming problem is adjusting surrounding lines when you hear something new in the data and need to make a change to what you'd previously transcribed. If you compare the early and final transcriptions in (7)–(10), you can see the problem.

It should be repeated that making a good transcription is very time-consuming indeed and that you can only find out by trial and error which kind of notation represents your data most accurately. Expect to listen to your recorder many times – you'll be surprised to find that even with high quality recorders there are tiny things that you misheard or had never noticed before. This is especially noticeable if you switch between different equipment (so this can be a good strategy too). And, just for security, always keep a back-up copy of your data and never use this when you're transcribing.

12.4 Investigable topics

Even before thinking about topics, you may want to think about the extent to which you want to be a rationalist or an empiricist. Do you want to work with naturally occurring data, or to elicit data? Do you want to collect or make use of an existing corpus? Or do you prefer the introspective approach in which invented examples are used to illustrate arguments? Will your data be contextualized or idealized or of both kinds? Will you adopt a discourse analytic approach in which you set out to find instances of pre-determined phenomena in your data or will you work in the CA tradition without *a priori* assumptions as to what you may find?

I suppose it may also seem rather odd to start discussing possible topics for project work after discussing technical issues as we've done in this chapter. But now that you've considered the nature of pragmatic investigation and the problems associated with data collection and transcription, you may have a better idea of what topic areas are practical.

This section shouldn't be taken as prescriptive or constraining. Indeed, there are many other areas that can be investigated besides the few suggested below and many ways of representing and analysing data other than the few outlined above. What follows is a short list of investigable areas – you'll notice that the first of these falls within the empirical framework and the second within the rationalistic:

1. Interactive pragmatics and conversational strategies: how does turn-taking work – in general terms and in a particular conversation? According to what principles and by what means does the speaker select the next speaker? Who self-selects at TRPs and with what effects? How does a potential speaker show their intention to be the next speaker? What sort of interventions occur: requests for clarification, confirmations of understanding, *aizuchi*, and both self- and other-initiated and self- and other-completed repair? What are the mechanics of interruption? Is interruption projected? If so, how far ahead is the intention to interrupt signalled? Are there interruption markers? What determines whether the existing speaker or the interrupter secures the floor? And relatedly, how does topic shift occur – is it natural or contrived? Is it preceded by a formulation of the gist of what had gone before? Is an agenda adverted to? Is 'topic' a viable unit of analysis? Do discussions of topic have internal structure? The units of conversation – insertion sequences, adjacency pairs, presequences. How are contributions cued and how does any contribution project beyond its moment of utterance?

2. Analysis within a rationalistic or means–ends framework of activity types, speech events and the institutional use of language. This is Levinson's definition of activity type: "[a] culturally recognized activity, whether or not that activity is co-extensive with a period of speech or indeed whether any talk takes place in it at all" which is "goal defined, socially constituted, bounded . . . with constraints on the participants, setting and so on, but above all on the kinds of allowable contributions. Paradigm examples would be teaching, a job interview, a jural interrogation, a football game, a task in a workshop, a dinner party and so on" (1979: 368). So, the structure and pragmatic properties of seminars, interviews, etc. Also talk types: the structure of telephone conversations, ordering sequences in restaurants, contributions to radio phone-ins, etc. To what extent are these speech events goal-oriented and to what extent do they determine their own structures? How are expectations signalled and how are prototypes, or best examples, implied and referred to? How is talk constrained and how do participants indicate constraints on allowable contributions? Determining the functional role assumed by a speaker and assigned to other speakers.
3. Focusing on power, distance and "relation indicating devices" (Matsumoto, 1988). How speakers encode social relativity; how speakers get their own way. Facework – how speakers use politeness strategies to acknowledge the face wants of others.
4. Audience design – how speakers signal that they take their audiences into account and how an audience is constructed by the speaker.
5. Reported speech – to what extent does a speaker relay what is said in a way that preserves the direct speech origo? How are speech act descriptions used? How does reporting the same utterance/conversation vary depending on speaker and addressee? Is there a pattern to what is reported and what is glossed? How does the context of reporting compromise the deictic origo of the direct speech context? By way of an example, notice how the Thursday context of the following exchange is accommodated in the reporting of a Wednesday telephone conversation:

(16) BRANKA: Did he definitely say tomorrow
PETER: Yes, he said he'd probably come on Friday morning

6. Co-authorship – how conversations and speech encounters are co-authored by participants; signals of agreement and mutual recognition of ends; anticipation; successful negotiation.
7. The acquisition of pragmatics: what is to be acquired and how it gets acquired – studies of infants and their recognition and production of pragmatic effects; how infants infer and invite inference; the role of pragmatics in enabling first language acquisition.
8. Cross-cultural pragmatics – pragmalinguistic knowledge and socio-pragmatic skills in a second culture; social structure and honorific encoding; distal contexts generally; achieving native-like pragmatic effects.
9. Intercultural pragmatics: how non-native members monitor understanding and negotiate meaning in a low-context, lingua franca situation; how socio-pragmatic differences are accommodated in intercultural communication.
10. Adding to sequential description: can you add a term of your own to the growing list of terms such as 'account', 'formulation', 'cue', 'repair', etc. which have been borrowed from everyday use and applied to conversational phenomena as descriptions of members' methods? Show how your term is motivated and how it accounts for a typical and repeated sequential phenomena.

11. Adding to pragmatic description: can you add a term of your own to the growing list of terms such as 'instruct', 'meetings talk', etc., which have been used to describe recognizable talk types?
12. Context: does the external social structure determine the way talk is organized and the type of contributions that occur? When is the context created by the talk itself?
13. Social context: are pragmatic variables and social structure associated? Can you repeat the Labovian 'fourth floor' experiment at the pragmatic level? What do different responses to a pragmatic stimulus tell us about social variables?
14. Ethnomethodological accounts of language use: showing how language use is expectable, regular and recognizable by members of a community. Providing an ethnographic account of the way that talk and life are entwined. Showing how membership and cultural affiliation are oriented to and have both including and excluding functions.
15. Metapragmatic and metasequential phenomena: how these are used by particular speakers and for what reasons.
16. The explanatory nature of pragmatics – show how some pragmatic feature such as a maxim hedge or an indirect speech act can account for systematic language behaviour.
17. Folk views of talk – investigating the extent to which people's beliefs about pragmatic uses of language (politeness, interruption, etc.) are oriented to in talk and reflect the phenomena that are actually observed. The degree of match between metapragmatic folk terms and pragmatic metalanguage.
18. When talk goes wrong – what is unexpectable but occurring and what might we hypothesize would never occur? Recognizing the regulative aspects of talk. Coping with pragmatic misunderstandings. How lasting are the effects of misunderstandings in talk-in-interaction and how are they repaired?
19. The pragmatic properties of written language.
20. Relating thought and language. How does what people say relate to what they appear to know? For example, I recently overheard the following fragment of conversation:

(17) STUDENT A: There's a girl on my course
STUDENT B: And is she pissing you off
STUDENT A: No no

In his second utterance, A denies the proposition that the girl is 'pissing him off'. Somewhere in his cognitive processing he's presumably thinking that B guessed wrong. Can you hypothesize the cognitive constructions that accompany talk exchanges?

12.5 Learning by doing

In this final part of the chapter I'll make some comments about ways of learning pragmatics by doing data-driven pragmatic analysis.

In order to do this kind of empirical pragmatics, it certainly helps to have a grasp of the kind of terminology associated with rationalistic pragmatics – in fact, it makes good sense to study rationalistic pragmatics of the kind presented in the earlier chapters in this book in your first year studying pragmatics and then to move on to empirical pragmatics later.

In the days when there was a Linguistics department at Durham, the students there used to 'do' empirical pragmatics in their second year. Their work consisted of recording naturally occurring data such as conversation, meetings talk, institutional talk, media talk, an instruct sequence, classroom talk, an interview – in fact, whatever interested them. They selected two minutes of this recording and described both the distal context and the immediate talk context in which it occurred. I listened to their tapes, and if I thought the data were transcribable and analysable, they'd move to the next stage of actually transcribing it. Inevitably, the transcription went through several drafts, a process which often helped them to work out the approach they were going to take in the analysis phase. Often they'd bring their data to class to try out suggestions on their classmates and to get feedback. When their approach was decided, they'd write about the analytic parameters they intended to use. Often they were fortunate enough to uncover a key which helped them to understand their data. Let me give a few examples.

One year, a student had recorded a visit to her flat by first year students looking to take it over the following year. As she worked on the data, she found several orientations by her flatmate to her status as a final year student. This was confirmed by the first year students, who were also orienting to this status. And then she got the idea – what she had in front of her was 'seniors talk'. She'd added a new semi-technical term to the inventory that includes 'instruct', 'meetings talk', etc.

Another student obtained fascinating data at the hairdresser. The first phase in the conversation was a negotiation which established the right of the hairdresser to alter the appearance of the customer. Thereafter the talk was sporadic, with long pauses between topics and sub-topics. What determined when talk would recommence and when lapse? And what sort of topics could be raised and how did they relate to the previous talk? How did the two parties in this service encounter reconcile differences in age, experience of life, family status, social class, occupation, etc.? How were misunderstandings resolved (such as the student's thinking that the hairdresser was happy because she wasn't busy)?

A third student recorded a mother/small child exchange in which the child was complaining vigorously about having to go home earlier than expected when out on a visit. Amid the shouting and the tears, two things became clear – the mother was constantly presupposing that they were going to leave and the child was constantly striving for different ways of making what had been implicatures in the early part of the exchange more and more explicit. So you could see a constancy in the mother's contribution and a progressive development in the child's contribution as she became more and more enraged. Put like this, it seems simple, but it takes a lot of hard study and careful analysis to uncover such patterns from complex data.

So let's take a case and study it.

Imagine you'd collected the data involving the porter and the student whose opening we studied in Chapter 10. The question then is: How can you find a key to unravel what's going on in it?

The first thing to realize about this method of collecting data, is that you don't know what you're going to get until you've actually got it and are faced with task of accounting for the talk that occurs. In the case of the porter/student data, two things we noticed in our preliminary study in Chapter 10 were the use of accounts and the participants' interest in determining who or what is to blame for the event that occurred. So perhaps we'll be able to analyse these in more detail. Let's look more carefully at the first two minutes of this six-and-a-half-minute conversation:

Participants:
Present throughout: P = Head Porter; S = Female student
Present from line 70: P1 = Postman

(18) P: hello young lady=
S: =hiya (1.5) em I was round yesterday I've had some CDs
nicked (.) [from Yoko]
P: [so they] tell me (.) and I put (1.0) in your
pigeonhole (.)
S: right
P: [you know] (.) a little parcel like that
S: that's what Magda said [she saw it yeah]
P: [and it was a little] bit torn mind
(.) but I put it [in] (.) and when Robin phoned me last
S: [well]
P: night (.) I said I remember (.) I can't remember which name
it was but I knew it was in the first pigeonhole
[A B] C or D
S: [yeah]
S: yeah that's what me and Magda had looked in [to see our
P: [that's right
S: mail]
P: and] it was there (. .) so after this (.) I mean it's (. .)
it's Durham students going in the bloody place (1.0) I
caught two yesterday (. .)
S: doing [what] (1.0) doing what=
P: [afternoon]
P: =just walking about (. .) [they] don't live there (1.0)
definitely English students (2.0)
S: wh wha what hh
P: in Yoko Hall (1.5)
S: all right hh
P: and I chased them out (1.0)
S: what were they doing there just
P: well they're just wandering about cos (. .) what the Durham
students have given (.) load (.) give the number (.) the
code number to anybody (. .) loads and loads of Durham
students
S: well I'm sure I've come in before and there's been a note
on the door you know so-and-so I'm in room whatever (.) the
code number is
P: that's right (.) and for that we have no control whatsoever
(.) so after this (1.8) what I intend to do (.) is any
parcel or anything (.) we leave in here
S: right
P: and we put a note in the pigeonholes
S: thanks [erm]
P: [that's] all we can do Joanna
S: I know
P: but I definitely put it in yesterday morning darlin I
remember it
S: so hh I mean I don't know what to do now to [be honest] cos
I've phoned (.) em (.) the company
P: that's right
S: and all I can get is this (.) bloody (.) answerphone if you
want if you want to make your payment press one if you want
to check [your balance press two] <hh> so that's all I
P: [that's right that's right]
S: can get from there

P: because Robin told me he says oh the other girls (.) some
of the other girls from (.) they saw it in the pigeonhole
(1.0) I says I put it in
S: yeah
P: and it was a little bit (.) it was was brown paper pet (. .)
and it was a little bit torn
S: yeah
P: (1.5) and I left it in the pigeonhole (.) cos if it's
recorded delivery or anything you see [we] we leave them
S: [yeah]
P: in here (. .) and we put a note on the pigeonhole (. .)
[on the door]
S: [okay I don't quite] think you know where I stand do you
(.) cos I mean (.) if they're going to sting me for (1.0)
<P1 enters>
P1: evening Reg

12.5.1 Doing accounting – first thoughts

Once we notice the importance of accounts in our data, a sensible course of action is to think through in a preliminary way what an account is for. Then, once we've an idea of the field we're interested in, we can turn to the literature. So what is an account for and how do accounts contribute to talk? Let me have a go at summarizing in a slightly more academic way what you may have sussed out about accounts and their contribution to talk based on what you read earlier in this book.

The purpose of negotiated talk is to arrive at a set of mutually agreed propositions which are an accepted outcome for all parties. It's in this sense that talk is consequential. Each turn in talk is, therefore, expected to be procedurally consequential, i.e. to forward the purpose of the negotiation. When a first pair-part such as a question can't be satisfactorily answered, an account is frequently provided as a next-best second pair-part. Accounts are dispreferred to the extent that it's their veracity rather than their explicit procedural consequentiality that's at stake, but are remedial to the extent that they prevent a breakdown in communication. Thus, accounts privilege veracity over procedural consequentiality.

Perhaps at this stage and before we turn to the literature, it's worth going back to the data to see just how accounts do privilege veracity over procedural consequentiality. When we return to our data, we straightaway see that the porter makes the proposition that he placed the parcel in the pigeonhole into a validity claim (i.e. he orients to its veracity) in a variety of sequential environments:

- by providing contextual detail: 'I left it in the pigeonhole' (l.63);
- in contrast to the previous part of the account: 'but I put it in' (l.10)
- when reflexively indicating a shift in members' method to accounting: 'but I definitely put it in yesterday morning' (l.46)
- within reported speech: 'but I knew it was in the first pigeonhole' (l.13); 'they saw it in the pigeonhole (1.0) I says I put it in' (l.57)
- when confirming an earlier account: 'and it was there' (l.19).

12.5.2 Doing accounting – reading the literature

You'll probably want to read as much as you can find in order to develop your understanding of the theoretical background. Often it's good to start with an early classic, follow up with a much cited work and then see whether there's anything new that provides an additional perspective. If you'd read Scott and Lyman's (1968) paper as your early work and Firth's (1995) paper as your much cited one, you'd have discovered that accounts are variously seen as:

- "statement[s] made by a social actor to explain unanticipated or untoward behavior" (Scott and Lyman, 1968: 46);
- remedial – they repair or prevent norm violations (Firth, 1995: 200);
- ways of responding to reproaches. For example, in our data, the porter takes the student's assertion that she doesn't know what to do (l.48) and her following account (l.48–55) as an indication that her wants aren't satisfied by his account, i.e. as a reproach. He therefore recommences his own account with 'because' (l.56), overtly signalling his obligation to account. And he embeds within this account (l.56ff) the account of his colleague which confirms the accuracy of his own original account.
- selective, i.e. they may be used to represent events in a way favoured by the speaker. For example, in our data, the porter goes on record as representing events from his own perspective: 'that's all we can do Joanna' (l.44). Although this validity claim is theoretically challengeable, given the unequal distribution of power, the challenge isn't easy to make.
- negotiable/co-constructed, so that an account may be modified through questioning, prompting, etc. "In that the account cannot 'tell the whole story', its detail, veracity and implied prudence will often be 'probed' by the account's recipient" (Firth, 1995: 212). For example, in our data, as we saw in Chapter 10, in the opening of the conversation (l.2–8), the porter acknowledges the student's account before commencing his own, which she acknowledges and then confirms as consistent with her own knowledge of events. In the co-construction that follows, the student's use of the past perfect, 'that's what me and Magda had looked in' (l.16), refers to a time before Robin's telephone call, thus co-constructing an agreed sequence of events.
- acknowledging that there's something to be accounted for by the speaker. Thus the porter reflexively orients to his need to account with 'because' (l.56) and 'cos' (l.63).

As you can see, we've already gone a long way down the road of explaining our data. However, in considering accounts as speaker-favoured representations, we noticed the difficulty the student has in challenging the validity claims made by the porter. And since the veracity of both accounts and outcomes needs to agreed by all parties, the question then is whether both parties in this speech event are equally well placed to agree or determine the 'truth' of the propositions. This suggests that it would be useful to read in this area too. If your search had led you to Harris's (1995) paper on 'Pragmatics and power', you'd have discovered that:

- " 'Truth' comes to be defined pragmatically as what is accepted explicitly as 'shared knowledge' " (Harris, 1995: 117). In our data, for example, the porter uses 'I' in the accounts that describe his own actions. His affiliation to institutional membership encoded by 'we' occurs in virtually all non-accounting talk (l.38, l.40, l.44, l.64).
- "Conflicting goals in the institutional contexts selected are power-laden and related to knowledge claims that must be negotiated linguistically" (ibid.: 120), as we saw above.
- It's "difficult for the less powerful participant to raise validity claims relating to the 'truth' of the utterances of the more powerful participant" (ibid.: 129).

This further reading suggests that we've found a key which will help us to unlock our data.

Summary

The investigative method sketched out above involves the collection of data whose analysis we expect will make a small contribution to knowledge. Preliminary analysis suggests a productive area for further study – in this case, the use of accounts. This is followed by background reading which reveals further productive lines of analysis, in this case the relationship of the representation of events to the power status of the participants in the talk exchange. An obvious next step would be to study the way the situation is resolved in the continuing conversation. This further study would be likely to raise our awareness of how particular outcomes arise, and, by implication, how such outcomes might be worked towards or avoided in future contexts.

12.5.3 Doing causal explanation – first thoughts

Why did the package go missing? Who, if anyone, is to blame? And what are the consequences for the porter and the student? The porter clearly has an interest in attributing the disappearance of the package to some cause other than his own actions and he clearly has his own ideas as to how to do this. These factors are immediately apparent from the data.

At this point, a wise researcher would stop and realize that further analysis along these lines couldn't proceed without knowing more about the attribution of blame. We wouldn't expect linguistics to provide such knowledge, but it seems reasonable to suppose that psychologists, anthropologists and sociologists would all be interested in the attribution of blame. The best strategy in such situations is often to talk to experts or to fellow students in these fields and ask for their advice on basic reading.

12.5.4 Doing causal explanation – reading the literature

If a helpful social psychologist had recommended Hewstone and Fincham's (2007) comprehensive textbook chapter on attribution theory and if you had found Hilton's (1991) paper on conversation and causal explanation, you'd have discovered that causal explanations rely on counterfactuality: if the event which did occur can be compared to a contrasting case in which the event wouldn't have occurred, then a cause is identified. Potential causes include:

- the person – in this case, the porter's actions;
- the stimulus – in this case, the parcel;
- the circumstance – in this case, the disappearance of the parcel.

There are tests which enable us to determine how each of these factors may have contributed to the event under investigation:

- To determine whether the porter's action contributed to the event, we test for **consensus**:
  High consensus = The porter's actions are the same as those of other porters.
  Low consensus = The porter's actions are different from those of other porters.
- To determine whether the parcel contributed to the event, we test for **distinctiveness**:
  High distinctiveness = The parcel is distinct.
  Low distinctiveness = The parcel is not distinct.
- To determine whether the disappearance of the parcel contributed to the event, we test for **consistency**:

High consistency = Parcels regularly go missing.
Low consistency = Parcels rarely go missing.

It's therefore in the porter's interest to establish *high consensus* (*low consensus* = his actions could be at fault), *high distinctiveness* (something about the parcel attracts the thief) and either *high consistency* (the situation is common and thus by implication uncontrollable) or *low consistency* (this is a new situation and thus couldn't have been foreseen).

Dispositional attributions. The literature shows that *high consensus* + *high distinctiveness* + *high consistency* configurations are associated with dispositional attributions. This means that the event is likely to occur anyway because the porter's actions are like anyone else's in his position, the parcel attracts attention and parcels regularly go missing. Dispositional attributions work on the principle of agreement – the situation is like others in which the event is likely to occur.
∴ The porter may be expected to orient to the characteristic nature of the event – as indeed he does.

Causal explanation. A *high consensus* + *high distinctiveness* + *low consistency* configuration makes the package the causal explanation since the porter's actions are like anyone else's in his position, the parcel attracts attention and parcels rarely go missing. Causal explanations work on the principle of difference between this and other events.
∴ The porter may be expected to orient to the exceptional nature of the event (as indeed he does), the particular characteristics of the parcel (as indeed he does), and to counterfactual cases where the event would not have occurred (as indeed he does).

The characteristic nature of the event: One point at which the porter orients to the characteristic nature of the event occurs just over two-thirds of the way through the conversation when he says:

(19) P: an' you see in Yoko (.) I've said it over and over again
you've got two keys (l.166–7)

This is followed by an explanation of the significance of the keys and then an account reflexively signalled by 'but what happens' (l.175). This is followed by a formulation ('so our hands is tied') (l.178) and a judgement ('but they're punishing their own (2.5) their own students') (l.180):

(20) P: an' you see in Yoko (.) I've said it over and over again
you've got two keys (.) one for the main door and one for
their own door
S: yeah
P: that main door's supposed to be locked all the time (.)
that stops anybody else getting in (2.0) Yoko
S: yeah
P: who hasn't got a key
S: yeah
P: but what happens (.) we go up and telling them lock it and
lock it all night at half past ten [what have you] we go
over at quarter to eleven (.) an' it's wide open again
(1.5) so (.) our hands is tied
S: (0.5) okay
P: but they're punishing their own (2.5) their own students

The exceptional nature of the event: The porter's orientation to the exceptional nature of the event is shown by his repeated formulations of future intentions involving a new strategy: 'so after this' (l.19); 'so after this (1.8) what I intend to do (.) is any parcel or anything (.) we leave in here' (l.39). This is because the need for a new strategy implicitly orients to the exceptional nature of what has occurred.

The distinctiveness of the parcel: The porter's orientation to the distinctiveness of the parcel is reflexively signalled by 'and it was a little bit torn mind' (l.9). Its distinctiveness is again oriented to at l.60: 'and it was a little bit (.) and it was brown paper pet (. .) and it was a little bit torn'.

Counterfactual cases: The porter invokes a counterfactual case where the event would not have occurred (l.63–7). He also suggests that events like this would not occur if the proper procedures had been adhered to (l.170–3).

Summary

In this second investigation of our data, our preliminary analysis suggests a productive area for further study – in this case, causal explanation. This is followed by background reading in a related discipline which enables us to explain significant portions of our data. An obvious next step would be to study the way the situation is resolved in the continuing conversation and in particular whether any causal explanation or dispositional attribution the interactants agree on reflects their relative power status and whether the outcome is favourable to one or the other party.

One more thing: our background reading in this case reveals the true value of our data. Not surprisingly, it turns out that the literature on causal explanation represents abstract cases rather than actual real-world instances. Although convincing, it isn't supported by empirical data of the detailed kind that we have been investigating. In other words, we've been *doing* causal explanation with a real instance in front of us. You'll very often find in your own project work that you're able to show with a real case that a theoretical construct is either sustainable or, sometimes, that it needs to be modified.

12.5.5 Conclusion

I hope the relatively detailed work that we've been doing in the final part of this chapter will inspire you to work on your own pragmatics project, either within a regular pragmatics class or as an individual project within your overall degree programme. Although it's slightly unnerving to collect data while still unsure of just what you're going to be able to do with it, you can be certain that all naturally occurred talk is pragmatically rich and offers opportunities for detailed analysis and explanation. Take heart from a student whose final year project I supervised in Hong Kong. She was extremely worried about collecting data first and only later deciding what to do with it. However, she plucked up courage and went to the airport where she had a useful airline contact who made it possible for her to record transactions at a check-in desk. One of the first passengers she recorded was travelling from Shanghai to Sydney *via* Hong Kong. But instead of getting his Hong Kong–Sydney boarding pass at the air-side transit desk, he'd made a mistake and passed through immigration to the land-side. At the land-side check-in desk, he was asked to pay the departure tax that at that time was levied in Hong Kong. He was not happy.

The student's analysis of the resulting data earned her an A grade.

Afterword

> **Life is short, and Art is long; the occasion fleeting, experience deceitful, and judgement difficult.**
> *(The first aphorism of Hippocrates, the physician of Cos)*

Thank you for buying this book, and thank you especially for reading to the very end of it. Now that you've reached the end, I have to share with you the sad news that Eleanor, whose portrait appears on the front cover and whose utterances you've overheard at various places in the book, was killed in a car crash in 2005. After a lot of thought, I decided that it would be wrong entirely to remove her voice from this new edition. Since this is a book about the real things that real people say, it would also be wrong to let you suppose that she continues to 'do pragmatics'.

Eleanor's portrait was painted posthumously from photographs by the gifted artist and winner of the 2004 BP Portrait Award, Stephen Shankland, about whom you can find out more at www.stephenshankland.com. Art, and painting in particular, are important to us because they openly declare that they are representations of reality. This portrait is especially clever in that it also includes a photograph, or perhaps painting. This representation of a representation acts like a metapragmatic cue, encouraging us to look for meaning in a particularly directive way. In fact, the portrait is full of implied meanings – if you want a few ideas, email me at grundypeter@btinternet.com and I'll send you some suggestions. Alternatively, you can try some of the categories discussed in the opening chapter: What meanings do the butterfly, the Bonsai, the leafless sapling, the riderless horse, the partially raised blind, the shadows communicate indirectly? What contexts do they prompt you to recover? In what ways are they appropriate? What has to be accommodated to understand their relevance?

The painting is also appropriate to a pragmatics book in a more literal way: Eleanor communicates a non-verbal, pragmatic meaning to someone on her left outside the frame of the photograph in which she appears on a horse. In the main portrait, she wears an enigmatic expression as she tries to puzzle out what is meant by what is said in the message she reads.

Returning to the notion of representation and art, painting reminds us that everything is a representation. We think we know what *learning* and *teaching* and *language*, or for that matter *brother* and *sister* and *parent* are, but in fact all we have are our own representations of *learning, language, parent*, etc., representations that may be very different from someone else's, whether from our own or a different culture. So although the representation of pragmatics in *Doing Pragmatics* is, like Stephen Shankland's portrait of Eleanor, the very best I can do, it's only a representation, painted, as it were, from photographs.

More personally, you might be interested to know that Eleanor cared about horses above all else. When we registered her second pony with the British Show Jumping Association, we agreed that she'd have first choice of a show-name and, should a horse already be registered with that name, I'd have second and third choices. The names we submitted to the BSJA were, in order of preference, Irish Instinct (the pony came from Ireland), Conversational Implicature and Relevance Theory. I'm sorry to say that no other horse was registered as Irish Instinct. True to his name, he very often aimed straight for the bar.

Finally, to end with an imperative whose most salient meaning is to be recovered at the level of what is said, if you drive a car, take real care. And if, like Eleanor, you're a passenger in a car, remind your driver to take real care.

Checking understanding: solutions and suggested answers

1 Using and understanding language

(1.1)

(3) PHARMACIST: Do you usually have this sort
PETER: Yeh I think so
PHARMACIST: They make you drowsy mind
PETER: Oh are there others that don't

Do you usually have this sort
The pharmacist presupposes that I've had cold capsules before. Given the speaker, I'm much more likely to understand, her utterance as a professional rather than a social inquiry.

Yeh I think so
My informal 'Yeh' shows that I'm being friendly. I know that I usually have the sort I've asked for (and so, probably, does the pharmacist), but I hedge my reply with 'I think' because it's more friendly to appear slightly uncertain. My use of 'so' is anaphoric and refers back to 'have this sort' – she and I are beginning to co-construct our conversation.

They make you drowsy mind
I take the pharmacist's 'you' to refer not to me in particular but to people in general (unlike the 'you' in her first utterance). Her use of 'mind' signals that she is warning me of something. Her utterance also makes sense of what she had said before: if she had just given me this warning straight away, it might have sounded rather abrupt.

Oh are there others that don't
My use of 'Oh' shows that I'm a bit surprised by what she has just said. My question shows that I think she is trying to find an indirect way of recommending a different kind of capsule, and so I invite her to give me the information that I assume she has.

(4) STALLHOLDER: Do you want two boxes of grapes for 80p
PETER: No I don't think so. There aren't any black ones at the moment, are there
STALLHOLDER: No they're just green ones
PETER: No my wife's very saucy
STALLHOLDER: <laughs>
PETER: No I didn't mean that – you know what I mean
STALLHOLDER: It's just the way you said it

Do you want two boxes of grapes for 80p
The stallholder begins by making an offer.

No I don't think so. There aren't any black ones at the moment, are there
The preferred response to an offer is acceptance, so I take care when I decline, hedging my 'no' with an expression of uncertainty, 'I don't think so', with the pro-form 'so' helping to co-construct the conversation as in (3) above. My statement and addressee-including tag imply that had the grapes been black, I would have accepted the offer.

No they're just green ones
The stallholder confirms what I suspect with 'no' and adds the redundant confirmation that 'they're just green ones'.

No my wife's very saucy
I feel obliged to provide an explicit reason for not wanting the green grapes. My initial use of 'no' doesn't negate a proposition but indicates that what I'm about to say may be slightly unexpected.

<laughs>
Laughter often occurs in response to something incongruous. The stallholder's laughter seems to indicate that she takes 'saucy' to mean flirtatious rather than fussy about food.

No I didn't mean that – you know what I mean
I correct the stallholder's misunderstanding (this use of 'no' contradicts the proposition that my wife is flirtatious) and choose a form of words ('what I mean') which presupposes that I mean something and asserts that the stallholder knows what it is.

It's just the way you said it
The stallholder continues our discussion of how the wrong meaning was conveyed, minimizing the fault attributable to me with her use of 'just'. Could it be that what caused her to think I was suggesting my wife was flirtatious was my use of 'no'?

(1.2)

(68) Even Presidents have private lives

Appropriateness – Clinton obviously thought this was the most appropriate way to deal with the revelation that he had had a relationship with a White House intern.

- Indirectness – This seems to be an indirect way of saying that it was no one else's business.
- Inference – I infer that Clinton is implying that he has a right to do things like this if he wishes.
- Indeterminacy – 'have' = are entitled to.
- Context – The meaning we infer depends on Clinton saying it rather than you or me saying it.
- Relevance – In order to understand this utterance, I need to consider what would make it relevant – for example, he is talking about himself rather than some other president.
- Accommodation – In order for this to be an appropriate utterance and in order to recover the intended meaning, Clinton's audience need to know about his affair with Monica Lewinsky.
- Reflexivity – Clinton's use of 'even' tells me that what he says may be contrary to the general view and therefore surprising.

(69) I don't know how you say this in English but for me it was ooh-la-la-la

- Appropriateness – Peslier obviously thought this was the most appropriate way of expressing his delight.
- Indirectness – Peslier does not say directly what he feels.
- Inference – I infer from the third 'la' that Peslier is very happy indeed.
- Indeterminacy – It's hard to imagine anything more indeterminate than a meaningless segment 'la' which is added to the more conventional but still strictly meaningless vocalization 'ooh-la-la'.

- Context – It would clearly need to be a context as exceptional as winning a major race for the speaker to add the third 'la'.
- Relevance – The most relevant way to take this utterance is not as a request for language tuition (as it might be in the context of a second language classroom) but as an expression of delight.
- Accommodation – There are many assumptions required for this to be an appropriate utterance: the speaker must be a speaker of English as a second language and the addressee/s must be native speakers aware of the context referred to by 'it'.
- Reflexivity – Peslier begins by commenting on his inability to convey the meaning he feels. His use of 'but' then contrasts this comment with his attempt to express what he feels, which he does in a mixture of English and pastiche French.

(70) Shane Warne can't bowl from both ends (Radio commentator at an England vs Australia Test Match)

- Appropriateness – The commentator feels that it's appropriate to comment on as well as to describe the game that's in progress.
- Indeterminacy – There are two credible candidate interpretations for 'can't bowl': (a) the rules of the game do not permit Warne to bowl from both ends, and (b) Warne can only bowl successfully from one end.
- Indirectness – Candidate interpretation (a) seems to be an indirect way of saying that Australia's only hope of winning would be for Warne (to be allowed) to bowl from both ends; candidate interpretation (b) seems to be an indirect way of criticizing Warne's bowling performance.
- Context, inference, relevance – Since this comment was made on one of those rare occasions when England were in the ascendancy, (a) seems to be the most relevant inference. Or perhaps by saying that Warne can't bowl from both ends, the commentator implies that England are in the ascendancy.
- Accommodation – To understand this utterance fully, the overhearing audience needs to know some of the rules of cricket, to understand what is mean by 'bowl' and 'both ends', and to know why Shane Warne would be an appropriate subject of the assertion.
- Reflexivity – Although the utterance does not appear to have overt reflexivity, one might ask whether the use of 'Shane Warne' rather than 'Warne' indicates some sort of speaker involvement in the utterance.

2 Deixis – the relation of reference to the point of origin of the utterance

(2.1)

1a) Which finger did he bite?/*This* little finger on the right; Are you ready? Wait for it! Wait for it! *NOW*!; *Behind* you.

1b) I bet you weren't expecting *this*; I'm off *now*; I always hide *behind* a tree (i.e. behind in relation to the seeker).

1c) And *this* strange guy walks in and vomits; *Now* that wasn't a very nice example; I hide my money *behind* the bookcase (the back of the bookcase does not require any context to be fully determined because bookcases have backs and fronts, so the use is intrinsic).

3) 'You just have to read this chapter' appears to address the hearer directly. But the use of 'just' and our real world knowledge that reading chapters takes time might tempt you to take 'you' non-deictically. This would certainly be a preferred reading

if your friend was addressing several people. Although even in this case it's clear that an empathetic utterance such as this wouldn't be used when talking to just anyone. It's as though 'you' are taken to belong to a particular group, perhaps people who might be expected to appreciate chapters of the kind the speaker is reading. This in turn suggests that the notion that demonstratives like *you* can be used entirely non-deictically may be problematic. Compare utterances like 'You (just) have to come/go with me'. By comparison, 'this chapter' is deictic and might or might not be gestural, perhaps depending on whether your friend offers you the book or not.
4) How about *According to the map, the last mile of this walk is the most difficult*? Or an analytical sentence like *The last mile is always the most difficult*?

(2.2)
1) How about *We're not all daft you know* or *Our understanding of history will always stand us in good stead*?

2) If Salman Rushdie is using 'we' and 'us' exclusively, he means that only he should be tolerant. But if he is using the pronouns inclusively, he means that those who have declared the *fatwa* and who are addressed by Rushdie's statement should also show tolerance. The exclusive reading is apologetic and the inclusive reading is more accusatory. If the use is non-deictic, then he is treading a middle course between apology and accusation – but it's difficult to see why he should have used *we* and *us* at all if he intended this meaning. Perhaps the writer intends it to be difficult to determine the status of the pronouns here.

(2.3)
1) I would normally say (23), but I would say (23′) if I was talking to someone who lived in the same house as John or who was very close to him. If I was asking John for an invitation, I would always use *come*.

3) I'm indebted to Zhang Qian for posing this neat problem and to Kelly Glover for helping me to tidy up the explanation. It seems to me that 'to the left of Mark' is deictic because it will always be interpreted as to the left from the speaker's (or addressee's) perspective and it therefore identifies Sue as referent. 'On the left of Mark' could be deictic, i.e. left from speaker's or addressee's perspective, thus identifying Sue as referent, or non-deictic, i.e. left from Mark's perspective, thus identifying Dave as referent. 'On Mark's left' is typically regarded as non-deictic, i.e. identifying the referent does not depend on knowing the point of origin of the utterance. If you agree with these judgements, you need to think about why it should be the case. One explanation could be to do with English being a Head+Adjunct order language, i.e. we expect the head word (for example, the preposition in a preposition phrase) to come first. 'On the left' is the head in *on the left of Mark* so the order is expectable. But in *on Mark's left*, the head word, 'left', comes second. When this word order occurs in a predominantly Head+Adjunct language, the whole phrase will tend to be viewed as a single compound word, so that *Mark's left* becomes a new non-deictic term to describe what is on the left in relation to Mark irrespective of the speaker's perspective.

4)
(28) [–D],S and [+D],A
(28′) [–D],S and [+/–D],A; if [–D],A then [–D],anyTP
(29) [+D],S and [–D],A
(29′) [+/–D],S and [–D],A; if [–D],S then [–D],anyTP
(30) [+D],S and [+D],A,face-to-face or [–D],A,telephone; [+D],anyTP
(30′) as (30) or [–D], S and [–D],A,face-to-face or poss[+D],A,telephone; [–D],anyTP

Notice how adding 'permanently' to these utterances sets up other possible contexts.

(2.4)

1) The change from the first to the second edition is from a deictic ('Now . . .') whose origo you would probably have taken as the time of reading rather than the time of writing to a deictic ('Half-a-lifetime later . . .') whose origo is the time of an event mentioned in the discourse. Because the default assumption for written discourse is that the deictic origo is the place and time of reading, if I wanted to refer to an event that had occurred twelve months earlier, I'd be much more likely to write 'about a year before writing this' than to write 'about a year ago'. Both are deictic, but 'about a year before writing this' instructs you to identify the time indicated by treating the publication date of the book as the origo. Although in principle you could equally easily identify the time picked out by 'about a year ago', I want to save you the trouble of reasoning that the reading-time default origo isn't the time in relation to which 'about a year ago' is to be interpreted. In 2000, when the second edition of *Doing Pragmatics* was published, 'Half a lifetime later . . .' seemed preferable to 'Now . . .' because, like 'about a year before writing this', it enabled readers to pinpoint a time reference accurately relative to an origo in the discourse which was relatively easy to identify. By the time we get to the third edition in 2008, 'Half a lifetime later . . .' is no longer accurate, hence the return to 'Now . . .'.

2) I suggest

(38a) *Now* what have you found to say of our past (probably non-deictic)
(38b) What have you *now* found to say of our past (deictic, but barely grammatical in this position; what Hardy wrote)
(38c) What have you found *now* to say of our past (deictic)
(38d) What have you found to say of our past *now* (deictic and gestural)

It seems that the use of *now* is progressively more gestural when it occurs towards the end of the sentence. Where there are several possible placements for an item in a sentence, placement-to-the-right will usually attract focus.

(2.5)

1) The British announcement is the most direct in that it lexicalizes those whom the announcement is aimed at, 'Passengers for Sunderland . . .' Both the British and the MTR announcements are more direct than the KCR announcement as they give advice ('should') rather than suggest an option ('may'). It seems that 'there' co-occurs with a more indirect way of giving information or advice. We might argue that 'here' is deictic and 'there' anaphoric, with either 'the next station' or, more probably, 'Kowloon Tong' as its antecedent. This makes me think again about (47/47′) – perhaps it's less natural to get an anaphoric reading for a proximal than for a distal deictic.

2) The proximal *here* sits more easily with the less formal 'Passengers please . . .' than does the distal *there*:

(51′) The next station is Kowloon Tong. Passengers please change to MTR trains here/?there

This seems to support the claim above that 'there' co-occurs with a more indirect way of giving information or advice. The conclusion I draw from 'Passengers please' is that the KCR now wants to deal less formally with passengers. The conclusion I draw from the bizarre repetition of 'Kowloon Tong' (are there two Kowloon Tongs perhaps?) is that the KCR still doesn't refer to the MTR circuit with the expectable proximal because the city-slicker:country-boy conceptualization is alive and well.

(2.6)

(57) There are two deictics here, one, 'this point', embedded in the other, 'beyond'. Presumably the person who places the sandwich-board facing the wrong way pays more attention to 'this point' which indexes the point where platform and car park meet than to ensuring that the message is read from the car park rather than the platform side. (This might prompt us to ask whether he approaches 'this point' from the platform side when he places the notice.) There's the further issue of whether the deictic centre of written messages is the location of the message (perhaps for 'this point'?) or of the reader (perhaps for 'beyond this point'?). Notice that the direction the notice faces doesn't make the determination of 'this point' problematic.

(58) What we know about syntax tells us that the antecedent of the anaphor 'that' ought to be 'the applicant's native tongue'. What we know about the world tells us that we are being asked to evaluate the applicant's English. Would a cooperative referee be guided by the pragmatics rather than the syntax?

(59) The spoken answer 'Thursday or Friday' is implicitly deictic with the addressee inferring something like 'on Thursday or Friday of *next week*'. The reason for arguing this is that if the answer had been given on a Monday or a Tuesday, 'on Thursday or Friday of *this week*' would have been understood. As the day of the week on which the programme is to be broadcast is unknown and may not coincide with the day of the actual conversation, a Friday, the sub-titler opts for the non-deictic translation 'just a few days' which answers the 'how long' question. (Note that the point of time indexed by '*in* just a few days' is deictic.)

(60) If I was unable to confirm by looking through the window that the train had arrived at Terminal 2, my destination, I think I'd have taken 'are stopping' to index a future time and would have stayed on the train, thus missing my flight. This is why most such signs say something like 'This is Terminal 2'. You might like to consider the pragmatic conditions that help us to determine the time referred to by *be+ing* in utterances like 'I'm cooking the dinner', 'I'm staying with John', 'This train is stopping at Terminal 2', etc.

(61) Presumably we are meant to infer the deictic meaning of 'local' although the context calls for an intrinsic reading. If you live in Britain, you'll probably have noticed the coach company which claims to be 'Your local company – nationwide'.

3 Presupposition – accommodating background knowledge

(3.1)

(13) 'the' → <the ladies' room exists>; 'where's' → <the ladies' room is (to be found) somewhere>.

(14) 'what' → <they all say something>.

(15) 'your' → <your attention exists>; 'the' → <the fact . . . exists>; 'I draw your attention to the fact that' → <smoking is not allowed in this aircraft by law>; 'this' → <this aircraft exists>.

(16) 'how' → <there is a way of showing him . . .>; 'how' → <you feel in a certain way>.

(3.2)

(32) 'last time' → <the addressee had said on a previous occasion what he/she said on this occasion>.

(33) 'your' → <the addressee has a name>; 'again' → <the speaker had asked the addressee's name on a previous occasion>.
(34) 'return' → <the addressee had been to Durham on a previous occasion>.
(35) 'other' → <there has been at least one previous 'thing' mentioned by the speaker>.
(36) 'my' → <the speaker's son exists/existed>; 'second' → <the speaker had a husband before>.
(37) 'my' → <the speaker's varlet exists>; 'again' → <the speaker was unarmed before>; 'un-' → <the speaker had armed>.
(38) 'again' → <the speaker and (her) two colleagues had met before>; 'when' → <the speaker and (her) two colleagues will meet again>.
(39) 'who' → <someone keeps the gate>; 'the' → <the gate exists>.
(40) 'who' → <someone is there>.
(41) 'the' → <the king exists>; 'how' → <the king escaped our hands somehow>.
(42a) treats their having dogs as presupposed and asserts that they are expensive. ('No' denies that they are cheap.)
(42b) treats their having stock as presupposed and asserts that their stock consists of cats. ('No' denies that they have [cheap] dogs.)
(42c) treats their having dogs as presupposed and asserts that they go bow-wow. ('No' denies that they go 'cheep', the sound associated with birds.)
(42d) treats their having stock (dogs) as presupposed and asserts that the stock which goes 'cheep' are birds. ('No' denies that their dogs go 'cheap', or perhaps 'cheep'.)

4) 'the' → <the young lady who . . . exists>; 'her' → <the young lady has a shapely backside>; definite description → <President Bush exists>; 'would not have been' → <the young lady was daring>; definite description → <Mr Clinton exists>; 'had . . . still been' → <Mr Clinton is no longer President>.

(3.4)
1) These are my suggested examples – are yours as good or better?

- Temporal: I chickened out before I got married.
- Factive: The potty prince never ignores the fact that his plants like being talked to.
- Definite descriptions: The straightforward pragmatics book can never be written.
- Change-of-state: The second time I began learning Russian I found it even harder.

2) 'I'm concerned about losing my watch' seems to presuppose either P1 <the speaker might lose their watch> or P2 <the speaker has lost their watch>, i.e. a possibility or an actuality. Both survive negation. 'I'm concerned that I might lose my watch' seems to presuppose P1, but I'm not sure that it always survives negation. 'I'm concerned that I might have lost my watch' seems to presuppose possibility and probably to survive negation. *Be concerned about* seems to me to have some filter properties although it fits the factive paradigm in terms of the environments in which it may occur. In the two boys example, the epistemic modal 'might' tends to suggest a reading that what occurs in the complement clause exists at least as much in their minds as in actuality.

4 Speech acts – language as action

(4.1)
1) You will have listed lots of situations and speech acts. One of my favourites is the contrast between the use of *Sorry* to invite the speaker to repeat their utterance and

the use of *I'm sorry* with an accompanying scowl to dare the speaker to do this. Here the same proposition seems to be used for entirely opposite purposes.

2) My former student was perhaps re-establishing our acquaintance. As she went on to remind me who she was, she perhaps did not expect me to remember her. Hamlet's father's ghost was urging Hamlet to avenge his murder.

4) Hiroko misheard 'It's OK' and thought instead that I had said 'OK'. The same proposition conveyed in minimally different ways can thus be used either to accept or to reject an offer.

(4.2)

1) Giving someone flowers might count as many things, including thanking or apologizing or expressing sympathy or indicating affection or expressing the wish that the person receiving them should recover from illness.

2) *Locution*: conveying the proposition that the addressee has returned to a place they were in on a previous occasion.
Illocution: likely to be an expression of the speaker's irritation with the addressee.
Perlocution: variable, perhaps causing the addressee to go away, feel insulted, make a retort of some kind, etc.

(4.3)

Examples of explicitly performative utterances that are often cited include *I second the motion, I name this ship <Queen Victoria>, I promise <you won't regret it>, I bet you <£5 you can't eat a kilo of chocolate>, I apologize, I refuse <to accept your explanation>, I plead (not) guilty*. I have a life insurance policy which contains the sentence 'The within-named proposer . . . is hereby admitted as a member of the society'.

(4.4)

The counter clerk takes 'Do you sell postage stamps?' as an indirect speech act requesting a stamp or stamps. In fact, Mr Logic asks whether one of the felicity conditions on buying stamps obtains, from which she infers that he wishes to buy some. While she responds to the illocutionary force of his utterance, his 'logic' consists in treating it only as a locutionary act. The absurdity of this strategy is confirmed by the question mark that appears over her head when he does this a second time. Mr Logic could hardly have calculated the perlocutionary effect of treating the address term 'smart arse' as a mistaken attempt to use his name.

(4.5)

(32) *Illocution*: my wife expresses irritation with our daughter. *Perlocution*: She probably intends me to get our daughter to tidy her room. In fact, I felt reprimanded. It was as though I was partly to blame for my daughter's untidy bedroom.

(33) *Illocution*: the chair informs the addressee of something of which he appeared unaware and finds a witty way of doing this so as to spare the addressee embarrassment. *Perlocution*: The chair intends the speaker to stop and give way to the speaker on the chair's left.

(34) Eleanor's *illocution*: prepares the ground for asking a favour. *Perlocution*: Eleanor intends me to ask what she'd like me to do. Peter's *illocution*: grudgingly agrees to Eleanor asking her favour. *Perlocution*: I intend Eleanor to realize that what suits her is likely to cause me inconvenience.

(35) *Illocution*: a warning. *Perlocution*: the speaker intends me to show more respect/stop taking the mickey. In fact, the consequence was that the two people

who were with me, and who had been ready to leave, kindly waited for me to finish my drink before we all left together.

(4.6)

(45) The Postmaster treats 'Have you a biro' as a speech act in its own right. 'Yes you can borrow it' would be more appropriate for objects of value.

(46) The Caretaker meets me at the seminar room and explains that the key pad on the door is broken and that we therefore have to keep the door open until he's able to remove the pad. My response is intended as a complaint, the preferred outcome being that the Caretaker removes the pad right away. His 'ha ha ha' could be taken as an IFID! I don't suppose it ever occurred to him that one perlocutionary effect of his childish and uncooperative attitude would be naming (it's Graeme!) and shaming here.

(47) The interesting question is whether this counts as an apology. And if so, for what. Determining whether the time reference of the locutionary act is present or future seems to be important. Also determining whether the formula *I can <offer, promise, etc.>* implies that the apology/offer/promise isn't satisfactorily completed until the addressee indicates acceptance. (Notice also that *I apologize for* . . . and *I'm apologizing for* . . . are not identical illocutionary acts.)

(48) My response is triggered by what I take to be a marked way of asking whether I want white or black coffee. This seems to show that there are more and less expectable formulas for making offers of this sort, a topic taken up in the final section of the chapter. However, the waitress was surprised at the perlocutionary effect of her offer, so perhaps we affiliate to different sub-cultures.

5 Implicit meaning

(5.1)

1)

- Quantity – a helper will pass just one light-bulb rather than two to their colleague on the stepladder;
- Quality – a helper will supply a light-bulb of the appropriate quality (i.e., new rather than burnt out) and kind (bayonet-type or screw-type, as required);
- Relation – a helper will supply assistance that is relevant to the stage in the operation (e.g., will secure the stepladder when their colleague is climbing it rather than before or after);
- Manner – a helper will make the nature of their assistance clear (e.g., will make it evident that they are really securing the stepladder rather than being ambiguous or dilatory about it).

2)

(17) QUANTITY$_1$ <not a good job>

(18) QUANTITY$_1$ <possibly drinking games are the cause of declining academic standards>, <possibly drinking games aren't the cause of declining academic standards>

(19) QUANTITY$_2$ <a mixed case of wine>

(20) QUANTITY$_2$ <Oxford university>

(21) QUALITY <the interviewer doesn't know the answer to his question, wants to know it, thinks the interviewee knows the answer>

(22) RELATION <the dealers will be selling the dollar again>

(23) MANNER <the penalty is for adding graffiti> (not for not adding graffiti)

(5.2)
1)
(27) Flouts Quantity$_2$ because it's insufficiently informative.

(28) This isn't a sincere question (my wife knows that I haven't seen the room) and flouts Quality. 'that room of hers' is prolix and flouts Manner.

(29) By providing a response which isn't an answer to the question asked, Eleanor intends to direct me away from an unwelcome line of questioning. It's an attempt to flout relevance. Many pragmaticists doubt whether any utterance can ever be irrelevant as an addressee will always attempt to work out how even an apparently irrelevant utterance, such as this one, is related to what has gone before. Perhaps we should say of Eleanor's reply that the relevance is given but not obvious.

(30) This flouts manner because it plays on the ambiguity of 'fly'.

2)
(31) Quantity – tautology
(32)–(36) Quality – metaphor, overstatement, understatement, rhetorical question, irony

3)
(37) 'Current' is ambiguous. 'Ahead' is given a spatial sense by the television advertisement which shows human-like pylons striding 'ahead' across open country.

(38) 'We have the lead' is ambiguous, with one sense contradicting what is entailed by 'cordless'.

(39) The second multiplication symbol is used in a less than maximally perspicuous way to represent the lexical item 'by' in the phrase 'by far'.

(40) 'Fourmost' is an obscure blend of *four(-wheel drive)* and *(fore)most* and creates a new pair of homophones *foremost/fourmost.*

(41) 'Wafer' and the arrow is an obscure way of conveying the message <this is the way for happiness>.

(42) Since the power of computers is measured in megahertz, the homophone *hertz/hurts* is an obscure way of suggesting that this company makes buying a computer easy.

(43) The name 'Walter Wall' and 'wall-to-wall' are homophones. 'Walter Wall Carpeting' is obscure.

(44) This advertisement plays on the ambiguity (of the inappropriateness) of helping oneself to food and helplessness in the face of temptation.

(45) Two ambiguities: BA and 'Be a', and the ambiguity between connotations of 'better connected' – connected to more flights and having an impressive social network. The same obscurity occurs in the legend written on the side of Air Baltic planes: 'Air Baltic. Well connected with SAS'.

(46) 'On the spot' is an obscure way of conveying both the idiomatic meaning *immediately* and the literal meaning *on the spot or pimple.*

It seems that if we can pass the understanding test that newspaper headlines and advertisements sometimes pose, we feel good about ourselves and so are motivated to read the stories or have positive feelings towards the products advertised. Passing these understanding tests is a kind of initiation rite which makes us members of the privileged group of those who get the message.

4)
'It's the taste' flouts Quantity$_1$ (insufficient information) and Manner (obscure) and therefore triggers an inference process in which the addressee looks for the likeliest meaning that is relevant in the context that obtains. So the taste is good when something's being advertised on television and bad when referring to a school dinner.

(5.3)
2) Here are some tentative suggestions – do they coincide with your ideas?
'Well' – hedge on Quantity; 'if you asked me for a straight answer, . . . I shall say that . . . in terms of the averages of departments . . . you would . . . find that . . . there . . . wasn't very much in it one way or the other' – the proposition; 'as far as we can see' – hedges Quality; 'looking at it by and large' – ?hedge on Quality, ?intensifies Quantity; 'taking one time with another' – ?intensifies Quantity, ?has truth value; 'then' – intensifies Relation; 'in the final analysis' – intensifies Manner; 'it is . . . true to say that' – intensifies Quality; 'probably . . .' – hedges Quality; 'at the end of the day' – intensifies Relation; 'in general terms' – ?hedges Quality, ?hedges Manner; 'probably . . .' – hedges Quality; 'not to put too fine a point on it' – ?intensifies Relation, ?intensifies Manner; 'probably . . .' – hedges Quality; 'as far as one can see' – hedges Quality; 'at this stage' – hedges Quantity.

(5.4)
Because (68) appears at the beginning of the academic year and because of the pictorial representation, we infer that WH Smith sell everything necessary for study except uniforms. (69) implies that the videos sold at WH Smith are tear-jerkers for which you will need a handkerchief. We say that implicatures are non-conventional because they aren't part of the meaning of the expressions which invite them. These examples show the non-conventional nature of implicature in a particularly obvious way because the reasoning processes that enabled us to calculate the implicature in (68) won't work algorithmically for (69): i.e. you would be wrong to infer that (69) implies that WH Smith sell everything necessary for Christmas except hankies. Thus the implicatures recovered from (68) and (69) are non-conventional just because they are implicatures. Even recovering one of them fails to provide an algorithm by which the other can be recovered.

(5.5)
(70) flouts Quality and Manner. The question isn't a sincere question and the utterance is a deliberately obscure way of drawing attention to the misspelling of *necessary* by highlighting the homophone in 'seeing double'/double 'c'. The speaker might be taken to imply that the optician does not inspire confidence.

(71) flouts Manner. The speaker implies that the manufacturer of the fireworks is less than successful by suggesting the brand-name is inappropriate. The speaker is obscure in the sense that he treats the brand-name as a description. 'Sub-standard' also implies <not-standard> as a Quantity$_2$ implicature. I found myself doing the same thing after we had a new boiler fitted bearing the brand name 'Ideal', or, as I put it after one or two mishaps, 'far from ideal'.

(72) flouts the maxims of Quality and Manner. The graffiti suggest that the car is dirty by implying that it is not white. This is an obscure way of recommending that the car should be washed.

(73) flouts Manner. It might be taken to imply that the dessert menu is a kind of afterthought, or that diners are entitled to a dessert (i.e. it's what they deserve, even maybe as a kind of punishment as in *just deserts*). So both 'just' and the homophone 'desserts'/*deserts* are ambiguous.

(5.6)
(74) Normally we talk about teams *failing to win*, with the default expectation that a team plays to win. But after a recent series of defeats, this headline implies that England are expected to lose. Like all the examples in this set of *Checking Understanding* questions, there's a flout on Manner. There's typically a further relevance derived implicature, here probably that the England team are of poor quality.

(75) Normally we expect things to improve so that they become *better than ever*. Here Manner is flouted because 'worse' is 'better' when assessing a museum of horrors. The relevance derived implicature is perhaps that you should visit the museum now.

(76) Normally we expect our investments to increase in value. The relevance derived implicature is perhaps that we should think carefully before buying the financial product on offer.

(77) 'But' advises you that I'm going to say something that contrasts with the first stated proposition. The default expectation is that I am going to contrast my stupidity with Alister's cleverness. Manner is flouted because 'If you're as clever as me' is more obscure than the expectable 'If you're as stupid as me'. The relevance derived implicatures are that really clever people get someone else to do the task for them and that the addressee should follow my example.

(5.7)
(78) *Even* conventionally implicates that the proposition to which it's attached, in (78) 'the Labour Party front bench', is at one end of a scale. Knowing who the speaker is enables us to work out which end of a scale the Labour Party front bench is at, and further to infer the conversational implicature that the Labour Party front bench is nothing special.

As in (78), 'even' in (79) gives rise to the conventional implicature that the action of bringing a wife into Horley Town Hall is at one end of a scale. Thus 'I have not even brought my wife into Horley Town Hall' conversationally implicates that Horley Town Hall is nothing special. (79) shows that such implicatures are psychologically real as the speaker goes on to confirm it by saying 'That's what I think of Horley Town Hall'.

(5.8)
(80) Implicature recovered from Hugh's message: <The election will reveal which of us is the better candidate for the position>. (This is by no means the only implicature.)
Calculation: Although Hugh says that the best person will win, we can't know the outcome of the election in advance. And given that our colleagues form the electoral college, we expect them to judge wisely. There is also the default set expression *May the best man/woman win*, which suggests that elections are reliable ways of selecting better candidates. Therefore the most relevant way to take what Hugh says in the context in which he says it is that the outcome will determine who is the better candidate.

(81) Implicature recovered from my comment: This is obviously obscure and therefore flouts Manner, and possibly Quantity and Quality as well. Am I implying that I want to win the election or that I don't want to win the election?
Calculation: For a start, my comment suggests that I don't accept the default assumption implicit in Hugh's message that elections do determine who the better candidate is. So in order to understand what I meant, first it's necessary to recover an implicated premise. But which of the two possible implicated premises, <Hugh is the best person>, <I am the best person>, is the one I intend our Administrator, Sara, to recover? Unless you have sufficient contextual information about Hugh and me, you cannot determine this. However, I calculate that Sara knows enough about both of us to be able to determine it, as there wouldn't be any point in making the comment if I didn't make this assumption. If we take <Hugh is the best person> as the implicated premise, then 'I hope not' implies that I want to win. If we take <I am the best person> as the implicated premise, then 'I hope not' implies that I don't want to win. Again, it would help you a lot in determining what I might mean by 'I hope not' to know whether I was an ambitious candidate or had been pressured to stand and had agreed reluctantly. Or whether I am the kind of person who is boastful, or falsely modest, or genuine and sincere, etc. Again, I expect Sara to be able to recover this contextual information. So we see that calculating implicatures depends on being able to adduce appropriate contextual knowledge.

(5.9)
On the one hand, 'you know what trains are like' is less than fully informative, and therefore flouts Quantity$_1$. But if it's true, as it presumably is, that the speaker does know what trains are like, then the utterance seems to abide by Quantity$_2$. It might be also be argued that the formula *you know what x is like* is an economical way of suggesting that '*x*' isn't up to much.

(5.10)
(104) Drinking alcohol and smoking cigarettes are I-inferred to be same type activities, an inference that the fuller form of (105) does not invite. Notice that Cantonese is a pro-drop language, so subject pronouns are inferred unless a potentially unresolvable indeterminacy or a marked interpretation licenses the presence of a subject pronoun. Notice also that 'alcohol' is explicit, although 'drink' does I-imply <drink alcohol> in Cantonese. The order of the concepts may also be culturally significant.

(106) <the speaker is a student> conventionalized I-inference, the most economical way of expressing the meaning that the referent is performing the institutionally likely action. Cf. *go to prison, church, market, hospital, school.* (107) tends to favour <located at the university at the present time> over <a student at the university>. Because 'the university' isn't said, (108) tends to Q-imply <the speaker is a student> rather than <lost at some university>.

(109a) I-implies <the Library was the place of registration>.

(109b) is like (109a) unless taken as a marked utterance M-implying that the two events are unconnected.

(110a) I-implies <she opened the door with her key>. (110b) is like (110a) unless taken as a marked utterance M-implying that <the two events are unconnected or connected in some unexpected way>.

(111) The joke turns on requiring us to re-analyse 'a husband' in such a way as to replace the I-inference <someone as yet unmarried and willing to become a

husband>. Although the speaker's father intends the default I-inference, the joke turns on the speaker's drawing (or pretending to draw) a marked M-inference.

(112) shows how 'thicker' prompts different utterance-token readings in different contexts.

The construction in (113) has two possible syntactic interpretations, <'horny' is a more appropriate word than 'Hornby'> based on interpreting 'Hornby' negatively, and <(even) more horny than Hornby is> based on interpreting 'Hornby' positively. (You need to know that 'horny' means *sexually excited* and that 'Hornby' is the brand name of a kind of model train.) The first reading may be prompted by the 'horny' / 'Hornby' trope, which is marked, suggesting that an M-inference is required for an utterance that has obvious 'type' properties.

In (114) 'Wrong ticket' I-implies <do you have the wrong ticket>. While 'That's fine by us' I-implies <the speaker is content with the addressee's conduct>. In the context, 'That's fine by us' prompts the M-inference <anyone with the wrong ticket risks a fine>.

The I-inferred determination of 'the other half' as either <those more privileged> or <those less privileged> depends both on the speaker's own absolute position in the social structure (and is thus indexical) and, for speakers in middle of the social structure, on the relative position of those referred to by 'the other half' on the occasion of use. Like (114), (115) has stereotypical implied meaning but also an utterance-token meaning determined by the context of use.

(5.11)

1) Perhaps 'eat' to a child making poor progress with a meal, 'please eat' to someone hesitating before eating/waiting for the speaker to be ready to eat, 'you eat' to someone whose food might go cold waiting for the speaker's food to be ready to eat, 'do eat' to reassure someone reluctant to start eating, 'do please eat' when you want to make it especially hard for your invitation to eat to be ignored. You may have other and better intuitions as to the optimal interpretations. The point is that the same proposition has many different implied meanings.

2) (116a) was the one used. If the preference is for '*x*' to be less than '*y*' in 'would you like *x* or *y*', (116b) would be unusual. Perhaps (116a) favours the interpretation that the car advertised looks like a supermini but is in fact a sensible saloon, thus providing the best of both worlds. (117a) is the conventional order and (117b) a marked order, chosen on this occasion to convey the less expected, or marked interpretation that men can be victims of a crime usually thought of as having female victims.

3) In (118), a reader needs default procedures to generate the unmarked I-inference invited by 'fit the bill' and an additional procedure to generate the marked reading of 'bill' and incorporate it in the default inference. In (119), the stewardess needs a means of blocking the default implication of 'same' as <same as I had before> and generating <same as the previous speaker> if she is to understand the male passenger. Her 'sorry' indicates that the male passenger produces a less than optimal form for which she cannot generate an optimal meaning consistent with the background.

(5.12)

In (122), Chris invites an M-inference by referring to the colour of my clothes in a context where it would be unmarked to comment on a person's appearance or mood. My 'oh' conventionally implicates that I find his comment surprising, and his response indicates that he took me to understand 'blue' as <sad> and therefore as applying to me rather than to my clothes, which he hadn't intended. As 'blue' can also imply <pornographic> and <on the right in politics>, I ask Chris to confirm that he didn't mean these things either. Of course, I'm teasing a bit. In (123), <be successful in a career>, the conventionalized I-inference invited by 'go far', wouldn't normally be stated in the context of a short journey in physical space. The writer acknowledges this abnormal collocation by the use of 'only', which enables the default I-inference to go through.

6 Relevance theory

(6.1)

1) The more problematical items include determining the modality of 'attend' – was I obliged or recommended to attend? Determining the meaning of 'attend' – be physically present at meetings and keep quiet or be physically present at meetings and contribute to them? 'Course planning and examiners' meetings' – a single type of meeting at which two different kinds of business are conducted or two different types of meeting? Is 'in future' in Alice's ideolect equivalent to 'in the future' in my ideolect, i.e. from the time the message is written onwards? Or does 'in the future' imply that there had been a meeting in the past that I was expected to attend?

2) The explicatures which help trigger the recovery of each of the two implicatures include the relation of 'my' to 'book' – one of ownership or authorial proprietorship? The sense of 'seen' – awareness of physical presence or knowledge of contents? The sense of 'book' – physical object or contents? The higher level explicatures will provide us with speech act descriptions such as (put very crudely) <the speaker is asking about the whereabouts of property she wants returned> or <the speaker is advising of the need to become familiar with the contents of a book she has written>.

(6.2)

(16) You need to know that 'alcohol in moderation' is not harmful so as to recover the explicature <drinking alcohol in moderation>.

(17) You need to know that there's a risk of mad cow disease spreading to sheep and that slaughtering infected animals is official policy. It might also help to know that sheep do not, so far as we know, have higher cognitive functions.

(18) You need to know that the Equitable Life is unique among life insurance companies in never paying commission to agents.

(19) You need to know that a mouse is a device for pointing to items on a computer screen.

(20) You need to know that white rather than red is usually classified as 'sweet', 'medium' or 'dry' so as to understand that three varieties of white wine and one red wine are available.

(21) The only way to determine whether the cancellation applies to the first or the second of the two scheduled sessions is to turn up at the time the first session is scheduled.

(6.3)

The speaker's utterance is guaranteed relevant (1). She has used an idiomatic expression because she thinks I have the abilities and resources to provide a relevant interpretation of the metaphor (2). But I have a problem explicating 'life' (3): am I to infer <life span>, in which case the speaker is stating that the person referred to will cause her to die ten years earlier than she would otherwise have done? Or am

I to infer <stage in life reached at present>, in which case the speaker is stating that the person referred to has added ten years to her life expectancy? I certainly need non-linguistic information (such as knowing the mood of the speaker and the circumstances she's referring to) and paralinguistic information (such as the tone in which the utterance is delivered) to help me to determine which of the two explicatures I'm intended to recover. Having determined this, there will be an accessible assumption <the speaker is unhappy with the person she is speaking about> or <the speaker is happy with the person she is speaking about> (4, 5). Thus by recovering the appropriate context I'm able to prove the relevance of the utterance (6). (I'm grateful to Laurence Brushi for this very neat example.)

(6.4)
Without more of the surrounding conversation, it's not possible to know whether the speaker of (26) wanted to convey only what is entailed in her utterance once enriched by explicatures or whether she intended an implicature. However, 'only' in (25) tells the addressees that it'll be worth their while processing the utterance for an implicit meaning and that the speaker's purpose is not merely to convey neutral information. First, there are several explicatures: does 'we' refer to the speaker and her partner only or to the speaker, her partner and other members of their family? Since the conversation takes place in Florence, 'are' cannot denote present location and must be conceptually enriched to *live* or some equivalent. 'London' is presumably *the city named London in the UK*. These explicatures are necessary because this same utterance might have occurred 30 miles from London, Ontario, with very different explicatures. We also need to consider relevant contextual factors – the addressees are American visitors to Europe and are thus likely to spend time in London. Perhaps they are being offered a place to stay or being invited to visit the couple's home. On the other hand, it's possible that the speaker is boasting and intending to convey to the addressees that she is no ordinary tourist. Once again, you need more of the surrounding conversation to be sure. As I had been eavesdropping for some while, I knew that the speaker was boasting and was seeking to convey to her addressees that she was more cultured than they. But without the help of 'only', I wouldn't have been able to recover the implicature conveyed by the speaker.

(6.5)
1) Part of the decoding process is to explicate 'handed down', which appears to be used here as a phrasal verb meaning *bequeathed*. This explication is presumably based on the inference that when 'handed down' occurs in close proximity to someone referred to as a 'dear old grandfather', the phrasal verb reading is the most relevant assumption. Thus one implicature of the explicated utterance is that the joke-teller's grandfather is no longer alive. There is then a pause just long enough to cause the studio audience to think the sentence is complete and therefore to confirm to themselves that the explicature and implicature recovered are the most relevant understandings. But the joke-teller then continues 'the other night as he was clearing out our attic'. Discovering that the joke-teller's grandfather is still alive causes us to revise the original explicature and substitute the new explicated meaning that 'handed down' isn't a phrasal verb at all but a regular verb followed by an adverb. Unless you recovered the inappropriate explicature the first time (i.e. the phrasal verb determination), you couldn't get the joke, which consists in denying an implied meaning. It turned out that the participants weren't able to process 'handed down' before the continuation of the joke confirmed it as verb + adverb, and therefore didn't get the crucial explicature.

2) The participants didn't have the contextual resources to know what sort of place Scarborough is and that Rugby players would not usually choose it as a holiday destination.

3) The participants weren't able to recover the explicatures that Ivan is terrible in bed and hence Blodwen is disappointed. Perhaps this is to do with language knowledge – they are unaware that 'terrible in bed' is a permitted colligation. Perhaps there's insufficient time to revise the first reference assignment and recognize that it isn't the Ivan who was a savage ruler who is referred to – or, at least if it is, it's not his savagery that's salient.

4) (31): Clearly a considerable processing effort is required to draw the inference that the tooth was knocked out by a scene shifter who felt insulted by the joke-teller. But since any other conclusion would require more effort, the studio audience therefore assumes that this is the relevant inference. However, the participants had problems with this utterance – the effort required to process it was too great for the implicature to be recovered. Perhaps the reference to 'the BBC emergency dental service' was taken at face value and therefore the relevance of what followed was especially difficult to determine.

(32): 'she's doing very well' can only be understood as ironic when what follows the pause is understood. Therefore the first-pass reading has to be rejected and an extra processing burden is placed on the audience. Moreover, the audience is required to infer that she is not doing very well, although the joke-teller appears not to draw this inference himself. The non-standard use of English is regarded as humorous by the regular native speaker audience, but the non-native speaker participants first have to identify it as non-standard; even if they do this, they lack the native speaker context in which it is comic because incongruous. In 'you'll be forgiving', the *au pair* treats 'forgive' as dynamic rather than stative; for speakers of languages where there's no English-type co-occurrence constraint on progressive aspect and stative verb, it's by no means intuitive that 'forgive' is a stative verb. The audience needs to explicate the non-native speaker errors in two ways – both in their own right (i.e. 'bad language' = swearing) and by inferring likely intended meanings (i.e. 'bad language' = ungrammatical English). Similar explicatures are required for 'grandmaster' and 'touching up'. The humour partly derives from the implicature that the speaker does not know what she is saying. As well as the innuendo associated with 'touching up', there's also the association with painting, so that 'my grandmaster needs touching up' maintains a consistent, if unlikely, colligation. The processing effort required to infer all these meanings is very considerable. This is an understanding test that even native speakers/members find challenging.

5) The first pause is an on-record invitation to take sufficient time to process 'she's been doing a bit of work for us this weekend at home' to recover the implicature that the speaker has been taking advantage of her. This inference is then confirmed by the time allowed for processing by the second pause after 'and'. Having led his audience up the garden path in this way, the joke-teller then denies that this implicature is well founded ('no') and insists ('it's true') that the purpose of her stay is to learn the language. So it turns out that 'the first hypothesis consistent with the principle of relevance', that there's something going on between the joke-teller and his *au pair* girl, is inappropriate, or at least it is a contrivance of the joke-teller. The participants weren't able to infer this implicature at the pauses, perhaps through lack of contextual resources, perhaps because pauses give rise to weak implicatures. Thus they weren't able to construct a first hypothesis, were consequently unable to understand the significance of 'no' and 'it's true' as denials of that hypothesis, and could not therefore understand the joke.

7 Metapragmatic awareness

(7.1)
(12) The word (metalinguistic term) 'well' (mention) is a hedge (metalinguistic term)

(13) Pragmatics (metalinguistic term), the module with four assignments (gloss)

(14) Hedging (metalinguistic term) is typical in lecturer-speak (comment about language)

(15) He said (speech act description), 'You're nuts' (quotation)

(16) She criticized me (gloss)

(17) Let's put it this way (speech act description)

(18) I give you my word (explicit performative)

(19) All the same (discourse marker)

(20) Fortunately (sentence adverb), it's unlikely (higher level predicate)

(21) By the way (hedge), the seminar (speech event description) was yesterday

(22) I guess (evidential) this exercise (self-referential expression) has been challenging

(23) OK (contextualization cue), enough's enough

(7.2)
(Key: * = implicit)

(24) INTERVIEWER: Can (tense*, modal) you tell us (speech act description) what the possible benefits of this new vaccine (deictic*) are (tense*)
INTERVIEWEE: Well (discourse marker) we (deictic*) desperately need (tense*) a vaccine against this dreadful killer (deictic*)

(25) PETER: But (discourse marker) they still get (tense*) coffee made in Old Shire Hall
CARLA: But (discourse marker) there is (tense*) the seat of power
PETER: Well (discourse marker) here is (tense*) the receipt of power
Notice also how the speakers show awareness of each other's encoding (but → but → well, there is → here is, seat → receipt)

(26) ASSISTANT: Is (tense*) it for a sink or a bath
CUSTOMER: Haven't (tense*) a clue mate I'd (modal*) be guessing
ASSISTANT: My (IFID) you're (tense*) quick off the mark in Newcastle. Right on the ball like (discourse particle)

(27) BLAIR: Well (discourse marker) it's (tense*) only (hedge) if I mean (hedge) you know (discourse particle) if she's (tense*) got a or if she needs (tense*) the ground prepared as it were (hedge) because (intertextual link) obviously (sentence adverb) if she goes (tense*) out she's (tense*) got to (modal) succeed if it were (hedge) whereas (intertextual link) I (deictic) can (tense*, modal) go out and just talk (speech act description)

(7.3)
1a) turn, account, interruption, topic, response; 1b) debate, argument; 1c) so, still, then

2) How about *this conversation* (self-referential expression), *to sum up* (sentence adverb), *following that* (explicit intertextual link), *I didn't mean to interrupt* (gloss), various linguistic and paralinguistic ways of signalling intention to interrupt (contextualization cue).

(7.4)

[Key: 1 = logical connective; 2 = speech act description; 3 = evidential; 4 = IFID; 5 = metalinguistic term; 6 = discourse marker]

W: So (1) that comment (2) I heard from the vice-chancellor reminded (3) me

THE CHAIRMAN: You have not told (2) us what that comment was (2), nor to whom it was made (2). Could you please (4) say (2) what it was – say (2) it in English (5) or in Cantonese (5) – and say (2) who else was there at the time.

Page 108

W: Mr Chairman, I cannot recall exactly (3) the wording (5). It was in Cantonese (5), but (6) I cannot recall exactly (3) the phrasing (5) of it. I can only remember (3) the gist (5), that because (1) the name of the University was involved, and he did not want the University to be involved in political debates.

THE CHAIRMAN: To whom was that comment made (2)?

W: I remember (3) it was in the open area of the vice-chancellor's office, where the newspapers were put. So (1) it was in the general area. There are secretaries around.

THE CHAIRMAN: To whom was the vice-chancellor speaking (2)?

W: I think (3) the vice-chancellor was reading the newspaper. I just came in, if I remember (3), to the general office. His secretary was there. I do not remember (3) whether other people were there. But (b) he mentioned (2) that, and I heard that comment (2). Therefore (1), when I went back to my office, I took that copy of the Morning Post and read it myself.

(7.5)

l.3 'if you want to' = metapragmatic indication of the illocutionary force of the utterance as a suggestion / a permission

l.6 'like' disaffiliates the speaker from an unlikely possibility; the tag 'is it' is a metapragmatic indication of the propositional attitude of the speaker.

l.8 'virtually' = metalinguistic gloss on 'a full packet'.

l.9 'yeah' = metasequential indication of an upcoming contribution with a supporting propositional content; 'actually' = a metapragmatic indication that the proposition is well founded if unexpectable.

l.11 'yeah' = as in l.9.

l.12 'and' = metapragmatic indication that the propositions are consequentially linked.

l.40 'right' = metasequential marker of the speaker's intention to break into a conversation from which he had been excluded.

l.41 'all right then' = metapragmatic acceptance of the previous speaker's proposal, with 'then' marking the present speaker's agreement.

(7.6)

'(1.5)' = metasequential indication of search for new method; 'but' = metapragmatic indication of contrast between previous and upcoming item or method; 'I think' = hedge advising on quality of upcoming proposition; 'it it' = self-check; 'was my fault (0.5)' = metasequential signal of upcoming gloss; '(.) um (. .)' = metapragmatic indication of search for upcoming item; 'maybe' = hedge; 'of my poor English (. .)' = metapragmatic indication of search for upcoming item; 'or maybe' = hedge; 'of (. .)' = metapragmatic indication of search for upcoming item; 'some other' = unspecifying practice signalling disaffiliation and licensing the interruption that follows; 'and I think' = hedge advising on quality of upcoming proposition; 'um (1.0)' = metapragmatic indication of search for upcoming item; 'therefore' = metasequential signal of upcoming formulation; '(.)' = metapragmatic signal of upcoming propositional content for formulation; 'I (1.8)' = metapragmatic indication of search for formulation; 'I suggest' = metapragmatic indication of speech act; '(. .)' = metapragmatic indication of search for formulation.

9 Politeness phenomena

(9.1)
(9) The volunteered explanation 'It's quite slow at the moment' redresses my face loss. I ask for a reason, thereby showing an interest in my interactant's problem. Her joke 'perhaps it's having a rest' shows concern for my self-esteem.

(10) I'm careful not to threaten the stranger's face in the way I offer help. My formula allows him the option of saying he's lost without losing too much face.

(11) The hedge 'I think' reduces the threat to the student's self-esteem and the redundant 'here' helps to show the supervisor's interest.

(9.2)

1. I'd certainly have written a more informal, less distance encoding message. I guess that older people and people of higher social status would find the formal message more appropriate. As we'll see later in the chapter, the over-classes tend to favour distance encoding strategies.

2)
(15) The redundant 'I know' is a way of expressing empathy; 'but it was very helpful to me' gives a reason for imposing; 'I appreciate' is an overt expression of gratitude and 'what you did', because it is verbal, rather than a nominal such as *your action/your help*, is strongly on record; 'I feel indebted to you' makes a small act of assistance look more than it is. Going on record as incurring a debt is very rarely meant sincerely in a non-debt culture like Britain. Why does the writer say 'for agreeing to register' rather than *for registering* – does this imply that I had a real choice in the matter? (I did not feel good when I got this letter. I thought it was over the top.)

(16) This text is discussed at two points in the chapter where you can check your ideas against mine.
(I thought the notice was a bit stuffy. And I thought the reason was doubtful – I often drink coffee 'to promote a better learning environment' for myself and I'm not sure that it damages the learning environment of others. If it's necessary to remind people of classroom etiquette, what's wrong with the usual iconic signs? Or are we to M-infer that we're in a classroom/department with a particular problem, which is therefore signalled by abnormal means?)

(17) The emboldened strap-line exaggerates interest and directs me to react enthusiastically to a gift. 'Your home' is friendly and (over?) familiar. The nominalized 'Following your recent energy assessment by Newcastle Warm Zone'

(rather than *we've assessed your energy situation*) appears deferential, as does 'I am pleased to inform you' and redundant 'will' and 'measures'.

(The problem with this letter is that the familiar tone of the strap-line contrasts with the stuffy tone of the body of the letter, so that I wonder if it's a con. The writer seems to have a congruence problem.)

3) This postcard, which we get all too frequently, brings us very bad news (no water for several hours) but is set out to look more like an invitation to a Buckingham Palace garden party with a variety of font sizes, colours and types. One notable feature is the movement towards a less formal register, perhaps suggesting that the culture increasingly favours less distance encoding strategies.

Comparison of (18a) and (18b): The nominal 'INTERRUPTION OF WATER SUPPLY' is replaced by the much more informal, elliptical 'WATER OFF'. In (18a), the capital 'W' and 'S' in line 2 and the full date in line 3 are more formal and therefore distance encoding. (18a) prefers 'period' to 'time' and mentions 'drawing' rather than 'using' hot water – because these are inflated terms, they are deferential. In (18a), there's an attempt to minimize the inconvenience with the warning that using water would be 'inadvisable'. (18a) also implies a powerful position with the use of 'It is essential'. The impersonal structures in this sentence and in the previous sentence are typical politeness strategies which try to give the impression that things have to be as they are and happen without any responsible agent. (18b) contains an overt apology for a situation whose imposition is played down by the minimizing use of 'any' and 'may'. 'Help' in (18b) is a natural, friendly term – in the final line of (18a), distance is encoded by the use of 'please', which suggests that getting advice is an imposition.

Comparison of (18b) and (18c): (18c) begins by explaining why the water will be disconnected and in this way treats the customers as equals entitled to know why they are being inconvenienced. By beginning with an apology, replacing 'regret' with 'apologize', and omitting 'this may cause you', (18c) is more friendly and natural than (18b). Again, (18c) favours the more down to earth 'turned off' rather than 'remain shut' and 'so that the water does not run' rather than 'to prevent the risk of flooding'. If you imagine someone speaking to you, (18b) sounds much more formal than (18c), which, having provided a reason for the imposition, offers advice.

Comparison of (18c) and (18d): The first three sentences of these texts are identical. Thereafter (18d) continues the move to a less formal register with plain 'central heating' in place of 'conventional heating systems' and 'may be used' in place of 'may be operated', although 'the hot water should not be used' in (18c) is less elaborate than 'do not run off any hot water from the system' in (18d).

(9.3)

1) When this happened to me in quite a smart café, I found myself saying to a woman about my own age 'Excuse me, it isn't your umbrella'. My redressive language includes an apology for intruding on her right to unimpeded action ('Excuse me') and a negative declarative. By asserting that it isn't her umbrella, there's nothing to redress if it isn't, and I minimize the face loss if it is.

2)

(19) My 'yeah' indicates that I concur in the obscurity of 'Oxon' and my hedge ('I suppose') redresses having to spell out something that I actually think is fairly obvious.

(20) The speaker types what he says as unpredictable ('news'), which he treats as 'bad' from the addressee's point of view, with which he empathizes ('I'm afraid'), although a less serious injury to someone would normally be good news. The first part of what he says provides a reason for the second part, as encoded by 'so'. 'Needing you' is also redressive and shows the value of the addressee to the speaker. The speaker then apologizes.

(9.4)

1) Distance differentials

(24) treats you as an equal by claiming kinship ('mate'). The elliptical structure 'Got' (rather than 'have you got') implies closeness.

(25) begins with an apology ('Excuse me') and is pessimistic about whether the request will be met ('would you by any chance').

The speaker of (24) encodes much less distance between themselves and the addressee than the speaker of (25). I might make the assumption that the speaker of (24) was 'working class' and the speaker of (25) 'middle class' since it's in the interests of those who suppose themselves to be 'under' to claim equality and those who suppose themselves to be 'over' to try to maintain distance between themselves and others. This is why the kind of politeness middle-class parents teach their children is like that of (25) rather than that of (24), hoping by these means to give their children a head-start in life.

2) Power differentials

(26) is a direct order made all the stronger by the use of 'up', which has the effect of making the verb 'eat' perfective, so that it means 'eat till you have finished'.

(27) is an indirect way of telling the adult to eat. In (26) the parent shows how much more powerful they are than the child, and in (27) the child shows how much less powerful they are than the parent.

3) Imposition

I don't know what you decided to say. I might say something like

(28) Would it be all right if I left Honey with you on Wednesday morning – I'd really, really like to go shopping by myself for a change

(29) I don't know how to put this, but I don't suppose you could do me an immense favour. We've been invited to stay with the Trolls on Saturday night and you know how they hate babies. I don't suppose there's any chance that we could possibly leave Howler with you is there? I can let you have everything you'll need.

What's being requested in (28) is much less of an imposition than what's being requested in (29).

Taken together, these three pairs of utterances show that the social distance between speakers, the extent to which their power statuses are equal or unequal and the degree to which one speaker imposes on the other all affect the way we talk to each other.

(9.5)

Now that we know about face, we can see that the British announcement is closest to the way a friend would talk to us ('should') and is therefore addressed to our positive face. The original KCR announcement is more careful not to impose on us ('may') and therefore respects our negative face to a greater degree. The second generation KCR announcement appeals to negative face with the use of redressive 'please'. All the announcements respect negative face in not addressing their illocutionary target directly. In not even lexicalizing the illocutionary target, both the KCR and MTR announcements are especially respectful of negative face.

(9.6)
1) Hotels want to deter guests from stealing items from the bedrooms. But to suggest that hotel guests are thieves is very face-threatening. In (37) this is minimized by the scalar implicature triggered by 'should', by the term 'collect' and by offering items for sale. In (38), it's minimized by the scalar implicature triggered by 'if', by appealing to the positive face of the guest with whom the writer of the notice empathizes ('can't leave without') and by offering the item for sale. Do you agree that 'souvenir' can mean both something paid for and something taken as a kind of trophy? Do think it's odd that we can simultaneously feel our self-esteem appealed to by 'can't leave without it' and at the same time know that it's a euphemism for steal? Is the literal meaning or the inferred meaning more salient? [(38) is an English translation – hence 'fluppy' – of a standard French formula.]

2)
- Agentless passives: 'who are required to provide samples for analysis'; 'Patients . . . are reminded'; 'they may only be accepted'; 'if they are presented'; 'which are presented in non-sterile containers . . . and therefore cannot be accepted'.
- Deference strategies = elevated uses of language, some of which are euphemistic: 'samples'; 'are reminded'; 'on request'; 'hazard'.
- Impersonal statements of general rules: the first and third sentences.
- Powerful first person plural: 'our staff'.
- Reason / explanation: the third sentence.

Basically this message encodes power and distance. Since doctors have the power to cure us when we cannot cure ourselves and since we only visit them when we are in a weaker state than usual, it may not be surprising to find these relative positions encoded in notices like this. Try talking to your friends like this and see what happens.

3) The more redressive language you use, the greater the imposition your request will appear to be. For this reason, I find it best to say 'Sorry, could you turn your music down' accompanied by a watery smile. 'Sorry' and 'could' are negative politeness strategies. The smile is faintly positive.

(9.7)
(15) Positive politeness: 'Dear Peter' (I'm addressed by my first name, i.e. as an equal); 'I know it must have made a very difficult day even more fraught' (the writer can see the world from addressee's perspective); 'it was very helpful to me' (gives a reason for imposing).
Negative politeness: 'I appreciate what you did and I feel indebted to you' (goes on record as incurring a debt).

(16) Positive politeness: 'In order to promote a better learning environment' (provides reason); 'remember to' (attends to addressee's wants); 'Thank you' (gives thanks).
Negative politeness: 'to promote a better learning environment' (elevated language is deferential); 'please' (conventional redressive request marker); 'mobile telephone' (deferential).

(17) Positive politeness: '**Your home qualifies for free insulation**' (exaggerates interest); 'you will qualify for free insulation measures' (gift)
Negative politeness: 'Dear Mr Grundy' (deferential use of title and family name); 'your recent energy assessment' (deferential); 'I am pleased to inform you' (deferential); 'insulation measures' (deferential).

(9.8)
You cannot take the view that 'everyone's anything nowadays' unless you are a relatively older member of a group. We might expect a rapidly changing or more egalitarian society to make less use of negative politeness. If you'd been used to orienting to the negative face of older people when you were young, you might notice the difference between your former behaviour and the way younger people orient to your face wants as you get older.

10 Empirical pragmatics, interactive pragmatics, talk-in-interaction

(10.1) These are my suggestions – you've probably found equally good examples of your own.

1) DOCTOR: (. .) and on the pantry door it's just the one upstairs isn't it next to the showers (2.0) so I mean it's likely [it's] to be someone (1.0) around that area you would've thought wouldn't you (1.5)

'So I mean', which indicates an upcoming formulation, and the turn-final tag 'wouldn't you' project the end of the turn. Interestingly, as in many other places in this encounter, the students don't take up the turn at this TRP and thus oblige the Doctor to continue.

2) SUSIE: yeah no erm Nicole wants to no we need a word with you
DOCTOR: oh ⌈right⌉

The addressee must respond either verbally or by means of a non-verbal signal.

3) DOCTOR: how's it doing
SUSIE: yeah no erm Nicole wants to no we need a word with you

Susie self-selects after the Doctor's initial greeting.

4) DOCTOR: right erm (2.0) there not a lot (.) can do about it I can sort of like .hh (2.0) have a word with people if you want

This turn is followed by a 1.5 second gap, presumably because the students don't think the offer is worth responding to.

5) VICKY: will you help me with my [linguistics work] <laughs>
DOCTOR: [right I'm off]

The Doctor sees his opportunity to escape when Vicky asks Susie for help.

(10.2)
1) First pair-part of an adjacency pair:

DOCTOR: how's it doing

2) Use of address term:

VICKY: Susie

3) Clarification request:

DOCTOR: which one

4) Clarification request involving repetition:

NICOLE: cheese
VICKY: cheese

5) Tag used as an exit technique:

NICOLE: yeah a sign'll do won't it

6) Place where there's a natural next-turn taker:

SUSIE: yeah no erm Nicole wants to no we need a word with you
DOCTOR: oh [right]
NICOLE: [no] someone's been nicking stuff out the fridge

After the Doctor's turn, Nicole is the only licensed speaker.

(10.3)
1) Long single-unit turn:

DOCTOR: yeah just seeing people using your cheese again and you cannot really accuse someone cos they might have bought (.) bought it themselves

This turn is unlike most of the Doctor's long turns in not containing several units.
2) Short single-unit turn:

DOCTOR: oh [right]

3) Long turn resulting from lack of next speaker self-selection:

DOCTOR: right erm (2.0) there not a lot (.) can do about it I can sort of like .hh (2.0) have a word with people if you want
(1.5)
DOCTOR: erm .hh (3.0) I mean (.) do you do you want to sort of like have a word with everyone or just (.) do you want us to put a sign up or

4) Pauses within turns and lapses between turns in (3).

(10.4)

NICOLE: yeah a sign'll do won't it

'yeah' orients to the Doctor's previous turn, 'a sign'll do' is Nicole's contribution to consequentiality, and 'won't it' orients to the next turn.

11 Intercultural pragmatics

(11.1)
In working through the exercise, I hope you took into account the nationality of each passenger and the languages you felt entitled to assume they spoke as well as the extent to which you felt you were representing your national airline to each of them.

(11.2)
(22) The intended meaning is recovered as either an I- or an M-inference. Translate using the appropriate formula.

(23) Could be problematic depending on cultural norms. Probably translate as a description along the lines of '<name of speaker> wonders if we're all here or if we need to go and find anyone'.

(25) This form is used with the same force in some languages but not all. Probably translate as 'I'm sorry, I don't remember your name'.

(26) Possibly problematic. Translate literally. This meaning is recovered from the context in which the person referred to is patently stupid and the speaker, who isn't from Barcelona, conveys his attitude paralinguistically.

(28) Likely to be problematic. Translate finding a formula that conveys the same implicature.

(29) Could be problematic. 'Long' conversations may be good or bad, depending on the context.

(30) Likely to be problematic because of the idiomatic meaning. Try to find a formula with the same two meanings.

(31) Translate literally to convey whichever meaning is intended.

(33) Perhaps translate literally – i.e. 'never agree to' or 'never be able to', depending on meaning intended.

(34) Likely to be problematic. Translate using an equivalent indirect formula if available.

12 Doing project work in pragmatics

(12.1)
1) 'tsuh' in (7′) indicates that what follows is a distraction from the main business. 'um' is a poor transcription of what might be either a hesitation marker ('er') or an indefinite article. The decision to transcribe the segment as an indefinite article is based on it being impossible to detect any difference between the realization of this segment and of the segment following 'left', which is clearly an indefinite article. The consequences of this decision are far-reaching – as pointed out in Chapter 10, 'a' pre-empts 'my' and the option of indicating the colour of the folder ('orange'), seemingly going against the speaker's pre-planned strategy and causing him to pause in mid-utterance.

2) The early stage transcription indicates how easy it is to be misled by expectations even when listening carefully. Recognizing the past tense after 'I think' and the putative past 'it[d]' is what causes us to infer that the student distances himself psychologically from a traumatic event.

3) It's difficult to see why there should be a TRP after '.hh oh dear' since the librarian has nothing new to respond to, so the one-second pause is treated as being turn internal in the final transcription.
The more accurate final transcription 'happen to' captures the negative politeness of the student; accurately transcribing the librarian's turn as an interruption rather than a simultaneous onset shows her exasperation.

4) The self-edited 'telepho-' and 'num-' in the final version again show how easy it is for the transcriber to be misled by what they expect to find. The more accurate final transcription of self-edited items and latching rather than overlap show the librarian as more sympathetic towards a more troubled student.

In the final transcription, the student's 'great thank you' is represented as an overlap of 'if we find it' and therefore as an expression of gratitude for 'we can send it you'. If it was accurate, the early stage transcription would be problematic since the student's effusive expression of thanks appears to be a response to being asked if he has email.

Glossary

accommodation the willingness of a hearer to accept a proposition which is conveyed or presupposed rather than formally asserted.

activity type (or speech event): a goal-directed, culturally recognizable routine (Levinson, 1979).

adjacency pair a fundamental unit of talk consisting of a sequence of two paired units produced by different speakers so that the 'first pair part' triggers an appropriate 'second pair part'. Examples include greeting + greeting, invite + acceptance/refusal (Schegloff and Sacks, 1973).

anaphora a reference to a previous item, or 'antecedent', in a discourse.

communication the act of conveying a meaning from one party to another.

constraint a means of limiting available interpretations.

context any relevant element of the social structure or of encyclopedic knowledge. Context may impinge on or be created by the use language. Presumptive contexts are said to be 'distal' or 'macro' and contexts created in talk are said to be 'micro'.

contextual resource the term Sperber and Wilson (1995) use to describe the knowledge schema(ta) required by a hearer in order to understand an utterance.

conversation a series of utterances exchanged between two or more speakers which follow a regular pattern of turn-taking.

cooperative principle the central presumption underlying Grice's theory of conversational implicature (1967) which enjoins speakers to make relevant, expectable contributions to conversation.

defeasibility the term used to describe the cancellability status of a meaning. Some meanings are defeasible (e.g., that I have only one child in *I have a child*), others are not defeasible (e.g., that I have at least one child in *I have a child*).

deixis the indexical property of a closed class consisting of demonstratives such that their reference is determined in relation to the point of origin of the utterance in which they occur. Examples include *I, here* and *now*.

E-language, I-language a distinction drawn by Chomsky (1986) between language which is externalized (E) and internalized knowledge of language (I).

entailment a meaning that is always associated with an expression so that on every occasion when the expression occurs the meaning arises. For example, I can never say that one football team *beat* another without entailing that the first team scored at least one goal more than the second.

ethnomethodology the study of social behaviour, including linguistic communication, which looks for regularities common to members of a particular group.

explicature a term used by Sperber and Wilson (1995) to describe the 'full propositional form' of a sentence whose indeterminacies have been resolved by a process of inference.

face a person's sense of self-esteem (positive face) and desire to determine their own course of action (negative face) postulated by Brown and Levinson (1978) as the psychological feature addressed by politeness expressions. Hence face-wants (= need to have face respected), face-threat (threat to self-esteem or to freedom of action), facework (= language addressed to the face-wants of others). B&L suggest face is a universal feature of personality which politeness addresses, but some commentators think this view of face too western-oriented.

factivity the property of a set of predicates in whose domain subject or complement clauses are presupposed (Kiparsky and Kiparsky, 1971).

felicity conditions the conditions which must be in place for a speech act to be performed appropriately (Austin, 1962).

form linguistic structure (as opposed to function). Thus a sentence is a form, while an utterance is a sentence put to use, i.e. given a function.

grammaticalization the process by which an item comes to have a systematic relation to other items.

hedge a means of indicating weak adherence to a conversational maxim; contrast with **intensifier**, a means of indicating strong adherence to a maxim.

higher level explicature a term used by Sperber and Wilson (1995) to describe the propositional attitude of the speaker of an utterance, including speech act descriptions, which the addressee must recover inferentially.

historical pragmatics the study of the role that pragmatics, and particularly pragmatic inference, plays in language change.

honorific language forms used to encode the (high) social status of the addressee.

implicature an inferred meaning (Grice, 1967), often with a different logical (i.e. non-truth-preserving) form from that of the original utterance. In Grice's theory, the inferential process by which a hearer derives a conversational implicature is calculable, and the implicature is defeasible and non-detachable (if the context holds, any item with the same meaning will have the same implicature); according to Grice, implicatures may be 'generalized' (inferred irrespective of context – e.g., *some* will always implicate <not all>) or 'particularized' (particular to the context of the utterance in which they arise).

indeterminacy a property of linguistic forms such that their semantic value is underspecified and needs to be enriched in ways particular to the contexts in which they occur.

indexicality the encoding of points of reference relative to the speaker and the time and place of the utterance.

indirect speech act a functional use of language effected by the use of a form other than the one prototypically associated with the function concerned. For example, *Would you mind opening the window* is a request expressed in an interrogative form.

inference a conclusion derived from premises. A deductive or 'logical' inference is necessarily valid; inductive inferences 'project beyond the known data' (Honderich, 1995) and are probabilistic, i.e. an inductive inference may not yield the same conclusion when additional premises are adduced. Pragmatic inferences are usually presumed to be inductive, although Sperber and Wilson argue that explicatures and implicatures in relevance theory are deductive inferences. A hearer will frequently be led to infer a meaning as the result of a trigger, a feature of the utterance or its correspondence to known facts that leads the hearer to suspect that the literal meaning is not the (only) meaning that the speaker seeks to convey.

intercultural communication the use of language between speakers who represent different cultures.

iterated learning the process of language evolution that takes place as a result of the transmission of an increasingly learnable language from one generation to the next.

literal meaning it's generally (but not universally) held that words and sentences have an invariant literal meaning.

logical form the representation of the propositional content of a sentence in a form that may be adjudged true or false.

maxim the term Grice uses for the four sub-principles of his cooperative principle. The four maxims enjoin the speaker to strive to provide appropriately informative, well-founded, relevant contributions to conversation in a perspicuous manner. These may be hedged by metalingual glosses which indicate the extent to which the speaker is abiding by one or more of them.

meaning the sense that is conveyed in a communicative act. Conventional linguistic meaning is usually thought of truth-theoretically, i.e. if you know whether a sentence is a true or false description of some state of affairs, then you know what it means (truth-conditional semantics). Grice distinguishes conventional meaning and non-conventional or inferred meaning.

membership a central notion in ethnomethodology reflecting the extent to which a person shows cultural affiliation. Hence members' method, a generic term used in Conversation Analysis for the knowledge of conversational methods, such as turn taking, accounting, formulation, etc., which are demonstrated in conversational practice.

metalanguage the self-reflexive use of language so as to comment on or gloss itself. Hence metapragmatic uses of language gloss the pragmatic function of (parts of) an utterance and metasequential uses of language gloss the conversational function of (parts of) a talk sequence.

negation negation maps one value (false) on to another by means of a negative particle; the negative particle is also used metalinguistically as a way of objecting to some aspect of an utterance on any grounds except its conventional, semantic meaning.

optimality the highest level of match between an abstract representation and a form, or between a form and an abstract representation.

performative the use of language to accomplish action.

politeness the relationship between how something is said and the addressee's judgement as to how it should be said. In Brown & Levinson's model, politeness phenomena are seen as redressive and computed as a function of speaker–hearer power–distance differential and degree of imposition.

pragmalinguistics, socio-pragmatics terms coined by Leech (1983) to capture a user's knowledge of appropriate pragmatic forms and the contexts in which it's appropriate to use them.

pragmatic strengthening an umbrella term for the process of determining and enriching meaning by means of pragmatic inference.

pragmatics the study of language used in contextualized communication and the usage principles associated with it.

preference theory contributions to talk are said to be preferred and dispreferred. When it's necessary to make a dispreferred contribution, such as refusing an invitation, this may well be linguistically redressed.

presupposition a meaning taken as given which does not need to be asserted; variously defined as 'semantic presupposition' (non-defeasible, contributes to the truth-conditional meaning of the sentence), 'conventional implicature' (non-defeasible, non-truth-conditional) and 'pragmatic presupposition' (cancellable where inconsistent with speaker/hearer knowledge about the world).

presupposition projection the property of some complex sentences to inherit the presuppositions of the component sentences embedded within them.

procedural encoding an indication of how to process the proposition to which it is attached in order to determine its relevance. Distinguished by Blakemore (1987) from the conceptual encoding of propositions.

proposition a linguistic representation of a state of affairs with a truth value. Utterances may also encode the attitudes of speakers to the propositions which they contain.

rationalistic pragmatics a theory-driven approach to pragmatics based on the assumption that the use of language is based solely or essentially on reason.

reference most descriptions refer to persons, objects, notions on each occasion when they are used. The function of picking out an object in the world which matches a linguistic description is called referring.

relevance according to Sperber and Wilson (1995), every utterance is relevant merely by virtue of being uttered. If we know how it's relevant, we know the meaning the speaker intends to convey.

repair a term used in conversation analysis to describe the correction or adjustment by speaker or hearer of some part of what is said.

sentence the formal output of a grammar in which constituent items are combined in a limited set of rule-derived configurations.

sequence a term used to describe the 'grammar' of conversation as a variety of sequentially ordered turn-types and members' methods.

speech act the performative, or action accomplishing, aspect of language use, and particularly the (illocutionary) force associated with an utterance.

speech event see 'activity type'.

talk/talk-in-interaction a term used to describe conversation, which draws attention to the underlying principle of turn-taking.

turn (turn constructional unit) the principal unit of description in conversational structure.

universal a form or function found in all languages.

usage the principles which underlie allowable use.

utterance a sentence used by a speaker for some purpose. Thus 'I'm Peter' is both a sentence (it has a determinate grammar) and an utterance (I use it to introduce myself).

utterance-type meaning 'a level of systematic pragmatic inference based *not* on direct computations about speaker-intention but rather on general expectations about how language is normally used' (Levinson, 1995). As distinct from utterance-token meaning which is context-sensitive.

References

Alexander, J.C., Giesen, B., Munch, R. and Smelser, N. (eds) 1987: *The Macro-micro Link*. Berkeley: University of California Press.

Atkinson, J.M. and Heritage, J. (eds) 1984: *Structures of Social Action*. Cambridge: Cambridge University Press.

Atkinson, M., Kilby, D.A. and Roca, I. 1988: *Foundations of General Linguistics* (2nd edn). London: Allen and Unwin.

Austin, J.L. 1962: *How to Do Things with Words*. Oxford: Clarendon Press.

Austin, J.L. 1970: *Philosophical Papers*. Oxford: Oxford University Press.

Austin, J.L. 1971: Performative-Constative. In Searle, J.R. *Philosophy of Language*. Oxford: Oxford University Press, 13–22.

Basso, K.H. and Selby, H.A. (eds) 1976: *Meaning in Anthropology*. Albuquerque: University of New Mexico Press.

Bauman, R. and Sherzer, J. (eds) 1974: *Explorations in the Ethnography of Speaking*. Cambridge: Cambridge University Press.

Black, M. (ed.) *Philosophy in America*. Ithaca, NY: Cornell University Press, 221–39.

Blakemore, D. 1987: *Semantic Constraints on Relevance*. Oxford: Blackwell Publishers.

Blakemore, D. 1992: *Understanding Utterances*. Oxford: Blackwell Publishers.

Bloom, P., Peterson, M., Nadel, L. and Garrett, M. (eds) 1996: *Language and Space*. Cambridge, MA: MIT Press.

Blum-Kulka, S., House, J. and Kasper, G. (eds) 1989: *Cross-cultural Pragmatics: Requests and Apologies*. Norwood, NJ: Ablex.

Blutner, R. 2004: Pragmatics and the lexicon. In Horn, L.R. and Ward, G. (eds) *The Handbook of Pragmatics*. Oxford: Blackwell Publishing, 488–514.

Bolinger, D. 1967: Adjectives in English: Attribution and Predication. *Lingua* 18, 1–34.

Briggs, C.L. 1997: From the ideal, the ordinary, and the orderly to conflict and violence in pragmatic research. *Pragmatics* 7/4, 451–9.

Brown, P. and Levinson, S.C. 1978: Universals in language usage: politeness phenomena. In Goody, E.N. *Questions and Politeness*. Cambridge: Cambridge University Press, 56–311; reprinted with new introduction and revised bibliography as *Politeness: Some Universals in Language Usage* (1987). Cambridge: Cambridge University Press.

Burton-Roberts, N. 1989: *The Limits to Debate*. Cambridge: Cambridge University Press.

Carston, R. 1988: Implicature, explicature, and truth-theoretic semantics. In Kempson, R.M. *Mental Representations*. Cambridge: Cambridge University Press, 155–81.

Chafe, W.L. 1994: *Discourse, Consciousness and Time: The Flow and Displacement of Conscious Experience in Speaking and Writing*. Chicago: University of Chicago Press.

Chomsky, N. 1976: *Reflections on Language*. Glasgow: Collins.

Chomsky, N. 1986: *Knowledge of Language: Its Nature, Origin, and Use*. New York: Praeger.

Christiansen, M.H. and Kirby, S. (eds) 2003: *Language Evolution*. Oxford: Oxford University Press.

Cole, P. (ed.) 1978: *Syntax and Semantics 9: Pragmatics*. New York: Academic Press.

Cole, P. (ed.) 1981: *Radical Pragmatics*. New York: Academic Press.

Cole, P. and Morgan, J.L. (eds) 1975: *Syntax and Semantics 3: Speech Acts*. New York: Academic Press.

Comrie, B. 1976: Linguistic politeness axes: Speaker-addressee, speaker-reference, speaker-bystander. *Pragmatics Microfiche* 1.7.
Corbett, J. 2003: *An Intercultural Approach to English Language Teaching*. Clevedon: Multilingual Matters.
Crystal, D. and Davy, D. 1969: *Investigating English Style*. London: Longman.
Cutting, J. 2007: *Pragmatics and Discourse* (2nd edn). London: Routledge.
Davis, S. (ed.) 1991: *Pragmatics: A Reader*. Oxford: Oxford University Press.
Diessel, H. 1999: The morphosyntax of demonstratives in synchrony and diachrony. *Linguistic Typology* 3, 1–49.
Dirven, R., Frank, R. and Ilie, C. (eds) 2001: *Language and Ideology:* Vol. II. *Descriptive Cognitive Approaches*. Amsterdam: John Benjamins.
Dirven, R., Hawkins, B. and Sandikcioglu, E. (eds) 2001: *Language and Ideology:* Vol. I. *Theoretical Cognitive Approaches*. Amsterdam: John Benjamins.
Drew, P. and Heritage, J. (eds) 1992: *Talk at Work*. Cambridge: Cambridge University Press.
Drew, P. and Woolten, A. (eds) 1988: *Erving Goffman: Exploring the Interaction Order*. Cambridge: Polity Press.
Duranti, A. 1997: *Linguistic Anthropology*. Cambridge: Cambridge University Press.
Duranti, A. and Goodwin, C. 1992: *Rethinking Context*. Cambridge: Cambridge University Press.
Fauconnier, G. 1997: *Mappings in Thought and Language*. Cambridge: Cambridge University Press.
Firth, A. 1995: 'Accounts' in negotiation discourse: A single case analysis. *Journal of Pragmatics* 23, 199–226.
Foley, W.A. 1997: *Anthropological Linguistics: An Introduction*. Oxford: Blackwell Publishers.
Glover, K.D. 2000: The sequential analysis of proximal and distal deixis in negotiation talk. *Journal of Pragmatics* 32/7.
Glover, K.D. and Grundy, P. 1996: 'Why do we have these': When reconstructing the indexical ground is disfavoured. In Romary, L. and Reboul, A. (eds) *Time, Space and Identity*. Nancy: CRIN-Loria, 117–33.
Goody, E.N. (ed.) 1978: *Questions and Politeness*. Cambridge: Cambridge University Press.
Graddol, D. 1999: The decline of the native speaker. *AILA Review* 13, 57–68.
Green, G.M. 1996: *Pragmatics and Natural Language Understanding* (2nd edn). Mahwah, NJ: Lawrence Erlbaum Associates.
Greenberg, J.H. (ed.) 1978: *Universals of Human Language*. Los Angeles: Stanford University Press.
Grice, H.P. 1967: *Logic and conversation. Further notes on logic and conversation*. The William James lectures. Published as Part 1 of Grice, H.P. *Studies in the Way of Words* 1989: Cambridge, MA: Harvard University Press.
Grice, H.P. 1968: Utterer's meaning, sentence-meaning, and word-meaning. *Foundations of Language* 4, 1–18. Reprinted in Searle, J.R. (ed.) 1971: *Philosophy of Language*. Oxford: Oxford University Press, 54–70, and in Davis, S. (ed.) *Pragmatics: A Reader* (1991). Oxford: Oxford University Press, 65–76.
Grice, H.P. 1989: *Studies in the Way of Words*. Cambridge, MA: Harvard University Press.
Grundy, P. 1998: Parallel texts and diverging cultures in Hong Kong: Implications for intercultural communication. In Niemeier, S., Campbell, C.P. and Dirven, R. (eds) *The Cultural Context in Business Communication*. Amsterdam: John Benjamins.
Grundy, P. 2002: Reflexive language in language teacher education. In Trappes-Lomax, H. and Ferguson, G. (eds) *Language in Language Teacher Education*. Amsterdam: John Benjamins, 82–94.

Grundy, P. 2007a: Language evolution, pragmatic inference and the use of English as a lingua franca. In Kecskes, I. and Horn, L.R. (eds) *Explorations in Pragmatics*. Berlin: Mouton de Gruyter, 219–56.

Grundy, P. 2007b: Salient meaning, culture and language teaching pedagogy. In Lynch, A. and Northcott, J. (eds) *Teacher Education in Teaching English for Academic Purposes*. Edinburgh: University of Edinburgh (CD-ROM).

Grundy, P. and Jiang, Y. 2001a: The bare past as an ideological construction in Hong Kong discourse. In Dirven, R., Frank, R. and Ilie, C. (eds) *Language and Ideology: Vol II Descriptive Cognitive Approaches*. Amsterdam: John Benjamins, 117–34.

Grundy, P. and Jiang, Y. 2001b: Ideological ground and relevant interpretation in a cognitive semantics. In Dirven, R., Hawkins, B. and E. Sandikcioglu (eds) *Language and Ideology*: Vol. I *Theoretical Cognitive Approaches*. Amsterdam: John Benjamins, 107–40.

Grundy, P. and Jiang, Y. 2005: Linguistic action verbs and logical prompting in political discourse. In Thiele, W., Schwend, J. and Todenhagen, C. (eds) *Political Discourse: Different Media – Different Intentions – New Reflections*. Tübingen: Stauffenburg, 97–123.

Gu, Y. 1990: Politeness phenomena in modern Chinese. *Journal of Pragmatics* 14/2, 237–57.

Hall, E.T. 1976: *Beyond Culture*. Garden City, NY: Anchor Press.

Hanks, W.F. 1992: The indexical ground of deictic reference. In Duranti, A. and Goodwin, C. *Rethinking Context*. Cambridge: Cambridge University Press, 43–76.

Harris, S. 1995: Pragmatics and power. *Journal of Pragmatics* 23, 117–35.

Hawkins, J.A. 1978: *Definiteness and Indefiniteness: A Study in Reference and Grammaticality Prediction*. London: Croom Helm.

Hewstone, M. and Fincham, F. 2007: Attribution theory and research: Basic issues and applications. In Hewstone, M., Stroebe, W. and Jonas, K. (eds) *Introduction to Social Psychology* (4th edn). Oxford: Blackwell Publishers.

Hewstone, M., Stroebe, W. and Jonas, K. 2007: *Introduction to Social Psychology* (4th edn). Oxford: Blackwell Publishers.

Hilton, D.J. 1991: A conversational model of causal explanation. In Stroebe, W. and Hewstone, M. (eds) *European Review of Social Psychology*. Vol. 2. Chichester: John Wiley & Sons Ltd.

Hofstede, G.H. 1980: *Culture's Consequences*. Beverley Hills, CA: Sage.

Honderich, T. (ed.) 1995: *The Oxford Companion to Philosophy*. Oxford: Oxford University Press.

Hopper, P.J. and Traugott, E.C. 1993: *Grammaticalization*. Cambridge: Cambridge University Press.

Horn, L.R. 1972: *On the Semantic Properties of Logical Operators in English*. PhD diss. UCLA.

Horn, L.R. 1984: Toward a new taxonomy for pragmatic inference: Q-based and R-based implicature. In Schiffrin, D. (ed.) *Meaning, Form, and Use in Context: Linguistic Applications*. Washington, DC: Georgetown University Press, 11–42. Reprinted in Kasher, A. (ed.) *Pragmatics: Critical Concepts*. Vol. IV, *Presupposition, Implicature, and Indirect Speech Acts* (1998), 389–418.

Horn, L.R. 1985: Metalinguistic negation and pragmatic ambiguity. *Language* 61/1, 121–74.

Horn, L.R. 1988: Pragmatic theory. In Newmeyer, F.J. (ed.) *Linguistics: The Cambridge Survey*, Vol. 1. Cambridge: Cambridge University Press, 113–45.

Horn, L.R. 1989: *A Natural History of Negation*. Chicago: University of Chicago Press. Re-issued with a new introduction, 2001. Stanford, CA: CSLI Publications.

Horn, L.R. and Ward, G. (eds) 2004: *The Handbook of Pragmatics*. Oxford: Blackwell Publishing.

Hutchby, I. and Wooffitt, R. 2008: *Conversation Analysis* (2nd edn). Oxford: Blackwell.
Jaworski, A. and Coupland, N. 1999: *The Discourse Reader*. London: Routledge.
Jenkins, J. 2000: *The Phonology of English as an International Language*. Oxford: Oxford University Press.
Kaplan, D. 1978: On the logic of demonstratives. *Journal of Philosophical Logic* 8, 81–98. Reprinted in Davis, S. (ed.) *Pragmatics – a Reader* 1991: Oxford: Oxford University Press, 137–45.
Kasher, A. (ed.) 1998: *Pragmatics: Critical Concepts*. Vol. IV, *Presupposition, Implicature, and Indirect Speech Acts*. London: Routledge.
Kasper, G. 1990: Linguistic politeness: current research issues. *Journal of Pragmatics* 14/2, 193–218.
Kay, P. 1990: Even. *Linguistics and Philosophy* 13, 59–111. Reprinted in Kay, P. *Words and the Grammar of Context* 1997: Stanford, CA: CSLI Publications.
Kay, P. 1997: *Words and the Grammar of Context*. Stanford, CA: CSLI Publications.
Kecskes, I. 2004: Editorial. *Intercultural Pragmatics* 1/1.
Kecskes, I. and Horn, L.R. (eds) 2007: *Explorations in Pragmatics*. Berlin: Mouton de Gruyter.
Kempson, R.M. (ed.) 1988: *Mental Representations: The Interface between Language and Reality*. Cambridge: Cambridge University Press.
Kiparsky, P. and Kiparsky, C. 1971: Fact. In Steinberg, D. and Jakobovits, L. (eds) *Semantics*. Cambridge: Cambridge University Press, 345–69.
Kirby, S. 2001: Spontaneous evolution of linguistic structure: an iterated learning model of the emergence of regularity and irregularity. *IEEE Transactions on Evolutionary Computation* 5, 102–10.
Kirby, S. 2002: Learning, bottlenecks and the evolution of recursive syntax. In Briscoe, E. (ed.) *Linguistic Evolution through Language Acquisition: Formal and Computational Models*. Cambridge: Cambridge University Press, 173–203.
Kirby, S. and Christiansen, M.H. 2003: From language learning to language evolution. In Christiansen, M.H. and Kirby, S. (eds) *Language Evolution*. Oxford: Oxford University Press, 272–94.
Kopytko, R. 1995: Against rationalistic pragmatics. *Journal of Pragmatics* 23, 475–91.
Kopytko, R. 2001: From Cartesian towards non-Cartesian pragmatics. *Journal of Pragmatics* 33, 783–804.
Lakoff, G. 1971: Presupposition and relative well-formedness. In Steinberg, D. and Jakobovits, L. (eds) *Semantics*. Cambridge: Cambridge University Press, 345–69.
Lakoff, R. 1972: Language in context. *Language* 48, 907–27.
Lakoff, R. 1973: The logic of politeness: or minding your P's and Q's. *Papers from the Ninth Regional Meeting of the CLS*. Chicago: CLS, 292–305.
Leech, G.N. 1983: *Principles of Pragmatics*. Harlow: Longman.
Levinson, S.C. 1979: Activity types. *Linguistics* 17, 365–99.
Levinson, S.C. 1983: *Pragmatics*. Cambridge: Cambridge University Press.
Levinson, S.C. 1988: Putting linguistics on a proper footing: explorations in Goffman's concepts of participation. In Drew, P. and Woolten, A. (eds) *Erving Goffman: Exploring the Interaction Order*. Cambridge: Polity Press, 161–227.
Levinson, S.C. 1992: Activity types and language. In Drew, P. and Heritage, J. (eds) *Talk at Work*. Cambridge: Cambridge University Press, 66–100.
Levinson, S.C. 1995: Three levels of meaning. In Palmer, F. (ed.) *Grammar and Meaning – Essays in Honour of Sir John Lyons*. Cambridge: Cambridge University Press, 90–119.
Levinson, S.C. 1996: Frames of reference and Molyneux's question: Cross-linguistic evidence. In Bloom, P., Peterson, M., Nadel, L. and Garrett, M. (eds) *Language and Space*. Cambridge, MA: MIT Press, 109–69.

Levinson, S.C. 2000: *Presumptive Meanings: The Theory of Generalized Conversational Implicature*. Cambridge, MA: MIT Press.

Levinson, S.C. 2004: Deixis. In Horn, L.R. and Ward, G. (eds) *The Handbook of Pragmatics*. Oxford: Blackwell Publishing, 97–121.

Lockwood, W.B. 1968: *Historical German Syntax*. Oxford: Oxford University Press.

Lucy, J.A. (ed.) 1993: *Reflexive Language: Reported Speech and Metapragmatics*. Cambridge: Cambridge University Press.

Lynch, A. and Northcott, J. (eds) 2007: *Teacher Education in Teaching English for Academic Purposes*. Edinburgh: University of Edinburgh (CD-ROM).

Matsumoto, Y. 1988: Reexamination of the universality of face: politeness phenomena in Japanese. *Journal of Pragmatics* 12, 403–26.

Matsumoto, Y. 1989: Politeness and conversational universals – observations from Japanese. *Multilingua* 8, 207–22.

McCawley, J.D. 1981: *Everything that Linguists have Always Wanted to Know about Logic*. Oxford: Basil Blackwell.

Mey, J.L. 2001: *Pragmatics: An Introduction* (2nd edn). Oxford: Blackwell.

Mey, J.L. 2004: Between culture and pragmatics: Scylla and Charybdis? The precarious condition of intercultural pragmatics. *Intercultural Pragmatics* 1/1, 27–48.

Mey, J.L. 2005: What is in a (Hand)book? *Intercultural Pragmatics* 2/3, 347–53.

Moeschler, J. 2004: Intercultural pragmatics: a cognitive approach. *Intercultural Pragmatics* 1/1, 49–70.

Moeschler, J. 2007: The role of explicature in communication and in intercultural communication. In Kecskes, I. and Horn, L.R. (eds) *Explorations in Pragmatics*. Berlin: Mouton de Gruyter, 73–94.

Morgan, J.L. 1978: Two types of convention in indirect speech acts. In Cole, P. (ed.) *Syntax and Semantics 9: Pragmatics*. New York: Academic Press, 261–80. Reprinted in Davis, S. (ed.) *Pragmatics – a Reader*. 1991: Oxford: Oxford University Press, 242–53.

Nunberg, G. 1993: Indexicality and deixis. *Linguistics and Philosophy* 68, 1–43.

Nwoye, O.G. 1992: Linguistic politeness and sociocultural variation of the notion of face. *Journal of Pragmatics* 18, 309–28.

Palmer, F. 1995: *Grammar and Meaning: Essays in Honour of Sir John Lyons*. Cambridge: Cambridge University Press.

Panther, K-U. and Thornburg, L. 1998: A cognitive approach to inferencing in conversation. *Journal of Pragmatics* 30, 755–69.

Peirce, C.S. 1932: Division of signs. In Hartshorne, C. and Weiss, P. (eds) *Collected Papers of CS Peirce*. Vol. 2. Cambridge, MA: Harvard University Press, 134–55.

Recanati, F. 2004: Pragmatics and semantics. In Horn, L.R. and Ward, G. (eds) *The Handbook of Pragmatics*. Oxford: Blackwell Publishing, 442–62.

Report to the Council of the University of Hong Kong by the Independent Investigation Panel. http://news.tvb.com/instant/n20000809_16190.htm.

Romary, L. and Reboul, A. (eds) 1996: *Time, Space and Identity*. Nancy: CRIN-Loria.

Rubin, E. 1915: Figure and ground. In Beardslee, D.C. and Wertheimer, M. (eds) *Readings in Perception* 1958: London: Van Nostrand, 194–203.

Russell, B. 1905: On denoting. *Mind* 14, 479–93.

Sacks, H. 1974: An analysis of the course of a joke's telling in conversation. In Bauman, R. and Sherzer, J. (eds) *Explorations in the Ethnography of Speaking*. Cambridge: Cambridge University Press, 337–53.

Sacks, H., Schegloff, E.A. and Jefferson, G. 1974: A simplest systematics for the organization of turn-taking in conversation. *Language* 50/4, 696–735. Reprinted with changes in Schenkein, J. (ed.) *Studies in the Organization of Conversational Interaction* 1978: New York: Academic Press, 7–55.

Sadock, J.M. 1974: *Toward a Linguistic Theory of Speech Acts*. New York: Academic Press.
Sadock, J. 2004: Speech acts. In Horn, L.R. and Ward, G. (eds) *The Handbook of Pragmatics*. Oxford: Blackwell Publishing, 53–73.
Sbisà, M. 1995: Speech act theory. In Verschueren, J., Oestman, J-A. and Blommaert, J. (eds) *Handbook of Pragmatics*. Amsterdam: John Benjamins, 495–505.
Schegloff, E.A. 1987: Between micro and macro: context and other connections. In Alexander, J.C., Giesen, B., Munch, R. and Smelser, N. (eds) *The Macro-micro Link*. Berkeley: University of California Press, 207–34.
Schegloff, E.A. 1992: In another context. In Duranti, A. and Goodwin, C. *Rethinking Context*. Cambridge: Cambridge University Press, 191–228.
Schegloff, E.A. and Sacks, H. 1973: Opening up closings *Semiotica* 7/4, 289–327. Reprinted in abbreviated form in Jaworski, A. and Coupland, N. *The Discourse Reader*. 1999: London: Routledge, 263–74.
Schenkein, J. (ed.) 1978: *Studies in the Organization of Conversational Interaction*. New York: Academic Press.
Schiffrin, D. (ed.) 1984: *Meaning, Form, and Use in Context: Linguistic Applications*. GURT'84. Washington, DC: Georgetown University Press.
Schiffrin, D. 1987: Meta-talk: Organization and evaluative brackets in discourse. *Sociological Inquiry* 20, 199–236.
Schiffrin, D. 1994: *Approaches to Discourse*. Oxford: Blackwell.
Scollen, R. and Scollen, S.W. 2000: *Intercultural Communication: A Discourse Approach* (2nd edn). Oxford: Blackwell Publishers.
Scott, M. and Lyman, S.M. 1968: Accounts. *American Sociological Review* 33, 46–62.
Searle, J.R. 1965: What is a speech act? In Black, M. (ed.) *Philosophy in America*. Ithaca, NY: Cornell University Press, 221–39. Reprinted in Davis, S. (ed.) *Pragmatics – a Reader*. 1991: Oxford: Oxford University Press, 254–64.
Searle, J.R. 1969: *Speech Acts*. Cambridge: Cambridge University Press.
Searle, J.R. (ed.) 1971: *Philosophy of Language*. Oxford: Oxford University Press.
Searle, J.R. 1975: Indirect speech acts. In Cole, P. and Morgan, J.L. (eds): *Syntax and Semantics 3: Speech Acts*. New York: Academic Press, 59–82.
Searle, J.R. 1979: *Expression and Meaning*. Cambridge: Cambridge University Press.
Seidlhofer, B. 2005: English as a lingua franca. *ELTJournal* 59/4, 339–41.
Seuren, P.A.M. 1998: *Western Linguistics: An Historical Introduction*. Oxford: Blackwell Publishers.
Silverstein, M. 1976: Shifters, linguistic categories and cultural description. In Basso, K.H. and Selby, H.A. (eds) *Meaning in Anthropology*. Albuquerque: University of New Mexico Press, 11–55.
Sperber, D. and Wilson, D. 1995: *Relevance: Communication and Cognition* (2nd edn). Oxford: Basil Blackwell.
Steinberg, D. and Jakobovits, L. (eds) 1971: *Semantics*. Cambridge: Cambridge University Press.
Strawson, P.F. 1950: On referring. *Mind* 59, 320–44.
Stroebe, W. and Hewstone, M. (eds) 1991: *European Review of Social Psychology*. Vol. 2. Chichester: John Wiley & Sons Ltd.
Tallerman, M.O. (ed.) 2005: *Language Origins*. Oxford: Oxford University Press.
Talmy, L. 1978: Figure and ground in complex sentences. In Greenberg, J.H. (ed.) *Universals of Human Language*. Los Angeles: Stanford University Press, 625–49.
Tarski, A. 1944: The semantic conception of truth. *Philosophy and Phenomenological Research* 4, 341–75. Reprinted in Tarski, A. *Logic, Semantics and Metamathematics* 1956: London: Oxford University Press.
ten Have, P. 2007: *Doing Conversation Analysis* (2nd edn). London: Sage.

Thiele, W., Schwend, J. and Todenhagen, C. (eds) 2005: *Political Discourse: Different Media – Different Intentions – New Reflections*. Tübingen: Stauffenburg.

Thomas, J.A. 1995: *Meaning in Interaction: An Introduction to Pragmatics*. Harlow: Longman.

Trappes-Lomax, H. and Ferguson, G. (eds) 2002: *Language in Language Teacher Education*. Amsterdam: John Benjamins.

Traugott, E.C. 1989: On the rise of epistemic meanings in English: an example of subjectification in semantic change. *Language* 65, 31–55.

Traugott, E.C. 1995: The role of the development of discourse markers in a theory of grammaticalization. Paper presented at ICHL XII, Manchester.

Traugott, E.C. 1999: The role of pragmatics in semantic change. In Verschueren, J. (ed.) *Pragmatics in 1998: Selected Papers from the Sixth International Pragmatics Conference*, Vol. II. Antwerp: IPrA, 93–102.

Verschueren, J. 1998: *Understanding Pragmatics*. London: Arnold.

Verschueren, J. (ed.) 1999: *Pragmatics in 1998: Selected Papers from the Sixth International Pragmatics Conference*, Vol. II. Antwerp: IPrA.

Verschueren, J. 2000: Notes on the role of metapragmatic awareness in language use. *Pragmatics* 10/4, 439–56.

Verschueren, J., Oestman, J-A. and Blommaert, J. (eds) 1995: *Handbook of Pragmatics*. Amsterdam: John Benjamins.

Wilson, D. and Sperber, D. 1993: Linguistic form and relevance. *Lingua* 90, 1–15.

Wilson, D. and Sperber, D. 2004: Relevance theory. In Horn, L.R. and Ward, G. (eds) *The Handbook of Pragmatics*. Oxford: Blackwell Publishing, 607–32.

Yule, G. 1996: *Pragmatics*. Oxford: Oxford University Press.

Zimmerman, D.H. and Boden, D. (eds) 1991: *Talk and Social Structure: Studies in Ethnomethodology and Conversation Analysis*. Cambridge: Polity Press.

Index